Music and International History in the Twentieth Century

Explorations in Culture and International History Series
General Editor: Jessica C. E. Gienow-Hecht

In the last two decades, an increasing number of scholars in the United States and in Europe have introduced culture into the historical study of international relations. They believed that this important dimension was missing from international relations. While some senior scholars have played significant roles, the bulk of the work has come from younger scholars who have brought insights from other disciplines to the study of international history. This series aims at presenting some of this innovative work, with the first volume setting the scene.

Volume 1
Culture and International History
Edited by Jessica C. E. Gienow-Hecht and Frank Schumacher

Volume 2
Remaking France
Brian Angus McKenzie

Volume 3
Anti-Americanism in Latin America and the Caribbean
Edited by Allan McPherson

Volume 4
Decentering America
Edited by Jessica C. E. Gienow-Hecht

Volume 5
Practicing Public Diplomacy
Yale Richmond

Volume 6
Searching for a Cultural Diplomacy
Edited by Jessica C. E. Gienow-Hecht and Mark C. Donfried

Volume 7
Music and International History in the Twentieth Century
Edited by Jessica C. E. Gienow-Hecht

Volume 8
Empire of Pictures:
Global Media and the 1960s Remaking of American Foreign Policy
Sönke Kunkel

MUSIC AND INTERNATIONAL HISTORY IN THE TWENTIETH CENTURY

Edited by
Jessica C. E. Gienow-Hecht

NEW YORK · OXFORD
www.berghahnbooks.com

First published in 2015 by
Berghahn Books
www.berghahnbooks.com

©2015, 2018 Jessica C. E. Gienow-Hecht
First paperback edition published in 2018

All rights reserved. Except for the quotation of short passages for the purposes of criticism and review, no part of this book may be reproduced in any form or by any means, electronic or mechanical, including photocopying, recording, or any information storage and retrieval system now known or to be invented, without written permission of the publisher.

Library of Congress Cataloging-in-Publication Data

Music and international history in the twentieth century / edited by Jessica C. E. Gienow-Hecht.
   pages cm. — (Explorations in culture and international history series ; v. 7)
   Includes bibliographical references and index.
   ISBN 978-1-78238-500-4 (hardback : alk. paper) —
   ISBN 978-1-78533-758-1 (paperback) — ISBN 978-1-78238-501-1 (ebook)
   1. Music—Political aspects—History—20th century. 2. Music and diplomacy. 3. Music and state. I. Gienow-Hecht, Jessica C. E., 1964–
   ML3916.M8725 2014
   7809'.04—dc23

2014033532

British Library Cataloguing in Publication Data

A catalogue record for this book is available from the British Library

ISBN: 978-1-78238-500-4 hardback
ISBN: 978-1-78533-758-1 paperback
ISBN: 978-1-78238-501-1 ebook

Contents

List of Illustrations — vii

Acknowledgments — ix

Notes on Contributors — xi

Introduction
Sonic History, or Why Music Matters in International History — 1
Jessica C. E. Gienow-Hecht

I. Music, International Relations, and the Absence of the State

Chapter 1
The Wicked Barrisons — 33
David Monod

Chapter 2
The International Society for Contemporary Music and
Its Political Context (Prague, 1935) — 58
Anne C. Shreffler

II. Music, International History, and the State

Chapter 3
Music and International Relations in Occupied Germany,
1945–49 — 93
Toby Thacker

Chapter 4
Instruments of Diplomacy: Writing Music into the History
of Cold War International Relations — 118
Danielle Fosler-Lussier

Chapter 5
"To Reach ... into the Hearts and Minds of Our Friends":
The United States' Symphonic Tours and the Cold War   140
Jonathan Rosenberg

Chapter 6
Music Diplomacy in an Emergency: Eisenhower's
"Secret Weapon," Iceland, 1954–59   166
Emily Abrams Ansari

Chapter 7
Intimate Histories of the Musical Cold War: Fred Prieberg
and Igor Blazhkov's Unofficial Diplomacy   189
Peter J. Schmelz

Chapter 8
"Where I Cannot Roam, My Song Will Take Wing":
Polish Cultural Promotion in Belarus, 1988   226
Andrea F. Bohlman

Index   256

Illustrations

Figures

Figure 1.1. The four youngest Barrisons, Sophie, Inger, Olga, and Gertrude, ca. 1890. *Source:* New York Public Library, Billy Rose Theatre Collection, Barrison Sisters' Clipping File.   38

Figure 1.2. Henri de Toulouse-Lautrec, *Lona Barrison avec son manager et epoux,* 1900. The horse is Maestoso. *Source:* Brooklyn Museum Collection.   41

Figure 1.3. The five Barrison Sisters as they would have appeared at the height of their notoriety, 1896. *Source:* New York Public Library, Billy Rose Theatre Collection, Barrison Sisters' Clipping File.   43

Figure 1.4. A German postcard produced by F. Schüler, Berlin, with the caption, "Hexenzug—Walpurgisnacht." Although the Barrison Sisters are not identified as the witches, the five figures clearly associate them with decadence and debauchery. *Source:* F. Schüler, Berlin N.W.6. and Meisenbach Riffarth & Co., Leipzig, 1902.   47

Figure 2.1. The program of the ISCM Festival in Prague, 1935, on the cover of the Austrian music journal *Anbruch* 17, no. 8 (1935). *Source:* Eda Kuhn Loeb Music Library, Harvard University.   63

Figure 2.2. Anton Webern, Concerto for Nine Instruments, op. 24, beginning of the first movement. Used by permission of European American Music Distributors Company, United States, and Canadian agent for Universal Edition, Vienna.   67

Figure 2.3. The first issue of the short-lived music journal *Musica Viva* (1936), p. 1. *Source:* Eda Kuhn Loeb Music Library, Harvard University.   79

Figure 5.1. Leonard Bernstein with a group of Peruvian musicians on the 1958 tour to Latin America. *Source:* New York Philharmonic Leon Levy Digital Archive. 153

Figure 5.2. Leonard Bernstein, stopping for a shoe shine, frolics with a group of children in Lima, Peru, on the 1958 Latin American tour. *Source:* New York Philharmonic Leon Levy Digital Archive. 155

Figure 5.3. Leonard Bernstein speaking with Vice President Richard Nixon on the 1958 Latin American tour. *Source:* New York Philharmonic Leon Levy Digital Archive. 156

Figure 6.1. Sergeant Haddix and Miss Iceland. *Source:* Demaree Bess, "Uncle Sam's Reluctant Ally," *Saturday Evening Post,* 29 December 1956. 171

Figure 6.2. The fence at Keflavík. *Source:* Demaree Bess, "Uncle Sam's Reluctant Ally," *Saturday Evening Post,* 29 December 1956. 172

Figure 6.3. Boston Symphony Orchestra musicians en route to Iceland, 1956. Roger Voisin (trumpet), Ralph Pottle (horn), and Arthur Kerr (trombone). Photographer unknown. *Source:* Boston Symphony Orchestra Archives. 174

Figure 7.1. Fred Prieberg. Photographer unknown. *Source:* public domain. 195

Figure 7.2. Galina Mokreeva. *Source:* Igor Blazhkov; date unknown. 201

Figure 7.3. Igor Blazhkov and Valentin Silvestrov, 1975. *Source:* Larisa Bondarenko. 213

Tables

Table 6.1. NSC 5426, Statement of Policy on Iceland: Courses of action (abbreviated from original). *Source:* Draft Statement of Policy proposed by the National Security Council on Iceland, NSC 5426, 12 July 1954, White House Office, NSC Staff, Papers, 1948–61, Disaster Series, Box 49, Iceland (1), EPL. 173

Table 8.1. The Distribution of Power in the Central Committee of the PZPR (1981–85). 230

Table 8.2. Musical associations receiving funds from the PZPR in 1983. 231

Acknowledgments

This book represents a symphony of efforts on the part of many people, and it is a great pleasure for me to thank them all. First, I should like to thank our publisher, Marion Berghahn, who has supported and believed in this series, Explorations in Culture and International History, since its inception twelve years ago. Next, I would like to express my personal ode to joy in gratitude to the contributors of this book, historians and musicologists alike who truly strove and worked hard to bridge the gap between two disciplines in order to seek a dialogue between both fields (rather than paying lip service to this endeavor). I know that harsh criticism from outside as well as scholastic disagreements on both sides of the disciplinary divide may have rendered writing and rewriting individual chapters an occasionally onerous and frustrating task. Thank you for your intellectual rigor, for your patience—and for hanging in there! Third, I wish to thank the two anonymous reviewers from Berghahn Books, whose nuanced criticism was a treasure of inspiration for our ideas. While one's uncommon tone raised eyebrows among the contributors, both reviewers ultimately made this a much better book. Thank you to Wayne Moquin for compiling the index and to the stellar team of editors at Berghahn Books: Adam Capitano, Elizabeth Berg, and Caitlin Mahon.

Over the years, I have had the great fortune to work with a number of young master's and doctoral candidates who gave far more to their respective institutes than time and "Dienst nach Vorschrift"; some of them played a vital role in the making of this book. Thank you to Carolin Viktorin, Jochen Molitor, and Marcel Will for their organizational support in the initial stage of this project; to Annika Estner for her tenacity in formatting and synchronizing the layout of the manuscript; to Tilman Pietz and Matthias Kreßner for being my assistants in Cologne; and to Alyn Euritt in Berlin for proofreading the full manuscript. You all deserve praise for your inspiration, your help, your upbeat spirit, and, most importantly, for forming a great team over the course of several years.

Thank you all for making this book sing!

Jessica C. E. Gienow-Hecht
Berlin, February 2015

CONTRIBUTORS

EMILY ABRAMS ANSARI is Assistant Professor of Music History at the University of Western Ontario in Canada. She received her PhD from Harvard University in 2010. Her research examines issues of national identity and politics as they pertain to music in the United States. Her current book project considers the effect of the Cold War on US musical nationalism through a study of composers' participation in government-funded cultural diplomacy, a topic on which she has also published articles in the *Journal of the Society for American Music* and *Diplomatic History*.

ANDREA F. BOHLMAN is Assistant Professor of Music at the University of North Carolina, Chapel Hill, and received her PhD in music from Harvard University. Her work concerns the music history of the recent past, in particular the musical cultures of East-Central Europe. A monograph in preparation is a study of the interaction between political action and music in Poland in the late twentieth century. She has also worked extensively on the composer Hanns Eisler and popular music in Europe, in particular the Eurovision Song Contest. Her current research addresses the history of sound media in twentieth-century Poland and engages economies of amateur music worlds, the persistence of "old" media such as magnetic tape and radio, and audiovisual documentary practices. She previously taught at the University of Pennsylvania as a Mellon Postdoctoral Teaching Fellow in Music.

DANIELLE FOSLER-LUSSIER is Associate Professor of Musicology at the Ohio State University. She is the author of a book entitled *Music Divided: Bartók's Legacy in Cold War Culture* (University of California Press, 2007) and a forthcoming book that describes musical performances sponsored by the US Department of State during the Cold

War. Fosler-Lussier's research on music and politics in Eastern and Western Europe and the United States has been supported by fellowships from the National Endowment for the Humanities, the American Council of Learned Societies, the Mershon Center for International Security Studies, the American Musicological Society, and the International Research and Exchanges Board.

JESSICA C. E. GIENOW-HECHT is Chair of the Division of History at the John F. Kennedy Institute for North American Studies at the Free University Berlin. She is the series editor of Explorations in Culture and International History (Berghahn Books, since 2003); her monograph *Transmission Impossible: American Journalism as Cultural Diplomacy in Postwar Germany* (hardback and paperback 1999) won both the Stuart Bernath Prize as well as the Myrna Bernath Prize of the Society for Historians of American Foreign Relations. Her most recent monograph, *Sound Diplomacy: Music and Emotions in Transatlantic Relations, 1850–1920* (2009, paperback 2012) won the Choice Outstanding Academic Title Award and is currently being translated into Chinese.

DAVID MONOD teaches history at Wilfrid Laurier University in Waterloo, Ontario. He is the author of *Settling Scores: German Music, Denazification, and the Americans, 1945–1953* (2005). Monod writes on American cultural history and has recently completed a book manuscript on the development of theatrical entertainments in the nineteenth century. He is currently researching a book on vaudeville.

JONATHAN ROSENBERG teaches US history at Hunter College and the Graduate Center of the City University of New York. His research focuses on the history of the United States in a global context. His current project, *From the New World: International Politics and Classical Music in Twentieth-Century America*, examines how classical musicians, composers, and performing organizations in the United States understood and responded to international developments from World War I to the Cold War. Rosenberg is the author of *How Far the Promised Land? World Affairs and the American Civil Rights Movement from the First World War to Vietnam* (Princeton University Press, 2006). He is the coauthor of *Kennedy, Johnson, and the Quest for Justice: The Civil Rights Tapes* (Norton, 2003), and he coedited *Cold War Statesmen Confront the Bomb: Nuclear Diplomacy Since 1945* (Oxford University Press, 1999). In addition to contributing articles and reviews to a variety of scholarly publications, Rosenberg has written for the *Christian Science Monitor,* the *Wilson Quarterly,* and the *Washington Post.*

PETER J. SCHMELZ is Associate Professor of Musicology and Chair of the Music Department at Washington University in St. Louis. He is currently completing a book on polystylism as cultural practice in the late USSR, focusing on the music of Alfred Schnittke and Valentin Silvestrov. He received a National Endowment for the Humanities Fellowship in 2011, and his first book, *Such Freedom, If Only Musical: Unofficial Soviet Music during the Thaw* (Oxford University Press, 2009), received an ASCAP Deems Taylor Award in 2010.

ANNE C. SHREFFLER is the James Edward Ditson Professor of Music at Harvard University, having served as Professor of Musicology at the Universität Basel in Switzerland from 1994 to 2003. Her current work focuses on the twentieth-century musical avant-garde in Europe and the United States, with special emphasis on the political and ideological associations of new music. Her most recent book, coauthored with Felix Meyer, is *Elliott Carter: A Centennial Portrait in Letters and Documents.* Awards include the Alfred Einstein Award of the American Musicological Society and a Guggenheim Fellowship.

TOBY THACKER is a Senior Lecturer in Modern European History at Cardiff University. His book *Music after Hitler, 1945–1955* (Ashgate, 2007) explored the development of music in occupied Germany after World War II and in the early years of a divided Germany after 1949. He has also written *The End of the Third Reich: Defeat, Denazification, and Nuremberg, January 1944–November 1946* (Tempus, 2006) and *Joseph Goebbels: Life and Death* (Palgrave Macmillan, 2009). He is currently working on a study of British culture and the memory of World War I.

INTRODUCTION
Sonic History, or Why Music Matters in International History

Jessica C. E. Gienow-Hecht

Call it *Audiogeschichte, histoire du son,* or "sonic history."[1] Historians of international relations have recently become quite fascinated with the history of sound and music, and the acoustic turn is well on its way to becoming the "next big thing." For both historiographical and historical reasons, this development should come as no surprise. First, the history of sound is the business of musicology, and many musicologists have been doing that kind of "international" history in one way or another for more than sixty years. Second, since the 1980s and 1990s, music and political history have gone through a period of rapprochement that was controversial at the time in some circles but has now been accepted as one of the ways in which musicologists work. Third, and most importantly, universal attitudes embedded in the liaison between music and internationalism have historically been used to divorce aesthetics from political realities, with sometimes negative consequences (take, for example, Schopenhauer, Pfitzner, and Palestrina). Moreover, statements like these can be read in different ways, either as poetical romantic expressions of belief in the power of music as an expressive but nonverbal art form, or as suggesting a literal cure for the woes of international relations. But either way, they reflect the typical nineteenth-century belief in music as a remedy for any number of conflicts, ranging from domestic violence to battlefield slaughter. The fact that in tandem with he-

Notes for this section begin on page 20.

gemonic tensions and military conflicts in Europe, civil war in the Balkans and Americas, colonial uprisings in Asia, and numerous international interventions (mostly in the Ottoman Empire) Western contemporaries cited music as a political remedy should catch our attention.

This book reflects the attempt to introduce students and scholars interested in the study of international history to the study of music as a useful tool and category of analysis. The contributors of this volume argue that music can be used as a measuring stick for the quantity as well as for the quality of an international relation. Music may reflect a relation when other ties are severed, it can help us to understand the nature of a relation operating on different levels, and it can introduce us to an entirely new dimension of what we deem an "international relation."

On the following pages, I will review the existing literature dedicated to music and international history, arguing that up to this point, musicologists have done far more for the advancement of our understanding of music as a force in international history than historians of international relations. Next, I shall outline the stories, strategies, and standpoints presented in this book. Five observations at the end of this chapter shall serve to define the most important methodological and historical findings of this book, along with recommendations for future research.

Musicology and History

Musicologists have long pondered the history of music. Working with material such as written sources (scores, reviews, memoirs) and approaches such as textual criticism, musical analysis, philology, and others, musicologists investigate, for example, a specific composer, the genesis of musical styles (for example, jazz), music's social function in a given period, and the varieties of musical performances in a given location at a particular time. Scholarly results can encompass edited volumes documenting and commenting on scores (often including the development of a piece over time), biographies of one composer or a group of composers, discussions on the function of music in a specific society (such as a social class, a region, or a nation), and the interplay of musical styles, texts, and harmonies over time. Music history in this sense is closely wedded to the production, performance, reception, and criticism of music. The closely related field of ethnomusicology concentrates on music as it is situated in social relations; historically, its focus has been on non-Western music. Another related field, music theory, is principally concerned with technical aspects of the style, notation, and creation of music.

In the past fifty years, and more so even in the past fifteen years, musicologists have produced a highly developed literature on musical change in the context of modernity. They have looked at traditional and folk music interacting with music from other localities, globalization, migration, and other transnational processes. In the same vein, many musicologists have turned to the political and social meanings of music. They have investigated issues of gender, class, and race as well as the hidden ideologies embedded in musical activity.[2] Looking at the works of Johannes Brahms, including *Ein deutsches Requiem,* composed after the Austro-Prussian War, Daniel Beller-McKenna, for example, has shown how Brahms infused his compositions with a moral and spiritual intensity that reflected what Beller-McKenna characterizes as a nineteenth-century "tendency of Germans ... to foresee the coming of a new Reich in millennial, apocalyptic terms."[3] Esteban Buch, in turn, has examined the international significance of Beethoven's Ninth Symphony over the course of nearly two hundred years. Buch argues that Beethoven became an important national symbol in Germany for the same reason that he appealed to other political and cultural groups: because his music embedded a universalism that made it accessible to people of all creeds. Romantics saw the "Ode to Joy" as the climax of their art, German nationalists as a symbol for heroism and "Germanness," French republicans as the *Marseillaise de l'humanité,* communists as a prophecy for a world without class distinctions, Catholics as the Gospel, Adolf Hitler as his favorite birthday tune, Rhodesia as a national anthem, the European Union as a unifying hymn, UNESCO as part of the world heritage register, and so on.[4]

Like in so many other fields in the humanities, the lines between musicology and other disciplines are becoming increasingly transparent. Traditionally, musicologists' interest in music differs from that of other researchers in other fields in the sense that for musicologists, music as a sounding activity will often be at the center of their research.[5] In his book *Nineteenth-Century Music,* Carl Dahlhaus warned musicologists to produce a history of *music,* not a *history* of music. Dahlhaus felt the need to state such a warning because musicologists crossed the traditional limitations of their field. Inspired by the work of sociologist Tia DeNora, for example, many musicologists now situate listening as part of everyday life. Ethnomusicology and musicology both allow the foregrounding of detailed consideration of the social aspects of music.[6]

One might argue that scholars from other fields, including history, tend to use music as a sounding board, a reflector, a measuring device to find out about something that, on first sight, may have nothing to do with music at all: the nature of power relations, continuities and changes in political culture, inner social rivalries, the long-term quest for cultural identity, or the negotiation of economic positions. But in many cases one can actually argue—and some musicologists have done so—that such phenomena do relate to music because music helps constitute those phenomena. Leslie Sprout's dissertation on music in Vichy France reveals that music was a key tool of the state, combining political power and musical style. The work of Beth Levy on music and the American frontier, the work of Peter Schmelz on music and dissent in the USSR—all these studies show that musical sound is not separate from other historical and social phenomena, but part of the fabric of history.[7]

Historians and Music

The musicological research on the sociopolitical meaning of music has intersected with the interests of social and cultural historians, many of whom originally had no or little background in the field. Similar to musicologists, historians are interested in studying music as a historical event or development, analyzing its change, form, development, and meaning over time. But unlike musicologists, who regard music as a sounding activity, their interests focus not on music as a process but as a "lens," an instrument to analyze questions of power, political hegemony, and cultural change. They view music less as a subject of investigation and more as a tool to reconstruct the past by shedding light on groups, individuals, organizations, events, objects, actions, and phenomena.

Celia Applegate, for example, whose early works focused on issues of identity, has since published widely on the political meaning of and the ways in which the music of the romantics reflected the desire for German unity.[8] Jürgen Osterhammel and Sven Oliver Müller's article "Geschichtswissenschaft und Musik" calls on historians to consider music as a central facet shaping the process, if not progress, of history. Essays in the volume analyze the mutual perception of music lovers, the exchange between the musical artist and the public, and the public radius of such musical relations.[9] The African studies scholar Kelly Askew has explored the close connection between music, economics, and political changes. Key to Tanzanian nation building, Askew argues, were musical and dance practices exhibited by everyone from government elites to participants in wedding ceremonies. Music and popular culture at large played a significant part in what Askew calls "performing the nation."[10]

From the investigation of music and nation building, it is only a short step to the investigation of music in the context of international history. Scholars of international history are typically interested in issues of domination and suppression, hegemonic rivalry, cultural exchange and affinity, consensus and confrontation—modes of relationships, that is. Musicologists, as we have seen above, have an interest in both the connecting power of music and its geographical and cultural peculiarity, as well as the social aspect and meaning of music and musical culture. Music thus constitutes one out of many devices by which individuals, regions, nations, and unions can be either united or driven apart. Similar to science, commerce, environmental interest, film, literature, and the performing arts, sound entails a form of communication and affiliation. While its language may strike the casual observer as more specialized than, say, the analysis of films, books, plays, and newspapers, and while to the political historian's eye, a musical score may look less accessible than a cable in Record Group 59 of the National Archives, in essence music fulfills the same purpose: it is a tool of communication reflecting a relationship between a producer/performer and the audience, possibly conditioned by a mediator such as a moderator (for example, a conductor), or through mediation by performance, broadcast, or recording.[11]

Recently historians have turned to sources and theories of musical creativity, performance, and audio records in the context of international relations. In this context, popular music—notably jazz, rock, and hip-hop—has received considerable attention. A number of scholars, such as Frederick Starr, have written on American jazz musicians' visits to the Soviet Union and other Warsaw Pact countries during the 1920s and 1930s and discussed Stalin's repression of popular music.[12] Others have highlighted the potential of folk music in borderland areas, such as the US-Mexico border, to accentuate the go-between nature of culture among nations and the emergence of a transnational culture.[13]

A considerable body of work has focused on the meaning of jazz in the context of the Cold War. Christian Schmidt-Rost's *histoire croisée* of Poland and the German Democratic Republic reveals that to many artists and consumers, jazz provided a space of interaction that was appealing precisely because it seemed to be removed from politics. Lisa Davenport's study on the meaning of jazz exports, in turn, shows that US-funded jazz protagonists such as Louis Armstrong, Dave Brubeck, Duke Ellington, Dizzy Gillespie, and Benny Goodman shaped foreign perceptions of the United States and capitalism in the Cold War. In all of these cases, US intentions always focused on winning the Cold War, an intention that shaped the United States' relationships with new postcolonial nations around the world.[14]

Likewise, the history of rock music has inspired quite a few international historians. Eric Zolov has investigated the development of Mexican counterculture, especially in relation to the impact of rock music, US influences, and foreign hippies. Zolov stresses Mexican resistance to perceived "musical imperialism," concerts, the crackdown on rock, and the activities of record companies in Mexico. In Mexico, Zolov contends, Elvis was "refried" to support the emergence of a new and young national identity.[15] A very important book, and early in recognizing the role of music in Cold War politics, Uta Poiger's *Jazz, Rock, and Rebels* analyzes the impact of jazz and rock in East Germany. As she shows, the perception of popular music genres differed tremendously in East and West; while the West German government understood popular music as a private affair, the East German government interpreted it, along with fashion and taste, as part of the class struggle threat to communism that needed to be repressed.[16]

Quite a few authors have investigated the instrumental character of jazz and rock music, that is, music as an instrument of political influence. Historians such as Penny Von Eschen, among others, have stressed the malleable character of particular genres of music, which made them perfect, if volatile, tools of cultural diplomacy in the propaganda between East and West. First, artists went off-message, such as Duke Ellington in 1963 in Baghdad, where he took a stroll with his unmarried companion and caused a storm of protest.[17] Second, the political briefings musicians did receive were often so vague that there was no clear "message" in the first place.

By far the most recent international research has focused on hiphop (notably rap), covered by students of musicology, ethnology, and media studies as well as cultural and regional studies, who investigate the global spread of this particular musical genre.[18] Identifying the genre either as a form of protest against discrimination, a way to assert regional identity (particularly on the part of youth), an avenue to hybrid cultural exchange, or all of the above, scholars have looked at specific regions of the world to retrace peculiarities and comparisons. For example, looking at the phenomenon of hip-hop in Germany, Osman Durrani asks why Turkish minorities in the state should take up an American musical form as a way of expressing their identity. Durrani's essay addresses international relations within a postmodern society; hip-hop, he argues, offers a variety of senses of identity to an increasingly diverse group of citizens.[19]

Scholars of hip-hop "think" internationally and politically, but—similar to Uta Poiger's interpretation of rock 'n' roll in East Germany—they see music as a tool of identification, demarcation, and protest, not state policy, and there is much that scholars of international history can learn from these analyses.[20] For example, in crisis-ridden Sierra Leone, local idioms merged with West African hip-hop to create a music that presented young peoples' "moral universe" as contrasting sharply with the world of their parents, teachers, and politicians.[21] In South Africa, as the works of Albert Grundlingh and Daniel Künzler show, rap and Voëlvry music emerged as a means to give a voice to antiapartheid social protest.[22]

In Asia, transnational cultural flows, regionalism—a politically and economically powerful policy—and local identities likewise played a significant role in the development of popular music. Thus, Stefan Fiol explores the emergence of subnational regionalism in postindependence India; vernacular popular music, he argues, often mixes manifestations of local cultural identity in order to create a "space" for regional belonging and political change in a globalized world.[23] Nationalism and regional self-identity articulated through the medium of popular music likewise play a tremendous role in Burma and South Korea, as Amporn Jirattikorn and Jeonsuk Joo have shown. Transnational and intense recognition of Korean pop, Joo finds, developed into a source of pride and distinctiveness for South Koreans, thus merging regional policy and national self-consciousness.[24] The emergence of a vibrant pop music scene has also led to transcultural flows between Japanese and Korean musicians, after the South Korean government abandoned the ban on Japanese culture in 1998, affecting the public debate regarding how to go beyond postcolonial relations while at the same time remembering the country's tragic history.[25]

Research on Latin American hip-hop has likewise focused on the context of identity and transnational/transcultural identities. In Brazil, hip-hop's "black identity" connected the composition and themes of North and South American musicians,[26] and quite a number of studies stress the genre's significance in the context of protest and mobilization. Thus, Paul Almeida and Ruben Urbizagastegui have pointed to the growth of musical protest groups in small nations that they believe played a vital role in the development of revolutionary mobilization,[27] while Hanna Klien, Tanya Saunders and others have delineated the role of hip-hop in Havana as a form of African American resistance against social discrimination, a sign of "Afro-diasporic activism," and a tool for transnational identity.[28]

Many historians and students of regional cultures have located the emergence and influences of hip-hop squarely in terms of "national rhythms"; in this tale, popular music represents forms of race mixture and transnational exchange between European, Latin American, African, and, recently, Asian compositions, giving way, in turn, to core symbols and expressions of national identity and local concerns over inequalities.[29] Tony Mitchell's review of Aboriginal hip-hop may thus apply to musicians around the world:

> As an educational format, a vehicle to express anger at discrimination and marginalization and pride in one's heritage, a way of binding communities together through dance and performance, a declamatory form of storytelling set to music, and a means of expressing oral history, hop hop's affinities with aboriginal cultural forms make it an ideal means for youth to get in touch with their tribal identity, history and cultural background. It is also a vital means of articulating their place in today's world.[30]

Thus, hip-hop has been globalized but has also gone native since its emergence in Jamaica in the 1970s. From Greenland—where it has morphed English, Danish, and Greenlandic elements—to Australia, from New Zealand to South America, it has highlighted forms of regional expressions and subaltern discourses as much as transcultural flows and global protest. There are varieties in the forms and motivations of musicians and compositions, but specific characteristics never change, notably the wish to express identity and the readiness to seek transborder communication and exchange.[31] This research's emphasis on nonstate or even antistate identity provides a telling glimpse into the study of music in international relations at large that we shall get back to further on.

Historians and Classical Music

Classical music is a latecomer in the debates on international relations and international history. The productions of (mostly) dead, white European males as well as concurrent notions of elitism and refinement did not lend themselves easily to the investigation of social and cultural history at a time when race, class, and gender had long ruled questions of how to analyze culture and how to interpret the past. Furthermore, the tradition of thinking of music as "apolitical," which was strongly advocated after World War II, meant that these readings were underplayed for a long time. Even the new international history, which borrows heavily from neighboring fields and disciplines, has been slow to pick up the pertinence of classical music as an element of interaction beyond mere aestheticism.

One of the most enticing recent interpretations comes from Jürgen Osterhammel, who has delineated the emergence of a global music scene during the five decades prior to 1930. During this period, he argues, European classical ("serious") and opera music thrived on all five continents, while early forms of mechanical music transmission "delocalized" the consumption of both European and non-European music all over the world, leading to an expansion but not a long-term mixture of both.[32] Here, music emerges as a possibility of communication among territories that was, however, not always fully realized; while European composers like Claude Debussy and Antonin Dvorak briefly flirted with non-European forms of music for a few years, in the end such efforts remained just that, brief flirtations, never definitive characteristics of their work.

A number of musicologists and historians have studied the impact of Cold War politics, divisions, and anxieties on the composition of music. In her 2009 dissertation, Emily Abrams Ansari, one of the authors in this book, examined the work of US composers—"masters of the president"—during the Cold War with a particular eye on their cooperation with the federal government for the purposes of US propaganda abroad. As Ansari points out in a related 2012 essay, musical composers were not hapless pawns directed by a federal state in the name of containment; rather, they were granted unprecedented power to shape the music (serious classical music, but no serialism or experimentalism) and, with that, the image of the United States exported to audiences worldwide.[33] Meanwhile, Danielle Fosler-Lussier has investigated the reception of the United States Information Agency's musical programs in Asia and elsewhere, pointing to the decisive impact of local demands for specific kinds and calibers of musical programs. As Fosler-Lussier recounts, the chief commissioner and president of the Pakistan Arts Council, for example, demanded in 1958 "that the U.S. Embassy provide an ice show 'or a really good jazz orchestra' for a Pakistani arts festival" because he had heard that the US government had favored India with an ice show.[34] These are important findings because they shed light on three of the most tantalizing questions of cultural propaganda—the inner workings of the information machine, the politics of identity, and the unforeseen tensions between audiences, organizers, and US officials. Evidently, many countries tended to see a musical event (including a visit by a US orchestra) as a political phenomenon, adding to their own national and geopolitical status. Collectively, these studies show that musicologists have already moved into the field of international history, notably Cold War studies.

Yet, even among historians of the Cold War, the topic has typically been subordinated to power politics and cultural exchange. Thus, David Caute, Hugh Wilford, and Francis Stonor Saunders have highlighted the manipulative role of music as an art form in the hands of secret services and cultural propagandists.[35] Even though snippets of information such as Van Cliburn's triumph at the International Tchaikovsky Piano Competition in 1958 or Leonard Bernstein and the New York Philharmonic's tour to the Soviet Union during the following year have been repeated endlessly in the respective scholarship dedicated to US cultural diplomacy,[36] we have not spent much time making sense of such moments besides stereotypical explanations referring to the arts as instruments of political power.

"Ah swear to goodness, ah just can't believe all this is happenin' to li'l ole Van Cliburn from the piney woods of East Texas!," *Time* magazine quoted the 23-year-old pianist on 19 May 1958, after he had received the stellar Russian award with the explicit approval of Nikita Khrushchev. Most Western observers at the time could not believe it either, and we need to begin to wonder what it meant that different forms of music, including classical music, played such a prominent role in the Cold War. What does it mean that Khrushchev did not seem to blink once before allowing the award to be presented to a US artist? Did national and geopolitical interests subside, if just for a moment? How did the engagement of soloists and entire orchestras change the nature and perception of the Cold War as a geostrategic and ideological battle? Was this a part of the Cold War we have not considered before?

While it is tempting to subordinate music to an instrumental function of power politics during the twentieth century, it is equally deceiving to echo nineteenth-century sentiments of musical internationalism. In a recent online comment dedicated to a roundtable on music in the Cold War featured in the journal *Diplomatic History*, Charles Maier argued that for all the classical topics of international relations—power, hegemonic drive, self-performance—the exchange of symphony orchestras in the Cold War may provide a glimpse of those "Dionysian fields" of universal harmony that humankind has aspired to since the beginning of time (or, one may add, has wanted to believe in for various, more worldly reasons). While it may be a consolation to believe that President Eisenhower, along with the chief organizers of US cultural and information programs, were driven by visions of peace in an age of statements, policies, and documents such as the National Security Council Report 68,[37] we are hard-pressed to make such arguments based on more than speculation. The sources we know plead for mutual understanding, but not for compromise. Whether liberal or conservative, at the end of the day, the organizers of musical tours in the 1950s and 1960s were hoping to win the Cold War, not to abandon it.[38] The question is: how do we make sense of the nexus of power and harmony, of politics and sound? Emphasizing one in disregard of the other will not get us any closer to understanding the link between the two.[39]

Clearly, the time and the scholarship are ripe for addressing these and other questions linking the study of music to the study of international history. There is even a surging debate: on both sides of the Atlantic Ocean, in France, Germany, and the United States, scholars are beginning to organize conferences, workshops, projects, and forums dedicated to the interplay of classical music and international history.[40] But why and how is music and all that is attached to it—musicology, performance, reception theory, emotions, and psychology—an attractive avenue for scholars interested in foreign relations? What can music tell us about international history that we did not know before? And what can experts of international relations and musicologists learn from each other?

Understanding Music and International Relations

Much of the scholarship on music as a historical phenomenon originates in the understanding that media—any kind of media—play a significant role both in our understanding of the past and, even more so, in historical actors' modes of self-perception and self-performance. Borrowing from communication studies, media theory, in particular, is concerned with the nature and impact of specific forms of communication tools—ranging from a show to a computer—on particular groups or societies.[41] Media and communication scholars point to any form of communication, ranging from face-to-face societies of the early modern type to online exchange, to ask how humans employ particular modes of communications—"symbols"—to create "meaning" and "messages" and how, then, these meanings meander into political, cultural, economic, and social dimensions of their respective societies. Music, in this sense, can be understood not merely as a "thing to bring" (such as in cultural diplomacy) but as a medium, a transmitter, and a symbol for a message as well as a reflector for identity and communication.[42]

In a thought-provoking dissertation, Lauren Erin Brown has looked at the interplay of US arts funding and the Cold War. Examining the introduction of Russian ballet to the United States and its successive evolution into a US art form, Brown, first, questions the existence of cultural hierarchy and status quo in the United States and, second, argues that ballet's new consecration as a US art form legitimized what it meant to be an American both at home and overseas.[43] Like ballet and like any form of media, music can be understood as a form of communication, either a reflection of social conditions (identity, racism, nationalism, unity, collective purpose, etc.) or an instrument of political and cultural aspirations (hegemonic power, quest for rapprochement, display of ideals). In both cases, historians are called upon to investigate music not simply as a tool but as a forum of values, customs, and ideas.

In this book, we do not propose one or the other understanding. Instead, we wish to highlight some of the most recent trends developing in the field. In accordance with these ideas, I asked the contributing authors to address the following queries in their essays: How have authors "used" music to understand and narrate the (hi)story they are telling? How does music help us to explain an international relation? More specifically, how does music highlight the nexus between culture and international history? What can music tell us about international history that other avenues of cultural inquiry cannot? And where do authors see avenues for future questions and investigations regarding the role of music in culture and international history? These are the questions addressed in the present book.

Contents of the Book

David Monod jump-starts the volume with an introduction to the Barrison Sisters, an American family troupe that achieved fame and notoriety in the 1890s. Dressed as children, the sisters sang about sex, using voices that spectators described as peculiarly impassive and uncomprehending. Monod's article documents the divergent readings that the Barrisons received in Europe and the United States and uncovers a shared transatlantic belief that the voice served as a window to the soul. But as this chapter shows, while there was agreement on both sides of the Atlantic on the voice as a window to the soul, the wickedness of the Barrisons' performances, and the artificiality of their singing, American and European critics drew very different moral lessons from that shared understanding. Monod's study uses international comparisons to decipher what would be otherwise unintelligible: the moral principles that drove shared aesthetic sensibilities apart. In the end, the Barrisons functioned less as a highway of cultural exchange and more as a reflector of differing ethical codes.

Anne C. Shreffler then turns to the link between modern music and the Popular Front. Specifically, she investigates the International Society for Contemporary Music (ISCM) and its transnational political context in the mid-1930s. Like the League of Nations and the other international organizations conceived in its spirit after World War I, the ISCM found its very survival threatened by the political turbulence that arose between the Nazi seizure of power in 1933 and the outbreak of war in 1939. As the European new music scene was drawn into the political whirlwinds in the summer of 1935, groups whose squabbles had been mainly of the familiar, internal "artistic politics" kind were suddenly confronted with actual state politics. The exiled Austrian composer Hanns Eisler, representing the Soviet-led Popular Front, worked during the summer of 1935 to bring the ISCM into the fold, while the Nazi government set up its own alternative to the ISCM, the Permanent Council for the International Cooperation of Composers. The president of the ISCM, the English musicologist Edward Dent, fended off both sides and articulated a vision for the organization that uncannily anticipated later Cold War notions of a politically "neutral" art. Larger questions about whether music could express a "national spirit" and still have international validity, music's role in creating social change, the link between contemporary music and its audience, and even the definition of "contemporary music" itself emerged from these confrontations. This moment of upheaval in the new music scene, Shreffler argues, provides an excellent opportunity to measure and evaluate the interactions between music and international affairs.

Toby Thacker casts new light on critical aspects of international relations in the occupation of Germany between 1945 and 1949. He argues that music—of different types—can highlight the tension in this occupation between military coercion and cultural persuasion, and demonstrates how the balance between these two central modes of relationship between Allied occupiers and occupied Germans shifted between the end of World War II in May 1945 and the emergence of two nominally independent German states in 1949. The chapter then explores how music illuminates the competition that developed between the separate occupying powers as they sought to win over German hearts and minds in the embryonic Cold War. Finally, Thacker argues that a consideration of the role of music in this complex play of international relations enables us to reconsider the role of German agency in a situation in which control of the traditional structures of power—military, economic, and political—lay firmly with the occupying powers. The chapter concludes that an analysis of the role of music in this occupation does not lead to a fundamental reappraisal of the international relations involved, but to a much more nuanced understanding, one that recognizes the ways in which cultural phenomena can "develop a life of their own" in these relations.

Danielle Fosler-Lussier, in turn, considers music as an instrument of diplomacy. She argues that music should not necessarily be treated as a by-product that merely reflects political conditions, but as an integral part of the mix of human activity humans seek to describe when they write history. Her chapter offers evidence from the history of cultural diplomacy to demonstrate that Cold War musical activity as it was contested on the ground allows historians an important perspective on the history of Cold War propaganda. Viewed from the top down, US musical propaganda in the Third World appeared to be a project of imperial cultural transmission. Yet the recipients were far from passive participants. In many cases, US cultural programs were drawn into a local rivalry and conditioned by local demands. Because embassy staff served as mediators of information to the State Department, they were also vulnerable to advice that served the locals' interests sometimes more than those of the United States. The outcomes of these cultural diplomacy events were not primarily about transmitting ideas; instead, these performances and the negotiations surrounding them built relationships in which demands could be made upon the United States and the connection with the United States could be deployed in local power relations. Understanding how cultural propaganda was contested on a local scale, among nonstate actors, Fosler-Lussier argues, admits a new perspective on Cold War propaganda as a global practice.

Jonathan Rosenberg sharpens our understanding of US symphony tours during the Cold War. His chapter explores the intersection between classical music and international politics during the Cold War; it probes the story of a key cultural export program initiated by the US government in the 1950s, which sent leading US symphony orchestras to perform around the world. The program's aim was to advance the political and ideological objectives of the United States during a time when the East-West competition dominated the attention of policy makers. More specifically, the chapter examines the practice of cultural diplomacy, in which the United States deployed symphony orchestras to Asia and Latin America to present American cultural achievements to allies in both regions in an effort to advance the idea that the United States was capable of impressive attainments in the realm of high culture. The chapter thus highlights three perspectives related to the nexus between music and international history: First, it considers the US government's reasons for initiating the program. Second, it considers the journeys from the perspectives of the performing musicians. And third, it assesses the reception of the tours by examining local press coverage. As Rosenberg shows, the tours by the Symphony of the Air in 1955 and the New York Philharmonic under Leonard Bernstein in 1958 showcased the accomplishments of liberal capitalism, which, it was argued, was not limited to producing Hollywood blockbusters, oversized automobiles, or nuclear weapons.

Emily Abrams Ansari likewise looks at musicians as rhetorical surrogates in US president Dwight Eisenhower's Cold War planning, this time for Iceland. Through an examination of US musical diplomacy to Iceland during the crisis in relations of the mid-1950s, she demonstrates that Eisenhower considered music and musicians a particularly potent tool of psychological warfare, capable of carrying clear messages to foreign nations without the need for words. In Iceland, Eisenhower and his staff used classical musicians in response to negative Icelandic reaction to perceived cultural imperialism occurring via the US Air Force base on the island. Eisenhower's use of music in Iceland demonstrates that his principle objective in that nation was to build prestige for the United States. He and his staff considered classical music an ideal vehicle for building such prestige while also, intriguingly, devoid of imperialistic features, and thus the ideal way to downplay perceptions of an American cultural invasion. In this case study, the story of a musical mission to win friends reveals new insights into Eisenhower's foreign policy and strategy toward this nation, a model that Ansari believes might usefully be employed in assessing US relations with other nations.

Peter J. Schmelz introduces us to what he and others call "intimate diplomacy." He examines the unpublished correspondence of

Ukrainian conductor Igor Blazhkov and West German music writer Fred K. Prieberg. Their correspondence, carried out mainly from the 1960s into the 1970s, presents a new perspective on music and international relations during the Cold War, and, as Schmelz argues, the type of history it exemplifies: an intimate history. The author believes that the public side of Cold War exchanges has received much recent scrutiny, but the intimate side remains understudied. In particular, unofficial, personal transnational networks between the USSR and the West have received little examination. Yet, as the Blazhkov-Prieberg correspondence demonstrates, they formed a critical nexus for information exchange during the 1950s and 1960s, especially for music. Their exchange, independent of any official channels, preserves a snapshot of crucial moments from the 1960s, including the various freezes and thaws of official Soviet artistic policy, the politics of tamizdat, and the role of unofficial spaces (whether virtual or actual) within Soviet musical life. As Schmelz demonstrates, exchanges such as Blazhkov's formed a significant type of international relation. They framed each side's opinion of the other on a personal level, producing significant and tangible results, alongside more diffuse changes in perspective and behavior. For both historians and musicologists, intimate history promises discerning the enormous in the miniature by offering models for tracing similar dynamic intersections of music and society, both close and vast.

Andrea F. Bohlman investigates Polish-Belarusian musical relations shortly before the fall of the Berlin Wall. In 1987, the governments of the Soviet Union and the Polish People's Republic issued a declaration urging Polish-Soviet cultural exchange. Building upon recent successes touring Moscow, Poland's Department of Culture set out to connect the Polish stage with that of a neighboring Soviet Socialist Republic (SSR) where the language barrier was minimal: Belarus. The Polish-Belarusian collaboration's most ambitious endeavor, as Bohlman shows, was the staging of a popular song festival, itself modeled on the Festival of Soviet Song in Zielona Góra, a vital event on the landscape of Polish festival culture. The program of the July 1988 Festival of Polish Song in Vitebsk performed the constructive and reciprocal influences of Soviet and Polish popular music cultures upon each other through the twentieth century at its gala concert. An analysis of the performance of international history on the stage and through music, Bohlman contends, sheds new light on the diplomatic relations between Poland and its neighboring SSR. Stars of the Polish stage sang Soviet songs in Russian, and there was even a tribute to one of the great voices of Soviet *estrada,* Anna

German, who was Polish. Bohlman argues that the effort to connect Poland with the Soviet Union culturally interpreted popular music previously assumed to be national as hybrid. This musical party line provides an important and underexplicated counterpoint to narratives of Polish postwar history because it emphasizes Poland's divergence from other Warsaw Pact nations on both the musical and the political level.

Concept and Theory

There is much that a thoughtful inclusion of music into the repertory of international history can tell us. Stylistic choices can sometimes convey allegiances. Concert reviews can be as revealing as some government documents, depending on circumstantial factors such as the reviewer and the context. Musical contexts can provide political clues. Musicians and audiences are both national and international. Musical performances can have—and have had—political significance. Collectively, the chapters presented in this book highlight five points.

1. Genres. Much of this book is dedicated to what the Germans call *ernste Musik* (serious music). At the same time, "music" in this book covers a wide range of genres. While the focus is on classical music, it also includes gestures to burlesque, ballet, folk, new music and other genres. We deliberately opted for this diversity to stress that our remarks are not limited to art music or to the kind of music that educators once declared to be "educational," "uplifting," or "romantic." Classical music has recently experienced a surge of interest among researchers, a movement that deserves attention. But the principal demands and convictions—music as a reflector, music as a transmitter, music as a sounding board— can easily be transferred to other sorts of music as well. Indeed, ethnomusicologists have done just that since the 1960s; here, historians and musicologists are presented with a stellar opportunity to cooperate..

2. Cold War. As musicologists such as Danielle Fosler-Lusier have argued, the impact of the Cold War on modern twentieth-century music was immense, but there remains a giant hole in the foreign relations literature on the role of music. Certain governments favored, pushed, and pulled specific kinds of music (like jazz and classical music) while others—such as experimentalism or modernism—were more selectively supported or even shunned by governments, universities, and cultural diplomats.[44] The East-West conflict manipulated, isolated, ridiculed, exiled, and channeled prewar musical trends. For composers, depending on their expertise and their standing, the bipolar conflict offered either opportunity or relentless discrimination. The freedom to compose left much time and room for creativity, but not necessarily an outlet for public performance, while state control often entailed the necessity to compromise artistic inspiration with popular appeal. Under communism, in particular, composers often had little time for creativity as they were frequently required to take on other work, such as conducting choirs or student ensembles and writing commissioned works in a state-approved style for grand public events. There is already a strong body of work on other aspects of cultural diplomacy, yet the component of music is a novel facet and should receive much more attention than it currently does.

3. Manipulation. The impact of music on international relations is equally influential, and on this general level, at least three possibilities of cooperation between the two fields are obvious. First, the most evident approach is to treat music as an instrument of diplomacy. This is the story that Emily Abrams Ansari, Jonathan Rosenberg, Andrea F. Bohlman, Toby Thacker, and Danielle Fosler-Lussier tell. In international history, music can function as a transporter of ideas as much as messages of hegemony. Second, music can serve as a reflector of international debates, anxieties, strength, and resistance. Anne C. Shreffler's and Peter J. Schmelz's analyses of the political plight experienced by modern musicians in the face of totalitarianism demonstrate that in situations where musical production is heavily controlled and politicized, striving for freedom of expression takes on larger significance—standing in/substituting for freedoms absent in other areas of life. Third, as David Monod reminds us, music can be analyzed as a relation all by itself, a forum of shared experiences but also opposing assessments, and a canvas for mutual national perceptions. Combined, these three approaches underline that rational decision-making processes, power schemes, and grand strategy may or may not be at play in an international relation. Furthermore, incoming students to the field may start to think about the circumstances under which music as an international relation operates in a specific way.

4. Communication. In a similar vein, music can be a mode of communication, including conflict and consensus where emotions are being played out in a manner otherwise invisible. Jonathan Rosenberg, Emily Abrams Ansari, and Danielle Fosler-Lussier all show how, in different contexts, foreign audiences perceived US music performances as a measuring stick for emotional commitment and high expectations as well as cultural frustrations: if a prestigious musician or orchestra visited one country in a region, other countries also desired to have that honor to increase their national prestige. Their chapters highlight questions about the status of music as a historical document as well as the relation between music and language. Today, even in the Western world, musicologists admit multiple definitions of multimedia, and they also point out that sound influences and directs sight (for example, costumes, scenery), language (such as programs, words), and associations (genre definition, etc.). Future researchers should ask how specific musical choices were supposed to influence diplomacy. Even if we cannot retrace the political agenda for an individual musical program, we still need to make sense of the fact that government officials made or agreed to particular programs for particular audiences in particular settings—or not.[45]

5. *The state.* Most importantly, music can help us understand the extent to which the state assumes control of international cultural venues. Chronologically, nearly every chapter in this book shows how the state, from World War I on, developed an increasing interest in the use and manipulation of music for political means. As such, music becomes an indicator for both state and nonstate activities. This observation does not mean that the production, performance, and reception of music as such became exclusive instruments of state policy; Anne C. Shreffler and Peter J. Schmelz show, clearly, how musical activities constituted a realm designed to subvert or resist state policy. Schmelz even contends that an investigation of musical relations reveals a cultural link across the Iron Curtain at the height of the Cold War, when most such contacts were unpalatable.

There is something surprising, even paradoxical, in the fact that the state included music in its move toward "total diplomacy." After all, such policy ran counter to ideas of increased formalism and apolitism/internationalism, especially in "classical" and "contemporary" music. This paradox, it seems to me, is an issue worthy of investigation for future research.

In conclusion, in the twentieth century music seemingly became an effective instrument of state diplomacy precisely because it seemed apolitical. At the same time, nonstate actors and institutions, including some German conductors in the United States, had already perceived and used music as a tool of political power during the nineteenth century. When the administration of music as an instrument of diplomacy switched hands from nonstate promoters to diplomatic agencies after World War I, it was a change in structure, but not in thought.

These, it seems, are the most trying questions for students of music and international history in the twentieth century: How and why did this transformation of musical diplomacy from nonstate to state control happen? And how does it relate to ideas and perceptions of music as increasingly apolitical and international? When and how does the national, the geopolitical, and the international come into play? Do Asian audiences listening to a European concert consider themselves national beings? Or do they forget their regional identities during a musical experience? Do listeners, musicians, and organizers switch identities according to their actions, identifying themselves as national and at other times as nonnational? We need to examine to what extent music and musical events became targets of state control while, at the same time, contributing to the decentering of the state and the transformation of international relations since the 1970s.

This book urges scholars of international history to consider music—classical, folk, modern, popular, and other genres—as an instrument of hegemony and resistance; a reflection of identity and protest; a means of communication; a forum of encounter; but most of all, as a transporter for atmosphere, mood, and emotion in the making of international affairs. True, music cannot tell us precisely what people said, thought, or believed. It cannot address many of the traditional questions of international history such as those dealing with rational decision-making processes, power schemes, and grand strategy. Nor can we read scores and reviews like cables and government documents. But at the end of the day, geopolitics come and go on a much more rapid scale than cultural developments. In this sense, culture—including music—proves more enduring than power.

Acknowledgments

I wish to thank Peter Schmelz, Anne Shreffler, Danielle Fosler-Lussier, Rebekah Ahrendt, and Damian Mahlet, the participants of the Friday Lunch Talks in the Department of Music at Harvard University, and the anonymous reviewers from Berghahn Books for their time and thoughtful comments.

Notes

1. Petra Meyer, ed., *Acoustic Turn* (Munich: Fink, 2008).
2. See, for example, Susan McClary, *Feminine Endings: Music, Gender, and Sexuality* (Minneapolis: University of Minnesota Press, 1991); McClary, *Desire and*

Pleasure in Seventeenth-Century Music (Berkeley: University of California Press, 2012); Philip Brett, *Music and Sexuality in Britten* (Berkeley: University of California Press, 2006); Bonnie Wade, *Thinking Musically: Experiencing Music, Expressing Culture* (New York: Oxford University Press, 2009); Suzanna Clark and Alexander Rehding, *Music Theory and Natural Order from the Renaissance to the Early Twentieth Century* (Cambridge and New York: Cambridge University Press, 2001); Mark Slobin, ed., *Global Soundtracks: Worlds in Film Music* (Middletown, CT: Wesleyan University Press, 2008).

3. Daniel Beller-McKenna, *Brahms and the German Spirit* (Cambridge, MA, and London: Harvard University Press, 2004). See also Philip Bohlman, *Focus: Music, Nationalism, and the Making of the New Europe,* 2nd ed. (London: Routledge, 2011).
4. Esteban Buch, *La neuvième de Beethoven: Une histoire politique* (Paris: Gallimard, 1999); Jessica C. E. Gienow-Hecht, "Trumpeting Down the Walls of Jericho: The Politics of Art, Music and Emotion in German-American Relations, 1870–1920," *Journal of Social History* 36, 3 (Spring 2003): 585–613; Gienow-Hecht, *Sound Diplomacy: Music, Emotions, and Politics in the Transatlantic Relations since 1850* (Chicago: University of Chicago Press, 2009).
5. See, in particular, works by Richard Taruskin, whose writings on the link between music and have been among the most referenced: *The Danger of Music and Other Anti-Utopian Essays* (Berkley: University of California Press, 2009); Taruskin, "Introduction: The History of What?," in *Music from the Earliest Notations to the Sixteenth Century,* vol. 1, *Oxford History of Western Music* (Oxford: Oxford University Press, 2009), xiii–xxii. See also Christopher Small, *Musicking: The Meanings of Performing and Listening* (Hanover, NH: University Press of New England, 1998); Lawrence Kramer, *Interpreting Music* (Berkeley: University of California Press, 2011); Gary Tomlinson, *Music and Historical Critique* (Aldershot, UK: Ashgate, 2007).
6. Carl Dahlhaus, *Nineteenth-Century Music* (Berkeley: University of California Press, 1989); Tia DeNora, *Music in Everyday Life* (Cambridge: Cambridge University Press, 2000); DeNora, *Beethoven and the Construction of Genius: Musical Politics in Vienna, 1792–1803* (Berkeley: University of Berkeley Press, 1995). See also Melanie Wald-Fuhrmann, *Ein Mittel wider sich selbst: Melancholie in der Instrumentalmusik um 1800* (Kassel and New York: Bärenreiter, 2010).
7. Peter Schmelz, *Such Freedom, If Only Musical: Unofficial Soviet Music During the Thaw* (Oxford: Oxford University Press, 2009). See also the essays in *The Journal of Musicology,* vol. 26.
8. Celia Applegate and Pamela Potter, "Germans as the 'People of Music': Genealogy of an Identity," in *Music and German National Identity,* ed. Celia Applegate and Pamela Potter (Chicago: University of Chicago Press, 2003), 13, 15, 31; Applegate, *Bach in Berlin: Nation and Culture in Mendelssohn's Revival of the St. Matthews Passion* (Ithaca, NY: Cornell University Press, 2005).
9. Jürgen Osterhammel and Sven Oliver Müller, "Geschichtswissenschaft und Musik," *Geschichte und Gesellschaft* 38, 1 (2012): 5–20; Osterhammel, "Classical Music in a Global Context, 1860–1930," *Geschichte und Gesellschaft* 38, 1 (2012): 86–132.
10. Kelly Askew, *Performing the Nation: Swahili Music and Cultural Politics in Tanzania* (Chicago: University of Chicago Press, 2002).
11. Jessica C. E. Gienow-Hecht, "The World Is Ready to Listen: Symphony Orchestras and the Global Performance of America," *Diplomatic History* 36, 1 (January 2012): 17–28.
12. Amy Nelson, *Music for the Revolution: Musicians and Power in Early Soviet Russia* (Philadelphia: Penn State University Press, 2004); Walter Ojakäär, "Jazz in

Estland," in *Jazz in Europa*, ed. Wolfram Knauer, Darmstädter Beiträge zur Jazzforschung 3 (Hofheim: Wolke, 1994), 95–106; Mark Edele, "Strange Young Men in Stalin's Moscow: The Birth and Life of the Stiliagi, 1945–1953," *Jahrbücher für Geschichte Osteuropas* 50, 1 (2002): 37–61; Frederick S. Starr, *Red and Hot* (Vienna: Hannibal-Verlag, 1990); Gertrud Pickhan and Rüdiger Ritter, *Jazz Behind the Iron Curtain* (Frankfurt: Peter Lang, 2010); Penny Von Eschen, *Satchmo Blows Up the World: Jazz Ambassadors Play the Cold War* (Cambridge, MA: Harvard University Press, 2004).

13. John Koegel, "Crossing Borders: Mexican Popular Music in the United States," in *From Tejano to Tango: Latin American Popular Music*, ed. Walter Aaron Clark (New York: Routledge, 2002). Guadalupe San Miguel, *Tejano Proud: Tex-Mex Music in the Twentieth Century* (College Station: Texas A&M University Press, 2002); Josh Kun, *Audiotopia: Music and Race in America* (Berkeley: University of California Press, 2005); Alejandro L. Madrid, ed., *Transnational Encounters: Music and Performance at the U.S.-Mexico Border* (New York: Oxford University Press, 2011). For a perspective on US–Latin American relations in classical music, see Carol Hess, "Ginastera's Bomarzo in the United States and the Impotence of the Pan-American Dream," *The Opera Quarterly* 22, nos. 3–4 (Summer–Autumn 2006): 459–76.
14. Christian Schmidt-Rost, "Verflochtene Kommunikation: Die Jazzszenen in der SBZ/DDR und der VR Polen" (PhD diss., Free University Berlin, 2012); Lisa Davenport, *Jazz Diplomacy: Promoting America in the Cold War Era* (Jackson: University of Mississippi Press, 2009).
15. Eric Zolov, *Refried Elvis: The Rise of the Mexican Counterculture* (Berkeley: University of California Press, 1999).
16. Uta Poiger, *Jazz, Rock, and Rebels: Cold War Politics and American Culture in a Divided Germany* (Berkeley: University of California Press, 2000).
17. Von Eschen, *Satchmo Blows Up the World*.
18. Tanya L. Saunders, "Black Thoughts, Black Activism: Cuban Underground Hip-Hop and Afro-Latino Countercultures of Modernity," *Latin American Perspectives* 39, 2 (2012): 42–60; Tony Mitchell, "Blackfellas Rapping, Breaking and Writing: A Short History of Aboriginal Hip Hop," *Aboriginal History* 30 (2006): 124–37; Andy Wood, "Original London Style: London Posse and the Birth of British Hip Hop," *Atlantic Studies* 6, 2 (2009): 175–90; Susanne Stemmler, ed., *Hip-Hop und Rap in romanischen Sprachwelten: Stationen einer globalen Musikkultur* (Frankfurt: Lang 2007); Hanna Klien, *Hip-Hop in Havanna: Afroamerikanische Musik im Widerstand* (Vienna: Lit, 2009).
19. Osman Durrani, "Popular Music in the German-Speaking World," in *Contemporary German Cultural Studies*, ed. Alison Phipps (London: Arnold, 2002), 197–218.
20. For Africa, see Albert Grundlingh, "'Rocking the Boat' in South Africa? Voëlvry Music and Afrikaans Anti-Apartheid Social Protest in the 1980s," *International Journal of African Historical Studies* 37, 3 (2004): 483–514; Moses Chikowero, "'Our People Father, They Haven't Learned Yet': Music and Postcolonial Identities in Zimbabwe, 1980–2000," *Journal of Southern African Studies* 34, no. 1 (March 2008): 145–60; Rekopantswe Mate, "Youth Lyrics, Street Language and the Politics of Age: Contextualising the Youth Question in the Third Chimurenga in Zimbabwe," *Journal of Southern African Studies* 38, no. 1 (March 2012): 107–27; Winston Mano, "Popular Music as Journalism in Zimbabwe," *Journalism Studies* 8, no. 1 (February 2007): 61–78; Mark Lamont, "Lip-synch Gospel: Christian Music and the Ethnopoetics of Identity in Kenya," *Africa* (Edinburgh University Press) 80, no. 3 (2010): 473–96; Anne Schumann, "A Generation of Orphans: The Socio-Economic Crisis in Côte D'Ivoire as Seen Through Popular Music," *Africa* (Cambridge University Press) 2011 (November 2012): 535–555.

21. Susan Shepler, "Youth Music and Politics in Post-war Sierra Leone," *Journal of Modern African Studies* 48, no. 4 (December 2010): 627–42.
22. Grundlingh, "'Rocking the Boat' in South Africa?"; Daniel Künzler, "South African Rap Music, Counter Discourses, Identity, and Commodification Beyond the Prophets of Da City," *Journal of Southern African Studies* 37, no. 1 (March 2011): 27–43.
23. Stefan Fiol, "Articulating Regionalism through Popular Music: The Case of Nauchami Narayana in the Uttarakhand Himalayas," *Journal of Asian Studies* 71, no. 2 (May 2012): 447–73; Sender Dovchin, "Performing Identity through Language: The Local Practices of Urban Youth Populations in Post-Socialist Mongolia," *Inner Asia* 13, no. 2 (2011): 315–33.
24. Amporn Jirattikorn, "Shan Noises, Burmese Sound: Crafting Selves through Pop Music," *South East Asia Research* 18, no. 1 (March 2010): 161–89; Jeonsuk Joo, "Transnationalization of Korean Popular Culture and the Rise of 'Pop Nationalism' in Korea," *Journal of Popular Culture* 44, no. 3 (June 2011): 489–504.
25. Hyunjoon Shin, "Reconsidering Transnational Cultural Flows of Popular Music in East Asia: Transbordering Musicians in Japan and Korea Searching for 'Asia,'" *Korean Studies* 33 (January 2009): 101–23. See also Craig A. Lockard, *Dance of Life: Popular Music and Politics in Southeast Asia* (Honolulu: University of Hawaii Press, 1998); Edgar Wright Pope, *Songs of the Empire: Continental Asia in Japanese Wartime Popular Music* (PhD diss., University of Washington, 2003). For Indonesia, see Andrew Noah Weintraub, *Dangdut Stories: A Social and Musical History of Indonesia's Most Popular Music* (Oxford: Oxford University Press, 2010).
26. Paulina L. Alberto, "When Rio Was Black: Soul Music, National Culture, and the Politics of Racial Comparison in 1970s Brazil," *Hispanic American Historical Review* 89, no. 1 (February 2009): 3–40; Antonio Barrenechea and Heidrun Moertl, "Hemispheric Indigenous Studies: Introduction," *Comparative American Studies* 11, no. 2 (June 2013): 109–23; Monika Fürst-Heidtmann, "Francisco Curt Lange: Pionier, Mittler, Nestor der Musikwissenschaft in Lateinamerika," *Ibero-Amerikanisches Archiv* 17, nos. 2–3 (1991): 245–258; Kariann Goldschmitt, "Doing the Bossa Nova," *Luso-Brazilian Review* 48, no. 1 (2011): 61–78.
27. Paul Almeida and Ruben Urbizagastegui, "Cutumay Camones," *Latin American Perspectives* 26, no. 2 (March 1999): 13–42.
28. Klien, *Hip-Hop in Havanna*; Saunders, "Cuban Underground Hip-hop," Tamara Elena Livingston-Isenhour and Thomas George Caracas Garcia, *Choro: A Social History of a Brazilian Popular Music* (Bloomington: Indiana University Press, 2005).
29. George Reid Andrews, "Remembering Africa, Inventing Uruguay: Sociedades de Negros in the Montevideo Carnival, 1865–1930," *Hispanic American Historical Review* 87, 4 (November 2007): 693–726.
30. Mitchell, "Blackfellas Rapping, Breaking and Writing"; Saunders, "Black Thoughts, Black Activism."
31. Ali Colleen Neff, "The New Masters of Eloquence," *Southern Cultures* 19, 1 (Spring 2013): 7–25; Steven Salm, "Globalization and West African Music," *History Compass* 8, 12 (December 2010): 1328–39.
32. Osterhammel and Müller, "Geschichtswissenschaft und Musik"; Osterhammel, "Classical Music in a Global Context."
33. Emily Abrams Ansari, "'Masters of the President's Music': Cold War Composers and the United States Government" (PhD diss., Harvard University, 2009); Ansari, "Shaping the Policies of Cold War Diplomacy: An Epistemic Community of American Composers," *Diplomatic History* 36, 1 (January 2012): 41–52; Jennifer Campbell, "Creating Something Out of Nothing: The Office of Inter-American

Affairs Music Committees (1940–41) and the Inception of a Policy for Musical Diplomacy," *Diplomatic History* 36, 1 (January 2012): 29–39; Campbell, "Shaping Solidarity: Music, Diplomacy, and Inter-American Relations, 1936–1946" (PhD diss., University of Connecticut, 2010), on the early history of US–Latin American music programs; Lisa Jakelski, "The Changing Seasons of the Warsaw Autumn: Contemporary Music in Poland, 1960–1990" (PhD diss., University of California at Berkeley, 2009); Schmelz, *Such Freedom, If Only Musical*; Danielle Fosler-Lussier, "Music Pushed, Music Pulled: Cultural Diplomacy, Globalization, and Imperialism," *Diplomatic History* 36, 1 (January 2012): 53–64; Fosler-Lussier, "The Tradition of Communism and the Legacy of Béla Bartók, 1945–1956" (PhD diss., University of California at Berkeley, 1999); Fosler-Lussier, *Music Divided: Bartók's Legacy in Cold War Culture* (Berkeley: University of California Press, 2007).

34. Fosler-Lussier, "Music Pushed, Music Pulled."
35. Hugh Wilford, *The Mighty Wurlitzer: How the CIA Played America* (Cambridge, MA: Harvard University Press, 2008); Frances Stonor Saunders, *The Cultural Cold War: The CIA and the World of Arts and Letters* (New York: New Press, 2000).
36. David Caute, *The Dancer Defects: The Struggle for Cultural Supremacy During the Cold War* (Oxford: Oxford University Press, 2003); Stephen J. Whitfield, *The Culture of the Cold War* (Baltimore: Johns Hopkins University Press, 1991). On Van Cliburn, see also Joseph Horowitz, *The Ivory Trade: Music and the Business of Music at the Van Cliburn International Piano Competition* (New York: Summit Books, 1990).
37. National Security Council Report 68 (NSC-68) was a top secret policy paper signed by US president Harry Truman in September 1950 and arguably among the most definitive US foreign policy statements during the first twenty years of the Cold War. NSC-68 outlined a strategy focusing on the containment of communist expansion until the collapse of the USSR and, consequently, the emergence of a new world order of liberal-capitalist values. Steven Casey, "Selling NSC-68: The Truman Administration, Public Opinion, and the Politics of Mobilization, 1950–51," *Diplomatic History* 29, 4 (2005): 655–90; David T. Fautua, "The 'Long Pull' Army: NSC 68, the Korean War, and the Creation of the Cold War U.S. Army," *Journal of Military History* 61, 1 (1997): 93–120; Paul Nitze, "The Development of NSC-68," *International Security* 4, 4 (Spring 1980): 170–76.
38. See Laura Belmonte, *Selling the American Way: U.S. Propaganda and the Cold War* (Philadelphia: University of Pennsylvania Press, 2009); Andrew Justin Falk, *Upstaging the Cold War: American Dissent and Cultural Diplomacy, 1940–1960* (Amherst: University of Massachusetts Press, 2010); Sarah Nilsen, *Film and Cultural Diplomacy at the Brussels World Fair* (Jefferson, NC: McFarland, 2011); Kenneth Osgood, *Total Cold War: Eisenhower's Secret Propaganda Battle at Home and Abroad* (Lawrence: University of Kansas Press, 2006).
39. See the introductory essay by Richard Taruskin in *Repercussions* 5, nos. 1–2 (Spring–Fall 1996), 5–20, esp. 7–8. See also Jann Pasler, ed., *Composing the Citizen: Music as Public Utility in Third Republic* (Berkeley: University of California Press, 2009).
40. See, for example, "Theaters, Globalization, and the Cold War" (featuring several contributions on music), organized at the Ludwig-Maximilian-Universität Munich by Christopher Balme and Berenika Szymanski, May 2012; "The Cold War and American Music, 1945–2000," an international conference organized at the University of Munich by Christof Mauch, Britta Waldschmidt-Nelson, and Michael Kimmage, May 2012; "Sound History," a panel at the German Historikertag in Mainz organized by Gernhard Paul, 28 September 2012; "Inklusion und Exklusion: 'Deutsche' Musik in Europa und Nordamerika 1848–1945," a conference

for historians and musicologists organized by Yvonne Wasserloos and Sabine Mecking, Universität Düsseldorf, December 2012; "Music and Diplomacy," a conference organized by Rebekah Ahrendt, Mark Ferraguto, and Damien Mahiet, Tufts and Harvard Universities, March 2013; "Musique et relations internationales," a conference organized by Anaïs Fléchet, Université de Saint-Quentin en Yvelines, May 2013.
41. Niklas Luhmann, *Die Realität der Massenmedien* (Opladen: Westdeutscher Verlag, 1996); Luhmann, *Soziale Systeme* (Frankfurt: Suhrkamp, 1984); Werner Faulstich, *Die Mediengeschichte des 20. Jahrhunderts* (Munich: Fink, 2012); Manfred Faßler, *Was ist Kommunikation?*, 2nd ed. (Munich: Fink, 2002).
42. Sven Oliver Müller et al., eds., *Die Oper im Wandel der Gesellschaft: Kulturtransfers und Netzwerke des Musiktheaters im modernen Europa* (Munich: Oldenbourg, 2010).
43. Lauren Erin Brown, "'Cultural Czars': American Nationalism, Dance, and Cold War Arts Funding" (PhD diss., Harvard University, 2008).
44. Amy Beal, *New Music, New Allies* (Berkeley: University of California Press, 2006); Danielle Fosler-Lussier, "American Cultural Diplomacy and the Mediation of Avant-garde Music," in *Sound Commitments: Avant-garde Music and the Sixties*, ed. Robert Adlington (Oxford: Oxford University Press, 2009), 232–53; Fosler-Lussier, *Music Divided*; Schmelz, *Such Freedom, If Only Musical*.
45. I am indebted to Damien Mahiet for this point.

Bibliography

Alberto, Paulina L. "When Rio Was Black: Soul Music, National Culture, and the Politics of Racial Comparison in 1970s Brazil." *Hispanic American Historical Review* 89, 1 (February 2009): 3–40.

Almeida, Paul, and Ruben Urbizagastegui. "Cutumay Camones," *Latin American Perspectives* 26, no. 2 (March 1999): 13–42.

Andrews, George Reid. "Remembering Africa, Inventing Uruguay: Sociedades de Negros in the Montevideo Carnival, 1865–1930." *Hispanic American Historical Review* 87, 4 (November 2007): 693–726.

Ansari, Emily Abrams. "'Masters of the President's Music': Cold War Composers and the United States Government." PhD diss., Harvard University, 2009.

———. "Shaping the Policies of Cold War Diplomacy: An Epistemic Community of American Composers." *Diplomatic History* 36, no. 1 (January 2012): 41–52.

Applegate, Celia. *Bach in Berlin: Nation and Culture in Mendelssohn's Revival of the St. Matthews Passion*. Ithaca, NY: Cornell University Press, 2005.

Applegate, Celia, and Pamela Potter. "Germans as the 'People of Music': Genealogy of an Identity." In *Music and German National Identity*, ed. Celia Applegate and Pamela Potter, 1–35. Chicago: University of Chicago Press, 2003.

Askew, Kelly. *Performing the Nation: Swahili Music and Cultural Politics in Tanzania*. Chicago: University of Chicago Press, 2002.

Barrenechea, Antonio, and Heidrun Moertl. "Hemispheric Indigenous Studies: Introduction." *Comparative American Studies* 11, 2 (June 2013): 109–23.

Beal, Amy. *New Music, New Allies.* Berkeley: University of California Press, 2006.

Beller-McKenna, Daniel. *Brahms and the German Spirit.* Cambridge, MA, and London: Harvard University Press, 2004.

Belmonte, Laura. *Selling the American Way: U.S. Propaganda and the Cold War.* Philadelphia: University of Pennsylvania Press, 2009.

Bohlman, Philip. *Focus: Music, Nationalism, and the Making of the New Europe.* 2nd ed. London: Routledge, 2011.

Brett, Philip. *Music and Sexuality in Britten.* Berkeley: University of California Press, 2006.

Brown, Lauren Erin. "'Cultural Czars': American Nationalism, Dance, and Cold War Arts Funding." PhD diss., Harvard University, 2008.

Buch, Esteban. *La neuvième de Beethoven: Une histoire politique.* Paris: Gallimard, 1999.

Campbell, Jennifer. "Creating Something Out of Nothing: The Office of Inter-American Affairs Music Committees (1940–41) and the Inception of a Policy for Musical Diplomacy." *Diplomatic History* 36, no. 1 (January 2012): 29–39.

———. "Shaping Solidarity: Music, Diplomacy, and Inter-American Relations, 1936–1946." PhD diss., University of Connecticut, 2010.

Casey, Steven. "Selling NSC-68: The Truman Administration, Public Opinion, and the Politics of Mobilization, 1950–51." *Diplomatic History* 29, no. 4 (2005): 655–90.

Caute, David. *The Dancer Defects: The Struggle for Cultural Supremacy During the Cold War.* Oxford: Oxford University Press, 2003.

Chikowero, Moses. "'Our People Father, They Haven't Learned Yet': Music and Postcolonial Identities in Zimbabwe, 1980–2000." *Journal of Southern African Studies* 34, no. 1 (March 2008): 145–60.

Clark, Suzanna, and Alexander Rehding. *Music Theory and Natural Order from the Renaissance to the Early Twentieth Century.* Cambridge and New York: Cambridge University Press, 2001.

Dahlhaus, Carl. *Nineteenth-Century Music.* Berkeley: University of California Press, 1989.

Davenport, Lisa. *Jazz Diplomacy: Promoting America in the Cold War Era.* Jackson: University of Mississippi Press, 2009.

DeNora, Tia. *Beethoven and the Construction of Genius: Musical Politics in Vienna, 1792–1803.* Berkeley: University of Berkeley Press, 1995.

Dovchin, Sender. "Performing Identity through Language: The Local Practices of Urban Youth Populations in Post-Socialist Mongolia." *Inner Asia* 13, 2 (2011): 315–33.

———. *Music in Everyday Life.* Cambridge: Cambridge University Press, 2000.

Durrani, Osman. "Popular Music in the German-Speaking World." In *Contemporary German Cultural Studies,* ed. Alison Phipps, 197–218. London: Arnold, 2002.
Edele, Mark. "Strange Young Men in Stalin's Moscow: The Birth and Life of the Stiliagi, 1945–1953." *Jahrbücher für Geschichte Osteuropas* 50, no. 1 (2002): 37–61.
Falk, Andrew Justin. *Upstaging the Cold War: American Dissent and Cultural Diplomacy, 1940–1960.* Amherst: University of Massachusetts Press, 2010.
Faßler, Manfred. *Was ist Kommunikation?* 2nd ed. Munich: Fink, 2002.
Faulstich, Werner. *Die Mediengeschichte des 20. Jahrhunderts.* Munich: Fink, 2012.
Fautua, David T. "The 'Long Pull' Army: NSC 68, the Korean War, and the Creation of the Cold War U.S. Army." *Journal of Military History* 61, no. 1 (1997): 93–120.
Fiol, Stefan Fiol. "Articulating Regionalism through Popular Music: The Case of Nauchami Narayana in the Uttarakhand Himalayas," *Journal of Asian Studies* 71, 2 (May 2012): 447–73.
Fosler-Lussier, Danielle. "American Cultural Diplomacy and the Mediation of Avant-garde Music." In *Sound Commitments: Avant-garde Music and the Sixties,* ed. Robert Adlington, 232–53. Oxford: Oxford University Press, 2009, pp. 232–53.
———. *Music Divided: Bartók's Legacy in Cold War Culture.* Berkeley: University of California Press, 2007.
———. "Music Pushed, Music Pulled: Cultural Diplomacy, Globalization, and Imperialism." *Diplomatic History* 36, no. 1 (January 2012): 53–64.
———. "The Tradition of Communism and the Legacy of Béla Bartók, 1945–1956." PhD diss., University of California at Berkeley, 1999.
Fürst-Heidtmann, Monika. "Francisco Curt Lange: Pionier, Mittler, Nestor der Musikwissenschaft in Lateinamerika." *Ibero-Amerikanisches Archiv* 17, 2–3 (1991): 245–58.
Gienow-Hecht, Jessica C. E. *Sound Diplomacy: Music, Emotions, and Politics in the Transatlantic Relations since 1850.* Chicago: University of Chicago Press, 2009.
———. "Trumpeting Down the Walls of Jericho: The Politics of Art, Music and Emotion in German-American Relations, 1870–1920." *Journal of Social History* 36, no. 3 (Spring 2003): 585–613.
———. "The World Is Ready to Listen: Symphony Orchestras and the Global Performance of America." *Diplomatic History* 36, no. 1 (January 2012): 17–28.
Goldschmitt, Kariann. "Doing the Bossa Nova," *Luso-Brazilian Review* 48, 1 (2011): 61–78.
Grundlingh, Albert. "'Rocking the Boat' in South Africa? Voëlvry Music and Afrikaans Anti-Apartheid Social Protest in the 1980s," *International Journal of African Historical Studies* 37, 3 (2004), 483–514.

Hess, Carol. "Ginastera's Bomarzo in the United States and the Impotence of the Pan-American Dream." *The Opera Quarterly* 22, nos. 3–4 (Summer–Autumn 2006): 459–76.

Horowitz, Joseph. *The Ivory Trade: Music and the Business of Music at the Van Cliburn International Piano Competition.* New York: Summit Books, 1990.

Jakelski, Lisa. "The Changing Seasons of the Warsaw Autumn: Contemporary Music in Poland, 1960–1990." PhD diss., University of California at Berkeley, 2009.

Jirattikorn, Amporn. "Shan Noises, Burmese Sound: Crafting Selves through Pop Music." *South East Asia Research* 18, 1 (March 2010): 161–89.

Joo, Jeonsuk. "Transnationalization of Korean Popular Culture and the Rise of 'Pop Nationalism' in Korea." *Journal of Popular Culture* 44, 3 (June 2011): 489–504.

Klien, Hanna. *Hip-Hop in Havanna: Afroamerikanische Musik im Widerstand.* Vienna: Lit, 2009.

Koegel, John. "Crossing Borders: Mexican Popular Music in the United States." In *From Tejano to Tango: Latin American Popular Music,* ed. Walter Aaron Clark. New York: Routledge, 2002, pp. 97–125.

Kramer, Lawrence. *Interpreting Music.* Berkeley: University of California Press, 2011.

Kun, Josh. *Audiotopia: Music and Race in America.* Berkeley: University of California Press, 2005.

Künzler, Daniel. "South African Rap Music, Counter Discourses, Identity, and Commodification Beyond the Prophets of Da City." *Journal of Southern African Studies* 37, 1 (March 2011): 27–43.

Lamont, Mark. "Lip-synch Gospel: Christian Music and the Ethnopoetics of Identity in Kenya." *Africa* (Edinburgh University Press) 80, 3 (2010): 473–96.

Livingston-Isenhour, Tamara Elena, and Thomas George Caracas Garcia. *Choro: A Social History of a Brazilian Popular Music.* Bloomington: Indiana University Press, 2005.

Lockard, Craig A. *Dance of Life: Popular Music and Politics in Southeast Asia.* Honolulu: University of Hawaii Press, 1998.

Luhmann, Niklas. *Die Realität der Massenmedien.* Opladen: Westdeutscher Verlag, 1996.

———. *Soziale Systeme.* Frankfurt: Suhrkamp, 1984.

Madrid, Alejandro L., ed. *Transnational Encounters: Music and Performance at the U.S.-Mexico Border.* New York: Oxford University Press, 2011.

Mano, Winston. "Popular Music as Journalism in Zimbabwe." *Journalism Studies* 8, 1 (February 2007): 61–78.

Mate, Rekopantswe. "Youth Lyrics, Street Language and the Politics of Age: Contextualising the Youth Question in the Third Chimurenga in Zimbabwe." *Journal of Southern African Studies* 38, no. 1 (March 2012): 107–27.

McClary, Susan. *Desire and Pleasure in Seventeenth-Century Music.* Berkeley: University of California Press, 2012.

———. *Feminine Endings: Music, Gender, and Sexuality.* Minneapolis: University of Minnesota Press, 1991.

Meyer, Petra, ed. *Acoustic Turn.* Munich: Fink, 2008.

Mitchell, Tony. "Blackfellas Rapping, Breaking and Writing: A Short History of Aboriginal Hip Hop." *Aboriginal History* 30 (2006): 124–37.

Müller, Sven Oliver, Philipp Ther, Jutta Toelle, and Gesa for Nieden, eds. *Die Oper im Wandel der Gesellschaft: Kulturtransfers und Netzwerke des Musiktheaters im modernen Europa.* Munich: Oldenbourg, 2010.

Nelson, Amy. *Music for the Revolution: Musicians and Power in Early Soviet Russia.* Philadelphia: Penn State University Press, 2004.

Nilsen, Sarah. *Film and Cultural Diplomacy at the Brussels World Fair.* Jefferson, NC: McFarland, 2011.

Nitze, Paul. "The Development of NSC-68." *International Security* 4, no. 4 (Spring 1980): 170–76.

Ojakäär, Walter. "Jazz in Estland." In *Jazz in Europa,* ed. Wolfram Knauer, 95–106. Darmstädter Beiträge zur Jazzforschung 3. Hofheim: Wolke, 1994.

Osgood, Kenneth. *Total Cold War: Eisenhower's Secret Propaganda Battle at Home and Abroad.* Lawrence: University of Kansas Press, 2006.

Osterhammel, Jürgen. "Classical Music in a Global Context, 1860–1930." *Geschichte und Gesellschaft* 38, no. 1 (2012): 86–132.

Osterhammel, Jürgen, and Sven Oliver Müller. "Geschichtswissenschaft und Musik." *Geschichte und Gesellschaft* 38, no. 1 (2012): 5–20.

Pasler, Jann, ed. *Composing the Citizen: Music as Public Utility in Third Republic.* Berkeley: University of California Press, 2009.

Pickhan, Gertrud, and Rüdiger Ritter. *Jazz Behind the Iron Curtain.* Frankfurt: Peter Lang, 2010.

Poiger, Uta. *Jazz, Rock, and Rebels: Cold War Politics and American Culture in a Divided Germany.* Berkeley: University of California Press, 2000.

Pope, Edgar Wright. *Songs of the Empire: Continental Asia in Japanese Wartime Popular Music.* PhD diss., University of Washington, 2003.

San Miguel, Guadalupe. *Tejano Proud: Tex-Mex Music in the Twentieth Century.* College Station: Texas A&M University Press, 2002.

Saunders, Tanya L. "Black Thoughts, Black Activism: Cuban Underground Hip-Hop and Afro-Latino Countercultures of Modernity." *Latin American Perspectives* 39, 2 (2012): 42–60.

Schmelz, Peter. *Such Freedom, If Only Musical: Unofficial Soviet Music During the Thaw.* Oxford: Oxford University Press, 2009.

Schmidt-Rost, Christian. "Verflochtene Kommunikation: Die Jazzszenen in der SBZ/DDR und der VR Polen." PhD diss., Free University Berlin, 2012.

Schumann, Anne. "A Generation of Orphans: The Socio-Economic Crisis in Côte D'Ivoire as Seen Through Popular Music." *Africa* (Cambridge University Press) 2011 (November 2012): 535–55.

Shepler, Susan. "Youth Music and Politics in Post-war Sierra Leone." *Journal of Modern African Studies* 48, no. 4 (December 2010): 627–42.
Shin, Hyunjoon Shin. "Reconsidering Transnational Cultural Flows of Popular Music in East Asia: Transbordering Musicians in Japan and Korea Searching for 'Asia,'" *Korean Studies* 33 (January 2009): 101–23.
Slobin, Mark, ed. *Global Soundtracks: Worlds in Film Music.* Middletown, CT: Wesleyan University Press, 2008.
Small, Christopher. *Musicking: The Meanings of Performing and Listening.* Hanover, NH: University Press of New England, 1998.
Starr, Frederick S. *Red and Hot.* Vienna: Hannibal-Verlag, 1990.
Stemmler, Susanne, ed. *Hip-Hop und Rap in romanischen Sprachwelten: Stationen einer globalen Musikkultur.* Frankfurt: Lang, 2007.
Stonor Saunders, Frances. *The Cultural Cold War: The CIA and the World of Arts and Letters.* New York: New Press, 2000.
Taruskin, Richard. *The Danger of Music and Other Anti-Utopian Essays.* Berkley: University of California Press, 2009.
———. "Introduction," in *Music from the Earliest Notations to the Sixteenth Century,* vol. 1, *Oxford History of Western Music.* Oxford: Oxford University Press, 2005, 2010. pp. xiii–xxii.
———. "Introduction." *Repercussions* 5, nos. 1–2 (Spring–Fall 1996): 5–20.
Tomlinson, Gary. *Music and Historical Critique.* Aldershot, UK: Ashgate, 2007.
Von Eschen, Penny. *Satchmo Blows Up the World: Jazz Ambassadors Play the Cold War.* Cambridge, MA: Harvard University Press, 2004.
Wade, Bonnie. *Thinking Musically: Experiencing Music, Expressing Culture.* New York: Oxford University Press, 2009.
Wald-Fuhrmann, Melanie. *Ein Mittel wider sich selbst: Melancholie in der Instrumentalmusik um 1800.* Kassel and New York: Bärenreiter, 2010.
Weintraub, Andrew Noah. *Dangdut Stories: A Social and Musical History of Indonesia's Most Popular Music.* Oxford: Oxford University Press, 2010.
Whitfield, Stephen J. *The Culture of the Cold War.* Baltimore: Johns Hopkins University Press, 1991.
Wilford, Hugh. *The Mighty Wurlitzer: How the CIA Played America.* Cambridge, MA: Harvard University Press, 2008.
Wood, Andy. "Original London Style: London Posse and the Birth of British Hip Hop." *Atlantic Studies* 6, no. 2 (2009): 175–90.
Zolov, Eric. *Refried Elvis: The Rise of the Mexican Counterculture.* Berkeley: University of California Press, 1999.

Part I
MUSIC, INTERNATIONAL RELATIONS, AND THE ABSENCE OF THE STATE

Chapter One

THE WICKED BARRISONS

David Monod

The Barrison Sisters' return to the United States after two years in Europe was eagerly anticipated. When they left New York in 1893, they were a nondescript group of blonde-haired children offering a cute song-and-dance act. But in Europe, they developed into a minor theatrical sensation: a musical ensemble known for sexual burlesque whose members wiggled their bottoms, did a striptease, and sang lewd songs in French and German. Their offstage behavior was even more shocking than their onstage naughtiness, and the miasma of their wickedness seemed to engulf all those who came into contact with them. Reports of the five pretty Americans' affairs with European aristocrats and the suicide of one male lover made shocking and titillating reading back home, and "The Wicked Barrisons" became a moniker the group energetically advertised. It was the "strength of the scandal they are said to have achieved" in Europe that made sold-out houses on their return home likely, which is why Koster & Bial's, the New York music hall, booked them for an unusually long run of eight weeks.[1]

Hardly surprisingly, the five wicked sisters sold out on opening night, even filling the seats in the third tier at Koster & Bial's, where the view was limited. The newspaper reviews, however, were scathing, and the only positive one came from a *Chicago Tribune* writer who knew no French or German and so understood only two of their songs. It was "the most innocent thing imaginable," he wrote, the naughtiest bit being that they smoked cigarettes when the curtain rose and blew kisses to the audience. Other commentators were decidedly less approving. The five girls opened with "a coarse vulgar

---

Notes for this section begin on page 54.

song; not naughtily suggestive with veiled or half-hidden meaning, but vulgar and coarse as unrefined minds are vulgar and coarse ... there wasn't a hint of art about it, nor a gleam nor a sparkle of intelligence," wrote the *Atlanta Constitution*'s critic. Alan Dale, the theater reviewer for the Hearst papers (his real name was Alfred J. Cohen), concurred: "Wickedness, without beauty, cleverness or chic, is hard to swallow and apt to nauseate." The "indecency of the Barrison Sisters," he wrote, "is crude, inartistic and pitiful ... it's a fraud ... if the stories are true ... there must be something more." Ordinary spectators seemed to agree. "What a fake," one disappointed young New Yorker was heard saying to his date, to which his companion, "a girl wearing all the colors of the rainbow," ruefully responded: "Oh, mamma!"[2]

Although American and European spectators agreed that the Barrisons were wicked, commentators on either side of the Atlantic were divided in their appreciation of the display of that wickedness. It is an axiom of popular scholarship that turn-of-the-century Americans were more puritanical than Europeans, even if, as Christina Simmons observed, this view was first expressed by reformers of the 1920s who were trying to encourage new behaviors by pillorying existing ones.[3] The case of the Barrisons, while ostensibly illustrating American prudery, actually casts doubt upon it, revealing American critics to be not so much squeamish about sex as aesthetically conservative with respect to its musical representation. Where European critics and audiences enjoyed the Barrisons' juxtaposition of innocence and experience, banality and knowledge, their American equivalents considered the sisters' musical insouciance to be offensive. While the Barrisons enjoyed success in Europe and excited Americans who read about their activities while they were abroad, they were a failure when New Yorkers actually saw and heard them. American audiences appear to have wanted stage sex to excite them; they wanted it to have a voice that suggested its dangerous or worldly attraction. The problem for the Barrisons was that what made them appealing on the Continent made them unintelligible in the United States: they did not look or sound wicked. Although naughtiness did have international valence, the divergent reactions of audiences and critics on either side of the Atlantic suggests the musical form the Barrisons gave it did not.

One thing was not in dispute: the lyrics and movements of the Barrison Sisters, at the peak of their notoriety in 1895–96, were exceptionally explicit. Their act normally consisted of four or five songs, with encores, meaning that they occupied the stage for about fifteen minutes all told. As was always the case in variety shows, other artists preceded and followed them onstage. When they performed at Koster & Bial's, for example, thirteen acts preceded theirs. The Barrisons' usual act began (as it did in New York) with the curtain slowly opening to reveal five performers seated on the stage with their legs straight out in front of them. They were dressed in frothy white dresses that exposed their shoulders. The focus of attention, however, was on their legs, not their busts, and the dresses they wore were designed to reveal the pinkness of their legs between their socks and their pantalets. On their heads they typically wore shade bonnets. They were, in fact, dressed in the clothing normally worn by well-to-do children in the 1890s.[4]

In the first iteration of their act, which they premiered in Paris and carried to London in 1893, the sisters rose and sang nonsense songs and nursery rhymes while stepping around and gesturing coquettishly. They ultimately used the nonsense song "Linger Longer Lucy" for this purpose, as it had pointless lyrics that the right movements might make suggestive. They frequently raised their skirts to reveal their bloomers, especially when standing with their backs to the audience. Even in this tame form, what they were offering was a variation on child pornography, three of the sisters being adolescents in the mid-1890s and all of them being dressed as little girls. It was also their youth that validated the shift of erotic attention from their breasts (the usual objects of sexual interest for mature fin de siècle performers) to their legs.

After their first stint at the Folies Bergère in 1893, the Barrison Sisters introduced a new opening number sung in German, "Do You Want to See My Pussy?" It was with this song that their act normally opened in Berlin and Vienna. Here the curtain would slowly rise to reveal the feet of the sisters, dressed as children. Their song began with them demanding a "dog":

Papa won't buy me a Wauwau Wauwau.
Papa won't buy me a Wauwau.
I have a little cat,
I like her like a pet,
But I want to have a Wauwau Wauwau

Each time they got to the chorus and asked "Do You Want to See My Pussy?," the curtain would rise a little in response to the affirmative shouts of the audience. On the final chorus, when the curtain was fully raised, the sisters would toss their skirts up over their heads to reveal small black cat faces on the crotch areas of their pantalets.

The most famous and graphic of the girls' songs, however, was added when the Barrison Sisters were in Vienna and Lona, the oldest of the five, was presented with a Lipizzaner stallion. Following a couple of opening group numbers, Lona would enter in male riding attire and sing about being uncomfortable dressing as a man when she went riding. She would then remove her clothing bit by bit, feigning increasing embarrassment as the striptease progressed. At the song's conclusion, she would be clad in an undershirt and shorts and would announce, rather oddly, that she was now comfortable enough to ride a horse. Exiting, she would return mounted astride (not sidesaddle) her white horse, Maestoso. As the horse high-stepped around the stage, she would sing "in happily unintelligible French" about riding/intercourse:

> But he has a big powerful muscle
> One doesn't notice it at once, but it stands out when he is caressed
> The first time one gets on him:
> Oh! Oh! Oh! It hurts!
> The second time it's strange:
> Eh! Eh! Eh! It goes better!
> If he is firm, that's for sure:
> Oh! Oh! Oh! It's pleasant.[5]

At Koster & Bial's the Barrison Sisters also performed a song in English about Jack, who kissed each of them in the dark. The song ended with the Barrisons lifting their skirts over their heads and shaking them until the curtain fell. Their other number had each performer singing solo turns in which she declared she was less innocent than she appeared because of a certain "Johnny." In the song the women referred in various coy ways to what Johnny had done with each of them in the dark. During the number they carried canes, and at the climax of each solo the singer would lift one of her legs and hang it over the top of the cane in a crude phallic reference. As in their other songs, the "Johnny" number emphasized the girls' youth, apparent innocence, and receptiveness to male sexual interest.[6] In combining the image of the innocent child and the willing sexual initiate, they offered the pornographic fantasy of the nymphet whose cravings were sexual satisfaction and the pleasure she gave a man.

Five Barrison sisters and at least two nonfamily members were at one time or another involved in performing these songs. The original Barrison Sisters—Abelone (Lona), Sophie, Inger (Inge), Olga, and Gertrude—were all born in Denmark, but they migrated to the United States with their parents in 1883 when Abelone (the oldest) was about twelve. Lyseus Barrison, their father, made a small income repairing and peddling umbrellas. Some accounts suggest that he was an alcoholic and an abusive husband. The actress Pearl Eytinge, who met him in 1889, later described him as "a dissipated, ignorant, anarchistic umbrella mender," while another writer remembered him as a "stern, taciturn man with rigid ideas." A longshoreman, one of his Brooklyn drinking partners, however, described him vaguely as "all right, just like the rest of us." His wife, who one reporter said "feared him," appears to have left him in 1893 when she went to Europe with her girls. In any case, the children were estranged from their father. When he died in 1906 none of them came to his funeral, and they ignored requests to pay for his burial. He was ultimately interred at the expense of the Artist's Fund. Mrs. Barrison is an even more elusive figure. She was, according to Eytinge, a "delicate, frightened looking little creature," barely able to hold her sixth and youngest child, the baby Sanders. Another reporter, however, rated her as "shrewd ... quiet and clever" and praised her for keeping a close watch on the girls early in their careers, dressing them stylishly and ensuring that they were clean and neat.[7]

In the fall of 1889 Mrs. Barrison responded to an advertisement for child performers for the "picturesque Irish drama" *Fairies' Well* at the 14th Street Theatre in New York. Apparently, Abelone had already appeared on stage at least once before, in a juvenile role in Denmark, though she may also have previously acted in a play at Daly's in New York. At the time of their audition, the family was living in a tenement on Huron Street in Greenpoint, Brooklyn. The girls were all fairly close in age; Abelone was around eighteen and, according to their landlord, roughly two years separated each of her siblings. They all had long, thick, light blonde hair and round, doll-like faces (see figure 1.1). The director of *Fairies' Well* later wrote that "they were the prettiest children I had ever seen"; as he simply wanted cute girls for the show, they secured the job and were taught to dance. Unfortunately, the critics did not think their frolicking helped "relieve the blankness of the stage"; the *Evening Telegram* even rated the dancing on opening night "very bad." This was possibly a result of the intervention of the Gerry Society (the New York Society for the Prevention of Cruelty to Children), which ensured, because of their ages, that the children "did not do much." Still, the audience apparently thought them sweet enough to applaud them encouragingly.[8]

The Barrison girls continued to perform after the close of *Fairies' Well*, but separately. Abelone joined the Clara Morris touring company, where she took on "ingenue" roles. The others picked up work

Figure 1.1. The four youngest Barrisons, Sophie, Inger (Inge), Olga, and Gertrude, ca. 1890.
Source: New York Public Library, Billy Rose Theatre Collection, Barrison Sisters' Clipping File.

where they could: Sophie, who would have been eleven or twelve in 1891, secured a child part in the comic opera *Wang*, which was set in Siam. She sang in a children's chorus cute enough to even eclipse in popularity the elephant that "Emperor Wang" rode in on. In the meantime, Inger joined Kate Claxton's dramatic company, and Olga got a child part in another musical, *Midnight Bell*. Only Gertrude, who was nine or ten, was kept from the stage, though she emulated her sisters by putting on plays in the parlor with the neighborhood children. Sometime late in 1892, Pearl Eytinge ran into the children at Mrs. Fernandez's acting agency in New York and decided that a group act, featuring all five sisters together, could have novelty interest. Eytinge wrote a short pantomime for them, *Mr. Cupid,* drilled them on their parts, and in March 1893 oversaw their performance of it as part of the variety show at the Eden Musee. The reviewers did not pay much attention, some writing them off as "hopelessly stupid, and incomparably tame and dull," while others considered them "clever little performers." Still, the sisters were sufficiently popular that the Musee kept them on through May—with Lona (as Abelone now called herself) dancing a solo performance and the five being featured all together in a second pantomime. The money they made from their acting appears to have been enough for the family to move out of the tenement and into a small house near the waterfront in Brooklyn. Eytinge, who was a morphine addict and drank too much, soon dropped out of their lives, but her lover, William Fleron, took over the management of their act. Apparently, he saw in the five girls "great possibilities." Fleron now became their "guide, philosopher and friend" and, within a year, Lona's lover as well.[9] Once in Europe, he would be responsible for completely altering the course of the Barrison Sisters' fledgling artistic careers.

Fleron, also an immigrant from Denmark, was in his midthirties when he began his relationship with the 21-year-old Lona. He had already earned notoriety in the United States as the author of two plays—both dramatizations of French novels—that most newspaper reviewers considered obscene. What both works shared, and what likely drew Fleron to the girls, was that they dealt with the sexual appetites of women. The first—and far more successful—of his works was a version of Alexandre Dumas's *L'Affaire Clemenceau,* a Dorian Gray–like novel about infidelity, art, and moral corruption. In the play, a sculptor falls in love with and marries his beautiful and innocent model. His preoccupation with her body stimulates her sexual interests and, unable to satisfy her curiosity and desire with her husband, she proceeds to seduce and ruin a series of men until, at the close, her husband kills her, to the hearty applause of the audience. The second play, *Elysium,* based on a Mario Uchard erotic novel, tells the story of a man who inherits a harem of eight girls. He "enjoys his possession to the full for a while," but eventually "settles down" and marries one of his former sex slaves.[10] In both works, Fleron explored what were for the time risqué issues: Was it immoral or fun to have multiple sexual partners? When were emotions like love and desire destructive or consuming? What was the relationship between beauty and moral corruption, love and sex? What was the nature of female sexual desire?

Without doubt, it was Fleron who oversaw the Barrisons' descent into wickedness while they were in Europe. He closely controlled the girls, wrote the songs for them, and managed their affairs; he even refused to allow them to talk to the press unless he was present. Toulouse-Lautrec captured his influence in a splendid 1896 portrait of Lona leading Maestoso onto the stage of the Folies Bergère. Although Lona and her horse are centered in the frame, it is Fleron's looming, leering figure that dominates the picture (figure 1.2). Fleron's preoccupation with the latent eroticism of the supposedly innocent was evident in his infantilization of the sisters. His technique of shocking the audience by having ostensibly respectable young women crudely revealing their sexual passions became the central feature of their act. It was also Fleron who encouraged them to describe sexual satisfaction as a form of empowerment, so that the women he wrote for—whether as characters in his plays or as singers in a variety show—expressed their personal independence in terms of the power they felt as objects of male desire. And it was Fleron's humor—his fondness for camp—that gave the show its burlesque feel.

American newspaper reporters did not choose to make these connections. Although they sensed Fleron's influence and generally depicted him as a sleazy promoter, they did not bother to probe too deeply. For American observers, the Barrisons' descent into wickedness simply showed the dangers empty-headed girls faced when they had dealings with debauched Europeans. As they pointed out, there was nothing shocking about them prior to the Barrison Sisters crossing the Atlantic. Fleron to their mind was a facilitator—a kind of pimp—but he was not the instigator. Wickedness, they believed, was due to the Barrisons' own moral failure.

There was some truth to this interpretation. Although their bodies had always been the main focus of attention—Lona's being considered "a vision calculated to entrance the mind and the senses alike"—their act was not naughty prior to their European engagement. The Barrisons spent the summer of 1893 traveling around the Midwest and the South, where they appeared at such places as the Dallas agricultural fair. Their hair and curves and legs did attract notice, but that was not unusual. The sisters were usually described as "pretty," "charming," and "amusing," unlikely adjectives to apply to an act of wickedness. Moreover, even at this point their singing and acting were rated as weak, and critics urged them to "throw more feeling into [their] phrases."[11]

The break for the Barrisons occurred in September 1893 when Fleron secured their engagement at the Trocadero, a new theater owned by the promoter Florenz Ziegfeld. The Trocadero was Chi-

Figure 1.2. Henri de Toulouse-Lautrec, *Lona Barrison avec son manager et epoux,* 1900. The horse is Maestoso.
Source: Brooklyn Museum Collection.

cago's high-class variety house, and it featured a Hungarian dance band and specialized in imported European performers. It was during their week in Chicago that they were contracted to appear at the Folies Bergère in Paris, possibly by a scout there to locate a successor act for another Chicago star, the dancer Loïe Fuller. However it happened, two months later the Barrison Sisters left New York in November 1893, after a final stint at the Eden Musee.[12]

As in their American act, their initial Paris performances emphasized the Barrisons' youth and prettiness. Mrs. Barrison apparently accompanied her children to Paris, and this probably guaranteed some measure of decency, despite the house. Their act opened with the girls sitting in children's costumes, singing nursery rhymes to dolls. They then moved and postured about stiffly as they sang nonsense songs. Some even then reported their movements to be stilted, impassive, and mechanical. An English reviewer thought they were "grotesque" and "graceless," showing "due disregard for the music and time," while an Austrian commentator likened their posturing to Egyptian frieze art. Nonetheless, the charm and prettiness of the five young Americans made them, according to *Le Figaro,* one of the delights of the season. Likely, the timing of their arrival helped them immeasurably. Loïe Fuller was an imaginative dancer, and she provided the Folies Bergère with a level of propriety that it had hitherto lacked. Middle-class women had begun to attend the theater, and the Barrisons, who were, at this point in their careers, sweet rather than decadent, probably appealed to the more genteel crowd that was attending matinees with their children in tow.[13]

For Parisian audiences, a large measure of the Barrisons' appeal also came from their embodiment of a beauty ideal that art nouveau's decorative objects was spreading through the French middle class. Like the women in Alphonse Mucha posters and on the lamps, parlor table statuary, and vases of the belle époque, they had masses of tussled hair, china doll faces, ruffled clothing, and hands that were forever artificially, if delicately, posed. As five living embodiments of the new rococo, the celebration of the feminine, the fluid, the intimate, and the sensuous, they were instantly appealing. Parisians appear to have found nothing subversive about them, and they made no initial impact on the circles of symbolists or on the impressionists, with their antiestablishment associations (Toulouse-Lautrec did not sketch Lona until the Barrison Sisters' return to Paris from New York). The Barrisons, like art nouveau itself, initially sold youth, renewal, and regeneration, not rebellion, decay, and social criticism. Admittedly, there was something oddly sexy about them, and Fleron's staging ensured that beneath the coldness and calm of their movements there was an erotic implication, something titillating, a kind of seductive energy. They were, wrote observers searching for the adjectives that align them with the fluid femininity so admired in the belle époque, "snakey," "wormlike," and even "rubbery."[14]

If the French were charmed by the performers' youth and erotic potential, German spectators found other things to interest them. As

Figure 1.3. The five Barrison Sisters as they would have appeared at the height of their notoriety, 1896.
Source: New York Public Library, Billy Rose Theatre Collection, Barrison Sisters' Clipping File.

in Paris, "it was the quintuple picture of prettiness that pleased, at first," but their act changed in the months they spent at the Wintergarten in Berlin, and they gained surprising admission into a society far above their own. Language was undoubtedly a factor—for the girls knew German but not French—as was the departure of their mother, who apparently returned to Denmark when they moved to Berlin under the exclusive care of Fleron. But an even more potent contact was Wilhelm von Bernstorff—the son of Albrecht Graf von Bernstorff, the former Prussian foreign minister and minister of state—who had fallen for Sophie Barrison in New York and now reconnected with her. Bernstorff quite probably introduced the girls to a society far removed from the one they had known in Greenpoint. In Berlin, they started associating with a group of aristocratic Guard Cavalry officers who drank excessively and gambled ferociously. Most were from prominent Prussian families: Puttkammers, Plessens, Kleists, Kardoffs, and Kanitzes. Lona became the especial favorite, and she often joined the officers for late nights of drinking and gaming. One scandalous report described her winning a bet by riding a horse in the imperial stables in the middle of the night in her underclothes (or less). Another story circulated that a Count Aldorf shot himself over his love for Gertrude. Still another described a Count Wedel who had pawned the family jewels in order to pay the gambling debts he had acquired in Lona's company. One has to be careful not to take the gossip too literally, but at least one of the scandals did have truth to it. Early in 1895, Sophie ran off to London with her aristocratic suitor, apparently marrying Bernstorff en route. The marriage caused a scandal: Bernstorff, who was in his midforties, apparently had a wife already (though it is not clear if they were divorced or separated) and Sophie was only sixteen. The marriage was quickly dissolved, Bernstorff was hustled off on a diplomatic mission to China, and the manager of the Wintergarten threatened Fleron with breach of contract—he had contracted five Barrisons, not four—if Sophie did not return. Lona went to retrieve her errant sister, and while she was in London she took the precaution of picking up an understudy, an English actor who went by the stage name of "Tutti Frutti" but was quietly admitted into the family as Ethel Barrison.[15]

The sisters increasingly played to the interests of an audience drawn to the stink of scandal. They became "the rage in the German capital." In Berlin "Do You Want to See My Pussy?" was added, and Lona introduced her striptease. As Lona had now moved into a featured spot in the act, Ethel replaced her as the fifth Barrison in the group numbers. Although this meant that there were six performing "Barrisons," they continued to advertise themselves as a five-sister act. The mathematical incongruities continued when, in Vienna, the Barrisons added another "sister": Mabel. In Germany the Barrison Sisters became pop icons: postcards, prints, and posters were produced of them; they were featured in liquor and cigarette advertising; and the Thuringian porcelain manufacturer Ernst Bohne Söhne produced them as a set of slightly naughty figurines (figure 1.4).

The Barrisons' wickedness attracted new followers when they moved to Vienna and Budapest after six months at the Wintergarten. Fun-loving, dissipated aristocrats continued to enjoy after-theater entertainments with the girls. One of them—likely Count Arthur Pallavicini—gave Lona the Lipizzaner stallion, Maestoso, and Fleron wrote the song about riding to follow her striptease. After the show, the men caroused with the sisters, gambled, and drank heavily. Some of them, cut from the same cloth as Wedel, had trouble paying the bills: a Kröcher ended up in court because his family refused to cover his losses at the table. In the most scandalous connection of all, the twenty-year-old Pallavicini, a member of one of the most venerable families in the Austro-Hungarian Empire, shot himself purportedly over his love for Ethel. His funeral in Budapest was a solemn event, with the hearse draped in taffeta and a troupe of army officers carrying a margrave's crown on a silk cushion followed by, of all people, Ethel, dressed in mourning black. At the church, she fulfilled the count's last wish, as specified in his suicide note (the text of which had been released to the public), by placing a kiss on the dead man's lips.[16]

It was a fantastic spectacle, and news of it shot across the United States, where it joined the growing list of articles dealing with the Barrisons' sexual escapades. No one appears to have asked how much was true and how much theater; the narrative of the Barrisons' decline into sin and old-world decadence fit too easily into accepted cultural fictions concerning nation and gender. For two years, the American press charted the Barrisons' moral degeneration with appalled interest. Europe, the journalists knew from the outset, was responsible for turning them wicked. For American newspapers, which sought to understand the Barrison phenomenon from within the context of familiar narratives, it was really very simple. Despite their father's financial and moral failure, they had been good girls when they left the United States, their only flaw (albeit an un-American one) being the sin of haughtiness. Looking for their roots in the streets of Brooklyn, a local reporter concluded: "Greenpoint was not responsible for the wickedness of Mr. Fleron's protégées, for nearly every one agrees that they were good little girls before they crossed the river." Naturally, their wickedness needed explaining, even by New Yorkers. The Barrisons upset the conviction that Americans were an exceptional people, distinct in their democratic inclinations and moral principles. They were a challenge to the oldest of all American themes: the dichotomization of election and damnation, saints and sinners, the New World and the Old. Americans saw themselves as a special people because they had escaped the corruption and oppression of Europe. They had freed themselves from the burden of repressive laws and false beliefs. "What a relief," Francis Peabody remarked in 1915, "it is to recall that in America religion is not primarily an institution, but an experience; not a form of government, but a way of life!"[17] As former immigrants, the sisters were seen to be moving in the wrong direction, back into moral laxity and old-world decay. And in order to maintain the myth of American exceptionalism, their career in Europe had to be read as a fable of contamination, of sweet (if fluffy-headed) American girls corrupted by old-world sin.

Of course, the sisters were engaged in mythmaking of their own. Cut loose from their American roots, the sisters energetically re-created their own lives, not just by replacing themselves with others—by the time they reached Vienna two members of the troupe were merely playing at being siblings—but also by raising their status: they now talked about having had servants in Greenpoint, and of singing at the Metropolitan Opera. Those who associated closely with them joined them in the world of deceit and make-believe that was international celebrity. The juxtaposition of elements—children's clothing and sexual knowledge, eroticism and the absence of expression or feeling—made them irresistible targets for burlesque. Dressing up as the Barrisons became a favorite male gag; the day before Pallavicini shot himself he and his fellow officers had even switched clothes with the girls and then played naughty suit to each other. In Germany, much to the horror of the emperor, young officers of his Guard Cavalry appeared on stage at a royal entertainment dressed up as the girls. Alfred of Saxe-Coburg and Gotha apparently did a Barrison cross-dressing act wearing Lona's actual gown and underskirts, and dozens of less pretentious female impersonators took Barrison acts to the popular stages. The burlesque extended even further: according to a Viennese correspondent who knew the margrave, Pallavicini had not shot himself because of Ethel, but because his family was broke, he was hopelessly in debt, and he was being hounded by his creditors. It was the family, the informant noted, who concocted the love connection with Ethel in order to cover their liabilities and add a romantic twist to the young man's death, which would explain why one of the noblest families in the Austro-Hungarian Empire allowed a variety show entertainer a place of honor at his funeral. Similarly, contrary to the story that circulated, Kröcher had not run himself into debt because of Lona; he had known her only three months, and she was certainly not the cause of his gambling.[18]

The Barrisons' outsider status made them potent symbols of a European cultural upheaval. They were without local roots, and so even though their act's naughtiness was less original or unusual than it was presented as being, the fact that there were five of them made them seem like moral marauders from the cultural periphery. Moreover, because they presented themselves as wholesome young women from a good family who trivialized sex (by singing dispassionately about it), they excited audiences and inspired artists, craftsmen, and advertisers. The writer, Hugo von Hofmannsthal, who saw the Barrisons in 1895 and thought they were English, described them as manifestations of a pre-Raphaelite ideal, with their tilting "childlike shoulders" and tousled golden hair (figure 1.3). They encapsulated, in his eyes, the incongruent tendencies in En-

Figure 1.4. A German postcard produced by F. Schüler, Berlin, with the caption, "Hexenzug—Walpurgisnacht." Although the Barrison Sisters are not identified as the witches, the five figures clearly associate them with decadence and debauchery.
Source: F. Schüler, Berlin N.W.6. and Meisenbach Riffarth & Co., Leipzig, 1902.

glish art—the combination of innocence and sensuality, coldness and eroticism—that he found deeply appealing but singularly alienating. To Hofmannsthal, the curious thing about the Barrisons was that they aroused sexual interest even though they were "mannered and pristine, ignorant that they have something exciting to offer." He described them not as brazenly erotic but as cold, detached, and elegant. He remembered them dancing a gavotte, the white folds of their dresses swaying silently and slowly, evoking for him Fragonard-like images of elegant ladies in a pastoral setting. What fascinated Hofmannsthal was the distance the actors created between their stage selves and the real women he knew he was watching; this attracted him to them and yet imposed distance.[19]

The journalist and critic Anton Lindner was similarly fascinated by the incongruities in the Barrisons' performances and wrote a bizarre book about them in which he depicted them as emblems of the fin de siècle, looking not forward to modernity but backward to a culture that was crumbling under the weight of its own contradictions. His imagery was, however, like that of the postcards and the porcelain maker, more graphic and physical than Hofmannsthal's. "They lift up their colored skirts," Lindner observed, "and in so doing emphatically reveal their awareness of the faded values of their time." But like Hofmannsthal, he was intrigued by the alienation of the girls from their own erotic performances. Emulating the contrarieties in their act in his book, he wrote in German, under an assumed French name, and with a supposed introduction by a translator who had rendered the book from its purported French original. To Lindner, the Barrisons were an antipodean inspiration, corrupt children, soiled angels, passionless exponents of passion. The contradictions were too much for his caustic imagination, and, like other Austrian intellectuals, Lindner concluded that the Barrisons were making intelligible the dead burden of tradition that was distorting life's free expression into grotesquery.[20]

Were the Barrisons aware of the cultural disturbance they represented? To Berlin's and Vienna's decadents, they must have been, and so they interpreted their act as a grand self-conscious comedy, a cold-hearted satire on the alienation of flesh and soul. From long range, American critics held to another view: the girls were simply untalented, foolish, morally rotten gold diggers. From what little Fleron allowed them to say, it is hard to know what they thought about themselves. They seemed to enjoy their notoriety and were happy to portray themselves as vamps, but why wouldn't they seek to enhance an image that had lifted them so far out of the poverty and anonymity of Greenpoint? Intriguingly, the one thing that never attracted the attention of commentators in either the United States or Europe was the amount of ink that was being devoted to the Barrisons. Had commentators done so they might have questioned the validity of the divergent meanings they were projecting onto the feckless sisters.

Certainly, the Barrisons made no effort to revise people's views about their eroticism. While in Europe they spoke as though they had long enjoyed the fast life, to Americans they emphasized their sexual conquests. Fleron's advertising for their return trip "sent their tarnished reputations on before them," and they were promoted as having "wrecked monarchies, ruined large armies, been excommunicated from all the leading cities of Europe and sent scions of noble families to early graves. In fact, he asserts that they have broken half the family trees of Europe."[21] It was considered alluring advertising in the United States, and together with their youth and beauty both Fleron and the manager of Koster & Bial's thought it would guarantee sell-out houses. Although the press reported the sisters' immoral behavior in Europe disapprovingly, wily theater folk believed that even bad publicity would be an audience draw.

What this suggests is that entertainment people knew American audiences would take the Barrison Sisters' moral corruption and physical display in stride. No one seems to have worried that their act was too raunchy, and they were right. Although "a little thrill of shame" coursed through Koster & Bial's when Lona removed her trousers, she "disclosed nothing more than tights and loose fitted trunks and a blouse"; audiences seemed untroubled, and no one moved to censor their performance. Bodies were presented in various states of undress on American stages just as much, if not more, than on European ones. This may be why the sisters' bodies attracted more prurient interest in Europe than they did in the United States; in Europe they were objectified on a mass scale in bawdy posters and postcards, photographs, and sculptures. American commentators and audiences did not avoid watching women sing or dance in sexy ways, and they were mature enough to accept the display of naked skin when they felt it helped the show. When the Barrisons returned to the United States, the curvaceous actress Anna Held was all the rage, and her clothes were considered far more revealing than the sisters'. The first striptease on an American stage actually antedated Lona's by three years, and in the 1890s, disrobing in front of the audience had become a normal routine for trapeze artists. Charmion, the vaudeville acrobat, was more famous for her extended striptease, which she did on the trapeze, tossing clothing items to the audience, than for her perilous stunts. The year before the Barrisons' return to the United States, the manager of the Casino Roof Garden caused a stir in New York when he painted three "naked" people—two men and a woman—bronze and had them pose as statues at the entryway to the theater.[22] In short, Americans had seen bodies much less clothed than the Barrisons. The reason the sisters flopped in the United States was musical, not visual.

Americans did not respond positively to the Barrisons, even though Fleron's advance publicity had created enough excitement to supposedly guarantee their success. On opening night at Koster & Bial's, Lona received one encore for her equestrian number, which was a sign of polite rather than vociferous endorsement. The group songs were not, apparently, encored. The *New York Times* reported that "there was applause for them—for all of them—even for Lona. It was not the applause of a crowded house, however. It was not applause in which women took any part ... there were not a few hisses." Alan Dale denied that Lona was encored at all and believed "they have fallen as flat as a pancake," their only enthusiasts being a few "boozy boys and décolleté women" among the audience. But even these, he felt, were smart enough to feel disappointed. Charlotte Smith, the women's rights activist and nativist, who attended opening night, shrugged off the performance as having nothing to recommend it "beyond notoriety and the indecency of the exhibition." Perhaps the surest sign that the Barrisons did not live up to their billing was the fact that in the third week of November, at the end of their eight-week contractual run, Koster & Bial's let them go. Their act was not picked up by any other American theaters, and the Barrison Sisters quickly returned to Europe.[23]

As a sister act, the Barrisons did not long survive the scolding they received in New York. A gossip columnist observed that the craze for them "lasted about as long as the blaze from a bunch of tissue paper." They returned to Paris, short one of the extra sisters (Mabel), who chose to remain stateside, and were again featured at the Folies Bergère. Lona had never done her striptease act there with Maestoso, and it was then that Toulouse-Lautrec captured her image. But within eight months, by August 1897, the sisters had drifted apart. Ethel went back to London, no longer a Barrison. Two of the girls joined their mother in Denmark for a time, though by 1898 one of them (Gertrude) had returned to Paris (in the 1930s she was running a dance school in Vienna). Sophie reportedly opened a *café chantant* in Ostend with another sister, and possibly also Fleron, who may have by this time been her lover. Lona and Maestoso kept up a solo act in Europe and they again made the news when, in 1901, she was banned from performing in Berlin after protests from clergymen and moral leaders. Lona was the Barrison with the greatest stage ambition, and she was also the first to die, killed in a car crash with her lover, a Philadelphian, Captain Clarence Weiner, in 1908.[24]

What is interesting is that American, French, and German-language spectators in the mid-1890s heard the same singers perform the same songs in the same ways, but drew very different conclusions about them. According to all commentators, they were mannered, uninvolved, and awkward on stage, and their movements and gestures were invariably characterized as angular and disjointed. Their dancing was portrayed as stiff and jerky as they moved about the stage "with angular elbows, spread out fingers and flying curly hair"; they appeared to some observers to be more like "monkeys" than people. A Viennese spectator rather generously likened their act to "dancing between mirrors," so similar was their appearance and so artificial their posturing.[25] Even their lyrics were everywhere misunderstood, because they sang some of their songs in German to French and American audiences and in French and English to German speakers. Their French was apparently so poor that it was hard to understand even when they performed in Paris. Most European critics did not know how to place them, as their German seemed fluent (they were Danish Americans), while American writers often noted that they were of foreign birth (even though they were small children when their family immigrated).

The truth is that dissonance was at the heart of the Barrisons' act, and as a result they were never clearly heard or seen by anyone. No one seemed to notice that two of them were not Barrisons, or that somehow five siblings had became six, and then seven. In Europe, their bodies were appropriated by men as types, reproduced in bawdy art and turned into cross-dressing burlesque. Their inability to sing or dance was there misconceived as exquisite; the fact that they sang so uncomprehendingly about sexual intercourse was read alternately as sublime alienation or an utter lack of talent. The fact that they were without clear national or artistic roots—that they were unidentifiably foreign—was crucial; as an American group (that was often mistaken as British) that obtained celebrity abroad, they flourished in the zone of misunderstanding that existed between cultures. Appearing in Europe at a moment of intense cultural turmoil, they became what their observers, critics, and fans projected onto them—never understood, but remorselessly interpreted. For European critics and audiences, they were destroyers of aesthetic, sexual, and linguistic conventions and taboos, and their potency was enhanced by their outsider status.

But where European audiences found the foreign sisters' campy acting and unmelodic voices curious and significant, Americans simply considered them bad. Alan Dale, the well-known theater critic for the Hearst newspapers, described their voices as "shrill" and "thin," and he observed that they seemed to pay little attention to the words they were singing. He described their voices as flat, high-pitched—childlike—and strangely unemotional and their mannerisms as detached from the message of their music. Excoriating their most famous song, Dale wrote: "[T]here was no tune to it, no metre to it, no rhythm to it, nothing chic, nothing clever." A song, agreed the *Atlanta Constitution*'s music critic,

> be it good or bad, must be intelligently understood by its singer. Otherwise, a talking machine of wood or iron could sing it as well. Intelligence, discrimination and appreciation are necessary to art, and the Barrisons have neither. They have no art. They are merely five simpering, inane little women, with baby faces, peroxide hair, frail pipe-stem calves, and voices that suggest the nursery.[26]

The Western approach to music in the late nineteenth century transcended national boundaries, but the appreciation of its performance remained culturally and temporally bounded. There was a dominant language in Europe and the North America upon which agreement existed, an agreement that began with octaves and floated upward into harmonies and melodies. It was normal in the late nineteenth century for popular tunes in Germany or France to make their way around the Atlantic world, and music by composers working in the Western classical tradition traveled with relative ease across national boundaries. But the performance of music and the meanings that were assigned to individual works and their interpreters translated less perfectly. That is because music was conceived as more than just a way of organizing sound. It was a reflection of a spirit or intent that had to be recognized by its interpreters, conveyed in its performance, and appreciated by its audience.

The idea that music emanated from the soul of the performer, and that it was therefore potentially divine, was pervasive in mid-nineteenth-century Western culture. For Thomas Carlyle, song was "the speech of angels" and "nothing among human utterances allowed to man is felt to be so divine." Similarly, Hegel described song as expressing the inner life more perfectly than any other activity; in fact, he conceived it as the product of the oscillations of the soul itself. Music was not a reflection of "the objective world itself, but, on the contrary ... of the inmost self," Hegel wrote, and it made manifest "the depths of its personality and conscious soul." Marcel Proust found in the "unique accent" of each singer—in their individual "unmistakable voice"—in the sameness of tone to which, despite their best efforts, they "rise and return ... proof of the irreducibly individual existence of the soul." Of course, not all singing was sublime, and some, like that produced by the Barrisons, had more in common with the sirens' song than the angels'.[27] But the conventional Western approach to song production was that it was heartfelt and that it manifested the soul of its performers.

Acceptance of the conventional aesthetic made the divorce of the Barrisons' performance from their music's meaning jarring for audiences. They sang about doing naughty things but sounded like sweet, if untalented, young ladies. They turned singing—that most incandescent of art forms—into something entertaining by neutralizing its passion while singing about passion. The banality of their wickedness is what made them attractive to European audiences (and probably allowed them to move beneath the radar of vigilant Prussian censors) moving toward a modernist aesthetic that separated art from morality. The Barrisons appealed to fin de siècle European audiences because they made a mockery of the sentimental nineteenth-century association of music and soul. German, French, and Austrian spectators interpreted the girls' mundane and mannered performance as evidence of a cool sensuality. The fact that the singers did not seem to understand what they were doing made them even more sexy, given that everyone knew how wildly passionate and amoral they were from the stories circulating about their private lives. The Barrisons' striking success on the Continent was produced by their combination of innocence and sexual knowledge, harmony and discord, the emotionally charged and the uninvolved, the musical and the unmusical.

Although Americans were no more puritanical than Europeans in what they watched and listened to, they were more conventional in their appreciation of music: they wanted performers dealing with sex to convey lust or pleasure. Eroticism divorced from emotion was not amusing to them; it was commercial and cheap. Critics like Alan Dale found it hard to understand the Barrisons or determine the spirit infusing their songs and dances. He took the incongruities in their act—their mannered and mechanical posturing, expressionless tone, and rhythmic freedom—as proof that their souls were so undeveloped that they could not manage something as spiritual as song and dance. Their neutrality made them appear businesslike in describing sex, and this made them seem to Americans like prostitutes. Dale and other critics made no effort to understand the Barrisons in unconventional ways in part because the sisters so easily fit into a national myth of moral degeneration that they did not need to ask aesthetic questions. What was involved here was not so much prudery as an old-fashioned approach to music making and an unspoken faith in the moral superiority of the great democracy.

Although wickedness resonated in similar ways on both sides of the Atlantic, the performance of music did not. What the different receptions received by the Barrison Sisters in Europe and the United States suggests is that music performance is culturally bounded even if the music being performed arises from a shared tradition. The artificiality of the Barrisons' singing and dancing, which Europeans considered new and amusing and alien, was viewed in the United States as evidence of either vapidity or a moral corruption that was entirely mercenary. The unfortunate fact that the sisters were Americans then made their lack of talent and scandalous behavior a source of embarrassment and anger.

An international approach allows us to see that music reception has a history and that it developed in different ways in different places. It helps us to understand how, as in the case of the Barrisons, a performance might be untranslatable. The sisters touched a vein of perception too tangled up in cultural predilections and national myths to cross borders. As the critic for the *Atlanta Constitution* explained, Americans wanted their theatrical temptresses to sound and look like they meant no good. What he saw on stage at Koster & Bial's was simply a group of young women trying "desperately" to appear wicked as "they wiggled and twisted about and displayed their lingerie and piped on with their little vulgar song." But as it was, to his eye and ear, they revealed merely their "conception of wickedness," nothing more. "Their idea of wickedness [was] hatched in an incubator," he wrote presciently, "it has been cultured as well as their feeble strength would admit. They have made a study of it." Alan Dale agreed; no red-blooded American male, he wrote, would consider killing himself for one of the Barrisons—they were simply too uninvolved and uninteresting. The fact that they were the toast of Europe's military aristocracy only showed how effete and febrile the Old World had become. The Barrisons' music making had "failed" to arouse Dale's sexual interest, and that, in the end, was the measure he applied to both their wickedness and their music making. The sexual appeal of what the fictitious showgirl Dixie Dugan would describe as "being cool and looking hot" was still some decades off in America. "What a miserable failure," the *Atlanta Constitution*'s writer concluded in disgust when reflecting on the Barrisons. It was simply a "farce, [and] ... fiasco!"[28]

Notes

1. Undated clipping titled "From Nothingness to Notoriety," Barrison Sisters' File, Harvard Theatre Collection, Harvard University Archive (hereafter HTC).
2. *Chicago Daily Tribune,* 6 October 1896; *Atlanta Constitution,* 8 October 1896; undated review by Alan Dale [October 1896], Barrison Sisters' File, Billy Rose Theatre Collection, New York Public Library (hereafter NYPL).
3. Christina Simmons, "Modern Sexuality and the Myth of Victorian Repression," in *Passion and Power: Sexuality in History,* ed. Kathy Peiss and Christina Simmons (Philadelphia: Temple University Press, 1989), 158.
4. Undated clipping [October 1896], Barrison Sisters' File, HTC.
5. *New York Journal,* 27 September 1896.
6. Undated clippings [1895 and October 1896], Barrison Sisters' File, HTC; Wolfgang Jansen, *Das Varieté: Die glanzvolle Geschichte einer unterhaltenden Kunst* (Berlin: Edition Hentich, 1990), 105–18; Rainer Otto and Walter Rösler, *Kabarettgeschichte: Abriss des deutschsprachigen Kabaretts* (Berlin: Henschelverlag, 1981), 28.

7. *Brooklyn Daily Eagle*, 4 October 1896; miscellaneous undated clippings [1894–98], Barrison Sisters' File, NYPL; *World* [New York], 3 April 1898.
8. *New York Times*, 10 September 1889; undated clippings, Barrison Sisters' File, HTC; *New York World*, 1 November 1908, Barrison Sisters' File, HTC; clipping dated October 1899, Barrison Sisters' File, HTC; clipping dated 1896, Barrison Sisters' File, NYPL; *New York Times*, 10 September 1889; *New York Evening Telegram*, 10 September 1889; *New York Dramatic Mirror*, 10 October 1896.
9. *Sunday World* [New York], 15 June 1891; undated clipping from *Sunday World* [New York] titled "'The Face of an Angel, the Heart of a Devil' Says Pearl Eytinge," Barrison Sisters' File, NYPL; *New York Dramatic Mirror*, 25 March 1893.
10. *New York Dramatic Mirror*, 5 October 1890; *World* [New York], 17 May 1892; *New York Dramatic Mirror*, 28 October 1891; *New York Clipper*, 21 May 1892; *Brooklyn Daily Eagle*, 17 February 1891; *World* [New York], 16 September 1890.
11. *New York Times*, 16 March 1893; for reviews of Abelone, see *Brooklyn Daily Eagle*, 8 October 1891; *Buffalo Morning Express*, 16 October 1891.
12. Undated clipping titled "The Barrison Sisters," Barrison Sisters' File, HTC; *New York Dramatic Mirror*, 13 May 1893; on the Trocadero, see *Chicago Daily Tribune*, 16 April 1893, 26 April 1893, 27 April 1893, and (on the Barrisons' performance there) 17 September 1893.
13. *Graphic* [London], 16 June 1894; Pierre d'Ubecq [Anton Lindner], *Die Barrisons: Ein Kunsttraum* (Berlin: Schuster and Loeffler, 1897), 76; Naoko Morita, "An American in Paris: Loïe Fuller, Dance and Technology," in *A Belle Epoque? Women in French Society and Culture*, ed. Diana Holmes (New York: Berghahn Books, 2006), 115–16; Rhonda Garelick, *Electric Salome: Loïe Fuller's Performance of Modernism* (Princeton, NJ: Princeton University Press, 2007), 33.
14. Deborah Silverman, *Art Nouveau in Fin-de-Siecle France* (Berkeley: University of California Press 1992); Catherine Hindson, *Female Performance Practice on the Fin de Siècle Popular Stage* (Manchester: Manchester University Press 2008); Elizabeth Menon, "Women on the Fringe," in *Montmartre and the Making of Mass Culture*, ed. Gabriel Weisberg (New Brunswick, NJ: Rutgers University Press, 2001), 37–71; *Le Figaro*, 5 January 1894; d'Ubecq, *Die Barrisons*, 75.
15. On Sophie and Bernstorff, see *Dallas Morning News*, 28 January 1895; undated clipping titled "The Barrison Sisters," Barrison Sisters' File, HTC. On the Barrisons' drinking companions, see *Le Figaro*, 6 October 1899. On Sophie's elopement, see *Chicago Daily Tribune*, 20 January 1895 and 27 January 1895; *Los Angeles Times*, 27 January 1895.
16. Undated clipping titled "The Barrison Sisters," Barrison Sisters' File, HTC. On Maestoso, see Melody Hull, "Maestoso Mystery Solved," *Haute École: Quarterly Publication of the Lipizzan Association of North America* 16, no. 3 (2008): 3–5.; clipping dated 17 April 1899, Lona Barrison File, NYPL. For Pallavicini's suicide, see *Chicago Daily Tribune*, 15 August 1896; undated clipping titled "Barrison Sister Followed Margrave Arthur to the Grave," Barrison Sisters' File, NYPL.
17. *Brooklyn Daily Eagle*, 4 October 1896; Francis Peabody, "Americans Abroad," *Antioch Review* 201, no. 712 (March 1915): 371.
18. Lona invented an operatic career for herself in Germany; see the interview quoted in Jansen, *Das Varieté*, 106. For the Kröcher case, see *Le Figaro*, 4 October 1899. On insight into the Pallavicini suicide, see undated clipping titled "Barrison Sister Followed Margrave Arthur to the Grave," Barrison Sisters' File, NYPL.
19. Hugo von Hofmannsthal, "Englischer Stil," in *Gesammelte Werke: Prosa*, vol. 1 (Frankfurt: Fischer, 1956), 194–98; Mary Gilbert, ed., *Hugo von Hofmannsthal—Edgar Karg von Bebenburg: Briefwechsel* (Frankfurt: Fischer, 1966), 107–8; undated clipping from *Moderne Kunst*, Barrison Sisters' File, NYPL; see also Jansen, *Das Varieté*, 111–12.

20. D'Ubecq, *Die Barrisons*, 47.
21. Undated clipping titled "The Barrison Pantalettes," Barrison Sisters' File, HTC.
22. Ibid.; David Monod, "The Eyes of Anna Held: Sex and Sight in the Progressive Era," *The Journal of the Gilded Age and Progressive Era* 10, no. 3 (July 2011): 289–328; Eva Golden, *Anna Held and the Birth of Ziegfeld's Broadway* (Lexington: University of Kentucky Press, 2000); *Chicago Daily Tribune*, 15 August 1890. Charmion was not exactly poetry in motion, as a 1901 Edison film of her disrobing act demonstrates. The film can be seen at http://www.youtube.com/watch?v=CdxoZcHG9BY. On the bronzes, see Rudolph Aronson, *Theatrical and Musical Memoirs* (New York: McBride, Nast, 1913), chap. 8.
23. *New York Times*, 6 October 1896; undated review by Alan Dale [October 1896], Barrison Sisters' File, NYPL; undated clipping titled "Lewd and Indecent Says Charlotte Smith," Barrison Sisters' File, NYPL; undated clipping titled "Should be Suppressed, Says Dr. Pankhurst," Barrison Sisters' File, NYPL.
24. Clipping dated 22 May 1898, Barrison Sisters' File, NYPL; clipping dated August 1897, Barrison Sisters' File, NYPL; "Lona Barrison's Last Victim," August 1897, Barrison Sisters' File, HTC; undated clipping fragment titled "The Sisters Separate," Barrison Sisters' File, NYPL; *Philadelphia Inquirer*, 30 October 1908.
25. D'Ubecq, *Die Barrisons*, 54.
26. Undated review by Alan Dale [October 1896], Barrison Sisters' File, NYPL; *Atlanta Constitution*, 18 October 1896.
27. Thomas Carlyle, "The Opera," in *Critical and Miscellaneous Essays*, vol. 4 (Boston: Brown and Taggard, 1860), 441; Georg Wilhelm Friedrich Hegel, *Aesthetics and Lectures on Fine Art*, vol. 2, trans. T. K. Knox (Oxford: Clarendon Press, 1975), 891; Marcel Proust to Mr. and Mrs. Sydney Schiff, in Marcel Proust, *Correspondence*, vol. 21, ed. Philip Kolb (Paris: Plon1993), 372–73. See also Nicky Losseff, "The Voice, the Breath, the Soul: Song and Poverty in Thyrze, Mary Barton, Alton Locke and the Child of Iago," in *The Idea of Music in Victorian Fiction*, ed. Sophie Fuller and Nancy Losseff (Aldershot, UK: Ashgate, 2004), 8–9; Leslie Dunn and Nancy Jones, "Introduction," in *Embodied Voices: Representing Female Vocality in Western Culture*, ed. Leslie Dunn and Nancy Jones (Cambridge: Cambridge University Press, 1994), 1–14.
28. *Atlanta Constitution*, 18 October 1896.

Bibliography

Archives

Billy Rose Theatre Collection, New York Public Library
Harvard Theatre Collection, Harvard University Archive

Printed Sources

Aronson, Rudolph. *Theatrical and Musical Memoirs*. New York: McBride, Nast, 1913.

Carlyle, Thomas. "The Opera." In *Critical and Miscellaneous Essays*, vol. 4. 397–403. Boston: Brown and Taggard, 1860.

d'Ubecq, Pierre [Anton Lindner]. *Die Barrisons: Ein Kunsttraum*. Berlin: Schuster and Loeffler, 1897.

Dunn, Leslie, and Nancy Jones. "Introduction." In *Embodied Voices: Representing Female Vocality in Western Culture,* ed. Leslie Dunn and Nancy Jones, 1–14. Cambridge: Cambridge University Press, 1994.
Garelick, Rhonda. *Electric Salome: Loïe Fuller's Performance of Modernism.* Princeton, NJ: Princeton University Press, 2007.
Gilbert, Mary, ed. *Hugo von Hofmannsthal—Edgar Karg von Bebenburg: Briefwechsel.* Frankfurt: Fischer, 1966.
Golden, Eva. *Anna Held and the Birth of Ziegfeld's Broadway.* Lexington: University of Kentucky Press, 2000.
Hegel, Georg Wilhelm Friedrich. *Aesthetics and Lectures on Fine Art.* Vol. 2. Translated by T. K. Knox. Oxford: Clarendon Press, 1975.
Hindson, Catherine. *Female Performance Practice on the Fin de Siècle Popular Stage.* Manchester: Manchester University Press, 2008.
Hofmannsthal, Hugo von. "Englischer Stil." In *Gesammelte Werke: Prosa,* vol. 1, 194–98. Frankfurt: Fischer, 1956.
Hull, Melody. "Maestoso Mystery Solved." *Haute École: Quarterly Publication of the Lipizzan Association of North America* 16, no. 3 (2008): 3–5.
Jansen, Wolfgang. *Das Varieté: Die glanzvolle Geschichte einer unterhaltenden Kunst.* Berlin: Edition Hentich, 1990.
Losseff, Nicky. "The Voice, the Breath, the Soul: Song and Poverty in Thyrze, Mary Barton, Alton Locke and the Child of Iago." In *The Idea of Music in Victorian Fiction,* ed. Sophie Fuller and Nancy Losseff, 3–27. Aldershot, UK: Ashgate, 2004.
Menon, Elizabeth. "Women on the Fringe." In *Montmartre and the Making of Mass Culture,* ed. Gabriel Weisberg. 37–72. New Brunswick, NJ: Rutgers University Press, 2001.
Monod, David. "The Eyes of Anna Held: Sex and Sight in the Progressive Era." *The Journal of the Gilded Age and Progressive Era* 10, no. 3 (July 2011): 289–328.
Morita, Naoko. "An American in Paris: Loïe Fuller, Dance and Technology." In *A Belle Epoque? Women in French Society and Culture,* ed. Diana Holmes, 113–25. New York: Berghahn Books, 2006.
Otto, Rainer, and Walter Rösler. *Kabarettgeschichte: Abriss des deutschsprachigen Kabaretts.* Berlin: Henschelverlag, 1981.
Peabody, Francis. "Americans Abroad." *Antioch Review* 201, no. 712 (March 1915): 366–71.
Proust, Marcel. *Correspondence.* Vol. 21. Edited by Philip Kolb. Paris: Plon, 1993.
Silverman, Deborah. *Art Nouveau in Fin-de-Siecle France.* Berkeley: University of California Press, 1992.
Simmons, Christina. "Modern Sexuality and the Myth of Victorian Repression." In *Passion and Power: Sexuality in History,* ed. Kathy Peiss and Christina Simmons. Philadelphia: Temple University Press, 1989.

Chapter Two

THE INTERNATIONAL SOCIETY FOR CONTEMPORARY MUSIC AND ITS POLITICAL CONTEXT (PRAGUE, 1935)

Anne C. Shreffler

Like the League of Nations and the other international organizations conceived in its spirit after World War I, the International Society for Contemporary Music (ISCM) found its very survival threatened by the political turbulence that arose between the Nazi seizure of power in 1933 and the outbreak of war in 1939. The ISCM, an institution based on voluntary international cooperation, was forced to defend its nonpolitical aims in an age of extreme ideologies. In this chapter, I seek to understand what happened when this purportedly neutral organization was thrust into confrontation with party politics. During the summer and autumn of 1935, the ISCM had to react constantly to rapidly changing external political events as well as to internal pressures while trying to continue its mission to support contemporary composition.[1] In the process, the organization was forced to articulate a political and aesthetic position for the first time; the result was a fuller commitment to modernist styles than before, along with a historically farsighted pledge to defend the artistic freedom of the composer.

Only part of the battle over the ISCM was about the proper relationship between music and the state—politics in the strict sense. Larger questions about whether music could express a "national spirit" and still have international validity, music's role in creating social change, the link between contemporary music and its

---

Notes for this section begin on page 83.

audience, and even the definition of "contemporary music" itself emerged from these confrontations. In a highly charged political environment in which nationalism, and with it a suspicion of all cosmopolitan blends, was embraced by both right and left, the notion of music as neutral ground where hostilities could be set aside was a position that was harder and harder to maintain. As public policy and private ambitions collided, even the very substance of music was drawn into the political maelstrom as its styles, techniques, and idioms acquired political associations.

This moment of upheaval involving the ISCM provides an excellent opportunity to think about the relationship between music and international history. As the European new music scene was drawn into the political whirlwinds in the summer of 1935, groups whose squabbles had been mainly of the familiar, internal "artistic politics" kind were suddenly confronted with actual state politics. The ISCM was caught in the cross fire between pressures from the Scylla of the National Socialist alternative organization, the Permanent Council for the International Cooperation of Composers, on the one hand and the Charybdis of the Moscow-based Popular Front on the other. The ISCM was put into a position of having to decide whether to align with one side or the other, or indeed whether to take sides at all. The decision was not a symmetrical one. The National Socialist embrace of nationalist and ethnic (*völkisch*) values clashed overtly with the ISCM's internationalist profile and especially with its avant-garde wing. Moreover, the ISCM's openness to emigrant and refugee composers, whether Jewish or not, was a thorn in the side of National Socialist cultural policy, as was the ISCM's tolerance of atonal and twelve-tone music. While these factors pushed the organization clearly away from Nazi Germany, the separation was not easy because of the ISCM's strong historical connections to the German-speaking musical world—the Austrian and German sections had always been by far the most influential. Given the Soviet Union's perceived openness to modernist music and to international organizations (temporary and opportunistic though these attitudes may have been), as well as its acceptance of Jewish emigrants, it would have been logical, and in the short term probably quite advantageous, for the ISCM to have aligned itself with the Soviet cultural apparatus, yet this course, too, was vehemently resisted.

It is worth recalling that at this time new concert music was important enough for politicians to struggle over. While performance institutions such as opera houses or symphony orchestras possess political significance because of their ability to represent and project economic and cultural power, the production of lasting new works can be viewed as an even stronger index of cultural and national vitality. Although contemporary classical music has never been dominant in mainstream concert life, its perceived capacity to renew and perpetuate the musical canon has given it disproportionate influence in aesthetic debates.[2] The battle over the ISCM, which was in effect a proxy debate over the future of music, was fueled by the shared and implicit conviction that the nation that could produce the next Mahler, Puccini, or Debussy would gain great respect and cultural power.

The story of the confrontation over the future of the ISCM in Prague in 1935, insofar as it has been remembered at all, is told in one of two ways: as a missed opportunity or as a dodged bullet. Either the ISCM is chastised for its failure to take advantage of Moscow's offer of partnership or it is praised for insisting on the primacy of artistic values over political ones.[3] I will seek a more differentiated verdict. The organization ultimately preserved its independence from party politics, but at the price of a loss of political innocence; for the first time, the ISCM was forced to define its previously unarticulated neutral space between right and left. While the ISCM's hard-won expression of political neutrality was literally untenable at the time, it turned out to be highly prescient, as it anticipated the later Cold War aesthetic divide between a politicized left and a purportedly neutral center based on the ideal of artistic freedom. Examining this moment in 1935 helps to uncover the acute political struggles that lay behind that notion of neutrality, which, reigning after World War II, reduced new music to an expression of the single, "free" individual unconnected with any social force and unencumbered by any earthly bonds.

History and Structure of the ISCM

The ISCM, founded in Salzburg in the wake of World War I, aimed to create an international forum for contemporary classical music as a way to compensate for a cultural environment that was often hostile or unaccommodating to it. Intended as a kind of League of Nations for contemporary composition, international collaboration was in the organization's DNA. There was a distinctly utopian flavor to the enterprise: countries that had fought each other on the battlefield could join together in the name of artistic progress.[4] Received notions of music's independence from politics made this possible, and the ISCM was accordingly constituted as an explicitly nonpolitical organization.

A fundamental, and unresolved, tension between national musical aspirations and their international scope was built into the ISCM's very structure. The organization, which still exists, is comprised of national "sections." These may or may not carry out yearlong programs of their own, but their main function is to nominate works to be played at yearly international festivals (now called World Music Days). An international jury selected by the delegates from each section chooses works for the festival. (In the time period under investigation, the host country was expected to cover all costs.) Committed to supporting the newest music, the ISCM avoided allying itself exclusively with any one style or school.[5] While the jury was supposed to make its choices on musical criteria alone, there was often tension between the dual aims of selecting the best compositions on the one hand and having a truly international program on the other. This problem was usually resolved in favor of a kind of informal quota system designed to ensure the representation of the most active sections, even if this meant that occasionally works of lesser quality were chosen.[6] The ISCM, as a loosely organized collective of voluntary participants, was more analogous to the (later) European Union than to the United States. Individual national sections differed greatly, with some of the larger sections, most notably Germany and Austria, enjoying generous state support, while others, like the American section, relying on private donations and unpaid volunteers. It would be a mistake to ascribe too much influence to the ISCM; performance opportunities and working conditions for classical composers were affected much more by the situation in their own countries than by the international organization. But in spite of the fact that the ISCM had no real authority and few resources of its own, its yearly festivals brought composers together and showcased their works before international audiences. There was no other institution of comparable legitimacy and scope.

The ISCM Festival in Prague, 1935

> "Thus the Soviet Union saved the Festival."
> —Alan Bush, "The I.S.C.M. Festival at Prague"

The thirteenth festival of the ISCM "was notable in the history of the Society for two reasons, firstly through the uncertainty that prevailed as to whether it would take place at all, secondly because of its astonishing success with the general public—all the concerts except the first having been sold out long before they were due to begin."[7] Thus the English composer Alan Bush described the artistic success of the festival as well as the turmoil that surrounded it. The festival was originally to take place in Karlsbad (now known as Karlovy Vary) in western Czechoslovakia. Karlsbad had been chosen over its competitors, Brussels and Berlin, for several reasons: First, the well-known resort town promised "an unlimited number" of rehearsals and generous hospitality. Second, the festival would mark the one hundredth anniversary of the well-known spa's famous Kurorchester.[8] Third, Czechoslovakia boasted a thriving classical music culture and, as an independent democracy, it had attracted a large community of German musicians who had fled Nazi Germany. Finally, the presence of a vital Czech new music scene, whose most prominent representative was the quarter-tone composer Alois Hába, made the choice of Karlsbad a logical one.

The festival jury, which included the exiled German conductor Hermann Scherchen, selected an ambitious program of sixteen works for orchestra (one with chorus) and fifteen chamber works.[9] (The program as pictured on the cover of the Viennese music journal *Anbruch* is shown in figure 2.1.) The Second Viennese School was well represented. Anton Webern's Concerto for Nine Instruments, op. 24, which was among the Austrian nominations, received its world premiere at the festival. Two other emblematic works of musical modernism, Arnold Schoenberg's Variations for Orchestra, op. 31, and Alban Berg's Symphonic Pieces from *Lulu*, were chosen by the jury unilaterally, without nomination by any national section.[10]

An announcement of the festival published in the January–February issue of the German-language Czech music journal *Der Auftakt* describes the works to be performed and indicates the nationalities of their composers. This list differentiates between "Czech" and "Sudeten German" composers living in Czechoslovakia; German nationals are described as *reichsdeutsche* composers.[11] These terminological distinctions foreshadow the changing political circumstances that led to the next turn of events.

In early July 1935, after months of apparently harmonious preparations, and less than two months before the starting date, the Karlsbad city council announced that it was canceling the ISCM festival. Reasons given included insufficient financing as well as competition from other festivals taking place that year in Hamburg, Dresden, and Salzburg. A much more likely reason, however, for Karlsbad's sud-

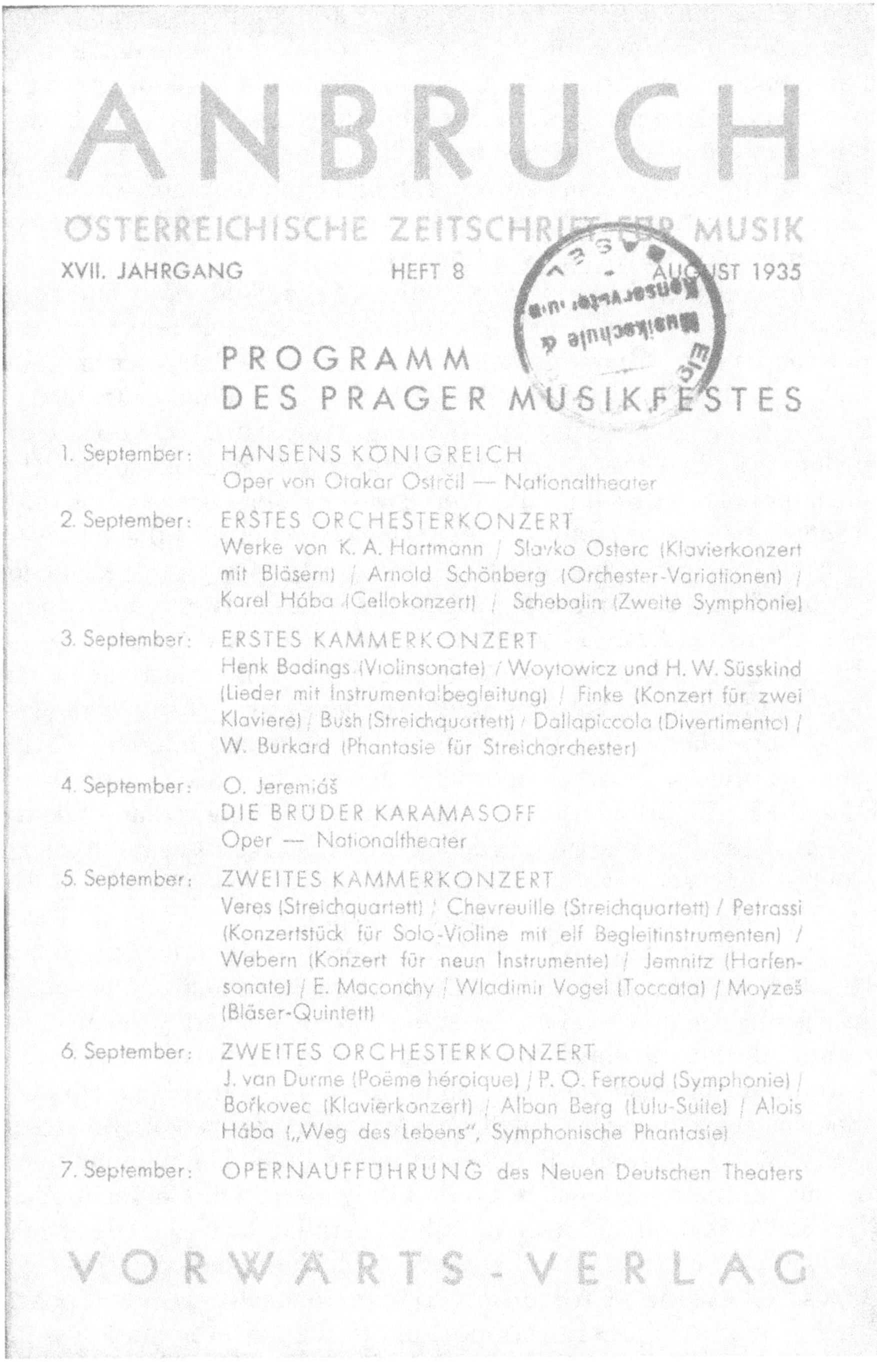

ANBRUCH

ÖSTERREICHISCHE ZEITSCHRIFT FÜR MUSIK

XVII. JAHRGANG HEFT 8 AUGUST 1935

PROGRAMM
DES PRAGER MUSIKFESTES

1. September: HANSENS KÖNIGREICH
Oper von Otakar Ostrčil — Nationaltheater

2. September: ERSTES ORCHESTERKONZERT
Werke von K. A. Hartmann / Slavko Osterc (Klavierkonzert mit Bläsern) / Arnold Schönberg (Orchester-Variationen) / Karel Hába (Cellokonzert) / Schebalin (Zweite Symphonie)

3. September: ERSTES KAMMERKONZERT
Henk Badings (Violinsonate) / Woytowicz und H. W. Süsskind (Lieder mit Instrumentalbegleitung) / Finke (Konzert für zwei Klaviere) / Bush (Streichquartett) / Dallapiccola (Divertimento) / W. Burkard (Phantasie für Streichorchester)

4. September: O. Jeremiáš
DIE BRÜDER KARAMASOFF
Oper — Nationaltheater

5. September: ZWEITES KAMMERKONZERT
Veres (Streichquartett) / Chevreuille (Streichquartett) / Petrassi (Konzertstück für Solo-Violine mit elf Begleitinstrumenten) / Webern (Konzert für neun Instrumente) / Jemnitz (Harfensonate) / E. Maconchy / Wladimir Vogel (Toccata) / Moyzeš (Bläser-Quintett)

6. September: ZWEITES ORCHESTERKONZERT
J. van Durme (Poëme héroique) / P. O. Ferroud (Symphonie) / Bořkovec (Klavierkonzert) / Alban Berg (Lulu-Suite) / Alois Hába („Weg des Lebens", Symphonische Phantasie)

7. September: OPERNAUFFÜHRUNG des Neuen Deutschen Theaters

VORWÄRTS-VERLAG

Figure 2.1. The program of the ISCM Festival in Prague, 1935, on the cover of the Austrian music journal *Anbruch* 17, no. 8 (1935).
Source: Eda Kuhn Loeb Music Library, Harvard University.

den lack of enthusiasm for hosting an international festival of contemporary music was the massive gains that the Sudeten German Party had made in the 1935 Czech parliamentary elections.[12] This party, supported and generously funded by the National Socialists, hewed closely to the NSDAP party line. (Three years later, the entire world would become aware of the Sudeten Germans when, at a summit in Munich, the Western allies ceded the border territory of western Czechoslovakia to Germany.)

The delegates of the Czech section of the ISCM, Hába and composer Erich Steinhard, first learned of the cancellation from the newspapers and tried frantically to regroup.[13] The delegates immediately launched inquiries into the possibility of holding the festival in Prague rather than Karlsbad. There were many practical obstacles, including finding an orchestra to substitute for the Karlsbad one (the members of the Czech Philharmonic were on summer vacation until 9 September, a week after the festival was to begin), and whether to bring the Karlsbad chorus or find a local one in Prague. These negotiations finally collapsed on 6 August. Less than twenty-four hours later, the exiled Austrian composer Hanns Eisler, working at that time with the Comintern's International Music Office (IMB) in Moscow, announced that the Soviet Union was prepared to host the festival in early November of that year. The Soviets promised to cover all the planned orchestra and chamber music performances. "In addition," Alan Bush, the British delegate, reported, "the hundred and twenty delegates and artists would receive free passage from the Russian frontier to Moscow and free hospitality during the Festival itself."[14]

The president of the ISCM, the English musicologist Edward Dent, was quick to turn down the Russian offer, in spite of its generosity. He cited two reasons, the first personal and the second professional. As a professor, he would not be able to attend a meeting in early November during the university semester. More importantly, Dent said, it would be impossible to hold an international festival in a country that was not a member of the ISCM. As a decentralized organization, the ISCM did not (and still does not) allow individual memberships on the international level, but rather only in the national "sections." The Soviet section had been dissolved in the wake of the large-scale reorganization of musical life that took place there during the early 1930s.[15] These formal reasons, correct in themselves, made it possible for Dent to express his opposition to the Soviet invitation without citing any political issues.

Finally, Dent "appealed to the artistic, national, and international prestige of Czechoslovakia."[16] This appeal to Czech patriotism and artistic pride set in motion processes at the highest political levels. A representative of no less than the prime minister called a meeting of the heads of all the relevant ministries and artistic organizations, at which it was decided to hold the ISCM festival in Prague after all. The political pressures on the Czech government were clear. To allow the festival to be snatched up by the USSR after being rejected by the Sudeten Germans of Karlsbad would look too much like fleeing into the arms of Moscow. As a result of the Czech government's engagement, the festival was reorganized over ten frenetic days and nights and opened in Prague on 1 September. (The members of the Czech Philharmonic even cut their vacation a week short.) While it might have looked as if Moscow had lost this round, Bush proclaimed that the Soviet Union had actually saved the festival by means of its intervention, without which it would have been canceled altogether.[17] Hába likewise later recalled the galvanizing effect of the Russians' offer on the Prague government, and claimed that keeping the festival in Czechoslovakia had been understood as "a cultural-political manifestation against Nazi aggression."[18]

This was the first of a chain of events in 1935 in which the ISCM was confronted with overt party politics. The Czech position, a volatile blend of the newly empowered Sudeten Germans in western Czechoslovakia and the more progressive forces in Prague (both German- and Czech-speaking), was a paradoxical mix of nationalism and internationality. The Czech delegates to the ISCM felt national pride for being able to host the festival in Prague under such difficult circumstances and for the works by their most prominent composers, including Hába, that were played at the festival. Yet as the Czechs welcomed the international delegates to Prague, they underlined the city's role as a European cultural capital. The prominent role of exiled composers and musicians at the festival (such as Eisler, Scherchen, Heinrich Jalowetz, Rudolf Kolisch, Wladimir Vogel, and Eduard Steuermann) bore witness to the organization's openness to persecuted emigrants. While by no means was all the music featured at the festival atonal or twelve-tone, the prominent selection (as a nonjuried piece) of the Variations for Orchestra by the exiled Schoenberg, as well as major works by Berg and Webern, served as an unmistakable marker of the distance from the political and aesthetical tenets of the German Reich.

This distance is most audible in Webern's Concerto for Nine Instruments, op. 24, which was performed for the first time at the festival, conducted by Webern's friend and fellow Schoenberg student Heinrich Jalowetz.[19] The concerto's spare, quiet texture eschews tonal centers, traditional phrase structures, or expressive rhetoric, yet is music of great subtlety, variety, and color. (The first two pages of the score are shown in figure 2.2.) Its pitch material is based on a twelve-tone row that is unusual in its minimalism; only two intervals, the major third and the minor second, are used. Each three-note segment of the row is related to all the others by one of the usual twelve-tone operations: inversion (mirror image), retrograde (backward), or retrograde inversion. That is, the available methods of transforming the row have been applied to the individual segments themselves, creating an extremely economical set of pitch materials for the piece. The opening measures, for example, sound the three-note figure in four different instruments, melodic shapes, and rhythms. The piano "answers" using the same three-note groups in reverse order, echoing the four rhythms of the beginning, also in reverse order.

The case of Webern is interesting because of the widespread misconceptions about his actual political beliefs at the time. Since he had been a student of Schoenberg, he was tarred with the brush of *entartete Musik*. And since he had conducted socialist choruses, he was believed to be a Social Democrat, and a victimized one, since he had lost his positions when the Social Democratic Party was banned in Austria in 1934. Few people knew of Webern's Nazi sympathies, which were fueled by an ardent German nationalism and influenced by members of his immediate family.[20] (He was, however, never anti-Semitic, and never turned his back on his venerated teacher, Schoenberg, or his Jewish friends.) Even though Webern imagined his music contributing to the grand tradition of German music, Nazi cultural officials did not see it that way. His music, while never officially banned, was not performed in Germany during the Third Reich. Regardless of Webern's own political beliefs, programming his concerto at the ISCM festival sent a dual message: first, it confirmed the organization's commitment to the most astringent modernism, and second, it signaled its rejection of the kind of popular nationalism espoused by the Nazis.

The Counterfestival of the Permanent Council

> "Die Erkenntnis von der Notwendigkeit der Pflege nationaler Eigenart ist Allgemeingut [geworden]."
> (The realization of the necessity of cultivating national character has become universally recognized.)
> —Herbert Gerigk, "Musikfestdämmerung."

Figure 2.2. Anton Webern, Concerto for Nine Instruments, op. 24, beginning of the first movement.
Used by permission of European American Music Distributors Company, United States, and Canadian agent for Universal Edition, Vienna.

The Permanent Council for the International Cooperation of Composers (Ständiger Rat für die internationale Zusammenarbeit der Komponisten) was called into being by the president of the Reichsmusikkammer, Richard Strauss, in the spring of 1934. At the organization's first business meeting, held at the Third International Music Festival at the Venice Biennale in September of that year, Strauss called for a thorough "reform" (*Neugestaltung*) of the current practice of music festivals. The musicologist Herbert Gerigk, an ardent Nazi who would go on to coedit the *Lexikon der Juden in der Musik*, reviewed the Venice Biennale in *Die Musik*, the "Amtliches Organ der NS-Kulturgemeinde" ("Official Journal of the National Socialist Cultural Community"). According to Gerigk, festivals of contemporary music relied too much on "foreign [*volksfremde*] elements."[21] As part of its reform, the Permanent Council would turn away from the prevailing trends in contemporary music and instead emphasize "the necessity of cultivating national character." The new organization did not dismiss internationality, according to a report in the Viennese newspaper *Das Echo*, but understood it as "the sum of different nations" rather than as a collaboration among equals.[22]

The emphasis on nationalism corresponded closely with the National Socialist *Blut und Boden* (blood and soil) ideology. In fact, Gerigk criticized the Italians, Germany's allies, at the Venice Biennale precisely because "Fascism [referring to Italian fascism] does not take into account the most primordial of all connections: that of blood and soil."[23] Gerigk found the inclusion of works by the French Jewish composer Darius Milhaud, the German Russian emigrant Vogel, the Schoenberg pupil Berg, and the Austrian Ernst Krenek shameful because this "unmusic" (*Unmusik*) and "musical nonsense" (*musikalischer Unfug*) was of the sort that had been driven out of Germany, and "it's high time that the rest of the world opens its eyes, too."[24]

While the Permanent Council did not explicitly claim to have been founded as an alternative to the ISCM, it was widely perceived as such. Scherchen quickly realized that whatever the ISCM's musical accomplishments that year, the Prague festival represented first and foremost "an artistic battle ... against *Blut und Boden* and musical pan-Germanism."[25] The Viennese journal *23*, whose name was taken from the paragraph of the Austrian press law dealing with the legal right to correct false statements published elsewhere,[26] provided a platform for Krenek to polemicize against the Permanent Council.[27] Krenek's title, "Die Blubo-Internationale," mocked the *Blut und Boden* ideology that lay at the heart of National Socialist music policy as well as its twisted definition of internationality. For the Permanent Council, Krenek pointed out, "international music" was used interchangeably with the derogatory terms "Neutöner" or "Atonaliker."[28]

Krenek also exposed the official state backing of the innocuously named Permanent Council for the International Cooperation of Composers and pointed out how its president, Richard Strauss, had absolute power to appoint national representatives.[29] In fact, Gerigk had made no bones about the fact that Strauss, the president of the Reichsmusikkammer, "leads the Permanent Council absolutely according to the Führer principle [*Führerprinzip*]. The vice president, Adriano Lualdi, was Mussolini's liaison for all matters pertaining to music."[30] The two fascist nations, however disparate their cultural policies were at that time, joined together—under firm German leadership—to provide an alternative to the democratically run, international ISCM.

The Permanent Council's emphasis on national origins as a basis for musical quality meant that much attention was paid to what constituted a German composer. In his review of the Venice Biennale, Gerigk was shocked to see Vogel's music programmed on an evening of "Nordischer Musik": "One was amazed to encounter here Wladimir Vogel, who now lives in Strassburg [France] and who a while ago wanted to be German, and now is identified as Russian."[31] The harshest words were reserved for Scherchen (who was not Jewish): "The emigrant [Scherchen], who in Germany had already overstayed his welcome, artistically speaking, before the 30th of January, still seems to want to present himself as German when it is to his advantage."[32] Gerigk similarly accused Krenek of trying to "pass" as a German. In an open letter in *23*, Krenek responded that he was not an emigrant, but a proud Austrian citizen living in his native city of Vienna, and that he never had the slightest desire to pretend he was German.[33]

In 1935, the Permanent Council presented a major festival in the French resort town of Vichy on the exact same September dates as the ISCM in Prague. In a clear attempt at one-upmanship, the Vichy festival was larger and more ambitious than the one in Prague, featuring representatives from more than fifteen countries and over seventy composers (as opposed to thirty-one composers in Prague).[34] Yet the Vichy program committee had made little attempt to focus on contemporary music, as the newest works were all at least five years old.[35] In addition, opulent staged performances of Verdi's *La forza del destino,* Saint-Säens's *Samson et Dalila,* and Strauss's *Salome* put the accent on repertory chestnuts rather than the avant-garde.[36] Of the contemporary composers, the festival featured chamber works by musically conservative figures such as Arnold Bax, Jean Binet, Philipp Jarnach, Mario Labroca, and Mario Castelnuovo-Tedesco. Krenek gleefully pointed out that the program committee had somehow overlooked (or managed to sneak in?) a work by Milhaud, whose orchestral suite *Les songes* was performed.[37]

Given the different repertoires and aesthetic focus of the simultaneous festivals in Prague and Vichy, in a sense they could hardly be seen as in competition with each other. Yet their overlapping membership caused problems for some delegates. The French composer Albert Roussel was a vice president of the Permanent Council[38] and very much in evidence at Vichy, although he was also a member of the ISCM. It was reported that the Italian delegate to Prague, Alberto Casella, attended both festivals, setting off for Vichy before the Prague festival was over.[39] Scherchen himself had evidently planned to do the same before Eisler convinced him otherwise.[40] Igor Stravinsky remained a vice president of the ISCM, although his music found favor with the Permanent Council, but he did not attend either festival.

Just as the cancellation of the ISCM by the Karlsbad authorities had forced the politically neutral organization to engage with international politics, the founding of the Permanent Council and the deliberate staging of its counterfestival at the same time led to even more fundamental questions about the ISCM's artistic principles. Should those with dual membership be tolerated or expelled from the ISCM?[41] Should the ISCM turn its focus to the most avant-garde music instead of simply representing a cross section of existing trends? Krenek offered the most polemical critique: the ISCM ought to articulate a clear alternative to the Permanent Council's aesthetic principles ("eine entsprechende Gegenwirkung zu entfalten") by emphasizing truly modern music. But, Krenek maintained, however well meaning, the organization would not be able to do this, because it had developed into a society "against new music." Rather than holding the modernist line, the ISCM had mindlessly gone along with the "entertainment music" (*Unterhaltung*) coming from the West, above all from France—he is referring here to neoclassicism—and the "folklore" from the East.[42]

Dent offered a spirited response to Krenek, implying that by so arguing, the Austrian section—by far the most radical musically—was in danger of splitting off from the main organization and succumbing to the same sort of nationalism that they were all trying to combat. Dent emphasized the international nature of the ISCM and reaffirmed its commitment to contemporary, even revolutionary tendencies in music while being open to a variety of styles, since no one was in a position to predict what kind of music would be significant in the future.⁴³

After being confronted with political events that dramatically interfered with their operations, the ISCM was forced to do some soul-searching. The organization had managed to function for the thirteen years of its existence with only an informal set of statutes that had never been voted on and were often revised.⁴⁴ Suddenly the organization's artistic goals and its place on the political spectrum had to be articulated and defended. The previous strategy of not having a strategy—that is, simply letting the national sections collaborate with a minimum of administration—was not up to the task of defending the ISCM against more centralized, explicitly political organizations like the Permanent Council. In fact, the question of legally binding statutes for the ISCM became one of the most urgent tasks in Prague.

The Permanent Council for its part avoided all mention of the ISCM and confined its public statements to uncontroversial issues such as support for music education and copyright protection for composers.⁴⁵ This approach muted the controversy. Some, like conductor Paul Sacher, the Swiss delegate to the Prague festival, regretted the absence of German composers; the ISCM could hardly call itself an international organization if one of the most significant musical cultures was not represented.⁴⁶ Others, including the Austrian music critic Paul Stefan, urged closer ties with fascist Italy, whose regime was so sympathetic to artists. At the same time, Stefan claimed, the ISCM, in response to the Permanent Council, needed to recall its founding principles, avoiding the extremes of right *and* left.⁴⁷ The traditional idealistic notion of music as intrinsically nonpolitical, a viewpoint shared by many in both the ISCM and the Permanent Council, made explicit protests difficult to articulate.

The Struggle Over the Future of the ISCM: Moscow versus Barcelona

> "Die neue Sprache der Musik muß jetzt konfrontiert werden mit der (konkreten) neuen gesellschaftlichen Situation."
> (The new musical language must now be confronted with the specific new situation in society.)
> —Hanns Eisler, "Einiges über die Lage des modernen Komponisten"

The most hotly disputed topic at the Prague ISCM festival was not the music, but rather where to hold the 1936 festival. This question was not an innocuous one, for the choice was between Barcelona and Moscow. As with the shift in venue from Karlsbad to Prague and the formation of the Permanent Council, political decisions made far away and outside the field of music again had a direct impact on the ISCM, forcing this traditionally nonpolitical organization to issue the first political statement of its existence.

At the Seventh Congress of the Comintern, which opened on 25 July 1935, the Soviet Union had shifted markedly from its previous policy of refusing to collaborate with social democratic parties and invoked the Popular Front.[48] All parties and organizations, even bourgeois-centrist ones, would be welcomed to fight side by side with the Soviets against fascism. The Soviet-controlled Popular Front cultivated the appearance of a voluntary collaboration of independent organizations, but this masked the control (and deniability) that Moscow sought to exert.

Eisler, who had been elected president of the Comintern's music division at the same congress, was expected to play a crucial role in the effort to bring together a broad network of international musical organizations. This role was very much in the spirit of Comintern, which Joy Calico has memorably described as "the evangelical missionary wing of the communist party."[49] One of Eisler's first outreach efforts, as we have seen, was to offer to host the 1935 ISCM festival in Moscow after Karlsbad's cancellation. After this offer was rejected, Eisler was sent as a delegate of Comintern to the festival in Prague in order forge ties between the ISCM and Comintern. Secretly, Eisler was planning with his Moscow allies a virtual takeover of the ISCM. For his part, Eisler hoped that bringing the ISCM into the fold would broaden Soviet cultural policies, allowing for a greater acceptance of contemporary Western concert music, much of which had been denounced as "formalist." (This was not to be.)

Eisler had prepared a major speech on the situation of the contemporary composer that was to be given at the Prague festival, but it is unclear whether he was given the chance. The text was published shortly afterward, and in any case Eisler would have communicated his ideas informally on the sidelines.[50] Music festivals have become sclerotic and fossilized, Eisler told the delegates. The main reason for this is that composers have been too focused on developing new musical languages, without considering how they relate to new developments in society. "The new musical language must now be confronted with the specific new situation in society," Eisler claimed.[51] One cannot simply work in isolation and expect to be ready for the future. One must participate in the movements that aim to change humankind. The composer has a real interest in doing this, Eisler stated (somewhat idealistically), since the new society naturally embraces artistic innovation ("Neue Menschen werden eben das Neue als selbstverständlich empfinden"). In words that surely resonated with the emigrants at the festival, Eisler said that this new society "will not treat composers with contempt, drive them into exile, rob them of their freedom and ultimately silence them."[52]

Eisler urged modern composers to become aware of the "front line": which side would be prepared to defend "progressive music" against the suppression and sabotage of the fascists? "The Soviet Union is the only country that would bring the festivals of the ISCM to a higher level, help them to overcome their conventional character, and thereby transform what has been a mere 'show' into a working meeting of potentially great significance." Referring indirectly to Dent's objection that the Soviet Union was not a member of the ISCM, Eisler urged the delegates to set aside "all formal reservations" and focus instead on the urgent artistic questions that needed to be resolved.[53] Eisler, sticking to generalities, did not spell out what a closer alliance with the Soviet Union would mean for the ISCM in terms of changes in policy and leadership. Eisler's argument was presented as his sincere personal opinion, which on its face seemed relatively noncontroversial.

Eisler traveled to Prague with his colleague Hermann Reichenbach, a German emigrant to the Soviet Union who was a member of the Soviet Composers Union and a cultural functionary for the Communist Party. Their confidential report (in German), entitled "Report on the Negotiations of the International Revolutionary Theater Association [IRTB, a division of Comintern] with the International Society for Contemporary Music on the occasion of the Festival in Prague," sketches the recent history of the ISCM as well as providing a behind-the-scenes description of their efforts to win the 1936 festival for Moscow.[54]

The fourteen-page, singe-spaced, typed report, dated 10 September 1935 and signed by Eisler and Reichenbach, not only gives a detailed account of the negotiations, but also provides names and evaluates each delegate's loyalty (or lack thereof) to the Soviet Union. Hába, for example, who as secretary of the Czech section of the ISCM had issued a formal invitation to the Soviet Union to participate in the Prague meeting, was dismissed as an anthroposophist and therefore unreliable in spite of his strong revolutionary sympathies.[55] The American section, however, according to Eisler and Reichenbach, "sympathizes with us completely, above all due to the important role played by Aaron Copland."⁵⁶ (Copland did not, however, attend the festival; the United States was represented by composer Louis Gruenberg.)

Eisler and Reichenbach quickly discovered they had been given a difficult brief, since Barcelona had already been promised the 1936 festival. Moreover, reversing this decision would in effect destroy the new Spanish section, led by the left-leaning composer Roberto Gerhard, who was quite favorably disposed to the Soviet Union and whom there was no reason to offend.⁵⁷ Finally, Dent reiterated his objection that since the Soviets were not members of the ISCM, it would be impossible to hold a festival in the Soviet Union, and he threatened to resign if the festival was taken away from Barcelona. Reichenbach pointedly reminded the delegates of Moscow's offer to host this year's festival after Karlsbad had canceled it, but the implicit quid pro quo was ignored.⁵⁸ Even though, according to Eisler and Reichenbach, "all delegates were convinced that only Moscow was the place where the ISCM's calcification could be melted away through the addition of fresh blood," most, whether reluctantly or not, saw the inadvisability of changing the venue for 1936.⁵⁹ In the end, the society voted to maintain its previous commitment to hold next year's festival in Barcelona. The Moscow offer, which had not been officially brought before the assembly for a vote, but had only been discussed behind the scenes, went unmentioned.⁶⁰

With this document, Eisler and Reichenbach sought to minimize the actual failure of their mission as they carefully laid the groundwork for a possible Soviet membership in the ISCM. Ultimately, they envisioned that the IMB could very quickly influence and lead the ISCM: "Because the composers are very unsure of themselves, there is the possibility that we can decisively influence and lead the ISCM relatively quickly due to the membership of [the Soviet] Composers Union and the influence of the IMB."⁶¹ This "spin" on what had proven to be an unsuccessful mission did not do very much to convince their Soviet partners, as we shall see.

The Popular Front and the ISCM

Another document in the Eisler collection at the Akademie der Künste, also in German, records the Prague festival from the point of view of the IRTB/IMB leadership. This document is unpublished and was first brought to the Akademie der Künste archive in Berlin in 2001.⁶² Entitled "Assignments and Results of the Delegation of the

International Music Office (IMB) at the Music Festival of the International Society for New Music [ISCM] in Prague," it was compiled from meeting notes by the secretary of the IMB, Margarete Lode, about a month after the festival. According to this document, the question of a "future collaboration" between the ISCM and Soviet music organizations was discussed at the very highest levels of government, the Central Committee of the Communist Party. There it was decided that comrades Eisler and Reichenbach would travel to Prague as representatives of the IMB in lieu of a delegation from the Soviet Composers Union.[63]

At a meeting attended by representatives from the Soviet Composers Union and the Comintern, Eisler and Reichenbach were given written instructions that included four main points:[64]

1. To issue an invitation from the Soviet Union to hold the festival in 1936, making sure to address the question of White Russian emigrants.
2. To organize a conference that would accompany the 1936 festival.
3. To explain why the Soviet Composers Union was not officially represented at the Prague festival (the invitation came too late, and there was not enough Soviet music programmed to make a visit worthwhile).
4. To begin negotiations about joining the ISCM, that is, about the Soviet Composers Union possibly constituting a Soviet section. The conditions are: "clarification of the relationship of the ISCM to the White Russian emigrants" and changing the passage in the statutes that grants membership to composers in the country of their residence.

The participation of Russian emigrants, Stravinsky being, of course, the most famous, was evidently a sore point. The German theater director Erwin Piscator, who was living in the Soviet Union at the time and directed the IRTB, had made it clear in the preceding discussion that they were willing to host the ISCM in Moscow only if these emigrants were excluded.[65] That is why it was considered necessary to revise the statute that granted membership on the basis of residence and not nationality (allowing Russian emigrants to be members of the French, Swiss, or American sections, for example). This request put the negotiators in a tricky position, since refugees from Nazi Germany would also have been affected by such a change. (If this were taken literally, Reichenbach himself, who lived in the Soviet Union, would have to be classified as a German delegate.) Eisler did not mention this question in his lecture to the ISCM, and it does not appear to have been emphasized. If we recall how the Permanent Council questioned the national status of German emigrants, we can see how both the Nazi and the Soviet governments had a problem with refugees, albeit with different groups of them.

As we have seen, the negotiations did not get that far. The first point, that of the Soviet Union's offer to hold the 1936 festival, took up all of Eisler's and Reichenbach's time and energy. Their position was made much more difficult by an additional directive handed to Reichenbach shortly before his trip: "Before we can propose Leningrad or Moscow as the next festival venue, one must be certain that Moscow does not lose the vote in favor of Barcelona. One can instruct the Czech section to ensure the outcome ahead of time; only then may we propose Moscow and issue the invitation."[66] In the end, these instructions to fix the outcome ahead of time ensured that the invitation was not officially extended, because the 1936 festival had already been promised to Barcelona and not enough delegates were prepared to vote against the Spanish section and against Dent's wishes.

The remainder of the report is devoted to the criticism that the two delegates received for allegedly letting themselves be perceived in Prague as representatives of the Soviet Composers Union as opposed to the IMB, along with a lengthy apology (*Erklärung*) by Reichenbach. The arguments against Eisler and Reichenbach were of the hairsplitting kind, seeking to gloss over the fact that the two men been sent to Prague precisely because the Soviet Composers Union had chosen not to send its own delegates; moreover, Reichenbach was himself a member of the Soviet Composers Union, so he had the right to represent himself as such. In any case, the criticism must have been humiliating for them. The point was to slap their wrists, presumably for their failure to carry out their directives.[67] While Eisler's reaction to the criticism is not known, it is probably not a coincidence that his Moscow activities came to a halt at this time, as he spent the next several years traveling and living in the United States, Spain, the United Kingdom, and Denmark before he finally settled in the United States in 1938.[68] Reichenbach was asked to leave the Soviet Union in 1937 and emigrated to the United States the following year.[69]

The ISCM's Resolution on Artistic Freedom

Amid all this turmoil, many delegates at the Prague festival, and especially Dent, were still reluctant to venture into overtly political waters. Although several delegates had pushed for resolutions condemning the simultaneous festival of the Permanent Council and expressing sympathy for a future meeting in the Soviet Union, these were not passed. Finally, after much debate, the general assembly did issue a resolution reiterating the organization's main tenets of artistic and political freedom. The proclamation, written in French (the official language of the society), states that the ISCM's primary aim is to defend the cause of "the most vital" (*les plus vivantes*) modern music. Given that artistic creation was necessarily threatened by a hostile environment, a paramount goal of the society was to ensure the artistic freedom of the composer. Furthermore, no discrimination on the basis of nationality, race, or religion would be tolerated as long as the creative work conformed to the spirit of the organization.[70] According to Haefeli, this resolution was the first political statement of any kind issued by the ISCM.[71]

Although abstractly worded, the resolution clearly seeks to steer a middle course by rejecting the nationalistic ideology of the Permanent Council as well as the Marxist position of putting the artist at the service of society. It accomplishes these things by placing the emphasis on the individual composer and his or her spiritual and intellectual liberty rather than on the guidance of any kind of collective, be it a nation, school, political party, or even the ISCM itself. Yet the resolution does not promise to protect the freedom of all composers everywhere, but rather addresses itself to those who work in the most "vital" kinds of modern music. Implicit in this concept of living new music is a certain distance from popular tastes, since the composer finds himself "necessarily" in a hostile environment.

The dividing line between music worthy of support by the ISCM— the most "vital" new music—and music that was unworthy was admittedly never clearly defined. The goalposts shifted constantly depending on who was on the jury each year. A typical example of a style that did not "conform to the spirit of the organization" may have been that of the young composer Erich Wolfgang Korngold. His work was more or less systematically excluded from the powerful Austrian section of the ISCM, which was controlled by the Second Viennese School and its allies.[72] In this case, new music was deemed to be synonymous with the atonal and twelve-tone idioms of Schoenberg, Berg, Webern, and Krenek. The music of Korngold, which, of course, later graced many well-known Hollywood film scores, was deemed to be so accessible that it did not need special protection by an organization like the Austrian section of the ISCM. The international organization's resolution reiterated and formalized what had been the understanding of only part of its membership before: that the ISCM's main goal was to support modernist music that was difficult for mainstream concert audiences to appreciate.

Echoes: Reactions to the Prague Festival

In 1936, the inaugural issue of the music journal *Musica Viva,* founded and edited by Scherchen, featured an extended account on the Prague ISCM festival entitled "Music Festivals and Music Every Day" (Musikfeste und musikalischer Alltag). There were short reports about the festival from the delegates Louis Gruenberg (United States), Luigi Dallapiccola (Italy), Paul Sacher (Switzerland), Jef van Durme (Belgium), and Alan Bush (United Kingdom).[73] The responses dealt overwhelmingly with the festival's political turmoil rather than the music. (There was no article devoted specifically to the works played.)

The following statement (originally in German) by the president, Edward Dent, was placed front and center as an epigraph to the entire feature: "I am of the definite opinion that the ISCM should remain a purely idealistic and artistic society—removed from everything commercial as well as political."[74] Dent's words echo the resolution passed in Prague and take it a step further. By removing itself not only from the political sphere, but also from the commercial one (which had not been mentioned in Prague), the ISCM could carve out a separate, protected space for advanced, serious music.

Musica Viva itself was the product of similar idealistic thinking about music's special place in the world. Scherchen's journal was at the center of an ambitious project encompassing multiple aspects of musical production and dissemination: the publication and distribution of scores, the production of radio music, special editions of scores for students, a music journal in four languages, and a record company. This project, called Ars Viva (Living Art), was designed to create an alternative infrastructure and support system for new music that could not flourish in Nazi Germany—in fact, analogously to the ISCM itself. Even though Scherchen supported left-wing causes, his own political views were carefully guarded, and there is no evidence that Ars Viva had any connection with the Popular Front's similar efforts to support international publications. With every article printed in four languages (German, French, Italian, and English), *Musica Viva*'s internationalism was visible on every page. (The first page of the first issue is shown in figure 2.3.) Yet this utopian impulse made the journal expensive to produce, and it lasted for only three issues.

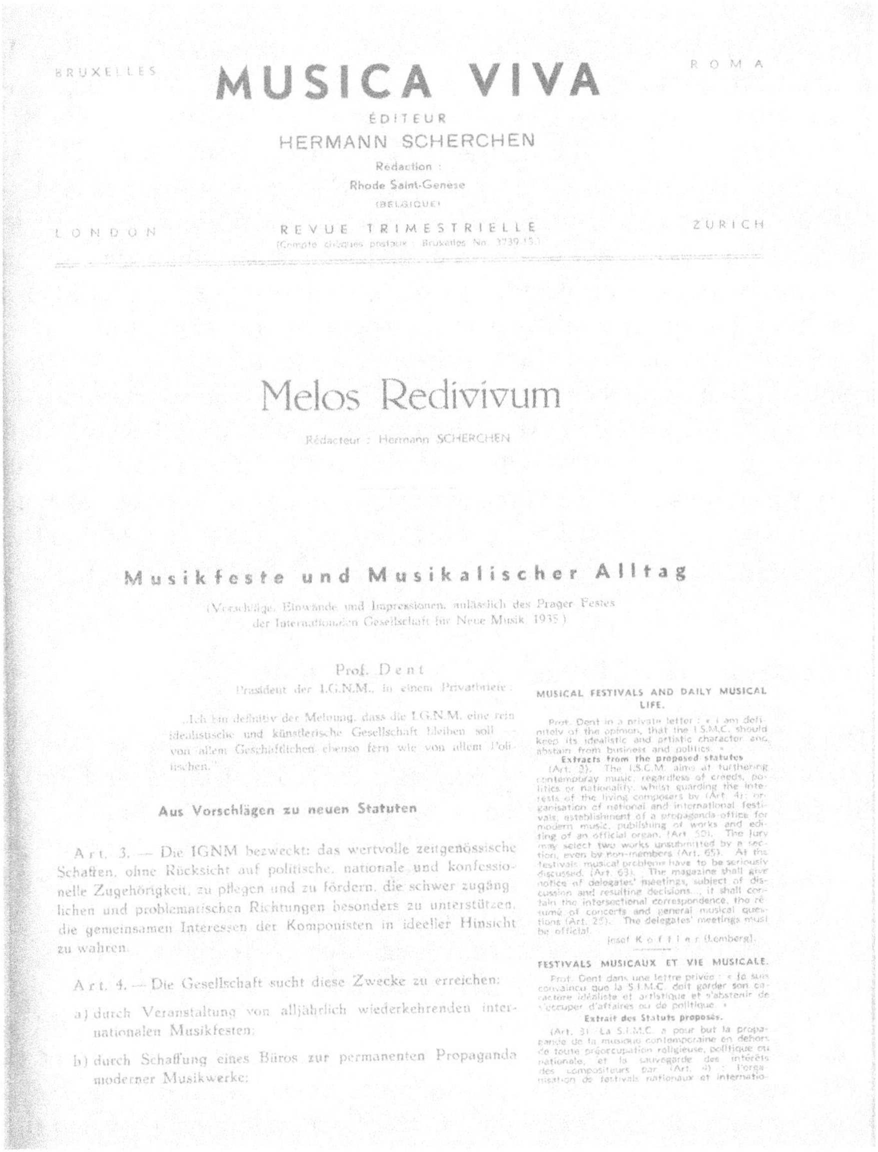

BRUXELLES **MUSICA VIVA** ROMA

ÉDITEUR

HERMANN SCHERCHEN

Redaction :

Rhode Saint-Genese

(BELGIQUE)

LONDON REVUE TRIMESTRIELLE ZURICH

(Compte chèques postaux : Bruxelles No. 3739.15.)

Melos Redivivum

Rédacteur : Hermann SCHERCHEN

Musikfeste und Musikalischer Alltag

(Vorschläge, Einwände und Impressionen, anlässlich des Prager Festes der Internationalen Gesellschaft für Neue Musik 1935.)

Prof. Dent

Präsident der I.G.N.M., in einem Privatbriefe:

„Ich bin definitiv der Meinung, dass die I.G.N.M. eine rein idealistische und künstlerische Gesellschaft bleiben soll — von allem Geschäftlichen ebenso fern wie von allem Politischen."

Aus Vorschlägen zu neuen Statuten

Art. 3. — Die IGNM bezweckt: das wertvolle zeitgenössische Schaffen, ohne Rücksicht auf politische, nationale und konfessionelle Zugehörigkeit, zu pflegen und zu fördern, die schwer zugänglichen und problematischen Richtungen besonders zu unterstützen, die gemeinsamen Interessen der Komponisten in ideeller Hinsicht zu wahren.

Art. 4. — Die Gesellschaft sucht diese Zwecke zu erreichen:

a) durch Veranstaltung von alljährlich wiederkehrenden internationalen Musikfesten;

b) durch Schaffung eines Büros zur permanenten Propaganda moderner Musikwerke;

MUSICAL FESTIVALS AND DAILY MUSICAL LIFE.

Prof. Dent in a private letter : « I am definitely of the opinion, that the I.S.M.C. should keep its idealistic and artistic character and abstain from business and politics. »

Extracts from the proposed statutes

(Art. 3). The I.S.C.M. aims at furthering contemporary music, regardless of creeds, politics or nationality, whilst guarding the interests of the living composers by (Art. 4): organisation of national and international festivals, establishment of a propaganda office for modern music, publishing of works and editing of an official organ. (Art. 50). The jury may select two works unsubmitted by a section, even by non-members (Art. 65). At the festivals musical problems have to be seriously discussed. (Art. 63). The magazine shall give notice of delegates' meetings, subject of discussion and resulting decisions..., it shall contain the intersectional correspondence, the résumé of concerts and general musical questions (Art. 25). The delegates' meetings must be official.

Josef Koffler (Lemberg).

FESTIVALS MUSICAUX ET VIE MUSICALE.

Prof. Dent dans une lettre privée : « Je suis convaincu que la S.I.M.C. doit garder son caractère idéaliste et artistique et s'abstenir de s'occuper d'affaires ou de politique. »

Extrait des Statuts proposés.

(Art. 3) La S.I.M.C. a pour but la propagande de la musique contemporaine en dehors de toute préoccupation religieuse, politique ou nationale, et la sauvegarde des intérêts des compositeurs par (Art. 4) : l'organisation de festivals nationaux et internatio-

Figure 2.3. The first issue of the short-lived music journal *Musica Viva* (1936), p. 1.
Source: Eda Kuhn Loeb Music Library, Harvard University.

The opening section of the article on music festivals was devoted to possible revisions to the ISCM's statutes. Launching his new music journal with an opening article on something so dry and bureaucratic may not seem like the most effective recipe for success. (Most people's eyes glaze over at the mere mention of bylaws.)

Yet the first proposed new statute, Article 3, struck at the heart of the controversies surrounding the ISCM in those years: "The I.S.C.M. aims at furthering contemporary music, regardless of creeds, politics or nationality, *especially the inaccessible and problematic tendencies*, whilst guarding the interests of the living composers."[75] This statement is rather more specific than the vague caveat from the Prague resolution: "as long as the creative work conforms to the spirit of the organization." By claiming a special place for complex modern music (as opposed to more accessible styles), the ISCM created an identity for itself that was necessarily distinct from that of the Permanent Council as well as from socialist realism. The implications are that such music is fragile but worthy of support, and that only the ISCM had the artistic integrity to support it. This viewpoint, if adopted consistently, would represent a clear shift away from the ISCM's previous practice of representing a panorama of existing contemporary tendencies. The new Article 3 was in fact included in the organization's first official statutes, which were approved in 1937.[76]

Conclusion: The Chimera of Political Neutrality

The ISCM emerged after the summer of 1935 with its independence intact and with a stronger political orientation than ever before. By claiming political neutrality—in the context of the tumultuous events of 1935, itself a political position—the dual principles of international collaboration and artistic freedom were articulated as the key to resisting the pressures from both left and right.

These principles were firmly anchored in traditional ways of thinking about music while also anticipating later Cold War attitudes. The main bone of contention in the debate over the future of the ISCM in 1935, as we have seen, was about the appropriate role of party politics in musical life. All the protagonists, whether left, right, or center, had inherited a belief in the basic disparity between the artistic and political spheres—between the realm of ideas and aesthetics and the realm of action and pragmatism—although they had radically different views on the separation. The notion that music's power comes precisely from its abstract and nonsemantic nature repeatedly came into conflict with the insistence on the part of the political leadership on both sides that music plays a leading role in the public representation of national interests.[77]

Here the powerful tradition of music's independence from politics, fed by and coupled with the nineteenth-century notion of "genius," proved stronger than local political interests. Indeed, the ISCM gained cultural capital by insisting on the independence of the individual artist, even if that meant sometimes sacrificing accessibility to an audience. That the IMB did not succeed in taking over the ISCM meant instability in the short term, but it also assured the organization's long-term survival, since its fate was not tied to that of a particular political regime. Similarly, Scherchen's emphasis on artistic rather than political standards with regard to his projects lent them a far greater legitimacy in the eyes of musicians and intellectuals than any party-oriented position would have.

The battle lines that were drawn during and after the Prague festival strikingly anticipated those of the later cultural Cold War. Although the anti-Semitic and nationalistic rhetoric of the Permanent Council more or less vanished (fortunately) from mainstream discourse, the arguments of Eisler as well as those contained in the ISCM's 1935 resolution bear a striking resemblance to the widespread and commonly accepted views on art that were propagated by the two superpowers after 1945. Although we know that actual practice on both sides was quite varied and often different from, or even contradictory to, the governing assumptions, these core ideas about music and its role in society—"as ideal types"—formed the blueprint for musical life on both sides of the Iron Curtain.

On the left, for example, Eisler's emphasis in his 1935 lecture on the composer's obligation to engage in the class struggle, to compose for children and for amateurs, and to employ new technology (radio, recording, and film) to propagate his music have clear parallels to aspects of postwar musical practices in the Soviet Union and Eastern Europe.[78] Eisler's warning that "the isolation, the uselessness [*Nutzlosigkeit*] of modern music has already become a disgrace for us all" was reiterated and amplified in another Prague manifesto, from 1948, which articulates the principles of the Zhdanov doctrine, which reestablished socialist realism and which Eisler had a hand in formulating as well.[79]

For the Western postwar ideal of art, on the other hand, the ISCM's insistence on art occupying a realm apart from politics strikes a very familiar note. In this view, not only does art need rarefied air to breathe, it is also necessarily dragged down by any political involvement at all, as André de Blonay had already claimed in his 1935 review of the Prague festival.[80]

Webern's Concerto for Nine Instruments, op. 24, which premiered at the festival, became one of the iconic works revered by the postwar avant-garde. Its sparse texture, uncompromising twelve-tone language, and rejection of traditional phrasing and rhetoric was considered by Erich Steinhard at the time of its premiere to be "uncompromising" but old-fashioned, as it drew upon idioms that had been established twenty years previously.[81] Louis Gruenberg concurred, writing that the concerto "is not essentially different from any of [Webern's] former works. There are the same shy bits, fastidious, birdlike pecks and squirts as before."[82] But almost twenty years later, the war-shattered young generation at the Darmstädter Ferienkurse für Neue Musik saw in the concerto a work of bracing avant-garde freshness, a musical analogue to erasing an unsavory past and an antidote to everything political.[83] Hardly a tabula rasa, the Webern work was actually a *Flaschenpost* (message in a bottle) from 1935 Prague, its otherworldly sounds transporting to later listeners not the implicit resistance to the nationalistic, conservative values of Nazi Germany that it seemed to articulate at the time, but rather the powerful evocation of an independent aesthetic realm.[84]

The efforts of Dent and others to articulate a politically neutral role for music were reactions to the immediate pressures facing the ISCM, but the results endured far beyond 1935. The ideas forged in the wake of the political turmoil surrounding the ISCM in 1935 uncannily anticipated later notions of a politically "neutral" art, whose actual connections with the state are hidden. The phrase that most readily conjured up this nonpolitical realm was "artistic freedom." The centerpiece of the ISCM's 1935 resolution, this phrase became a mantra in Western cultural diplomacy after World War II. These words are echoed in the name of the Congress for Cultural Freedom, funded by the Central Intelligence Agency (CIA), as well as occurring in countless emigration narratives of refugees from the Soviet Union.[85] The unpolitical stance of 1935 Prague, hastily forged as a simple exigency and a means for the survival of the ISCM, was not a brand-new idea, of course, as it drew on long-standing musical and aesthetic traditions. In the context of the political battles being waged in the mid-1930s, the notion of artistic freedom and political neutrality for music were completely at odds with the ideological fundamentalisms of those times. But the principles articulated in the Prague resolution had staying power; they were to reemerge after the war as unshakable truth for generations of Cold War artists and cultural functionaries in the West for years to come.

Acknowledgments

I am grateful to Dr. Thomas Ahrend for his helpful comments on the text.

Notes

1. The ISCM was founded in Salzburg in 1922. The standard and still indispensable work on the organization's history is Anton Haefeli, *Die Internationale Gesellschaft für Neue Musik (IGNM): Ihre Geschichte von 1922 bis zur Gegenwart* (Zurich: Atlantis Musikbuch-Verlag, 1982). Since the society was incorporated under its English name, there is some variance in the German translations used during the early years. It is now known as the Internationale Gesellschaft für Neue Musik (IGNM), although in the 1930s it was often referred to with a literal translation of the English name, the Internationale Gesellschaft für zeitgenössische Musik (abbreviated as IGM). In French, it is the Société internationale de musique contemporaine (SICM).
2. See Anne C. Shreffler, "Musikalische Kanonisierung und Dekanonisierung im 20. Jahrhundert," trans. Fabian Kolb, in *Der Kanon der Musik: Theorie und Geschichte—Ein Handbuch*, ed. Klaus Pietschmann and Melanie Wald (Munich: text + kritik, 2013), 611–30.
3. Haefeli's views on the Prague 1935 festival are clearly tilted toward the leftist, "missed opportunity" line; see Haefeli, *Die Internationale Gesellschaft für Neue Musik*, 190–99, 228–31. The centrist viewpoint comes from the contemporaneous writings of Edward Dent, Paul Sacher, and Paul Stefan, which will be discussed below.
4. Edward J. Dent, "Zum 13. Internationalen Musikfest in Prag 1935," *Der Auftakt* 15, nos. 7–8 (1935): 97.
5. Paul Stefan, "Ein freies Wort zum Internationalen Musikfest," *Anbruch* 17, no. 8 (1935): 205.
6. The Swiss critic André de Blonay noted this contradiction and commented that it would be more honest to simply recognize the right of each section to be represented. "Prague, un tournant décisif," *Schweizerische Musikzeitung* 75 (1935): 637.
7. Alan Bush, "The I.S.C.M. Festival at Prague," *The Musical Times* 76, no. 1112 (1935): 940.
8. H.W., "Zur Vorgeschichte des 13. Internationalen Musikfestes in Prag," *Der Auftakt* 15, nos. 9–10 (1935): 152.
9. Haefeli, *Die Internationale Gesellschaft für Neue Musik*, 492.
10. "Der Querschnitt: Das Internationale Musikfest in Karlsbad" [announcement], *Der Auftakt* 15, nos. 1–2 (1935): 31. As Schoenberg was already in exile in the United States, the Austrian section could probably not have nominated his works directly.
11. "Der Querschnitt," 31.
12. Alois Hába later confirmed that the motivation for the cancellation had been political: "Für Hanns Eisler: Beiträge von Freunden, Mitarbeitern und Schülern," *Sinn und Form*, 1964, 348.
13. H.W., "Zur Vorgeschichte des 13. Internationalen Musikfestes in Prag," 153.
14. Bush, "The I.S.C.M. Festival at Prague," 940. In H.W., "Zur Vorgeschichte des 13. Internationalen Musikfestes in Prag," 145, the number of invited delegates is given as 130.
15. There is considerable confusion about whether a Soviet ISCM section ever officially existed. Günter Mayer writes that there was a Soviet ISCM section from 1924 to 1934; see his notes to Hanns Eisler's essay "Einiges über die Lage des modernen Komponisten," in *Hanns Eisler: Musik und Politik. Schriften 1924–1948*, ed. Günter Mayer (Leipzig: VEB Deutscher Verlag für Musik, 1973), 327. Haefeli states that the Association for Modern Music (ASM) had served "indirectly" as the Soviet section of the ISCM; Haefeli, *Die Internationale Gesellschaft für Neue Musik*, 114, 231. The ASM was dissolved in 1932, according to Richard Taruskin;

16. see his *The Early Twentieth Century*, vol. 4, *The Oxford History of Western Music* (Oxford: Oxford University Press, 2005), 778.
16. H.W., "Zur Vorgeschichte des 13. Internationalen Musikfestes in Prag," 154. All translations are my own unless otherwise noted.
17. Bush, "The I.S.C.M. Festival at Prague," 940.
18. Hába, "Für Hanns Eisler," 349.
19. According to Hans and Rosaleen Moldenhauer, Webern had been scheduled to conduct the premiere of his Concerto for Nine Instruments, op. 24, but he decided not to attend the festival (even though he was president of the Austrian section) because he was "still annoyed over the [ISCM's] politics"; Hans Moldenhauer and Rosaleen Moldenhauer, *Anton von Webern: A Chronicle of his Life and Work* (New York: Knopf, 1979), 449. Webern was annoyed above all, it seems, by musical politics rather than the other kind: for example, by the fact that Berg's *Bruchstücke aus Wozzeck* had been removed from the program of the ISCM in Venice the year before, as well as by the ISCM's decision in 1935 to have George Szell instead of Heinrich Jalowetz conduct Berg's *Lulu* suite; see Moldenhauer and Moldenhauer, *Anton von Webern*, 678n5.
20. On Webern's Nazi sympathies, see Anne C. Shreffler, "Anton Webern," in *Schoenberg, Berg, and Webern: A Companion to the Second Viennese School*, ed. Bryan Simms (Westport, CT, and London: Greenwood Press, 1999), 301–4; Moldenhauer and Moldenhauer, *Anton von Webern*, 515–32.
21. Herbert Gerigk, "Musikfestdämmerung," *Die Musik* 27, no. 1 (1934): 50.
22. As quoted in Austriacus [Ernst Krenek], "Blubo-Sektion Oesterreich," *23: Eine Wiener Musikzeitschrift*, nos. 17–19 (15 December 1934): 40.
23. Gerigk, "Musikfestdämmerung," 45.
24. Ibid., 48.
25. Hermann Scherchen, letter to his wife, Auguste Maria Jansen-Scherchen, on 21 August 1935, in Hermann Scherchen, ... *alles hörbar machen: Briefe eines Dirigenten 1920–1939*, ed. Eberhardt Klemm (Berlin: Henschel, 1976), 253.
26. Ole Hass, "Introduction," in *23. Eine Wiener Musikzeitschrift (1932–1937)*, prepared by Ole Hass (Baltimore: RIPM Consortium, 2006), ix–xiii.
27. Austriacus [Ernst Krenek], "Die Blubo-Internationale," *23: Eine Wiener Musikzeitschrift*, nos. 17–19 (15 December 1934): 19–25.
28. [Krenek], "Blubo-Sektion Oesterreich," 41.
29. [Krenek], "Die Blubo-Internationale," 21.
30. Gerigk, "Musikfestdämmerung," 50.
31. Gerigk also used anti-Semitic rhetoric to describe Milhaud's suite from his opera *Maximilian*: "The soul of this music is mainly percussion orgies, in addition to, in this suite, an oriental color." Ibid., 48.
32. Ibid., 49.
33. Ernst Krenek, "Offene[r] Brief" [Open letter from Ernst Krenek to the editor of the journal *Musik im Zeitbewußtsein*], *23: Eine Wiener Musikzeitschrift*, nos. 17–19 (15 December 1934): 24.
34. Accounts differ: Henry Prunières indicates that seventy-one composers attended the Vichy festival ("Le Festival du Conseil Permanent pour la Coopération Internationale des Compositeurs de Musique, a Vichy," *La Revue Musicale* [numéro spécial], September–October 1935: 229), while Krenek cites seventy-nine composers ("Eau de Vichy auf unsere Mühle," *23: Eine Wiener Musikzeitschrift*, nos. 22–23 [10 October 1935]: 26). Max Unger cites the participation of eighteen countries: "Internationales Musikfest in Vichy," *Schweizerische Musikzeitung/Revue musicale suisse* 75 (1935): 620.
35. Prunières, "Le Festival du Conseil Permanent," 229.

36. Unger, "Internationales Musikfest in Vichy," 619. On the same page, Unger also criticizes the large number of works composed by the organization's delegates.
37. Krenek, "Eau de Vichy auf unsere Mühle," 26. The Milhaud work is identified in Unger, "Internationales Musikfest in Vichy," 620.
38. Gerigk, "Musikfestdämmerung," 50. Another vice president was Jean Sibelius.
39. Hanns Eisler and Hermann Reichenbach, "Bericht über die Verhandlungen des IRTB [Internationaler Revolutionärer Theaterbund] mit der Internationalen Gesellschaft für zeitgenössische Musik anläßlich des Festivals in Prag," in *Hanns Eisler: Gesammelte Schriften 1921–1935,* ed. Tobias Faßhauer and Günter Mayer (Wiesbaden: Breitkopf & Härtel, 2007), 292. This report will be discussed further later in the chapter.
40. Eberhardt Klemm, "Eisler und Scherchen: Prag oder Vichy," *Beiträge zur Musikwissenschaft* 28, no. 2 (1986): 118.
41. Eisler and Reichenbach viewed the dual memberships of Roussel, Honegger, Milhaud, Conrad Beck, and Ferroud as a serious threat to the ISCM. They also objected, on political grounds, to Stravinsky's role as vice president. Eisler and Reichenbach, "Bericht über die Verhandlungen," 287 and 290.
42. [Krenek], "Die Blubo-Internationale," 22.
43. Dent, "Zum 13. Internationalen Musikfest in Prag," 97, 99.
44. The first legally binding statutes were approved by the general assembly at the Paris festival in 1937; these are given in Haefeli, *Die Internationale Gesellschaft für Neue Musik,* 623–28. No previous versions of the statutes survive (ibid., 740n1). The question of a potential Soviet membership in the ISCM also forced the issue, as we will see below.
45. Unger, "Internationales Musikfest in Vichy," 620.
46. See Paul Sacher's letter in "Musikfeste und Musikalischer Alltag (Vorschläge, Einwände und Impressionen, anlässlich des Prager Festes der Internationalen Gesellschaft für Neue Musik, 1935)," *Musica Viva* 1, no. 1 (1936): 4. While the announcement in *Der Auftakt* had mentioned that works by two "reichsdeutsche" composers would be featured on the festival, one (by Edmund von Borck) was not played, and the other was by Karl Amadeus Hartmann, who was at that time a marginal figure and had no Nazi or nationalistic sympathies.
47. Stefan, "Ein freies Wort zum Internationalen Musikfest," 207–8.
48. The Seventh Congress of the Communist International "marked a turning-point in the history of Comintern." See E. H. Carr, *Twilight of the Comintern, 1930–35* (New York: Pantheon, 1982), 403, 424.
49. Joy Calico, "Eisler's Comintern File: F. 495, op. 205, d. 252"; this quotation appeared in an earlier version of the paper, now published in *Eisler in England,* ed. Oliver Dahin and Hermann Levi (Wiesbaden: Breitkopf & Härtel, 2014), 91.
50. See Hanns Eisler, "Einiges über die Lage des modernen Komponisten. (Anlässlich des 13. Festivals der I.G.N.M.)," in *Gesammelte Schriften,* 316. The text was published (in German) in Prague shortly after the festival as "Zur Avantgarde der Musik," *Die neue Weltbühne* 31, no. 38 (19 September 1935): 1189–92.
51. Eisler, "Einiges über die Lage des modernen Komponisten," 316.
52. Ibid., 317.
53. Ibid., 318.
54. Eisler and Reichenbach, "Bericht über die Verhandlungen," sig. 4686 (original) and 2786 (carbon copy), Hanns-Eisler-Archiv, Akademie der Künste, Berlin (hereafter cited as HEA/AdK). This report, which was published in Hanns Eisler's new *Gesammelte Schriften* edited by Tobias Faßhauer and Günter Mayer, and copies of other materials from the Soviet party archives are held in HEA/AdK. Calico, "Eisler's Comintern File," 92, explains how the IMB was ostensibly

a separate organization, but for all practical purposes it served as the continuation of the music division of Comintern, which had been established in 1932 as a subdivision of the Comintern's International Revolutionary Theater Association (Internationaler Revolutionärer Theaterbund, IRTB). This explains why the IRTB is mentioned in the report's title. Since the general assemblies at the festival were not open to the public, the most detailed descriptions we have of them are from this report.

55. Eisler and Reichenbach, "Bericht über die Verhandlungen," 289. Here and below, I cite the edition published in Hanns Eisler's *Gesammelte Schriften,* ed. Tobias Faßhauer and Günter Mayer.
56. Ibid., 293.
57. Ibid., 292.
58. Ibid., 301.
59. Ibid., 297. This passage is also quoted in Klemm, "Eisler und Scherchen," 120.
60. Eisler and Reichenbach were allowed to attend the general assembly as nonvoting observers. Here Reichenbach greeted the delegates on behalf of Soviet composers. In this speech, Reichenbach did emphasize that "we would look favorably on the possibility of holding a festival in Moscow at the earliest available opportunity." Eisler and Reichenbach, "Bericht über die Verhandlungen," 301. The report (p. 303) refers to a "gentleman agreement" [*sic*—original English] whereby Barcelona would be accepted as the venue for 1936, as long as Moscow would be a candidate for the 1937 meeting (which ultimately took place in Paris).
61. Ibid., 306.
62. "Aufgaben und Ergebnisse der Deleg[a]tion des I.M.B. zum Musikfest der Internationalen Gesellschaft für neue Musik in Prag," sig. 4548, HEA/AdK. This document is 5 typewritten pages, 1.5 spaced, dated "Moskau, den 7. Oktober 1935," and indicates that "Dieses Material wurde von der Genossin Lode, Sekretärin des IMB, zusammengestellt." The document bears a Russian archival stamp. According to notes in Hanns Eisler's *Gesammelte Schriften,* this typescript comes from the Russisches Staatsarchiv für gesellschaftspolitische Geschichte (RGASPI), formerly the Central Party Archive of the Communist Party of the Soviet Union (notes to Eisler and Reichenbach, "Bericht über die Verhandlungen," 490; excerpts from the "Aufgaben und Ergebnisse" text are cited on pp. 499–500). This typescript appears to be one of the sources that Günter Mayer brought back to Berlin in December 2001 after his trip to Russia to gather materials for the new critical edition of Eisler's works, the Hanns-Eisler-Gesamtausgabe (see Mayer's typescript report in Folder 4548 in HEA/AdK).
63. "Aufgaben und Ergebnisse," sig. 4548, p. 1, HEA/AdK.
64. The meeting was held in the IRTB offices on 28 August, about a week before the festival was to begin. The Soviet Composers Union was represented by "Genossen Tscheljapow [N. Chelyapov?] und Szabo [the Hungarian composer Ferenc Szabó]," and the IMB was represented by "[Erwin] Piscator, Reichenbach, Kreici, Reich, Lode"; "Aufgaben und Erbegnisse," sig. 4548, p. 1, HEA/AdK. In the typescript, the four points are erroneously numbered 2–5; ibid., 2.
65. Ibid., 1.
66. Ibid., 2. Eisler and Reichenbach mentioned this condition in "Bericht über die Verhandlungen," 295–96.
67. "Aufgaben und Ergebnisse," sig. 4548, pp. 3–5, HEA/AdK.
68. On Eisler's whereabouts between October 1935 and the spring of 1937, see Jürgen Schebera, *Hanns Eisler: Eine Biographie in Texten, Bildern und Dokumenten* (Mainz: Schott, 1998), 136, 141–50. Eisler continued to serve as president of

the IMB, from a distance, until April 1936; see notes to Eisler and Reichenbach, "Bericht über die Verhandlungen," 489.
69. Notes to Eisler and Reichenbach, "Bericht über die Verhandlungen," 491.
70. Cited in Haefeli, *Die Internationale Gesellschaft für Neue Musik,* 197. A German version was published shortly after the festival; "Die Delegiertenversammlung der Internationalen Gesellschaft für Neue Musik," *Der Auftakt* 15, nos. 9–10 (1935): 175.
71. Haefeli, *Die Internationale Gesellschaft für Neue Musik,* 199.
72. Ibid., 180–83.
73. See "Auszüge aus Briefen," in "Musikfeste und Musikalischer Alltag," 2–6. It is curious that there were no responses from Hába or Steinhard, the Czech delegates, or Eisler.
74. This quotation is described as being from a private letter, which, however, could not be found in the Hermann-Scherchen-Archiv of the AdK.
75. "Musikfeste und Musikalischer Alltag," 1. The phrase in italics was given in German only ("schwer zugänglichen und problematischen Richtungen") and was not included in the English, French, or Italian translations.
76. Haefeli, *Die Internationale Gesellschaft für Neue Musik,* 623.
77. Krenek, for example, claimed that trying to produce national music is likely to lead to mediocre results. Goethe's Germanness, and Balzac's Frenchness, are undeniable, but they achieved their greatness not by trying to be German or French, but by their genius; see his article "Das Nationale und die Kunst," *Der Auftakt* 14, no. 10 (1934): 166–69.
78. Eisler, "Einiges über die Lage des modernen Komponisten," 323–25.
79. Two versions of the manifesto are included in Hanns Eisler, *Musik und Politik 1948–1962* (Leipzig: VEB Deutscher Verlag für Musik, 1982), 26–31.
80. Blonay, "Prague, un tournant décisif," 637–38.
81. Erich Steinhard, "Internationales Musikfest in Prag," *Der Auftakt* 15, nos. 9–10 (1935): 151. Alan Bush wrote, more perceptively: "Written in Schönberg's twelve-tone system this work is nevertheless absolutely unlike Schönberg in its effect." He added, however, that "[i]t must have sounded very odd to many of those present." Bush, "The I.S.C.M. Festival at Prague," 941.
82. Louis Gruenberg, "Modern Youth at Prague, 1935," *Modern Music* 13, no. 1 (November–December 1935): 42.
83. See the legendary analysis of this movement by Karlheinz Stockhausen, "Weberns Konzert für 9 Instrumente, op. 24: Analyse des ersten Satzes," *Melos* 20 (1953): 343–48.
84. The idea of art as a message in a bottle (*Flaschenpost*) comes from Theodor W. Adorno, *Philosophie der neuen Musik,* vol. 12, *Gesammelte Schriften* (Frankfurt: Suhrkamp, 1991), 126. Translated by Robert Hullot-Kentor as *Philosophy of New Music* (Minneapolis and London: University of Minnesota Press, 2006), 102.
85. The standard work on the Congress for Cultural Freedom is by Frances Stonor Saunders, *Who Paid the Piper? The CIA and the Cultural Cold War* (London: Granta Books, 1999). For an account of the congress's musical activities, see Ian Wellens, *Music on the Frontline: Nicolas Nabokov's Struggle against Communism and Middlebrow Culture* (Hants, UK, and Burlington, VT: Ashgate, 2002).

Bibliography

Archives

Paul Sacher Collection, Paul Sacher Foundation, Basel, Switzerland

Hermann-Scherchen-Archiv and Hanns-Eisler-Archiv, Akademie der Künste, Berlin

Printed Sources

Adorno, Theodor W. *Philosophy of New Music*. Translated by Robert Hullot-Kentor. Minneapolis and London: University of Minnesota Press, 2006.
Austriacus [Ernst Krenek]. "Die Blubo-Internationale." *23: Eine Wiener Musikzeitschrift*, nos. 17–19 (15 December 1934): 19–25.
———. "Blubo-Sektion Oesterreich." *23: Eine Wiener Musikzeitschrift*, nos. 17–19 (15 December 1934): 39–44.
Bedford, Herbert. "The Permanent Council for the International Co-operation of Composers." *The Musical Times* 77, no. 1116 (1936): 159.
Blonay, André de. "Prague, un tournant décisif." *Schweizerische Musikzeitung* 75 (1935): 634–41.
Bush, Alan. "The I.S.C.M. Festival at Prague." *The Musical Times* 76, no. 1112 (1935): 940–42.
Calico, Joy. "Eisler's Comintern File: F. 495, op. 205, d. 252." In Eisler in England, ed. Oliver Dahin and Hermann Levi, 91–104. Wiesbaden: Breitkopf & Härtel, 2014.
Calvocoressi, M.-D. "Music in the Foreign Press." *The Musical Times* 76, no. 1114 (1935): 1098–99.
———. "Music in the Foreign Press." *The Musical Times* 77, no. 1121 (1936): 632–34.
———. "The Permanent Council for the International Co-operation of Composers" [Letter to the editor]. *The Musical Times* 77, no. 1117 (1936): 256.
Carr, E. H. *Twilight of the Comintern, 1930–35*. New York: Pantheon, 1982.
"Die Delegiertenversammlung der Internationalen Gesellschaft für Neue Musik" [announcement]. *Der Auftakt* 15, nos. 9–10 (1935): 175.
Dent, Edward J. "Zum 13. Internationalen Musikfest in Prag 1935." *Der Auftakt* 15, nos. 7–8 (1935): 97–99.
Eisler, Hanns. *Gesammelte Schriften 1921–1935*. Edited by Tobias Faßhauer and Günter Mayer. Wiesbaden: Breitkopf & Härtel, 2007.
———. *Musik und Politik: Schriften 1924–1948*. Edited by Günter Mayer. Leipzig: VEB Deutscher Verlag für Musik, 1973.
———. *Musik und Politik: Schriften 1948–1962*. Edited by Günter Mayer. Leipzig: VEB Deutscher Verlag für Musik, 1982.
Gerigk, Herbert. "Eine Lanze für Schönberg! Anmerkungen zu einem Geburtstagsaufsatz." *Die Musik* 27, no. 2 (1934): 87–91.
———. "Musikfestdämmerung." *Die Musik* 27, no. 1 (1934): 45–51.
———. "Triumph Nordischer Musik." *Die Musik* 27, no. 10 (1935): 733.
———. "Vergreisung oder 'Fortschreitende Entwicklung'? Bemerkungen zum Hamburger Musikfest 1935." *Die Musik* 27, no. 10 (1935): 721–27.
———. "Von Rauschebärten, vom ADMV. und von deutscher Musikpolitik." *Die Musik* 28, no. 2 (1935): 126–28.

Goldschmidt, Harry. "Hermann Scherchen." In *Um die Sache der Musik: Reden und Aufsätze,* 180–206. Leipzig: Reclam, 1970.
Gruenberg, Louis. "Modern Youth at Prague, 1935." *Modern Music* 13, no. 1 (November–December 1935): 38–44.
Hába, Alois. "Für Hanns Eisler: Beiträge von Freunden, Mitarbeitern und Schülern." In "Hanns Eisler," special issue, *Sinn und Form,* 1964, 348–52.
Haefeli, Anton. *Die Internationale Gesellschaft für Neue Musik (IGNM): Ihre Geschichte von 1922 bis zur Gegenwart.* Zurich: Atlantis Musikbuch-Verlag, 1982.
Hass, Ole. *23. Eine Wiener Musikzeitschrift (1932–1937).* Baltimore: RIPM Consortium, 2006 (http://www.ripm.org).
H.W. "Zur Vorgeschichte des 13. Internationalen Musikfestes in Prag." *Der Auftakt* 15, nos. 9–10 (1935): 152–55.
Klemm, Eberhardt. "Eisler und Scherchen: Prag oder Vichy." *Beiträge zur Musikwissenschaft* 28, no. 2 (1986): 117–21.
Krenek, Ernst. "Eau de Vichy auf unsere Mühle." *23: Eine Wiener Musikzeitschrift,* nos. 22–23 (10 October 1935): 22–29.
———. "Das Nationale und die Kunst." *Der Auftakt* 14, no. 10 (1934): 166–69.
———. "Offene[r] Brief" [Open letter from Ernst Krenek to the editor of the journal *Musik im Zeitbewußtsein*]. *23: Eine Wiener Musikzeitschrift,* nos. 17–19 (15 December 1934): 24–25.
———. "Zur Situation der IGNM." *Anbruch* 16 (1934): 41–44.
Lucchesi, Joachim, ed. *Hermann Scherchen: Werke und Briefe.* Vol. 1. Berlin: Peter Lang, 1991.
Moldenhauer, Hans, and Rosaleen Moldenhauer. *Anton von Webern: A Chronicle of his Life and Work.* New York: Knopf, 1979.
"Musikfeste und Musikalischer Alltag (Vorschläge, Einwände und Impressionen, anlässlich des Prager Festes der Internationalen Gesellschaft für Neue Musik, 1935)." *Musica Viva* 1, no. 1 (1936): 1–8.
"Das nächste (14.) Internationale Musikfest" [announcement]. *Der Auftakt* 15, nos. 9–10 (1935): 175.
Pauli, Hansjörg, and Dagmar Wünsche, eds. *Hermann Scherchen: Musiker, 1891–1966—Ein Lesebuch.* Berlin: Edition Hentrich, 1986.
Prunières, Henry. "Le Festival du Conseil Permanent pour la Coopération Internationale des Compositeurs de Musique, a Vichy." *La Revue Musicale* [numéro spécial], September–October 1935: 229–32.
"Der Querschnitt: Das Internationale Musikfest in Karlsbad" [announcement]. *Der Auftakt* 15, nos. 1–2 (1935): 30–31.
Raabe, Peter. "Nationalismus, Internationalismus und Musik." *Die Musik* 27, no. 11 (1935): 801–3.
Reich, Willi. "Internationale Verlagsgenossenschaft für neue Musik." *23: Eine Wiener Musikzeitschrift,* nos. 22–23 (10 October 1935): 29–31.
Schebera, Jürgen. *Hanns Eisler: Eine Biographie in Texten, Bildern und Dokumenten.* Mainz: Schott, 1998.

Scherchen, Hermann. ... *alles hörbar machen: Briefe eines Dirigenten 1920–1939* [Letters to his wife, Auguste Maria Jansen-Scherchen]. Edited by Eberhardt Klemm. Berlin: Henschel, 1976.

Shreffler, Anne C. "Anton Webern." In *Schoenberg, Berg, and Webern: A Companion to the Second Viennese School,* ed. Bryan Simms, 251–314. Westport, CT, and London: Greenwood Press, 1999.

———. "Musikalische Kanonisierung und Dekanonisierung im 20. Jahrhundert." Translated by Fabian Kolb. In *Der Kanon der Musik: Theorie und Geschichte—Ein Handbuch,* ed. Klaus Pietschmann and Melanie Wald, 611-30. Munich: Edition text + kritik, 2013.

Stefan, Paul. "Ein freies Wort zum Internationalen Musikfest." *Anbruch* 17, no. 8 (1935): 205–8.

———. "Das Internationale Musikfest in Prag." *Anbruch* 17, no. 9 (1935): 246–48.

Steinhard, Erich. "Internationales Musikfest in Prag." *Der Auftakt* 15, nos. 9–10 (1935): 150–52.

Stockhausen, Karlheinz. "Weberns Konzert für 9 Instrumente, op. 24: Analyse des ersten Satzes." *Melos* 20 (1953): 343–48.

Stonor Saunders, Frances. *Who Paid the Piper? The CIA and the Cultural Cold War.* London: Granta Books, 1999.

Stuckenschmidt, H. H. "Verbotene Musik." *Der Auftakt* 15, nos. 11–12 (1935): 177–79.

Taruskin, Richard. *The Early Twentieth Century.* Vol. 4 of *The Oxford History of Western Music.* Oxford: Oxford University Press, 2005.

Unger, Max. "Internationales Musikfest in Vichy." *Schweizerische Musikzeitung/Revue musicale suisse* 75 (1935): 618–21.

Wellens, Ian. *Music on the Frontline: Nicolas Nabokov's Struggle against Communism and Middlebrow Culture.* Hants, UK, and Burlington, VT: Ashgate, 2002.

Part II
MUSIC, INTERNATIONAL HISTORY, AND THE STATE

Chapter Three

MUSIC AND INTERNATIONAL RELATIONS IN OCCUPIED GERMANY, 1945–49

Toby Thacker

As the Battle of Britain was raging in the late summer of 1940, a debate started in Britain about how to treat a defeated Germany after the war. Mindful of the apparent failure of the Treaty of Versailles, which had sought to punish Germany after World War I, the idea was mooted that what was needed was a "spiritual regeneration" of that country and its people. When in 1942 and 1943 these discussions were broadened to include Britain's allies, the United States and the Soviet Union, it was agreed between them that a defeated Germany would be subjected to military occupation and its people to a program of "reeducation." This was a unique experiment intending no less than to change the way a whole people thought. In the final months of World War II, the plans for the "reeducation" of Germany were developed further, attention being paid to specific areas such as politics, education, the media, and the arts. As part of the "reeducation" program, the Allies planned a complete restructuring of the arts in Germany, including music.[1]

On 10 June 1945, only weeks after the end of World War II in Europe, General Zhukhov, the commander in chief of the Red Army, was invited with his staff to a victory celebration held by the Supreme Commander of the Allied Expeditionary Force Dwight Eisenhower at his new headquarters in Frankfurt. The senior British officer in Germany, Field-Marshal Bernard Montgomery, was also present with his staff. Before being wined and dined by their American hosts in the requisitioned buildings of the giant chemical company IG Farben,

---

Notes for this section begin on page 111.

Zhukhov, Montgomery, and their entourages were taken outside to a balcony. Together these representatives of the world's greatest military powers stood for some time while no fewer than 1,700 American and British aircraft flew overhead in a huge procession. One can only imagine what an awe-inspiring spectacle this must have been, as the air was rent with the pulsating sound of thousands of powerful engines. According to Montgomery, this "impressive display of air power" was "not lost on the Russians."[2] Eisenhower wrote: "In the bright sunlight it was a tremendous show and Zhukhov seemed much impressed."[3] Montgomery, in his account, went on to describe how those present were then entertained by "a coloured cabaret show, with swing music and elaborate dancing by negro women who were naked above the waist line. The Russians had never seen or heard anything like this before and their eyes almost popped out of their heads!"[4]

Two years later, in September 1947, a slightly different ceremony celebrating Allied unity and achievement was held at the Staatsoper in Berlin; it was similarly attended by representatives from the wartime Allies. This time the hosts were the French, who wished to commemorate the efforts of their own Resistance movement. An American report on the ceremony described how the Soviets "offered dances and music by their famous soldier chorus." The British were apparently represented by "a famous Scottish bagpipe band." With some disgust, the report described how "the United States Special Services supplied a small jazz band and a parody skit on 'Carmen' in which four soldiers participated." The "inappropriateness of the American offering" was apparently commented on by representatives of the different military governments attending, and the report noted also "the effect that these performances have … upon the Germans attending such performances. It requested that in future the United States Army is obligated to send as an example of the culture of our country, material and talent more representative and of greater dignity than was supplied for the French festival."[5]

These two vignettes provide fascinating insights into the complex and changing relationships in Germany after 1945 between the four occupying powers and the occupied Germans, and they point also to the importance of music in these relations. In the victory celebration staged by the Americans in Frankfurt in June 1945, music played only a marginal role. It was used as amusing entertainment after the central event, which was a huge display of military power, clearly intended to impress the Soviets. Significantly, neither Eisenhower nor his aide Harry Butcher (who also described the event in his memoir) felt the "coloured cabaret show" and "swing music" even worthy of mention in their accounts.[6] The Germans, too, were notable by their absence. Defeated and humiliated, none of their representatives were invited to the ceremony, although presumably thousands of them must have been aware of the huge procession of American and British aircraft that flew overhead that day.

Two years later, in occupied Berlin, music was center stage and being used in a solemn diplomatic occasion to express commemoration and to represent the national cultures of the four occupiers. Invited German representatives were clearly present, and the occupiers evidently wished not to overawe them but to impress them, and one another, with their separate musical offerings. The emphasis in the occupation had clearly shifted from physical coercion to cultural persuasion; the most senior officers in the American military government in Germany were dismayed with the way in which their national culture had been represented by jazz. Here we see the transition from military conflict to embryonic Cold War, in which the forces of culture have supplanted the guns, tanks, and warplanes that were used to force Germany into unconditional surrender in May 1945.

This chapter will explore ways in which music can be used to provide a much more nuanced account of the relations between the four occupying powers in Germany between 1945 and 1949 and their relations with the Germans themselves. It will argue first that music can illuminate the delicate and often uncomfortable balance that the occupiers sought to establish between coercion and persuasion, between punishment and "reeducation," in their separate zones of occupation. It will then use music to show how keen the competition was between the occupiers as the balance tipped from coercion to persuasion and the struggle developed to win over German hearts and minds. By examining the place of jazz in Allied programs and its reception in Germany after 1945, it will argue, as Jessica C. E. Gienow-Hecht has commented in another context, that "[c]ultural relations occasionally overlap with, but do not necessarily reflect political realities; instead they develop a life of their own."[7]

Throughout, music will be used to highlight the role of German agency in the years of occupation. This situation was, after all, one in which the occupiers appeared to hold all the cards: they had abolished all German organs of government and abrogated to themselves legislative authority. They controlled the physical movements of the German population and exercised a strict surveillance over all branches of the media. Where necessary, they used force to impose their will on the Germans. But in the sphere of culture, they depended on a significant degree of German cooperation, goodwill, and mutual involvement. Music not only provided a unique opportunity for the occupiers to impress and influence the Germans temporarily under their control, but also offered a significant cultural space in which the occupied Germans could express their own sense of autonomy and, within certain limits, a sense of national pride.[8]

The Soviet Union, the United States, Britain, and France occupied Germany in 1945 with a clear set of short-term objectives, but without a long-term plan for the future of Germany. They were united in their determination to destroy Nazism in all its institutional forms and to prosecute war criminals. They were equally committed to the dismantling of German military power and to the idea of "decartelization," the breaking up of the giant industrial combines that had supported Nazism and militarism. The fulfillment of these objectives necessarily involved a draconian repression in Germany. At its most brutal, this repression involved the arrest and confinement of tens of thousands of Germans, soldiers and civilians, men and women. It led to the prosecution of many of these people on newly created charges and to the execution of many hundreds found guilty of the most serious crimes. Thousands of ex-Nazis were imprisoned or subjected to restrictions on their future employment. Eventually—and it took some months for the occupiers to establish the machinery for this—far-reaching programs of "denazification" were implemented, requiring huge sections of the German population to fill out questionnaires and appear before tribunals to establish how far they had been involved with the activities of the Nazi Party before 1945.[9]

To add to the tension and hostility between occupiers and occupied that were generated by denazification, there was a catastrophic decline in economic conditions in Germany after May 1945. Although this was in large part caused by wartime damage and dislocation, it was significantly exacerbated by the policies of the occupiers. In the Soviet and French zones, there were extensive programs to dismantle German industrial plants and buildings and to remove these wholesale to the Soviet Union and France to help rebuild the shattered economies there. Although the British and the Americans were less interested in moving German industrial facilities to their own countries, they were determined to destroy or at least seriously to reduce the German capacity for manufacturing armaments and therefore deliberately held down the production of coal and steel. The results of these occupation policies were the same everywhere, varying only in degree. The standard of living of the German population was relentlessly forced down. Living in cramped and often ruined buildings, lacking fuel for heating in the winter, and often dressed in little more than rags, large sections of the population were barely subsisting by 1947. Official rations fell below the level needed to maintain health, and children went barefoot. Diseases such as tuberculosis reappeared, young women were forced into prostitution, and cigarettes became the most widely accepted medium of exchange in a flourishing black market.[10]

Underneath and often preceding the official policies of the occupiers, there was widespread violence, intimidation, and looting, often carried out by occupying soldiers without the sanction of military governments. The most shocking manifestation of this was the mass rape of German women that occurred in areas occupied by the Soviets; less well-known today but equally terrifying and traumatic for those affected at the time was a similar phenomenon in areas occupied by French troops.[11] Across Germany, there was looting after the arrival of Allied soldiers, and even when the structures of occupation had been established and a greater degree of military discipline had been enforced, German property was liable to be requisitioned to provide accommodation for the occupiers. Ironically, musical instruments were often taken from the Germans. An American report from Württemberg-Baden in June 1945 bluntly stated that "[o]ne harp, 3 Wagner tubas, and 2 Contra bass fiddles ... were requisitioned and used by 6th Army Corps."[12]

In this bleak and gloomy situation—which hardly augured well for the future—music appeared as a ray of light, an area in which occupiers and occupied might work together. As mentioned at the beginning of this chapter, from as early as 1940, a debate had developed in wartime Britain about how to treat Germany after the war, and by 1943 a consensus had developed among the Allies that punishment would have to be balanced with a program of "reeducation." Imagined in different ways, this idea of "reeducation" had developed by early 1945 into an ambitious project aimed at nothing less than the spiritual conversion of a whole people, away from ideas of Nazism and racial supremacy toward ideals of humanism and internationalism. Inevitably, the four wartime Allies imagined "reeducation" as a process that would reflect their own national ideals. The British and Americans hoped to implant the values of liberal democracy and pluralism in Germany; the Soviets—with reservations[13]—intended to develop the ideals of Marxism; the French fondly imagined that their own traditions as the land of liberty, human values, and finesse made them the ideal agents for a *mission civilisatrice* in Germany.

What is striking is the importance all attached to music in their "re-education" programs.[14]

Thus, from literally the first days and weeks of the occupation of Germany, all four occupying powers set about restoring musical life in the shattered areas of Germany they controlled. In towns and cities all over Germany in May, June, and July 1945, concerts were staged with the approval and support of local occupying authorities, often in semiruined buildings. Military vehicles were used to find and transport instruments and officers were detailed to locate musicians, above all conductors and directors of repute who could lend prestige to these events. Great efforts were made to find scores and parts for the actual music to be played, and strikingly similar programs were performed all over Germany. Typically, they highlighted music by Bach, Mozart, and Beethoven, alongside pieces by Mendelssohn and Tchaikovsky. In areas occupied by the Americans and the British, strict rules about "fraternization" applied and separate concerts were held for Allied service personnel and for Germans; in Soviet- and French-controlled areas, despite the severity of other aspects of the occupation, this segregation was not universally followed and "mixed" audiences were encouraged to attend.

One might imagine that these concerts would have been boycotted by German musicians and audiences, perhaps seen as propaganda stunts or exercises in a disreputable collaboration, but there is no record of this. On the contrary, everywhere across Germany, German musicians demonstrated enthusiasm and a desire to work with local representatives of the respective military governments. Listeners crowded in to the actual concerts, often—because of the lack of public transport—walking considerable distances to attend. The archival record from all four occupation zones provides striking testimony. The Soviets set the pace in the ruins of Berlin, encouraging the remaining members of the Berlin Philharmonic to perform in a cinema auditorium on 26 May 1945. The program was Mendelssohn's *Overture to a Midsummer Night's Dream,* Mozart's A Major Violin Concerto, and Tchaikovsky's Fourth Symphony.[15] In Munich, where the daily reports of the "Music Section" established by the Americans survived, world-famous musicians such as Richard Strauss, Eugen Jochum, Hans Knappertsbuch, and Oswald Kabasta vied for the honor of conducting the inaugural concert on 8 July 1945.[16] In Dresden, occupied by the Soviets, Gerhart Wiesenhütter had already conducted the Philharmonic Orchestra on 6 June, and on 1 July Rudolf Mauersberger directed the internationally renowned Kreuzchor singing Bach in the Church of the Resurrection.[17]

In Hamburg, Hans Schmidt-Isserstedt emerged to help the British to establish a new symphony orchestra, which was broadcasting and recording as early as July 1945. The adviser to the British foreign secretary toured the British zone in June and July 1945, and although his report to the government was overwhelmingly gloomy in its contents, he saw some of the work of this new orchestra: "In one studio we witnessed the German musical director, the German conductor, and the British control officer listening with great pride and pleasure to the first recording of a Mahler symphony, and it was very evident that in this sphere at least there are no political barriers to the closest cooperation between ourselves and the Germans."[18] In Stuttgart, occupied by the French at the end of the war, concerts for "mixed" audiences of German citizens and French troops were held on 17 June, 21 June, and 24 June. Everywhere, these performances attracted large, unusually attentive and appreciative audiences.[19]

It would be possible to interpret these events in a cynical way, to see them as exercises in Allied propaganda and German opportunism. Although these elements were present, they are not the whole story. It is abundantly clear that the music being performed spoke to the deepest feelings of occupiers and occupied alike. Some of these feelings, a reverence for senses of beauty and humanity that transcended chronological and national boundaries, may have been shared. It is entirely possible that others were not. For many Germans, this was undoubtedly an area, possibly the one last area, in which they could publicly express national pride after the catastrophic collapse of the Third Reich and the revelation of Nazi crimes. For some Germans, it was an opportunity to hear music by composers such as Mendelssohn and Mahler again, which had been forbidden under the Nazis and now symbolized a larger cultural freedom. For the Allies, the "German" composers performed at these first postwar concerts represented a strand of German history and culture that they had long interpreted more broadly as part of an international heritage and that, in their eyes, was not—despite the best efforts of the Nazis—tainted by the criminal record of the Third Reich.[20]

Nor was this a flash in the pan. Over the next four years, as material conditions in Germany deteriorated, the initial rush to restore German musical life developed into a keenly fought rivalry between the erstwhile Allies. All four occupiers sponsored the reconstruction of orchestras, opera houses, and music academies and the development of radio stations with elaborate music facilities. These radio stations typically employed first-class symphony orchestras, choirs, chamber ensembles, and dance bands. The radio stations paid large salaries to attract star conductors and soloists and sought to carve out individual profiles, some specializing in the classical repertoire, others in "early music," and others, such as Northwest German Radio in Cologne, in experimental and electronic music. The Soviets took the lead in allocating extra rations to professional German musicians; the French led the way in introducing virtuoso musicians from their own country to Germany. All four occupiers quickly sought to move beyond the early postwar repertoire of classical composers and introduce more modern and contemporary music. Modernist and avant-garde music—which had been condemned by the Nazis as "degenerate"—was widely perceived in postwar Germany as a language of antifascism and given special support, for example, in broadcasting and in the establishment of festivals and summer schools.[21]

These music programs were undoubtedly used for national propaganda. All four occupiers promoted their own national composers and performers in Germany, using them to represent symbolic aspects of their own cultures. Thus, the British used Britten and Tippett operas to represent ideals of a modern British culture; the French promoted a whole canon of their own composers to contest the idea that music was an area of exclusively German achievement; and the Soviets used Shostakovich above all as representative of their own progressive communist music culture. Belatedly, the Americans sought to introduce works by Barber, Piston, Harris, and Schuman to show that they too had a distinctive national music, and they arranged tours by black singers to counter accusations of racism. More striking, though, than these national efforts in postwar Germany is the extent to which all four occupiers, until the onset of the Berlin blockade in April 1948, actually cooperated and supported the performance of one another's music in their own zones.

The template for this cooperation was established by a French cultural festival held in Konstanz in June 1946 that included separate days set aside to showcase the national music from the four occupying powers, a formula that was then used in similar festivals around Germany.[22] We can see it replicated in miniature at the French commemorative festival in Berlin in September 1947 referred to at the start of this chapter. The Soviets, stereotypically imagined as exclusive and hostile to capitalist cultural influences, were for their part keen to see performances in their zone of works from Britain and the United States that had been successful in other parts of Germany. Most notably, the transparently communist Kulturbund zur demokratischen Erneuerung Deutschlands (Cultural League for the Democratic Renewal of Germany) supervised a series of chamber concerts in Berlin between 1946 and 1948 that performed a whole raft of international and German modernist composers. This concert series was as internationalist and forward-looking as anything sponsored in the Western zones. Perhaps the Soviets felt comfortable in having as one of their own the most widely performed single living composer in postwar Germany, Shostakovich, well established by 1945 as an international symbol of antifascism.[23] His music was the most frequently borrowed from the Inter-Allied Music Lending Library established in Berlin in September 1946, an institution that was perhaps the most tangible product of this shared vision.[24]

In this unique international situation, fundamentally defined by war and marked for the Germans by growing poverty, insecurity, and the repressive denazification programs of the occupiers, music occupied a unique place in the public sphere. It provided a cultural terrain where the occupiers could highlight the positive and constructive reasons for their presence in Germany. Through support for Bach, Mozart, Beethoven, and the "German" classics they could demonstrate their own love of and respect for German humanist culture and history; by insisting on performances of Mendelssohn and Mahler they were able to signal their distance from the Nazis, who had condemned these composers on racial grounds. By promoting modernist internationalism they proclaimed their open-mindedness, their commitment to contemporary artists and evolving ideals of culture. By giving preference to their own national composers and virtuoso performers they proclaimed—albeit quietly—their own singular achievements. All of this activity allowed them at the same time to win sympathy from elite sections of German society and make important personal and institutional links.

The tension between the idealism of these music programs and the harsh realities of everyday life in occupied Germany was obvious to many, not least to the "Music Officers" who had the responsibility in different zones for implementing these programs. In the French zone, René Thimonnier, the Chef du Bureau des Spectacles et de la Musique, had to plead for extra security measures to be implemented to protect concert goers from assaults by colonial French troops.[25] Thimonnier was undoubtedly aware of the particular outrage caused in Germany in 1923 by assaults allegedly committed by black French troops and hoped to avoid a repetition of this. His superior, Jean Arnaud, was aware of the desperately low rations for Germans in the French zone and complained publicly in 1947 that "[c]ulture and democracy are no replacement for calories."[26] From Munich in the American zone in April 1946, information control officers complained that German actors had forgotten their lines and even fainted from malnourishment during rehearsals.[27] In many different cities, concerts had to be staged in buildings that, at least initially, were partially open to the elements. The few surviving large concert halls in the Western zones, such as in Stuttgart, were typically reserved as places of entertainment for occupying troops. The American music critic Virgil Thompson published a scathing article about this in the *New York Herald Tribune,* complaining that "the pampering of our soldiers is considered everywhere to take precedence over the reconstruction of German cultural life, even where this has been thoroughly de-Nazified."[28]

This tension was also embodied within the music program, in that music officers in occupied Germany had a dual role. As well as reconstructing music culture as part of the "reeducation" program, they were tasked with the denazification of musicians. This was a complex and evolving process that was carried out with wide zonal and regional variations. It could be harsh and often appeared to Germans as arbitrary. Individual musicians, and these might be humble second violinists in a municipal orchestra or internationally known celebrity soloists, could find themselves summarily dismissed from employment, their reputations besmirched, and facing—in 1946 and 1947—a completely uncertain future. As directives from higher authorities in military governments changed, music officers found themselves sometimes having to revoke earlier decisions and dismiss musicians they had already approved for employment. Many complained bitterly about the difficulties this caused them, and it is clear that most were mightily relieved when denazification was first scaled back in 1947 and finally turned over in 1948 to German tribunals.[29]

In both constructive and repressive aspects of music programs in postwar Germany, competition was a defining feature of international relations. Indeed, the intensity of the competition points again to the importance of music in this situation, and we can see this intensity particularly clearly in parts of Germany initially occupied by one of the Allies and subsequently transferred to the control of another. In the final days of the war, French troops occupied Karlsruhe and Stuttgart and immediately encouraged performances of music in front of "mixed" audiences. After diplomatic wrangling, it was agreed that both cities should be included in the American zone, but by the time American troops arrived formally to take control, they had to combat widespread apprehensions that they would clamp down on musical activity. Their preparations were extraordinary: at 12:00 AM on 8 July 1945, the US 100th Division formally took control of Stuttgart. A license to perform music was given to a German municipal official at 12:01 AM, and at 12:02 AM Schubert's *Trout* Quintet was performed to an audience of dignitaries. Later that day, at 5:00 PM, the Philharmonic Orchestra performed, and a recording of the concert was broadcast at 10:00 PM.[30]

A similar situation arose in Leipzig, which was first occupied by the Americans in April 1945. They allowed the renowned conductor of the Thomanerchor, Günther Ramin, to perform some Bach motets before relinquishing the city to the Soviets in July, leaving them with the more thorny question of how to judge Ramin's previous involvement with the Nazi Party. The Soviets, for their part, took full advantage of their unfettered control of Berlin for the first weeks of the occupation to encourage concert performances and license the operation of a German organization, the Kulturbund zur demokratischen Erneuerung Deutschlands (Cultural League for the Democratic Renewal of Germany), which was given the grandiose task implied in its title.[31] Music by Beethoven and Tchaikovsky was performed by the Berlin Philharmonic at the formal inauguration of the Kulturbund on 4 July 1945.[32] By the end of the month, when the Americans, British, and French were allowed into Berlin to administer their own sectors, the Kulturbund was active in all of them.

This competition continued and even intensified over the next three years. Clearly, music served as the most important public symbol of an occupying power's cultural credentials in Germany and its respect for German traditions. This shared perception undoubtedly played a major part in the confused efforts made to denazify musicians. This aspect of the denazification program appeared particularly perverse to many Germans and, it should be said, to many individuals in the occupying forces. There was a widespread perception that musicians had been apolitical creatures, and deeply felt controversies developed particularly over the degree to which famous composers, conductors, and soloists should be punished for having continued their musical careers in the Third Reich. The four occupying powers made efforts to devise and implement a common policy, but there were widespread variations in individual zones in how this policy was implemented, and the four powers fell out over individual cases. This was an area where there was potentially enormous prestige to be gained or lost and, conversely, where great damage could be done to the public image of an occupier. The most celebrated case was that of the conductor Wilhelm Furtwängler, "the most august of all the Olympians,"[33] who had directed the Berlin Philharmonic throughout the Nazi period. Furtwängler had conducted at Nazi ceremonies and had taken the orchestra to perform in armaments factories after Goebbels's call for "total war" in February 1943. He had never been a Nazi Party member, however, had tried to protect the Jewish members of the orchestra in the early years of the regime, and had tried unsuccessfully to defend Hindemith when that composer was criticized by the Nazis.

The story of Furtwängler's denazification has been thoroughly investigated.[34] After being placed on a "blacklist" in the American zone, he was prevented from appearing in public until April 1947, when he was cleared by a denazification tribunal in Berlin, much to the chagrin of the Americans. Well before this, the French and the Soviets had tried to get Furtwängler to perform in their zones and had undermined the American effort to exclude him. Clearly, in this long-drawn-out saga, the French and the Soviets more highly valued the sympathy they might gain from German audiences by appearing to give greater weight to Furtwängler's musicianship than to his alleged support for Nazism. The Americans were prepared to forego this German sympathy in order to carry out their denazification program. The initial discomfiture of the American military government in Germany at Furtwängler's triumphal return to the public sphere was further compounded by his subsequent performance, in Berlin in September 1947, with Yehudi Menuhin.

This was a gesture with enormous symbolic importance, and it is frequently interpreted in narratives of postwar Germany as a landmark moment in the broader process of international reconciliation and restitution after World War II. The spectacle of a great Jewish musician and a great German conductor performing the Beethoven Violin Concerto together appears in this light as a triumph of the human spirit and internationalism over the forces of intolerance and racial hatred. How much more unfortunate, then, for the Americans that their own military police appeared to have done their best to spoil the concert, making the 1,900-strong audience enter in single file and taking so long over this that some, including German newspaper critics, "were not permitted to take their seats." An internal American report went on to note that "[d]uring the playing of the Beethoven concerto MP's walked up and down the aisles asking for passes from Germans and Allies. Persons without passes were ejected. This not only disturbed the audience and Mr. Menuhin but completely nullified the effect the concert was supposed to make."

Lest it be thought that the Americans did not understand the symbolic importance of music in postwar Germany, we should note that the same report described this concert as "[o]ne of the most important steps thus far undertaken in Berlin by the War Department in connection with the reorientation policy."[35]

The divergences in music policy between the occupying powers, particularly in attitudes toward denazification, are best explained in terms of this jockeying for prestige and a shared recognition of the potential damage done to relationships with the Germans by appearing overly vindictive. But how should we interpret the extraordinary convergence in policies toward music in occupied Germany between May 1945 and May 1948? It is tempting, but perhaps naïve, to imagine that it simply reflected a common belief in the redemptive power of music to heal the German soul. It certainly tells us something about the long-shared internationalism of European musical culture and the transplanting of this culture onto American soil.[36] The language of European art music, even in its modernist forms, was by the 1940s one that was equally well understood by cultivated people in Britain, France, Germany, the Soviet Union, and the United States. It also speaks of the strength of conviction, clearly shared in elite political and even military circles, that European art music had a particular cultural weight and influence in Germany and that it was worth supporting there. Britain, France, and the Soviet Union were all impoverished by the war; these were not countries that could afford to waste money or resources on pointless luxuries in their foreign policies. The Unites States was, of the occupiers, economically as well as militarily the strongest, and it is striking how its military government in Germany, sometimes reluctantly, felt obliged to try to match the music programs of the others.

We should not overlook the role of individuals in this unique situation, which have been called "the golden hunger years." The music programs of the occupiers were implemented by relatively junior figures, often musicians who had been given military rank who found themselves with powers in Germany that they could not have aspired to in their home countries. People such as Jack Bornoff, the first British "music controller" at the Northwest German Radio (NWDR) in Hamburg, René Thimonnier in the French military government in Baden-Baden, or Newell Jenkins, who supervised the American Music Control office in Württemberg-Baden in 1946 and 1947, worked with energy and idealism to implement the briefs given to them. Less is known about the corresponding figures in the Soviet military administration, but it is clear that men such as Sergei Barski, who was responsible for music in the administration between November 1946 and May 1948, and Ivan Peresvetov, who supervised the musical reconstruction in Dresden after May 1945, behaved similarly.[37] David Monod's comments about the American Music Control officers as a type may be extended to cover those who worked in similar roles for the British, French, and indeed the Soviet military governments in Germany: "Most of them were young artists and arts administrators who shared a certain idealism about music and its place in society."[38]

These "music officers" depended in large measure for their success on working with equally talented and committed Germans. Thus, Bornoff's success in founding the NWDR Symphony Orchestra in Hamburg owed much to his fruitful collaboration with Schmidt-Isserstedt, who was for many years its principal conductor; the emergence after 1949 of the NWDR's subsidiary branch in Cologne as a world leader in electronic music owed much to Hans Eimert, employed there by the British since 1945. German communists and fellow travelers—once approved by the Soviet authorities—were given particular autonomy in the Soviet zone. The exciting program of the Kulturbund in Berlin was almost entirely due to the zeal of Hans-Heinz Stuckenschmidt and a group of German colleagues; Karl Laux played a similarly important role in Dresden. The journalist Wolfgang Steinecke was supported in his application to work as a cultural official in Darmstadt by the American military government, and he went on to use its support to establish the hugely influential Darmstadt Ferienkürse für Neue Musik.[39] If the repressive aspects of the occupation of Germany—notably the war crimes trials and the denazification program—were marked by mistrust and obstruction between occupiers and occupied, the constructive music programs in all four zones were characterized in large part by genuine cooperation.

Music as a cultural force takes many forms, and these forms are constantly changing. Thus far we have seen how European art music acted as a common language in Germany between 1945 and 1948 and how it was used on all sides as a commonly understood symbol of prestige. The two international ceremonies referred to at the start of this chapter also displayed more confused reactions to another kind of music, one largely associated in Europe in the 1940s with the United States, and with black Americans—jazz. Curiously, the Americans in 1945 did not make jazz a part of their official music program in Germany. This decision was partly because of a desire not to conform to Nazi stereotypes of the United States as a land without culture, and partly because American planners knew that their troops would bring plenty of jazz with them in any case. Similar considerations were applied by the Oxbridge-educated planners in London, who considered what music should be broadcast and performed in postwar Germany. Although these men were well aware of the popularity of jazz in wartime Germany, and of its propaganda use by British broadcasting to Germany during the war, they were reluctant to associate jazz, or "light music," with the projection of British culture abroad. The BBC German Service, which was working hand in hand with the Foreign Office, drew up detailed plans for broadcasting to postwar Germany and concluded in January 1945 that there should be "no direct propaganda in Light Music."[40]

The Soviet Union was ideologically opposed to jazz, which it saw as escapist and vacuous. Although jazz may earlier have had some credibility among communists as the original expression of an exploited black subproletariat, by the 1930s it was seen as a commodified product of the capitalist entertainment industry. It was with great reluctance that jazz was tolerated by the Soviet military administration in Germany. Significantly, a document from 1945 on the "practical work" of the Kulturbund, which continued through the occupation years as the main cultural organization in the Soviet zone, listed one of its tasks "in the area of art" as "the struggle against trash and material of lesser worth."[41] Although at this early stage of the occupation this material was not further defined and was not described as American, this was clearly a reference to jazz and other forms of popular culture. This highbrow disdain formed the underlying bedrock of official communist views of jazz throughout the occupation of Germany and into the later German Democratic Republic (GDR).

The French alone took a different view, one that may have reflected their own experience of German occupation. It was decided that in the French zone, jazz would be promoted and broadcast as an antidote to the bland popular music that had been favored by the Nazis and, in French eyes, had been used as a propaganda tool by them. The journal of the French military government, reviewing the situation in August 1947, declared that "American jazz has been introduced and maintained, despite numerous protests, as a reaction against the march music and sentimental light music which was too complacently exploited by German stations."[42] Not only did the French insist on broadcasting jazz from their radio station in Baden-Baden, the Südwestfunk, but they also sponsored concert tours in their zone by jazz groups such as the "ensemble Jacques Hélian" from Radio France.[43] In 1949, the French sanctioned the appointment of the writer Joachim-Ernst Berendt to the position of "Jazz Editor" at the Südwestfunk, a position that he used to great effect, campaigning through the 1950s and beyond for jazz to be accepted as a serious art form in the Federal Republic of Germany (FRG).[44]

The extraordinary spread of jazz in Germany after May 1945 demonstrates how difficult culture is to control and regulate. For all the reservations expressed in London and Washington DC, jazz was available to German radio listeners through the American Forces Network and the British Forces Broadcasting Service, to say nothing of the BBC German Service, and later the Südwestfunk. There were many amateur jazz bands among American and British servicemen, and officers' clubs in particular employed German jazz musicians to entertain them. From the start of the occupation, jazz was widely performed and heard in Germany. "Hot clubs" were formed in larger cities, even in the Soviet zone. Rudolf Käs has described how, in the first year of the occupation, these were often the only form of nightlife available to Germans.[45]

Jazz provides another example of German agency in an almost powerless situation. German jazz musicians and jazz lovers, many of whom, like Hans Blüthner and Joachim-Ernst Berendt, had had to keep a low profile under the Nazis, were able to come out into the open and exploit the occupation to earn money and pursue their musical interests in spite of official Allied disapproval. In some cases, German jazz lovers were able to form alliances with junior officers in the occupation forces who shared their enthusiasm. Thus, a "hot club" was formed in Heidelberg "by military personnel of the Stardust Club" in 1947. This venue was apparently popular with locals, but membership was "restricted to young people seriously interested in jazz."[46] In a similarly earnest spirit, the Americans sponsored a "Contemporary Music Festival" in Stuttgart in June 1947 that attempted to provide a history of jazz in what they described as their "first serious jazz concert,"[47] but this was an isolated event in their official music program.

Many German jazz musicians, such as Kurt Henkel and his orchestra, who worked with Radio Leipzig in the Soviet zone, found employment with the radio stations, which used house bands to fill many hours of their broadcasting schedules with music mixing elements of genuine American jazz and more traditional German dance music. Younger Germans, identifying jazz with a whole way of life, formed amateur bands and often played inside the institutional frameworks offered by the newly formed youth organizations set up by the occupiers to replace the Hitler Youth. By the time Germany was partitioned in 1949 and the GDR was established, the craze for jazz within the communist youth movement—the so-called Free German Youth (FDJ)—was already a matter of great concern to the authorities there. From correspondence between the Central Committee of the Socialist Unity Party[48] and the FDJ it is clear that the younger, "hotter" jazz musicians of the FDJ were taking business away from the more staid, adult dance bands. In the eyes of the party's trade union organization, this was not because they were better musicians, but because they played "so-called Hot music" better than professional orchestras. Evidently the audiences already preferred this "so-called Hot music."[49]

This passion for Western popular music was indeed firmly established on both sides of the Iron Curtain before 1949 and it has proved to be much more than a passing fad. Successive waves of Western popular music, such as boogie-woogie, bebop, rock 'n' roll, the "beat music" of the 1960s, punk rock in the 1970s, and hip-hop in the 1980s, have been at the heart of generational conflict and cultural debates in Germany since then. There can be no doubt that the identification of generations of young people in East Germany with jazz and later forms of Western popular music was a significant factor in their alienation from the communist values that were being propagated there with increasing force in 1947 and 1948, and that became the official values of the new state after 1949. But, paradoxically, this most powerful propaganda weapon of the Cold War was not seen as or used as part of the formal propaganda arsenal of the Americans or the British in Germany between 1945 and 1949.

An analysis of the distribution and reception of jazz in occupied Germany suggests a number of interesting points about international relations. It reinforces the sense in which music was seen as an important symbol of identification. The occupying powers were all determined to be identified with high culture, and particularly with European art music; they were, with the exception of the French, unwilling to be officially associated with jazz. As the ideological differences between the Western Allies and the Soviets became more apparent after 1947, the Soviets became more willing publicly to identify jazz as a capitalist malaise with its origins in the United States. By the time the GDR was established with Soviet support in October 1949, in response to the formation of the FRG in the West, the communist hostility to jazz was hardening and it was being seen as a weapon in the Cold War confrontation between East and West. The musical theorists of the early GDR formulated the analysis that jazz was an imperialist tool consciously used by the West to anaesthetize the German working class and detach this class from its own cultural roots. This theory was the basis of the extraordinary and totally unsuccessful campaign against jazz waged by the communists in the early GDR.[50]

Conversely, the Western powers and, by 1949, their supporters in the newly emerging FRG, were committed to an ideal of cultural freedom and had to put to one side whatever snobbish prejudices they might have held about jazz as a musical form. They had to recognize that the genie was out of the bottle and that musical taste was not something they could easily control or manipulate. Kaspar Maase has analyzed this as part of a larger "cultural turn," stating that "[a]fter World War II, the pioneering role was played by the champions of a youth culture centered around international pop music."[51] In the FRG, different branches of the music industry were quick to see the huge potential for making money out of jazz and other forms of popular music and went on to make this a salient aspect of the "economic miracle" and the development of consumerism in the FRG.[52] The Western Allies learned at first to make a public virtue out of their slightly uncomfortable tolerance of jazz and then to use it as a Cold War propaganda weapon. They still preferred to do this discreetly, reserving the full force of their publicity machines for more respectable music.[53] Uta Poiger has demonstrated that it was not until "the second half of the 1950s" that "U.S. and West German policies towards East Germany" were prepared to use "some forms of American popular culture as a Cold War weapon."[54] Since the early 1950s, the British had consciously used jazz as a propaganda tool in the broadcasting schedules of the BBC German Service, which they aimed specifically at listeners in the GDR.[55]

As the Cold War developed, although both sides continually developed their military forces and maintained these in a state of readiness, these forces were never used in Europe. A partitioned Germany remained on the front line of the divide, and it was here that the cultural confrontation was played out most publicly, with both sides seeking to promote their ideals and win the affiliation of Germans on both sides of the Iron Curtain and, after 1961, the Berlin Wall. A whole body of literature has now established the importance of music in this confrontation, tracing the origins of this particular cultural contest back to the "Music Control" programs introduced into Germany under the aegis of occupation in 1945.[56] And strangely, it has become increasingly clear that for all the emphasis given by both sides to European art music, it was forms of popular music and the lifestyles they represented that were the most powerful weapons in the Cold War arsenal.[57]

It is in this light that we should revisit the victory celebration at the American headquarters in June 1945 and the French memorial concert held in Berlin in September 1947. The vast fleet of aircraft that so impressed the military leaders at the celebration, and of which Eisenhower and Montgomery were so proud, was in the end never used to terrorize their opponents. But perhaps the amazed Soviet response to the "coloured cabaret show," the "swing music," and the dancing of half-naked "negro women" was more justified. They and the "small jazz band" supplied by the US Special Services for the memorial concert in 1947, for all the misgivings of their superiors, proved to be formidable cultural weapons. And, sadly for those who love the tradition of European art music, it is difficult to imagine that it will ever again be considered such an important factor in international relations as it was in Germany between 1945 and 1949.

Notes

1. See, for sources on the British wartime debate, Robert Vansittart, *Black Record: Germans Past and Present* (London: Hamish Hamilton, 1941); Victor Gollancz, *Shall Our Children Live or Die?* (London: Gollancz, 1942); H. N. Brailsford, *Our Settlement with Germany* (Harmondsworth, UK: Penguin, 1944). On the genesis of the Allied reeducation program and the place of music in the plans of the separate occupiers, see Toby Thacker, *Music after Hitler, 1945–1955* (Aldershot, UK: Ashgate, 2007), 17–29.
2. Viscount Montgomery, *The Memoirs of Field-Marshal the Viscount Montgomery of Alamein, K. G.* (London: Collins, 1958), 362.
3. Dwight Eisenhower, *Crusade in Europe* (New York: Doubleday, 1948), 348.
4. Montgomery, *The Memoirs of Field-Marshal the Viscount Montgomery*, 362.
5. Report from Brigadier General Gailey to Major-General White, 22 October 1947, OMGUS 5/267-3/4, Institut für Zeitgeschichte, Munich (hereafter IfZ).
6. See Harry Butcher, *Three Years with Eisenhower* (London: Heinemann, 1946), 716–18.
7. Jessica C. E. Gienow-Hecht, *Sound Diplomacy: Music and Emotions in Transatlantic Relations, 1850–1920* (Chicago and London: University of Chicago Press, 2009), 219.
8. A representative example of the way this sense of German agency and pride has been expressed is a large book celebrating the renaissance of German cities after 1945. The reconstruction of musical life in each city is here recounted with pride and virtually no reference to the occupying powers. See Hermann Glaser, Lutz von Pufendorf, and Michael Schöneich, eds., *So viel Anfang war nie: Deutsche Städte 1945–1949* (Berlin: Siedler, 1989).
9. There is a huge literature on the prosecution of Nazi war criminals and the denazification program. See, for an introduction and a full bibliography, Toby Thacker, *The End of the Third Reich: Defeat, Denazification and Nuremberg, January 1944–November 1946* (Stroud: Tempus, 2006).

10. There is a growing literature on the occupation of Germany after 1945, but much of it deals either with individual zones of occupation or with particular themes. See, for a concise introduction, Mary Fulbrook, *Divided Nation: A History of Germany 1918–1990* (London: Fontana, 1991). On the Soviet zone, see Gareth Pritchard, *The Making of the GDR 1945–53: From Antifascism to Stalinism* (Manchester: Manchester University Press, 2000). On the British zone, see Noel Annan, *Changing Enemies: The Defeat and Regeneration of Germany* (London: HarperCollins, 1995). For representative older narratives, see Lucius Clay, *Decision in Germany* (London: Heinemann, 1950); John Gimbel, *The American Occupation of Germany: Politics and the Military, 1945–1949* (Stanford, CA: Stanford University Press, 1968); Frank Roy Willis, *The French in Germany 1945–1949* (Stanford, CA: Stanford University Press, 1962). For more recent studies, see Klaus-Dietmar Henke, *Die amerikanische Besetzung Deutschlands* (Munich: Oldenburg, 1996); Stefan Martens, ed., *Vom "Erbfeind" zum "Erneuerer": Aspekte und Motive der französischen Deutschlandpolitik nach dem Zweiten Weltkrieg* (Sigmaringen: Thorbecke, 1993); Volker Koop, *Besetzt: Französische Besatzungspolitik in Deutschland* (Berlin: be.bra Verlag, 2005); Norman Naimark, *The Russians in Germany: A History of the Soviet Zone of Occupation, 1945–1949* (Cambridge, MA, and London: Belknap Press of Harvard University Press, 1995). For a concise analysis of the "collapsed economy" of the postwar period, see Arnold Sywottek, "From Starvation to Excess: Trends in the Consumer Society from the 1940s to the 1970s," in *The Miracle Years: A Cultural History of West Germany, 1949–1968,* ed. Hanna Schissler (Princeton, NJ, and Oxford: Princeton University Press, 2001), 341–58.
11. On rape in the Soviet zone, see Naimark, *The Russians,* 69–140. On rape in the French zone, see 'Ein schwieriges Erbe: VerGEWALTigungen bei Kriegsende' in Annemarie Hopp and Berndt Warneken, eds., *Feinde, Freunde, Fremde: Erinnerungen an die Tübinger Franzosenzeit* (Tübingen: Universitätsstadt Tübingen, Kulturamt, 1995), 57–62; Edgar Wolfrum, "Das Bild der 'Düsteren Franzosenzeit': Alltagsnot, Meinungsklima und Demokratisierungspolitik in der französischen Besatzungszone nach 1945," in Martens, *Vom "Erbfeind" zum "Erneuerer,"* 87–114.
12. Weekly Situation Report of the Film, Theater, and Music Control Section, 6871st DISCC, 9 June 1945, OMGWB 12/91-1/7, Generallandesarchiv, Karlsruhe (hereafter GLAK).
13. The Soviets only proceeded gradually to the imposition of a Soviet model of society in their zone of Germany. Stalin himself had grave misgivings, arguing famously that communism suited Germany as much as a saddle suited a cow. See Anne McElvoy, *The Saddled Cow: East Germany's Life and Legacy* (London: Faber and Faber, 1993).
14. Thacker, *Music after Hitler;* see pp. 15–38 on the genesis of the reeducation project and the place of music in the plans of the separate occupiers. For more details on British planning, see Toby Thacker, "'Liberating German Musical Life': The BBC German Service and Planning for Music Control in Occupied Germany, 1944–1949," in *"Stimme der Wahrheit": German-Language Broadcasting by the BBC,* ed. Charmian Brinson and Richard Dove, Yearbook of the Research Centre for German and Austrian Exile Studies 5 (Amsterdam: Editions Rodopi, 2003), 77–92.
15. See the poster for the concert reproduced on the front of Maren Köster, *Musik-Zeit-Geschehen: Zu den Musikverhältnissen in der SBZ/DDR 1945 bis 1952* (Saarbrücken: Pfau, 2002).
16. See Music Section, Daily Diary, 4 July 1945, OMGB 10/48-1/5, Bayerisches Haupt-

staatsarchiv, Munich (hereafter BHA), which states that the program for the first postwar concert for a German audience in Munich was to consist of Mendelssohn's *Overture to a Midsummer Night's Dream*, Mozart's Fortieth Symphony, and Tchaikovsky's Fourth Symphony.

17. See Karl Laux, *Nachklang: Autobiographie* (Berlin: Verlag der Nation, 1977), 322–23.
18. Strang to Secretary of State, 11 July 1945, p. 17, PRO/FO 898/401, National Archive, London.
19. Annex to Weekly Situation Report, Film, Theater, and Music Control Section, 6871st DISCC, 7 August 1945, p. 3, OMGB 10/48-1/5, BHA; see also Weekly Situation Report of the Film, Theater, and Music Control Section, 6871st DISCC, 30 June 1945, pp. 2–4, OMGWB 12/91-1/7, GLAK.
20. For a detailed recent account of the Nazi efforts to appropriate one of these "German" composers, see Erik Levi, *Mozart and the Nazis: How the Third Reich Abused a Cultural Icon* (New Haven, CT, and London: Yale University Press, 2010).
21. For an account focusing on the competition between the Soviets and the Americans in Berlin, see Elizabeth Janik, "'The Golden Hunger Years': Music and Superpower Rivalry in Occupied Berlin," *German History* 22, no. 1 (2004): 76–100.
22. "La Quinzaine Culturelle de Constance," *La France en Allemagne* 1 (July 1946): 20–24.
23. See Thacker, *Music after Hitler*, chap. 3, "Anti-Fascism and Music."
24. Ibid., 94–95.
25. Thimonnier to Colonel Boucher, Chef de la Section des Beaux-Arts, 15 September 1945, AC 490/7, Archives de l'Occupation française en Allemagne. The papers of the French occupation were seen by this author in Colmar, but have since been rehoused in Paris.
26. *La France en Allemagne, Numéro Special: Information et Action Culturelle*, August 1947, p. 61.
27. Report on Information Control Meeting, 29–30 April 1946, 11 May 1946, OMGUS 5/348-3/4, IfZ.
28. Virgil Thomson, "German Culture and Army Rule," *New York Herald Tribune* (Paris edition), 22 September 1946.
29. For a comparative survey of the denazification of musicians, see Thacker, *Music after Hitler*, 39–73. The most detailed study of denazification in an individual zone is David Monod, *Settling Scores: German Music, Denazification, and the Americans, 1945–1953* (Chapel Hill and London: University of North Carolina Press, 2005).
30. Weekly Situation Report of the Film, Theater, and Music Control Section, 6871st DISCC, 14 July 1945, p. 2, OMGWB 12/91-1/7, GLAK.
31. Jelissarow, Chef der Garnison und Militärkommandant der Stadt Berlin, to Becher, 25 June 1945, DY 27/841, Stiftung Archiv der Parteien- und Massenorganisationen im Bundesarchiv, Berlin (hereafter SAPMO-BArch).
32. *Berliner Zeitung*, 5 July 1945.
33. George Clare, *Berlin Days 1946–1947* (London: Macmillan, 1989), 78; see pp. 78–90 for an account of Furtwängler's record under the Nazis and his return to Berlin in 1946.
34. The best treatment of Furtwängler's denazification is in Monod, *Settling Scores*, 128–66.
35. Howley to Commanding Officer, Berlin Command, OMGUS, 1 October 1947, OMGUS 5/267-3/4, IfZ. For a fuller account, see Humphrey Burton, *Menuhin: A Life* (London: Faber, 2000).

36. This was, of course, an idea refuted by the Nazis, who held that music was a reflection of racial character and wished to reassert an ideal of an imagined, pure "German" music.
37. On Barski, see Köster, *Musik-Zeit-Geschehen,* 54–67; on Peresvetov, see Laux, *Nachklang,* 313–17.
38. Monod, *Settling Scores,* 37.
39. See Michael Custodis, "'Unter Auswertung meiner Erfahrungen aktiv mitgestaltend': Zum Wirken von Wolfgang Steinecke bis 1950," in *Deutsche Leitkultur Musik? Zur Musikgeschichte nach dem Holocaust,* ed. Albrecht Riethmüller (Stuttgart: Franz Steiner, 2006), 145–62.
40. Post War Music Programmes for Germany, 12 January 1945, E1/758/1, BBC Written Archive, Caversham.
41. „Über die praktische Arbeit der Kulturbund-Gruppen", DY 27/2751, SAPMO-BArch. This document is undated, but from its contents it can be reliably placed before October 1945.
42. *La France en Allemagne: Information et Action Culturelle,* August 1947, p. 35.
43. *La France en Allemagne* 2 (August 1946): 59.
44. On Berendt, see Andrew Wright Hurley, *The Return of Jazz: Joachim-Ernst Berendt and West German Cultural Change* (New York and Oxford: Berghahn Books, 2009).
45. See Rudolf Käs, "Hot and Sweet: Jazz im befreiten Land," in Glaser, von Pufendorf, and Schöneich, *So viel Anfang war nie,* 250–55, esp. 251.
46. Heidelberg Detachment, Theater and Music Control, Activities Report from 3 March–9 March 1947, 7 March 1947, OMGWB 12/91-1/9, GLAK.
47. Quarterly History of Theater and Music Control Branch, period 1 April–1 July 1947, pp. 1–2, OMGWB 3/407-3/3, GLAK.
48. The Socialist Unity Party of Germany was the official name given to the party formed by the merger of the Social Democratic and Communist Parties in the Soviet zone of Germany in April 1946, which was then assigned a "leading role" in the zone and subsequently in the German Democratic Republic.
49. See Deutscher Musiker-Verband in der Gewerkschaft für Kunst und Schrifttum im FDGB Gross-Berlin an das Sekretariat des Zentralrates der FDJ, 20 November 1948, DY 30/IV 2/9.06/286, SAPMO-BArch; SED Zentralsekretariat Abt. Kultur und Erziehung an den Zentralrat der FDJ, 3 August 1949, DY 30/IV 2/9.06/286, SAPMO-BArch.
50. See Toby Thacker, "The Fifth Column: Dance Music in the Early GDR," in *The Workers' and Peasants' State: Communism and Society in East Germany under Ulbricht 1945–71,* ed. Patrick Major and Jonathan Osmond (Manchester: Manchester University Press, 2002), 227–43.
51. Kaspar Maase, "Establishing Cultural Democracy: Youth, 'Americanization,' and the Irresistible Rise of Popular Culture," in Schissler, *The Miracle Years,* 428–50, 429.
52. On the reception of jazz in the Western zones and in the Federal Republic of Germany, see Reinhard Fark, *Die mißachtete Botschaft: Publizistische Aspekte des Jazz im soziokulturellen Wandel* (Berlin: Spiess, 1971).
53. On the role of jazz in Germany during the Cold War, see Uta Poiger, *Jazz, Rock, and Rebels: Cold War Politics and American Culture in a Divided Germany* (Berkeley: University of California Press, 2000); Reginald Rudorf, *Jazz in der Zone* (Cologne: Kiepenheuer and Witsch, 1964).
54. See Poiger, *Jazz, Rock, and Rebels,* 6–7, 61.
55. See, for example, Thacker, *Music after Hitler,* 190–91, on the British use of Karl Walter's dance band, which had fled from the GDR as a result of political hostility toward them there.

56. See, for example, Frances Stonor Saunders, *Who Paid the Piper? The CIA and the Cultural Cold War* (London: Granta, 1999).
57. See Jolanta Pekacz, "Did Rock Smash the Wall? The Role of Rock in Political Transition," *Popular Music* 13, no. 1 (January 1994): 41–49.

Bibliography

Archives

Archives de l'Occupation française en Allemagne
Bayerisches Hauptstaatsarchiv, Munich
BBC Written Archive, Caversham
Generallandesarchiv, Karlsruhe
Institut für Zeitgeschichte, Munich
National Archive, London
Stiftung Archiv der Parteien- und Massenorganisationen im Bundesarchiv, Berlin

Printed Sources

Annan, Noel. *Changing Enemies: The Defeat and Regeneration of Germany*. London: HarperCollins, 1995.
Brailsford, H. N. *Our Settlement with Germany*. Harmondsworth, UK: Penguin, 1944.
Burton, Humphrey. *Menuhin: A Life*. London: Faber, 2000.
Butcher, Harry. *Three Years with Eisenhower*. London: Heinemann, 1946.
Clare, George. *Berlin Days 1946–1947*. London: Macmillan, 1989.
Clay, Lucius. *Decision in Germany*. London: Heinemann, 1950.
Custodis, Michael. "'Unter Auswertung meiner Erfahrungen aktiv mitgestaltend': Zum Wirken von Wolfgang Steinecke bis 1950." In *Deutsche Leitkultur Musik? Zur Musikgeschichte nach dem Holocaust*, ed. Albrecht Riethmüller, 145–62. Stuttgart: Franz Steiner, 2006.
Eisenhower, Dwight. *Crusade in Europe*. New York: Doubleday, 1948.
Fark, Reinhard. *Die mißachtete Botschaft: Publizistische Aspekte des Jazz im soziokulturellen Wandel*. Berlin: Spiess, 1971.
Fulbrook, Mary. *Divided Nation: A History of Germany 1918–1990*. London: Fontana, 1991.
Gienow-Hecht, Jessica C. E. *Sound Diplomacy: Music and Emotions in Transatlantic Relations, 1850–1920*. Chicago and London: University of Chicago Press, 2009.
Gimbel, John. *The American Occupation of Germany: Politics and the Military, 1945–1949*. Stanford, CA: Stanford University Press, 1968.
Glaser, Hermann, Lutz von Pufendorf, and Michael Schöneich, eds. *So viel Anfang war nie: Deutsche Städte 1945–1949*. Berlin: Siedler, 1989.
Gollancz, Victor. *Shall Our Children Live or Die?* London: Gollancz, 1942.
Henke, Klaus-Dietmar. *Die amerikanische Besetzung Deutschlands*. Munich: Oldenburg, 1996.

Hopp, Annemarie, and Berndt Warneken, eds. *Feinde, Freunde, Fremde: Erinnerungen an die Tübinger Franzosenzeit.* Tübingen: Universitätsstadt Tübingen, Kulturamt, 1995.
Hurley, Andrew Wright. *The Return of Jazz: Joachim-Ernst Berendt and West German Cultural Change.* New York and Oxford: Berghahn Books, 2009.
Janik, Elizabeth. "'The Golden Hunger Years': Music and Superpower Rivalry in Occupied Berlin." *German History* 22, no. 1 (2004): 76–100.
Käs, Rudolf. "Hot and Sweet: Jazz im befreiten Land." In *So viel Anfang war nie: Deutsche Städte 1945–1949,* ed. Hermann Glaser, Lutz von Pufendorf, and Michael Schöneich, 250–58. Berlin: Siedler, 1989.
Koop, Volker. *Besetzt: Französische Besatzungspolitik in Deutschland.* Berlin: be.bra Verlag, 2005.
Köster, Maren. *Musik-Zeit-Geschehen: Zu den Musikverhältnissen in der SBZ/DDR 1945 bis 1952.* Saarbrücken: Pfau, 2002.
Laux, Karl. *Nachklang: Autobiographie.* Berlin: Verlag der Nation, 1977.
Levi, Erik. *Mozart and the Nazis: How the Third Reich Abused a Cultural Icon.* New Haven, CT, and London: Yale University Press, 2010.
Maase, Kaspar. "Establishing Cultural Democracy: Youth, 'Americanization,' and the Irresistible Rise of Popular Culture." In *The Miracle Years: A Cultural History of West Germany, 1949–1968,* ed. Hanna Schissler, 428–50. Princeton, NJ, and Oxford: Princeton University Press, 2001.
Martens, Stefan, ed. *Vom "Erbfeind" zum "Erneuerer": Aspekte und Motive der französischen Deutschlandpolitik nach dem Zweiten Weltkrieg.* Sigmaringen: Thorbecke, 1993.
McElvoy, Anne. *The Saddled Cow: East Germany's Life and Legacy.* London: Faber and Faber, 1993.
Monod, David. *Settling Scores: German Music, Denazification, and the Americans, 1945–1953.* Chapel Hill and London: University of North Carolina Press, 2005.
Montgomery, Viscount. *The Memoirs of Field-Marshal the Viscount Montgomery of Alamein, K. G.* London: Collins, 1958.
Naimark, Norman. *The Russians in Germany: A History of the Soviet Zone of Occupation, 1945–1949.* Cambridge, MA, and London: Belknap Press of Harvard University Press, 1995.
Pekacz, Jolanta. "Did Rock Smash the Wall? The Role of Rock in Political Transition." *Popular Music* 13, no. 1 (January 1994): 41–49.
Poiger, Uta. *Jazz, Rock, and Rebels: Cold War Politics and American Culture in a Divided Germany.* Berkeley: University of California Press, 2000.
Pritchard, Gareth. *The Making of the GDR 1945–53: From Antifascism to Stalinism.* Manchester: Manchester University Press, 2000.
Rudorf, Reginald. *Jazz in der Zone.* Cologne: Kiepenheuer and Witsch, 1964.
Stonor Saunders, Frances. *Who Paid the Piper? The CIA and the Cultural Cold War.* London: Granta, 1999.
Sywottek, Arnold. "From Starvation to Excess: Trends in the Consumer Society from the 1940s to the 1970s." In *The Miracle Years: A Cultural*

History of West Germany, 1949–1968, ed. Hanna Schissler, 341–58. Princeton, NJ, and Oxford: Princeton University Press, 2001.

Thacker, Toby. *The End of the Third Reich: Defeat, Denazification and Nuremberg, January 1944–November 1946.* Stroud: Tempus, 2006.

———. "The Fifth Column: Dance Music in the Early GDR." In *The Workers' and Peasants' State: Communism and Society in East Germany under Ulbricht 1945–71,* ed. Patrick Major and Jonathan Osmond, 227–43. Manchester: Manchester University Press, 2002.

———. "'Liberating German Musical Life': The BBC German Service and Planning for Music Control in Occupied Germany, 1944–1949." In *"Stimme der Wahrheit": German-Language Broadcasting by the BBC,* ed. Charmian Brinson and Richard Dove, 77–92. Yearbook of the Research Centre for German and Austrian Exile Studies 5. Amsterdam: Editions Rodopi, 2003.

———. *Music after Hitler, 1945–1955.* Aldershot, UK: Ashgate, 2007.

Vansittart, Robert. *Black Record: Germans Past and Present.* London: Hamish Hamilton, 1941.

Willis, Frank Roy. *The French in Germany 1945–1949.* Stanford, CA: Stanford University Press, 1962.

Wolfrum, Edgar. "Das Bild der 'Düsteren Franzosenzeit': Alltagsnot, Meinungsklima und Demokratisierungspolitik in der französischen Besatzungszone nach 1945." In *Vom "Erbfeind" zum "Erneuerer,"* ed. Stefan Martens, 87–114. Sigmaringen: Thorbecke, 1993.

Chapter Four

INSTRUMENTS OF DIPLOMACY
Writing Music into the History of Cold War International Relations

Danielle Fosler-Lussier

In a well-known essay, Robert Buzzanco denied the relevance of "culture" as a "material factor" that might shape foreign policy. Buzzanco cautioned historians "not to eat dessert before the meat and potatoes," thereby suggesting that the study of culture offers little to nourish our histories.[1] Still, Buzzanco did acknowledge in the same essay that culture can be an "instrument of foreign policy,"[2] and that this subject constitutes an appropriate line of inquiry within the discipline.

Without necessarily accepting the confines Buzzanco has set out for our work, we might ask: what kind of instrument of foreign policy can music be? Certainly, it is neither a scalpel nor a weapon, neither precise nor menacing. To classify music as a kind of "soft power" only begs further questions.[3] I will argue here that music—in particular, US musical diplomacy during the Cold War—offers us ways of understanding the complex politics of allegiance that have shaped the behavior of individuals and populations. Music is not an "extra" as we write history: rather, it is part of the fabric we seek to describe, a site of interaction where people meet, work together, and learn from one another. In some cases, they leave this interaction with power relations among them altered or a new definition of self.[4]

Taking music seriously as a factor in diplomacy means not only its adoption as our subject of study, but also a commitment to knowing how music does its work in the world. Scholars of music have

---

Notes for this section begin on page 134.

long understood that musical performance is not only about sound, but also about status, affiliation, identity—in short, about social relations of many kinds.[5] Historical studies that fail to recognize music as a social activity run the risk of idealizing performance and thereby misunderstanding soft power. As the music critic Christopher Small has described it, music creates "relationships among the performers, between the performers and the listeners, among the listeners and anyone who may be present, and even between those who are present and those who are not. It is in those relationships ... that the meaning of a musical performance lies."[6] The case of cultural diplomacy is special, for some of the most important relationships it cultivates connect "those who are present and those who are not"— relationships built in the imagination between the United States as a mythologized sender of music and listeners who liked or disliked its music; between embassy staff and citizens in the countries where they worked; and between State Department staff in Washington DC and the people they hoped to reach through music.

Small's description of musical performance as a network of relationships affords us a new view of soft power. Seen from the perspective of its planners, US musical propaganda appears to be a project of imperial cultural transmission from a center to peripheral places—yet the recipients were far from passive.[7] Eyewitness accounts sent from diplomatic posts to the State Department attest to a tremendously complex set of negotiations about how and for whom music could be performed, what music should be chosen, and what the music meant. We see in the cases presented below a variety of ways in which individuals, organizations, and countries that hosted visiting musicians used the American program to make demands on the State Department, to compete with their neighbors, or to define their own places in the Cold War world. Here culture is not an overlay atop the "real" history: music is a means by which people determine their mutual and distinct interests, build personal relationships around these interests, and have their values changed or reaffirmed. Musical diplomacy was not enacted solely in the performance of musical works: it was made real in the negotiations about priorities that surrounded these performances and in the symbolic value the performances held for all the participants.

Ironically, the documents used in this chapter to examine this play of interests on the ground are mostly from the State Department's own archives. The detailed reports sent back to the State Department by its diplomatic posts constitute the most complete collection of sources available on this subject. These reports, often composed by embassy personnel who saw the performances firsthand, are subject to a number of biases. The budget of the Cultural Presentations Program was contingent on evidence of progress: State Department officials encouraged embassies to submit glowing reports that could be cited in the annual summaries sent to Congress. Yet the archives contain numerous accounts of failures or partial successes, suggesting that honest assessment was still valued; and apart from critics' reviews published in the foreign press, they are the only eyewitness reports preserved and accessible in quantity. (Newspaper reviews demand further scrutiny, for some of them were based on press releases composed by US embassy staff: diplomats' reports to the State Department are typically more revealing than some of the hagiographical articles appearing in foreign newspapers about American-sponsored concerts.) The accounts of frustrations, conflicts, and failures sent to Washington by diplomatic officers give us glimpses of how difficult it was to put on a show successfully abroad and describe the various situations that could prevent success or alter a performance's meaning. With the exception of the translated press excerpts that were routinely included with them, the information in these diplomats' reports is filtered through the lens of American aims and values; but the incidents they describe nonetheless have much to teach us about responses to American cultural diplomacy. In particular, the sources I consider here show ways in which the US musical program became embroiled with local issues and conflicts, placing its embassies and the State Department itself under a variety of pressures from the very people they were trying to please.

Local Aspirations

From July to September of 1957, N. M. Khan, the chief commissioner and president of the Pakistan Arts Council, demanded repeatedly that the US State Department provide an ice skating show or a "good jazz orchestra" for the International Festival of Culture to be held in Karachi in November of that year.[8] Khan had heard that the US government had presented an ice show in India and sought equal treatment for Pakistan. Though Khan expressed appreciation for the scheduled appearances of Marian Anderson at the festival, he undoubtedly knew, as did the US Embassy in Karachi, that classical music would not engage crowds as popular entertainment would.[9] The embassy's chargé d'affaires, Arthur Z. Gardiner, wrote of Khan:

"He is looking to the U.S. for a spectacular presentation that will draw and entertain thousands of Pakistanis."[10] Gardiner agreed with Khan's assessment: "Any performance where the appeal is visual would be preferable to a musical one in a country where only a small proportion of the population has been exposed to western music enough to begin to appreciate it."[11]

The relationship between Khan and the embassy was complicated by the fact that the State Department preferred not to act as impresario in the host countries; rather, embassies were asked to find local commercial or nonprofit sponsors for concerts. Commercial sponsors usually took a portion of the net profit from concerts, with the remainder returning to the embassy to defray the costs of the tours.[12] Even nonprofit sponsors benefited from their association with the State Department: they won a closer relationship with embassy officials, publicity for their organizations, and sometimes a cut of the proceeds for local charities. In many parts of the world, it was hard to find impresarios who could handle both logistics and publicity; many embassies, therefore, came to rely on a few sponsors who proved particularly able. Acting on behalf of the Pakistan Arts Council, Khan sponsored the successful October 1957 visit of the Minneapolis Symphony to Karachi. That Khan personally introduced the orchestra's conductor to the president of Pakistan during a concert intermission may have raised Khan's prestige both with the president (for having brought the American orchestra) and with the embassy (for having been able to arrange such a meeting).[13] Khan's proven ability to fill concert halls encouraged Gardiner to press the State Department more than once to send the music Khan wanted: citing Khan's previous accomplishments, Gardiner wrote, "I believe everything possible should be done [to] fulfill this request."[14] One year later, Khan would present the five successful performances of the Jack Teagarden Sextet in Karachi—having gotten his jazz band.[15]

This anecdote illustrates well the nature of American cultural diplomacy as paid for by the President's Emergency Fund for International Affairs and carried out by the State Department's Cultural Presentations staff.[16] We might imagine the concerts sponsored by the State Department as fly-by-night events centered around the act of musical performance itself: the band comes to town, plays, and leaves, having perhaps changed some hearts and minds through the sheer power of music. Yet Khan's involvement—and that of other figures like him—shows us other key elements of cultural diplomacy. First, local people were involved, not just for chance meetings with musicians when the band was in town, but also for months of planning before performances. The process of organizing concerts put knowledgeable citizens of the host countries into close working contact with embassy officials. Second, the US government's willingness to bring famous musicians to Pakistan who would not otherwise have come enhanced the impresario's prestige and that of local agencies, as well as that of the United States. Third, however much US officials imagined the relationships built by cultural presentations as simply binational, they were rarely straightforward: rivalries among neighboring cities, regions, or nation-states shaped the political significance of these events. Khan enlisted US support in building a Pakistani festival that would present Pakistan's national identity in a way that was legible to Pakistanis, but also internationally, to be read by India; and he used what he knew of US musical gifts to India to press the State Department for parity. This was "psychological warfare," not by the United States, but using the United States' resources.

The factor of international rivalries was closely observed by State Department personnel, even when the US government was not sponsoring a performance directly. For instance, when Louis Armstrong visited Uruguay under private sponsorship in November 1957, Public Affairs Officer Harold Urist wrote that "the people of Montevideo are somewhat sensitive about the standing of their city in relation to Buenos Aires across the river. It gave them a feeling of importance when the King of Jazz stopped off for a few days instead of bypassing them."[17] Because news of American, Soviet, and Chinese cultural presentations appeared frequently in newspapers and on the radio, citizens of potential host countries were well aware if they were being passed over. The State Department's decision to send the New Orleans Philharmonic to Bogotá and Guayaquil but not Quito during its 1956 Latin American tour was "bound to cause widespread criticism and resentment against U.S. and its cultural entities," according to Ambassador Sheldon Mills.[18] The desire to make populations feel "included" was especially pressing in Eastern Europe, where the aim of US information programs was to keep citizens informed and "to let them know they are not forgotten."[19] When the Polish press reported that the Boston Symphony Orchestra had appeared in Moscow and Prague but omitted Warsaw, the US ambassador to Poland requested an appearance by the Cleveland Orchestra to remedy hurt feelings.[20]

A sense of inclusion or exclusion was evoked not only by the presence or absence of concerts, but also by the content and quality of concerts sent by the United States. When the Merce Cunningham Dance Company performed in Caracas in August 1968, some audience members walked out during the concert, perhaps displeased by the abstract, avant-garde style of the presentation. Nonetheless, the English-language *Daily Journal* reported that the Cunningham dancers felt that "the Venezuelan audiences understood them better than all the others, were more sophisticated in their reactions and were more sympathetic to experimental and modern techniques—than the audiences in the great capitals of Mexico City, Rio and Buenos Aires."[21] By making a claim that Venezuelan audiences understood music in the most difficult and up-to-date styles, the music critic asserted Venezuela's place in a hierarchical value system. Art music in the European tradition had long commanded respect as the "highest" music in a hierarchy of prestige; this hierarchy was not honored or even known everywhere in the world, but for those individuals who had had contact with European culture through colonial institutions, travel, education, or other means, this music had cachet, especially in its latest incarnation as "modern music."[22] If Venezuelans understood this music, and the US performers acknowledged their understanding, then Venezuelans could consider themselves participants in this high-status music: they were good listeners and they mattered in the world of that music.[23] Christopher Small has noted that classical music "can often function as a vehicle for the social aspirations of upwardly mobile people—'This is who I am,' which can easily slip over into 'This is who I want to be,' and even, 'This is who I want to be seen as being.'"[24] It is apparent in this Venezuelan case that this aspiration can be enacted not only on an individual scale, but also on an international scale—wanting one's city and one's country to be taken seriously as part of a global musical scene, and wanting oneself and one's neighbors to be recognized as legitimate listeners.

Quality and Value

Nowhere was this hierarchical assessment of music's quality more pronounced than in Japan. Japanese critics were fiercely skeptical of American performers, and Japanese audiences demanded not only elite Western classical music but also impeccable performances by the United States' most famous musicians. At one point two competing music festivals in Osaka and Tokyo both sought a "top" American symphony orchestra. The US ambassador, Douglas MacArthur Jr., sent a terse telegram to the secretary of state detailing the scrutiny with which American orchestras were judged:

> Japanese regard Philadelphia only slightly below Boston but with New York definitely one of three great American orchestras. Possibility Boston visit widely known, and anything other than Philadelphia would be pronounced anti-climax. If Boston fails [to] come, Osaka festival management will be most unhappy. Without consulting them, embassy predicts they would happily settle for Philadelphia. Rather [than] Cleveland or Chicago, however, predict festival would go back to Belgian orchestra they have on string. Japanese do not consider Cleveland or Chicago as top orchestras. New Orleans definitely not acceptable.[25]

Anything less than the best—not the best in any absolute, measurable sense, but the best as perceived by the discerning Japanese audience—would compromise the effectiveness of the Cultural Presentations program. When the Little Orchestra Society, an accomplished chamber ensemble that revived neglected classical works, came to Japan from New York, Japanese critics who had never heard of the ensemble were unimpressed. Ambassador MacArthur reported that "reputation is at least as important as quality. The Little Orchestra tour was unsuccessful simply because the sophisticated Tokyo critics were not prepared to accept the Little Orchestra as one of the world's major symphony orchestras. I was not surprised."[26]

The Japanese press described the Cold War competition between the Soviet Union and the United States as a "cultural battle," with the Americans falling behind the Soviets in the number and quality of attractions presented.[27] The USSR routinely sent its most famous artists to Japan, and the Japanese public could compare the quality of American dancers with the Bolshoi Ballet and American actors with the Moscow Art Theatre, as well as with the most renowned European performers.[28] Under these conditions, it was not difficult for Japanese concert organizers to place the embassy and the State Department under duress: if the wrong attraction was sent, the State Department would lose the respect of the elite Japanese concertgoers it was courting.

Even in places where Western music was not widely preferred, audiences made careful estimations of the quality and prestige of the music they were offered. In Addis Ababa, Ethiopia, as in Japan, competition from Soviet and Chinese performers made it urgent that the program send first-rate artists. The US Embassy in Addis Ababa firmly rejected the proposed visit of a collegiate theater ensemble, "since any amateur group coming from [the] U.S. would automatically be compared with recent performance [of a] Soviet troupe. Only top professional performers would be effective here."[29] The prestige tours of the New York Philharmonic and the Boston Symphony Orchestra to Europe and the USSR in 1955 and 1956 had received worldwide press; it seemed only fair for people in the developing world to notice and ask for comparable treatment.[30] William Killea, public affairs officer of the US Embassy in Lima, Peru, requested repeatedly that the State Department send "only the best" musicians, for Peruvians were voicing suspicions that "the top U.S. performers are sent to Europe and other areas and the lesser known ones to Latin America."[31] Likewise, the embassy in Baghdad reported that "embassy personnel have been asked why the United States does not make it possible for Iraq to see and hear some of our 'top' cultural offerings such as symphony orchestras, opera, ballet, and so forth."[32] Because embassy staff served as mediators of information to and from the State Department, they were privy to complaints and requests from local people, and they developed a sensitivity to feelings of neglect on the part of the populations where they served. Consequently, the State Department routinely received lobbying messages from its embassies all over the world, asking for more "top" performers.

For some people, particularly those whose countries did not regularly receive foreign performers, a gift of music from the United States was a significant affirmation. After Iraq received concerts by Metropolitan Opera star Eleanor Steber, the dean of a college there said that "Baghdad now is on the musical map of the world, thanks to the Americans," and the embassy received "many calls from local citizenry expressing their deep appreciation."[33] The American consul in Lahore counted "the boost to Lahore's pride due to its inclusion" as a significant outcome of the Minneapolis Symphony's visit.[34] This combination of quality, prestige, and flattery was not merely about good feelings: it was a key component of US cultural diplomacy. The public affairs officer of the US Embassy in Rio de Janeiro, Aldo D'Alessandro, explained that

> the average Port-Alegran is more keenly aware of political implications of "President's Program" performances than of their pure artistic value. This results in a partly flattered, partly suspicious attitude which, however, at the end has always been overcome by an overwhelming appreciation of quality. If that quality were lacking, however, the feeling of suspicion about political activity would predominate.[35]

The perception of "quality" was not only a judgment about the appeal of the performance; as implied above, it was also a judgment about the perceived importance and significance of the artists on the world scene, itself a fluid and subjective category. It was only worthwhile for critics and audiences abroad to accept music sent by the United States if they received both excellent music and the signal that they were being taken seriously as an audience. In the absence of those elements, the sensation of being subject to propaganda made the concerts unattractive.

When "nonprestige" groups came, no matter how excellent, audiences and critics were sometimes harsh in their comments and published reviews; this happened frequently enough that embassy staff at some posts learned to anticipate criticism. The US Embassy in Argentina expressed reservations about the National Symphony Orchestra, slated for a 1959 tour, because it was not the best-known American orchestra. The State Department in return warmly defended the quality of the orchestra and of its selection process: "While Argentina critics may disagree with those in the United States, the New York reviews given the National Symphony Orchestra last winter and the unqualified judgment of the ANTA [music selection] panel is that this orchestra is absolutely top quality."[36]

When cellist Richard Kay, pianist Seymour Bernstein, and violist Kenneth Gordon toured Japan as the American Trio in 1955, students made pointed and critical comments to the musicians after a concert: "I don't think that the Trio played all movements of the piece as written"; "I heard some unnatural sounds" (referring to a missed note); "I imagine you were surprised to see so many students here today. In America the young people are not nearly as interested in classical music as in Japan, are they?" Indeed, part of the musicians' task was to answer such charges against the United States. According to the embassy's delighted report to the State Department,

> Bernstein, Gordon, and Kay in perfect harmony, but with solo breaks, performed a 10-minute USIS sonata, reciting statistics, recounting personal experiences, demonstrating quietly but surely that America is culturally-minded on a mass basis, with American youth sharing largely in the general devotion to the fine arts. The questioners were not prepared for such an eloquent, factual statement; and even the "baiters" in the room were obviously impressed.[37]

Critics often took pleasure in putting the United States in its place, frequently asserting the stereotype that "the United States is a purely materialistic country lacking in both spiritual and intellectual development, without a culture of its own and without interest in the cultural achievements of other nations."[38] Sometimes they used the stereotype more obliquely by comparing American musical interpretations unfavorably with those of other artists. American orchestras were typically commended by Japanese critics for their excellent technical skills. European orchestras, by contrast, were generally praised for their delicacy of interpretation, which was cited as lacking in the American performances—the latter regarded as an intellectual or spiritual rather than a mechanical achievement. Criticism of this kind was only secondarily about the performance: it was foremost an expression of concern about how people should relate to the United States and its offerings, cultural and otherwise. US officials took these musical criticisms seriously as a metonym for the perceived stature of their country in the world.

The Mediation of Prestige

The demand for musicians of quality was paradoxical: in many places the musical performance was less appealing than was the idea of inclusion. Where Western music was little known, the reputations of famous performers could not draw audiences. Yet in some cosmopolitan areas and places that had American cultural centers, the US media had the power to create reputation. For example, according to D'Alessandro, audiences in Rio de Janeiro were "very prestige-conscious," attending only events known to be the best. Yet music critics and journalists were all reading American magazines and newspapers to learn what music was highly regarded in the United States. If an attraction was unknown to Brazilian critics, they would discount its worth; but, D'Alessandro wrote, "if the attraction has been widely acclaimed in the United States, the group's success here will be almost guaranteed by favorable notices prior to the performance."[39] This relationship between music and other media meant that it was possible to cultivate fame where none had previously existed; indeed, this procedure was the norm. George Hellyer, counselor of the US Embassy in Tokyo, explained that "often name artists in Japan do not coincide with U.S. opinion. Names are usually built through motion pictures, records, and books. It is very difficult to build a name in Japan unless adequate materials and time are available."[40] By building artists' reputations far in advance of their arrival and carefully judging what to send, the State Department could best assure the success of its visiting musicians.

It is a curious irony that even though embassy staff perceived an acute demand for American music on the part of foreign publics, they had to work hard to get people to attend concerts. Howard Elting Jr., counselor of the US Embassy in Vietnam, explained that the embassy was catering to the tastes of "educated Vietnamese" in planning cultural presentations, yet the educational preparation undertaken by the embassy was dazzling in its scope. To publicize the concerts of the Jack Teagarden Sextet, the Golden Gate Quartet, and the Little

Orchestra Society, the three cultural presentations that would visit Vietnam in 1959, the United States Information Service (USIS) published one hundred thousand copies of a booklet in Vietnamese about these three concerts; embassy personnel gave twelve public lectures about American music and the specific performers who would visit, some of which were reprinted in newspapers; record-listening sessions were held; Voice of America aired advertisements; recordings of the three groups were given prominent placement on Radio Vietnam; footage of the groups was included in weekly newsreels in movie theaters; and when the groups actually arrived, two of the three concerts were broadcast nationally. To avoid selling many tickets to foreigners resident in Vietnam, all publicity was conducted in Vietnamese until the final week.[41] As Elting reported, the tremendous publicity effort was itself noteworthy in the public's eyes:

> A number of Vietnamese commented after the concerts that the wonderful thing about the visit of the Little Orchestra is that it enabled the Vietnamese to learn something about American organization and planning. "That," exclaimed a Vietnamese newsman, "is a lesson we Vietnamese have to learn." A curious commentary, this, in that no such thought ever crossed our minds in planning the concerts.[42]

US cultural presentations thus provided not only high-quality performances, but also an important glimpse into American strategies of mediation.

The process of educating Vietnamese audiences appears to have been effective. Likely as a result of the pervasive publicity, ticket sales for the American presentations in Vietnam were better in 1959 than ever before, even though the acts that had come before—Richard Tucker, Marian Anderson, William Warfield, and Eleanor Steber—were also first-rate. Younger Vietnamese appreciated the jazz and popular music, while the older generation's response "ranged from slightly condescending tolerance to disdain." Even though people came to the concerts, they reserved the right to judge the American music, and their judgments were not always positive. The review of Teagarden's jazz sextet in the newspaper *Ngon Luan* was chilly: "Jazz music, which is also commonly considered to be noisy music, reflects the American's animated, enthusiastic, and free way of life…. Jack Teagarden's jazz has enabled us to better know a friendly people, but it would be a mistake to conclude that jazz will become the musical idiom of our people."[43] Still, the excellence of the performances was recognized in the press. The French-language newspaper *Journal d'Extrême-Orient* even expressed respect for the performers regardless of the music's actual appeal: "[O]ne likes or does not like jazz. But such mastery one must call art."[44]

Of the three groups that came to Vietnam that year, it was the Little Orchestra Society—the same group that failed to impress the Japanese—that drew the warmest response. In Elting's assessment, the quality of the performance, the sense of a gift bestowed, and the financial prowess required to move an orchestra all played a role. Elting recognized that the audience of educated Vietnamese music lovers was tiny; he felt that perhaps half the audience "did not understand what they heard. Nor did they necessarily like what they heard." Nevertheless, the compliment of having been given good music mattered deeply to the audience. Elting wrote:

> There is good reason to believe that the great majority were very much impressed by the spectacular scope of the entire effort. Perhaps it would not be too much to say that they drew the conclusion that the people who bestowed their patronage on the Little Orchestra and arranged to have it sent around the world, must be the possessors of an opulent culture.[45]

Whether listening actually requires any kind of "understanding" (in the sense of mediation through formal education) remains a contested question among music scholars; but it was generally accepted by State Department personnel that people needed some familiarity with European classical music in order to like it.[46] The Cultural Presentations staff recognized that such education was unavailable in most of the world; yet even listeners who did not like Western music seemed to demand music that met European standards of prestige, so policy planners felt obliged to send what was mutually recognized as the "highest-quality" music. Even so, a group like the Little Orchestra Society might succeed in one place and fail in another on the basis of the embassies' ability to convince various publics that what they were hearing was valuable music.

Diplomatic officers in the field and State Department staff in Washington routinely used the regrettable shorthand of "sophisticated"/ "unsophisticated" to refer to various peoples as more or less conversant with Western artistic norms. However unfortunate the term, its use pointed to a real problem for US cultural presentations. Edmund H. Kellogg, the interim chargé d'affaires at the US Embassy in Phnom Penh, Cambodia, sent a sharply worded missive to the State Department describing the utter lack of connection Cambodians felt with Western music of any kind. As Kellogg told it, in the face of Soviet-American cultural competition, "Cambodians were willing to accept any and all entertainment offered by the rival government impresarios, but weren't sure if they would like it. We would be unreasonable if we expected more of a reaction. Cambodia has never heard an orchestra."[47] The US Consulate in Chiang Mai, Thailand, reported that although the public was very receptive to visiting musicians, they needed "careful education" provided through radio programs and "sound trucks saturating the towns with background information and samples of music" to ensure adequate familiarity with the music and thereby a successful concert.[48] The US Embassy in Bangkok characterized the project of cultural presentations as "principally an educational one," citing the need for lectures, demonstrations, and other means of cultivating an audience.[49] In places to which the Soviet Union would send circuses and the Chinese would send acrobats or Peking Opera, the State Department struggled to find the right way to address audiences, settling on a compromise program that would meet the demand for access to the "best" Western culture and teach people to enjoy that music while also entertaining audiences with the occasional marionette show or folk singer.[50]

Instruments of Soft Power

When Howard Elting Jr. looked back on the concerts given by the Jack Teagarden Sextet, the Golden Gate Quartet, and the Little Orchestra Society in Vietnam in 1959, he wrote that the United States "successfully 'reached' students and intellectuals through this medium. But this merely begs the question—What does this all add up to?"[51] We might well ask with him: what can we conclude about the nature of music as an instrument of US diplomacy?

It is not difficult to find evidence for the view that musical diplomacy was a mere accessory to more overt forms of advocacy, for US Foreign Service officers themselves sometimes saw cultural presentations as an adjunct to hard power or a substitute for it. In places where the press and broadcast media were censored, as in Portugal, cultural programs appeared to be an indirect but still functional means for communicating American ideas and values: "[I]t is through the information center, relations with the universities, lecture and concert audiences, and educational exchange that we must make our case."[52] Indeed, informational propaganda both supported and resulted from musical diplomacy, and the attractiveness of music brought people into contact with Americans and American ideas. This view of musical diplomacy corresponds closely to Joseph Nye's theory of soft power. Nye sees soft power as fulfilling an information function, allowing any country "to get its messages across and to affect the preferences of others."[53] Nye also identifies the sheer attractiveness of American cultural products—its music, its movies—as a major source of soft power.[54]

Nevertheless, Nye's theory does not fully encompass music's role, for in seeing soft power "as a resource rather than a relationship" he misses essential qualities of musical practice that define music's diplomatic effectiveness.[55] The musical events described above did not primarily transmit ideas, as other forms of propaganda did; instead, these performances and the negotiations surrounding them built complex social relationships. Requests for music communicated to the State Department by its embassies reveal how people assessed their own power in relation to the Cold War conflict: Were they bypassed, or in the same league with their neighbors? Did the United States consider them to be cultured, or not? The presence and nature of musical presentations was understood as a barometer of what Peter van Ham has called "social power": citizens of nation-states could judge the importance of their states vis-à-vis the United States and their neighbors by what music was sent.[56]

In identifying "attractiveness" as a factor in international relations, neither Nye nor Van Ham explore fully how that attractiveness functions. Nye writes that the attractiveness of music and other cultural products accrues soft power for the United States, but he does not account for the multifaceted interactive processes of musical programming and reception. Although in most cases Van Ham describes social power as generated through multilateral communication, he, too, explains music's appeal only as a form of consumerism that colonizes the global imagination—a unilateral imposition of cultural products.[57] Yet in the evidence presented above we have seen that power did not rest with the United States alone. Foreign publics made a variety of demands on the State Department through communications with its embassies and consular posts; the desire for this music was carefully cultivated through information propaganda, yet listeners abroad also requested and used music to suit their own purposes. The anxious missives from US diplomatic posts to Washington make it plain that the program was highly responsive to—even subject to—the tastes and aspirations of the publics it sought to reach. This collaborative element is not negated by the fact that the US government was simultaneously cultivating demand for this music. Rather, the top-down and bottom-up aspects of this process remained in productive tension with each other.

In Matthew Fraser's account of soft power, he distinguishes imperialism (a "deliberate project of a center extending influence and control over a periphery") from globalization ("infinitely subtler and more complex interplay among many interconnecting cultures and economies").[58] Fraser's distinction is well drawn; yet US musical diplomacy encompasses both of these contrasting elements at once. Indeed, music's soft power is a strange form of power because it includes choice and consent on the part of people in the host countries and vulnerability on the part of the United States.[59] If we look at musical diplomacy from the top down, we see the imperial desire to impress American values upon others; if we look at it from the bottom up, we see an intensive process of negotiation and engagement. Both views offer us true, if partial, pictures; both modes constitute Cold War ways of thinking about and engaging with other people as competitors, benefactors, or allies amid shifting hierarchies of influence and allegiance. Understanding music as a practice, not an object, helps us to see how these relationships were formed, sustained, and interpreted.

In a critique of Nye, Edward Lock correctly notes that "the possibility of attraction rests upon the existence of social norms defining what it means to be attractive"—and these norms are not fixed, but negotiated among the parties.[60] In its bid for prestige, the Cultural Presentations staff deployed a European hierarchy of musical value to assert American competence in cultural matters, and also tried to transmit that hierarchy abroad so that American music could be judged as worthy. Audiences the world over who received cultural presentations accepted the European norm to widely varying extents; for many, acceptance of the norm seemed like the price of admission to a prestigious worldwide elite. The freedom with which music critics abroad censured Western performers, however, suggests that citizens of host countries were active partners in making decisions about the meaning and value of the music given by the United States. The norms that the State Department's Cultural Presentations staff sought to affirm were not adopted wholesale; they were contested and adjusted at each concert, at each preconcert talk, and in each newspaper review or educational event. Any account of cultural diplomacy should take into account the nature and extent of this kind of "pushback," the extent to which norms were partially adopted, refused outright, or applied in ways the senders did not foresee—as in Japan, where the norms were turned against the very American performers who sought to introduce them.

Music is not the "dessert" to the "meat and potatoes" of material history. Once we understand music as a social practice, we can see that its use in diplomacy created a rich network of connections between embassies and local people, between audiences and musicians, and between nations. In a speech at once advocating and limiting the influence of the "cultural turn" in history, Melvyn Leffler wrote that "the post-modernist emphasis on culture, language, and rhetoric often diverts attention from questions of causation and agency."[61] Yet the relationships built through US musical diplomacy offered copious opportunities for the assertion of agency by impresarios, embassy staff, musical and cultural critics, and ordinary citizens, who became part of conversations about musical excellence. Further, these relationships paved the way for more direct kinds of diplomatic work: for instance, personal ties fostered by musical diplomacy aided in the selection of grantees to come to the United States, furthering more overtly political goals.[62]

I reject the view of cultural life as a symbolic veneer overlaid upon genuine political action because I regard music not only as ephemeral performance, but also as a form of human relationship bearing political stakes—personal connections to be made or refused, respect to be won or lost. When individuals demanded music from the United States, as did N. M. Khan in Pakistan, or critiqued American performers, as did Japanese critics, these acts were not merely a representation of Cold War political relations: they helped to define those relations. I will not go as far as Fraser, who writes that "America's most persuasive weapons were its values, way of life, and culture," for it is only reasonable to acknowledge the role of many kinds of hard power.[63] The wooing process between the United States and other nations enacted during the Cold War appears to us more like hard-headed confrontation in the context of treaties or negotiations about foreign aid, and more like simple "attraction" when presented through the arts—yet "hard" and "soft" strategies alike demonstrated close attention to power relations and a dynamic of careful negotiation. The soft power of cultural presentations encompassed not only the attractiveness of music and its ability to carry messages, as Nye suggests, but also its ability to foster reciprocal social interaction on small and large scales. The wide-ranging and substantive relationships formed around and through these musical performances constitute the essence of music's soft power.

Acknowledgments

The author gratefully acknowledges the financial support of the National Endowment for the Humanities and the Mershon Center for International Security Studies at the Ohio State University, as well as the research assistance of Deborah Ruhl, Angela Black, Jeannette Getzin, and Paul Covey. Thanks to Peter Schmelz and Emily Abrams Ansari for their helpful comments.

Notes

1. Robert Buzzanco, "Where's the Beef? Culture without Power in the Study of U.S. Foreign Relations," *Diplomatic History* 24, no. 4 (2000): 631.
2. Ibid.
3. The classic definition of soft power is that of Joseph Nye Jr., in *Soft Power: The Means to Success in World Politics* (New York: Public Affairs, 2004). Further literature is cited below.
4. Historians have critiqued Buzzanco's line of thinking and pursued alternative ways of examining the role of the arts and culture in history. For a concise summary of the "cultural turn" in diplomatic history, see Andrew J. Rotter, "The Cultural History of U.S. Foreign Relations," in *A Companion to American Cultural History*, ed. Karen Halttunen (Oxford: Blackwell, 2008), 425–36. An excellent review of the literature on cultural diplomacy appears in Kenneth Osgood and Brian C. Etheridge, "Introduction: The New International History Meets the New Cultural History—Public Diplomacy and U.S. Foreign Relations," in *The United States and Public Diplomacy: New Directions in Cultural and International History*, ed. Kenneth Osgood and Brian C. Etheridge (Boston: Martinus Nijhoff, 2010), 1–25; see also the detailed studies in Jessica C. E. Gienow-Hecht and Mark C. Donfried, eds., *Searching For A Cultural Diplomacy* (New York: Berghahn Books, 2010). On musical diplomacy, see Jessica C. E. Gienow-Hecht, *Sound Diplomacy: Music and Emotions in Transatlantic Relations, 1850–1920* (Chicago: University of Chicago Press, 2009); Lisa E. Davenport, *Jazz Diplomacy: Promoting America in the Cold War Era* (Jackson: University Press of Mississippi, 2009); Penny M. Von Eschen, *Satchmo Blows Up The World: Jazz Ambassadors Play the Cold War* (Cambridge, MA: Harvard University Press, 2004).
5. As only a few among many examples, see Tia DeNora, "Music Sociology: Getting the Music Into the Action," *British Journal of Music Education* 20, no. 2 (2003): 165–77; Thomas F. Johnston, "Power and Prestige Through Music in Tsongaland," *Human Relations* 27, no. 3 (1974): 235–46; Lisa Jakelski, "The Changing Seasons of the Warsaw Autumn: Contemporary Music in Poland, 1960–1990" (PhD diss., University of California, Berkeley, 2009).
6. Christopher Small, "Why Doesn't the Whole World Love Chamber Music?," *American Music* 19, no. 3 (2001): 345.
7. See Danielle Fosler-Lussier, "Music Pushed, Music Pulled: Cultural Diplomacy, Globalization, and Imperialism," *Diplomatic History* 36, no. 1 (2012): 53–64.
8. Ambassador James M. Langley, American Embassy Karachi, to Secretary of State John Foster Dulles, 032 Anderson, Marian/9-2557, Central Decimal File 1955–59, Record Group 59, General Records of the Department of State, National Archives, College Park, Maryland (hereafter CDF55-59). The dates for all doc-

uments from the Central Decimal File are encoded in the file numbers unless otherwise indicated: 9-2557 is shorthand for 25 September 1957.
9. Morris Dembo, Second Secretary, American Embassy Karachi, to Department of State (hereafter DOS), 032 Anderson, Marian/12-357, CDF55-59.
10. Arthur Z. Gardiner, Chargé d'Affaires ad interim, American Embassy Karachi, to DOS, 032 Anderson, Marian/7-1857, CDF55-59.
11. Ibid.
12. Secretary of State Christian Herter, DOS Instruction CA-265, to all diplomatic and consular posts, "Cultural Presentations: President's Program: Program Guide," 032/7-959, CDF55-59.
13. Arthur Z. Gardiner, Deputy Chief of Mission, American Embassy Karachi, to DOS, 032 Minneapolis Symphony Orchestra/10-357, CDF55-59.
14. Langley to Dulles, 032 Anderson, Marian/9-2557, CDF55-59.
15. W. Mallory-Browne, Counselor for Public Affairs, American Embassy Karachi, to DOS, 032 Teagarden, Jack Sextet/10-658, CDF55-59.
16. For an overview of the Cultural Presentations program, see Kevin Mulcahy, "Cultural Diplomacy and the Exchange Programs, 1938–1978," *Journal of Arts Management, Law, and Society* 29, no. 1 (1999): 7–29. For a more personal view, see Charles M. Ellison, "The Performing Arts and Our Foreign Relations," *Music Educators Journal* 52, no. 2 (1965): 49–50, 135–38.
17. Harold E. Urist, Public Affairs Officer, American Embassy Montevideo, to DOS, 032 Armstrong, Louis/12-1257, CDF55-59.
18. Ambassador Sheldon T. Mills, American Embassy Quito, to Secretary of State Dulles, 032 New Orleans Philharmonic Symphony/3-556, CDF 1955-59.
19. *IIA: The International Information Administration Program,* Department of State Publication 4939, International Information and Cultural Series 32, released April 1953.
20. Ambassador Joseph E. Jacobs, American Embassy Warsaw, to DOS, 032 Cleveland Symphony Orchestra/12-756, CDF 1955-59.
21. "The Caracas Audience: 'Receptive' and 'Sympathetic,'" *Daily Journal,* 21 August 1968, enclosed in Ambassador Maurice M. Bernbaum, American Embassy Caracas, to DOS, 27 August 1968, folder 23, box 59, Group II, MC468: Bureau of Educational and Cultural Affairs Historical Collection, Special Collections, University of Arkansas Library.
22. On European music in Latin America, see Rodrigo Herrera, "The Role of Classical Music in the Development of Nationalism and the Formation of Class in Quito, Ecuador" (PhD diss., University of Texas at Austin, 2000). On more general issues of prestige, see Joseph Bensman, "Classical Music and the Status Game," *Trans-action* 4, no. 9 (1967): 55–59.
23. See Danielle Fosler-Lussier, "American Cultural Diplomacy and the Mediation of Avant-garde Music," in *Sound Commitments: Avant-garde Music and the Sixties,* ed. Robert Adlington (Oxford: Oxford University Press, 2009), 240–44.
24. Small, "Why Doesn't the Whole World Love Chamber Music?," 351.
25. Ambassador Douglas MacArthur Jr., American Embassy Tokyo, to Secretary of State Christian Herter, 032 Boston Symphony Orchestra/11-1859, CDF1955-59.
26. Ambassador Douglas MacArthur Jr., American Embassy Tokyo, to Robert Thayer, DOS, 032/8-2659, CDF55-59. See also the embassy's more extensive report on the Little Orchestra Society's visit to Japan: George M. Hellyer, Counselor of Embassy for Public Affairs, American Embassy Tokyo, to DOS, 032 Little Orchestra Society/8-2159, CDF55-59.

27. Ambassador Douglas MacArthur Jr., American Embassy Tokyo, to DOS, 032 Cliburn, Van/6-1658, CDF55-59. The State Department acknowledged that Japan was a key target for both Soviet and US cultural diplomacy efforts: see R. Allan Lightner, Acting Assistant Secretary for Public Affairs, to MacArthur, 032/3-959, CDF55-59; C. Douglas Dillon, Acting Secretary of State, to American Embassy Tokyo, 032/4-2059, CDF55-59.
28. Ambassador John M. Allison, American Embassy Tokyo, to Secretary of State John Foster Dulles, 032 New York City Ballet/7-2056, CDF55-59. See also George M. Hellyer, Counselor of Embassy for Public Affairs, American Embassy Tokyo, to DOS and USIA, "President's Program Inadequate to Compete with Communist Cultural Offensive in Japan," 032/3-659, CDF55-59.
29. Ambassador Don C. Bliss, American Embassy Addis Ababa, to Secretary of State John Foster Dulles, 032 Florida Agriculture and Mechanical University Players/5-1358, CDF55-59.
30. See Emily Abrams Ansari, "'A Serious and Delicate Mission': American Orchestras, American Composers, and Cold War Diplomacy in Europe," in *Crosscurrents: American and European Music in Interaction, 1900–2000*, ed. Felix Meyer, Carol J. Oja, Wolfgang Rathert, and Anne C. Shreffler (Basel: Paul Sacher Stiftung, 2014); D. Kern Holoman, *Charles Munch* (Oxford: Oxford University Press, 2011), 146–54. Jonathan Rosenberg chronicles the New York Philharmonic's trips to Latin America and the USSR in 1958 and 1959: "Leonard Bernstein: An Idealist Abroad," in *Leonard Bernstein: American Original,* ed. Burton Bernstein and Barbara B. Haws (New York: Collins, 2008), 119–29.
31. William D. Killea, Public Affairs Officer, American Embassy Lima, to DOS, 032/12-1059, CDF55-59.
32. Lawrence J. Hall, American Embassy Baghdad, to DOS, 032 Minneapolis Symphony Orchestra/11-856, CDF55-59.
33. George A. Mann, Public Affairs Officer, USIS Baghdad, to USIA Washington, 032 Steber, Eleanor/2-2557, CDF55-59.
34. William F. Spengler, Consul in Charge, American Consulate General Lahore, to DOS, 032 Minneapolis Symphony Orchestra/9-2757, CDF55-59.
35. Aldo D'Alessandro, Country Public Affairs Officer, American Embassy Rio de Janeiro, to DOS, 032/11-2559, CDF55-59.
36. Secretary of State John Foster Dulles, DOS Instruction A-91, to American Embassy Buenos Aires, 032 National Symphony Orchestra/10-258, CDF55-59.
37. Joseph S. Evans Jr., Counselor of Embassy for Public Affairs, USIS Tokyo, to DOS, 032 American Trio/10-1955, CDF55-59. USIS stands for United States Information Service—the name used abroad for the United States Information Agency, or USIA.
38. Francis J. McArdle, Public Affairs Officer, USIS Lisbon, to DOS, 032/8-2459, CDF55-59.
39. Aldo D'Alessandro, Country Public Affairs Officer, American Embassy Rio de Janeiro, to DOS, 032/11-2559, CDF55-59.
40. George M. Hellyer, Counselor of Embassy for Public Affairs, American Embassy Tokyo, to DOS, 032/6-1559, CDF55-59.
41. Howard Elting Jr., Counselor of Embassy, American Embassy Saigon, to DOS, 032/5-2559, CDF55-59.
42. Ibid.
43. *Ngon Luan,* 2 December 1958, cited in translation in Elting to DOS, 032/5-2559, CDF55-59.
44. Cited in translation in Elting to DOS, 032/5-2559, CDF55-59.

45. Elting to DOS, 032/5-2559, CDF55-59.
46. See Frauke Hess, "Verstehen: Ein musikpädagogischer Mythos," in *Musikpädagogik als Aufgabe: Festschrift zum 65. Geburtstag von Siegmund Helms,* ed. Matthias Kruse and Reinhard Schneider (Kassel: Bosse, 2003), 119–35; Jerrold Levinson, *Music in the Moment* (Ithaca, NY: Cornell University Press, 1997), esp. 174–75.
47. Edmund H. Kellogg, Chargé d'Affaires ad interim, American Embassy Phnom Penh, to DOS, 032/4-659, CDF55-59.
48. American Consul William B. Hussey, American Consulate Chiengmai [Chiang Mai], to DOS, 032/3-2059, CDF55-59.
49. American Embassy Bangkok to DOS, 032/9-2859, CDF55-59.
50. R. Allan Lightner, Acting Assistant Secretary for Public Affairs, to Douglas MacArthur Jr., American Embassy Tokyo, 032/3-959, CDF55-59; C. Douglas Dillon, Acting Secretary of State, to American Embassy Tokyo, 032/4-2059, CDF55-59.
51. Elting to DOS, 032/5-2559, CDF55-59.
52. McArdle to DOS, 032/8-2459, CDF55-59.
53. Joseph Nye Jr., *Bound to Lead: The Changing Nature of American Power* (New York: Basic Books, 1990), 194.
54. Nye, *Bound to Lead,* 193–95; Nye, *Soft Power,* 46–55.
55. Edward Lock, "Soft Power and Strategy: Developing a 'Strategic' Concept of Soft Power," in *Soft Power and US Foreign Policy: Theoretical, Historical and Contemporary Perspectives,* ed. Inderjeet Parmar and Michael Cox (New York: Routledge, 2010), 36.
56. Peter van Ham, *Social Power in International Politics* (New York: Routledge, 2010), 8, 49.
57. Ibid., 33, 46–59, esp. 52.
58. Matthew Fraser, *Weapons of Mass Distraction: Soft Power and American Empire* (New York: St. Martin's Press, 2003), 29.
59. The necessity of consent opens the possibility of a neo-Gramscian reading. See Geraldo Zahran and Leonardo Ramos, "From Hegemony to Soft Power: Implications of a Conceptual Change," in Parmar and Cox, *Soft Power and US Foreign Policy,* 21.
60. Edward Lock, "Soft Power and Strategy," 37. Van Ham's definition of social power is "the capacity to establish the norms and rules around which other actors' actions converge," a definition that is relevant but not adequate for describing musical diplomacy (*Social Power,* 8).
61. Melvyn P. Leffler, "New Approaches, Old Interpretations, and Prospective Reconfigurations," *Diplomatic History* 19, no. 2 (1995): 180. Cited in Stephen Tuck, "Historiographical Review: The New American Histories," *The Historical Journal* 48, no. 3 (2005): 823.
62. See Danielle Fosler-Lussier, "Cultural Diplomacy as Cultural Globalization: The University of Michigan Jazz Band in Latin America," *Journal of the Society for American Music* 4, no. 1 (2010): 76–78.
63. Fraser, *Weapons of Mass Distraction,* 23.

Bibliography

Archives

National Archives, College Park, Maryland
Special Collections, University of Arkansas Library, Fayetteville, Arkansas

Printed Sources

Ansari, Emily Abrams. "'A Serious and Delicate Mission': American Orchestras, American Composers, and Cold War Diplomacy in Europe." In *Crosscurrents: American and European Music in Interaction, 1900–2000*, ed. Felix Meyer, Carol J. Oja, Wolfgang Rathert, and Anne C. Shreffler. Basel: Paul Sacher Stiftung, 2014.

Bensman, Joseph. "Classical Music and the Status Game." *Trans-action* 4, no. 9 (1967): 55–59.

Buzzanco, Robert. "Where's the Beef? Culture without Power in the Study of U.S. Foreign Relations." *Diplomatic History* 24, no. 4 (2000): 623–32.

Davenport, Lisa E. *Jazz Diplomacy: Promoting America in the Cold War Era.* Jackson: University Press of Mississippi, 2009.

DeNora, Tia. "Music Sociology: Getting the Music Into the Action." *British Journal of Music Education* 20, no. 2 (2003): 165–77.

Ellison, Charles M. "The Performing Arts and Our Foreign Relations." *Music Educators Journal* 52, no. 2 (1965): 49–50, 135–38.

Fosler-Lussier, Danielle. "American Cultural Diplomacy and the Mediation of Avant-garde Music." In *Sound Commitments: Avant-garde Music and the Sixties*, ed. Robert Adlington, 232–53. Oxford: Oxford University Press, 2009.

———. "Cultural Diplomacy as Cultural Globalization: The University of Michigan Jazz Band in Latin America." *Journal of the Society for American Music* 4, no. 1 (2010): 59–93.

———. "Music Pushed, Music Pulled: Cultural Diplomacy, Globalization, and Imperialism." *Diplomatic History* 36, no. 1 (2012): 53–64.

Fraser, Matthew. *Weapons of Mass Distraction: Soft Power and American Empire.* New York: St. Martin's Press, 2003.

Gienow-Hecht, Jessica C. E. *Sound Diplomacy: Music and Emotions in Transatlantic Relations, 1850–1920.* Chicago: University of Chicago Press, 2009.

Gienow-Hecht, Jessica C. E., and Mark C. Donfried, eds. *Searching For A Cultural Diplomacy.* New York: Berghahn Books, 2010.

Herrera, Rodrigo. "The Role of Classical Music in the Development of Nationalism and the Formation of Class in Quito, Ecuador." PhD diss., University of Texas at Austin, 2000.

Hess, Frauke. "Verstehen: Ein musikpädagogischer Mythos." In *Musikpädagogik als Aufgabe: Festschrift zum 65. Geburtstag von Siegmund Helms*, ed. Matthias Kruse and Reinhard Schneider, 119–35. Kassel: Bosse, 2003.

Holoman, D. Kern. *Charles Munch.* Oxford: Oxford University Press, 2011.

IIA: The International Information Administration Program. Department of State Publication 4939. International Information and Cultural Series 32. Released April 1953.

Jakelski, Lisa. "The Changing Seasons of the Warsaw Autumn: Contemporary Music in Poland, 1960–1990." PhD diss., University of California, Berkeley, 2009.

Johnston, Thomas F. "Power and Prestige Through Music in Tsongaland." *Human Relations* 27, no. 3 (1974): 235–46.
Leffler, Melvyn P. "New Approaches, Old Interpretations, and Prospective Reconfigurations." *Diplomatic History* 19, no. 2 (1995): 173–96.
Levinson, Jerrold. *Music in the Moment.* Ithaca, NY: Cornell University Press, 1997.
Lock, Edward. "Soft Power and Strategy: Developing a 'Strategic' Concept of Soft Power." In *Soft Power and US Foreign Policy: Theoretical, Historical and Contemporary Perspectives,* ed. Inderjeet Parmar and Michael Cox, 32–50. New York: Routledge, 2010.
Mulcahy, Kevin. "Cultural Diplomacy and the Exchange Programs, 1938–1978." *Journal of Arts Management, Law, and Society* 29, no. 1 (1999): 7–29.
Nye, Joseph, Jr. *Bound to Lead: The Changing Nature of American Power.* New York: Basic Books, 1990.
———. *Soft Power: The Means to Success in World Politics.* New York: Public Affairs, 2004.
Osgood, Kenneth, and Brian C. Etheridge. "Introduction: The New International History Meets the New Cultural History—Public Diplomacy and U.S. Foreign Relations." In *The United States and Public Diplomacy: New Directions in Cultural and International History,* ed. Kenneth Osgood and Brian C. Etheridge, 1–25. Boston: Martinus Nijhoff, 2010.
Rosenberg, Jonathan. "Leonard Bernstein: An Idealist Abroad." In *Leonard Bernstein: American Original,* ed. Burton Bernstein and Barbara B. Haws, 117–34. New York: Collins, 2008.
Rotter, Andrew J. "The Cultural History of U.S. Foreign Relations." In *A Companion to American Cultural History,* ed. Karen Halttunen, 425–36. Oxford: Blackwell, 2008.
Small, Christopher. "Why Doesn't the Whole World Love Chamber Music?" *American Music* 19, no. 3 (2001): 340–59.
Tuck, Stephen. "Historiographical Review: The New American Histories." *The Historical Journal* 48, no. 3 (2005): 811–32.
Van Ham, Peter. *Social Power in International Politics.* New York: Routledge, 2010.
Von Eschen, Penny. *Satchmo Blows Up The World: Jazz Ambassadors Play the Cold War.* Cambridge, MA: Harvard University Press, 2004.
Zahran, Geraldo, and Leonardo Ramos. "From Hegemony to Soft Power: Implications of a Conceptual Change." In *Soft Power and US Foreign Policy: Theoretical, Historical and Contemporary Perspectives,* ed. Inderjeet Parmar and Michael Cox, 12–31. New York: Routledge, 2010.

Chapter Five

"TO REACH ... INTO THE HEARTS AND MINDS OF OUR FRIENDS"
The United States' Symphonic Tours and the Cold War

Jonathan Rosenberg

In the spring of 1955, the Japanese composer Kosaku Yamada reflected on his experience in a Tokyo concert hall after hearing a program by the Symphony of the Air, one of America's leading orchestras. Describing May 3, 1955, the day of the concert, as one that would never be "forgotten in Japanese musical history," the elder figure wrote that his "eyes were blurred with deep feeling." All the country's music lovers had been waiting for such an event, he said, waiting "to hear the symphony unsurpassed in richness of power, in force, in freedom of style ... All through the concert, I kept on saying to myself, 'Ah, this is the real thing.'"[1]

From a distinguished Japanese musician pondering a memorable experience in a Tokyo concert hall, we shift our gaze to a less sublime setting, a gathering of the American Society of Newspaper Editors in Washington DC, where Dwight Eisenhower spoke in April 1953, delivering a speech titled "A Chance for Peace." In language of no small eloquence, the American president, having only recently taken office, declared that the "free world" was focused on one central question: "the chance for a just peace for all peoples." The former military leader considered the cost of the arms race in distinctly human terms, observing, "Every gun that is made, every warship launched, every rocket fired signifies, in the final sense, a theft from

---

Notes for this section begin on page 159.

those who hunger and are not fed, those who are cold and are not clothed." The ex-general reflected upon the chance for a better future and looked toward a time when the world's peoples might no longer have to live beneath "the cloud of threatening war." With the death of Stalin the previous month, it was possible, the president suggested, that a new era had arrived.[2]

These two moments, a concert-going experience described by a sensitive listener thousands of miles from the United States and an address given by a political leader in his nation's capital, help set the stage for the focus of this chapter, which explores the classical music initiatives undertaken by the United States during the Eisenhower years, a time when Washington sent esteemed ensembles across the world in order to compete with the Soviet Union in the cultural realm. As we shall see, the United States deployed symphony orchestras overseas to help advance its diplomatic objectives, an act that suggests the spheres of music and power politics might be far less discrete than one would imagine. One aim of this chapter is to examine the extent to which such musical initiatives shed light on American thinking about the character of the Cold War, while another is to consider whether music might illuminate the subject of international relations, which is, of course, the larger objective of this volume.

To return to Washington, some have argued that Eisenhower's 1953 address was mainly a propaganda exercise that aimed, in the wake of Stalin's death, to "wrestle the peace initiative away from the Kremlin."[3] If nothing else, the new president and his advisers were determined to devise an approach to counter the Soviet Union, which had positioned itself as the great power most willing to escape the constraints of the Cold War. What has been called Russia's worldwide peace initiative had clearly caught the attention of the United States, and the Eisenhower administration moved to develop a foreign policy comprising a variety of programs that would respond to the distinctive challenges of the post-Stalin era. Among those challenges was Russia's decision to raise significantly its commitment to cultural diplomacy, which was demonstrated by the fact that Moscow, between 1953 and 1955, had increased by a factor of three the number of dance groups, theater companies, and musical organizations it was exporting to other countries.[4] From an American vantage point, this belied Moscow's putative willingness to search for a peaceful resolution to the Cold War; it pointed, instead, to a purposive effort to convince the world's peoples that the Soviet Union was blessed with a rich creative culture, which, when compared with that of the United States, might incline others to emulate the socialist model. Government officials in the United States saw the worldwide implementation of the Soviet cultural initiative as proof of Moscow's determination to prevail in the East-West competition.[5] Thus, the Eisenhower administration was convinced that Soviet leaders, whatever their public stance, were prepared to do what they thought necessary to win the global struggle that had cast a shadow across the international landscape since the end of World War II.

In this context, the new administration began to construct a foreign policy that elevated the importance of cultural matters in interstate relations. Writing to his brother, the president evinced an acute awareness of the world's negative image of the United States, which he averred was intolerable in the current geopolitical climate. The world was "ignorant" about the United States, and it was critical that "some of the misunderstandings be corrected." Of particular concern was the way other peoples perceived America's "cultural standards and artistic tastes." Eisenhower worried that "Europeans ha[d] been taught that we are a race of materialists, whose only diversions are golf, baseball, football, [and] horseracing." Foreign peoples knew the United States for its automobiles, rather than for "worthwhile cultural works of any kind."[6] Thus, cultural diplomacy became one way to combat the negative perceptions of the United States held by peoples around the world.[7] From this geopolitical matrix, classical music—particularly high-profile overseas tours by leading American orchestras—would become an important piece of the diplomacy of the 1950s. It was hoped that such initiatives could help transform the world's perception of the United States, which would fortify America's position in the ideological battle for the allegiance of peoples across the globe.

Before considering this story, which focuses on the 1955 Asian journey by the Symphony of the Air and the New York Philharmonic's 1958 trip to Latin America under Leonard Bernstein, I shall consider some of the questions around which this volume is framed, the most important of which concerns the relationship between music and international relations, or, more specifically, how focusing on music can enrich our understanding of US international history. These reflections are offered as I continue to work on a sweeping study on the interrelationship between international politics and the culture of classical music in the United States from World War I to the Cold War. By the culture of classical music, I am referring to several aspects of the classical music sphere in the United States: the attitudes, activities, and ideas of singers, instrumentalists, conductors, and composers; the activities and repertoire of American performing institutions such as symphony orchestras and opera companies; and the ideas and attitudes of classical-music listeners (both professional reviewers and ordinary concertgoers). With that in mind, I would suggest that the culture of classical music in the United States was deeply enmeshed in twentieth-century international affairs, and I would contend that focusing on the intersection between the domains of classical music and international relations can offer insights into important aspects of American political culture and deepen our understanding of how and why the United States perceived and engaged the world as it did.

I approach this project as a scholar of twentieth-century US international history (and a former classical musician) who has been drawn to an emerging historiography that, over the last fifteen years or so, has sought to situate the history of the United States in a global context. As a growing cohort of scholars has demonstrated, the global embeddedness of the United States throughout American history has been crucial in shaping American political, social, economic, and cultural life. According to Thomas Bender, "American history cannot be adequately understood unless it is incorporated into [a] global context"; he notes, moreover, that "the zones of contact and exchange among people ... rarely stop at borders."[8] In considering the subject of music, one sees that the matter of a nation's embeddedness in the world is especially salient—for music is, after all, difficult to contain within the borders of the nation-state. Throughout the twentieth century (and before), musicians and performing organizations traversed state boundaries easily and often, and music itself—whether a Wagner opera, a Beethoven symphony, or a Mozart sonata—has always flowed readily across the boundaries of states. If one looks at contemporary America, for example, one can venture out on most nights in cities large and small to hear the works of composers from across the world—from Germany, Austria, Russia, Britain, France, Japan, China, and beyond—performed by musicians from Asia, Europe, and the Americas.

Thus, as one reflects upon the culture of classical music in the United States, it is clear that the nation's boundaries are permeable, the world of classical music demonstrating America's susceptibility to intercultural contact and influence, whether through exposure to compositions by foreigners or through the interactions Americans have with the diverse artists who perform in the nation's auditoriums. And significantly, much the same can be said about America's symphonic ensembles, which, while they are domestic cultural institutions, have, at times, played the role of dynamic actors on the international stage, their members well positioned to transmit values and ideas across the boundaries of states.

Such reflections lead one to ponder the link between music and international relations, and to consider how music can help us to understand a specific set of historical circumstances, which I want to discuss before turning to the Cold War journeys of the Symphony of the Air and the New York Philharmonic. To that end, I shall offer some additional thoughts on the larger project I am working on, which spans much of the twentieth century. In examining the source material on which the study is based—concert reviews and writings on music in newspapers, magazines, and music journals; the archival records of performing institutions; the personal papers of leading musical figures; and selected US government materials—I have repeatedly encountered evidence illustrating a key facet of twentieth-century American political culture, the ever-present fear of anti-democratic regimes, which has often been melded to America's determination to defend democracy against its perceived challengers. And both, of course, are inextricably connected to the subject of international relations. It is worth emphasizing, moreover, that the United States' concern with overseas threats and its commitment to defend democracy were not episodic aspects of twentieth-century U.S. history, but were, instead, persistent characteristics of America's international engagement over the years. Indeed, throughout the last century, the United States grappled with a variety of "dangerous regimes," from the Germany of Wilhelm II and Hitler, to Mussolini's Italy, to the Soviet Union of Stalin, Khrushchev, and Brezhnev, which, together, catalyzed America's fear of autocracy and totalitarianism and led the country to devote an enormous amount of energy, to say nothing of blood and treasure, to preparing for and fighting wars, hot and cold.

As I have combed through the relevant music-related sources—sources not typically of interest to foreign relations historians—it has become clear that the world of music can serve as an important window onto this enduring phenomenon in the history of the United States in the twentieth-century: the persistent fixation on overseas threats and the determination to defend both the United States and other countries against America's ostensible enemies. This research has convinced me that by exploring the intersection between the culture of classical music in the United States and twentieth-century international affairs, one can apprehend a great deal about how Americans understood themselves, the world, and their country's role on the international stage.

Not surprisingly, America's perception of foreign threats over the course of the twentieth century was not static. At times, such threats were thought to imperil the country's physical security, as in World War II, while at other moments, the nature of the threat was less concrete, as Americans became convinced that what the United States represented in the world—its principles, values, and ideas—were under siege. During World War I, for example, American intervention against Germany was not predicated on the notion that Wilhelm's Germans posed a threat to the territorial integrity of the United States. What was critical, instead, was the idea, ultimately embraced by Woodrow Wilson, that Germany threatened a particular kind of world order, an order that was thought essential to maintaining American security, broadly conceived. That world order, based on liberal democratic values and the rule of law, was one that leaders like Wilson thought the United States embodied more perfectly than any other nation, and, in Wilson's estimation, America was uniquely suited to help preserve it. In the end, Wilson came to believe that the United States could do so only by going to war. In more recent times, during the Cold War—as the symphonic tours demonstrate—American fears sprang less from the worry that the continental United States would be overrun by Soviet forces than from the notion that the continued expansion of communism overseas would undermine and delegitimize the American idea, causing American values to seem less relevant, which would, in turn, make the United States unworthy of emulation and thus less powerful.

Throughout the Cold War, American policy makers were concerned that the United States might become an endangered ideological species, a nation forced to survive in a turbulent communist sea. If such a world came to pass, many policy makers believed, it would be a less secure place, a conviction that compelled the United States to do whatever it could to prevent that from happening. It was essential, therefore, to defend liberal capitalism and, more specifically, the American political and economic model against any state that threatened its continued preeminence. And as one reflects upon America's global engagement over the course of the twentieth century, both before and during the Cold War, I would suggest that examining the world of classical music can shed light on the nature of the United States' international concerns and how the country sought to address them.

With those reflections in mind, let us turn to Dwight Eisenhower's effort to fortify America's international posture, as suggested by a 27 July 1954 letter from the president to the House Committee on

Appropriations that delineated the administration's belief in the importance of the cultural component of US foreign policy. "I consider it essential," the president wrote, "that we take immediate and vigorous action to demonstrate the superiority of the products and cultural values of our system of free enterprise." The administration sought five million dollars to support "presentations abroad by private firms and groups of the best American industrial and cultural achievements" in order to demonstrate America's devotion to "peace and human well-being" so as to "offset worldwide Communist propaganda charges that the United States has no culture and that its industrial production is oriented toward war."[9] The following month, on 26 August, Congress passed Public Law 663, which gave birth to the President's Emergency Fund for International Affairs. Divided into three categories, the fund allocated approximately half of the five million dollars to the Commerce Department to develop US involvement in international trade fairs. Another $2,250,000 was channeled to the State Department to support overseas cultural presentations, including dance, music, theater, and sports; and the remainder went to the United States Information Agency to help publicize the myriad cultural events that would be presented overseas.[10] With the establishment of the President's Emergency Fund, the groundwork was laid for government funding of overseas cultural programming in nearly every corner of the world, the objective of which was to advance the international standing of the United States.[11]

An example of Washington's decision to fund overseas cultural initiatives is the 1955 tour offered by the Symphony of the Air, one of America's leading orchestras, which plied its craft before ecstatic audiences in Japan, Korea, the Philippines, Taiwan, and Hong Kong. One of the virtuoso ensembles of the era, the orchestra, established in 1954, comprised players from the acclaimed but defunct NBC Symphony Orchestra, which Arturo Toscanini had directed for many years. On the Asian tour, two American conductors, Walter Hendl of the Dallas Symphony and Thor Johnson of the Cincinnati Symphony, led the orchestra in programs comprising standard orchestral fare, as well as some American compositions that aimed to expose foreign audiences to America's creative spirit. In announcing the tour, Robert C. Schnitzer, who headed the government's International Exchange Program, remarked (if awkwardly) that it was "a most auspicious attraction to inaugurate the Far East activities of our Program," especially since "our Asian friends have an excellent hearsay knowledge of Western music," but had never before had a "live demonstration of the importance and quality represented by this project."[12] As would be true of other US government–sponsored orchestral tours in these years, the concerts given by the Symphony of the Air had been organized under the auspices of ANTA, the American National Theater and Academy.[13]

Before, during, and after the trip, Americans at home were exposed to uniformly positive reporting on what the ensemble might achieve overseas. The idea that the United States was not culturally barren and could strengthen its international position if it displayed the attainments of American culture to other peoples received wide support on the American home front. Noting that orchestral tours were only part of an "extensive program to show our friends in other lands that we have an active artistic life," the *New York Times* commended US policy makers for recognizing that "the battle for men's minds and hearts [could] be waged on the cultural front."[14]

Beyond the national interest rationale, American readers also regularly encountered the notion that music could provide a balm for an unstable world. The capacity of classical music to soften the hard edges of international politics was remarked upon in *Musical America,* one of the country's leading music journals. Claiming the performances by the Symphony of the Air demonstrated that music had the power "to promote understanding ... among men," the journal described the orchestra's players as "America's most potent ambassadors of good will since the end of the war." And once the tour was over, it was suggested, those Asians who had harbored ill feelings toward the United States would have their work cut out for them, since the ensemble's visit was creating "excitement ... enthusiasm ... [and] admiration."[15] According to one writer, classical music, as performed by a distinguished American ensemble, could enhance the possibility of peace itself. Music, it seemed, was a language that would allow Americans to speak to the Japanese and the Japanese to speak to the Americans. If different peoples could communicate more effectively with one another, they could "meet upon a common ground," thus creating a mutually rewarding situation. And this, readers learned, was the "stuff out of which the permanent peace must be built."[16]

The stories filtering back to the United States about the response to the Symphony of the Air were bound to resonate powerfully with Americans, many of whom undoubtedly supported the country's strategy of advancing its Cold War objectives through the nation's cultural programs. Americans learned of an outdoor concert in Seoul attended by thirteen thousand "music-hungry" Koreans—including staunch anticommunist ally President Syngman Rhee—where, according to Hendl, countless "Koreans came into close contact and complete understanding with a group of Americans." Speaking in idealistic terms, the conductor claimed it was "the most positive proof of the universality of music."[17] A few days later, Americans learned that Generalissimo Chiang Kai-shek and Madame Chiang had joined seven thousand Chinese at the Armed Forces Stadium on the island of Taiwan to hear Beethoven, Mozart, and Gershwin. The concert, a benefit for the Chinese Women's Anti-Aggression League, was described as one of Taipei's "major social and artistic event[s] of the year," and the Nationalist Chinese leader, a key US ally, mingled with the orchestra's musicians (and with his cabinet), shaking hands and thanking them for their work. The intersection between politics and culture on the concert stage would have been impossible to miss, whether one was in the audience in Taiwan or reading the reports in the United States.[18]

By all accounts, local audiences were powerfully affected both by the orchestra's performances and by the presence on native soil of a large group of gifted musicians. This enthusiastic reception was hardly confined to the response of Asian music critics, whose pleasant task was to evaluate the quality of the performances. One is struck not by the critics' enthusiasm—this was a superb ensemble, after all—but by the rapturous response evinced by regular people who were lucky enough to hear the Symphony of the Air in person. Nowhere was this more true than in Japan, where nearly sixty-five thousand people heard the orchestra perform in a land where no Western orchestra had ever played. Millions more heard the orchestra through radio and television broadcasts, and the United States Information Service even produced a 35-millimeter film of a live performance that was distributed throughout Japan, along with one hundred albums the orchestra had recorded.[19]

While the US embassy was thrilled by the fact that the crowd wept at the final concert in Tokyo and claimed the response was "a dramatic rebuttal to Communist arguments that America is a nation without culture or sensitivity,"[20] more poignant—and less overtly nationalistic—aspects of the visit emerged, as was noted in the Japanese press. One paper, *Nagoya Mainchi,* said the "long-awaited concert" had turned the concert hall into "a place of deep emotion. The dream of our music fans to hear the world's best symphony orchestra was finally realized." The salutary power of music was considered by another paper, *Nagoya Chubu Nippon,* which observed that those attending the concert "forgot for the moment their social status. They forgot their nationalities and racial differences.

Their hearts all merged and converged on the universal beauty of music ... [which offers] ... solace for human beings."²¹ The collective emotion produced by the orchestra's performance was captured by another publication, which claimed the ensemble had "grasped the heartstrings of the Japanese people." And as we heard earlier, the Japanese composer Kosaku Yamada reflected on his experience in a Tokyo concert hall upon hearing the program by the Symphony of the Air on a day that would never be "forgotten in Japanese musical history."²²

The ensemble's visit was notable for the way it touched young Japanese music lovers, who showered the musicians with reverence and affection. Throughout their stay, the players were moved by the fan mail and small gifts they received from many Japanese youngsters. One player recounted his amazement at the musical knowledge of the young Japanese, claiming that a group of fourteen-year-old girls he encountered "knew as much about music as many older musicians." The members of the orchestra spent as much time with the young music aficionados as they could, he said, noting that the students, who were also deeply interested in government affairs, are "the future leaders of Japan." He recalled, too, that the orchestra's players were told by a US government representative in Japan that the ensemble had done "more toward establishing a close rapport between our two countries than a staff of attaches could hope to do in years."²³ A particularly memorable episode saw the orchestra further endear itself to the country's young people by presenting a special outdoor concert for thousands of youths who were unable to afford the regular performances. (For the equivalent of about twenty-five cents, they were able to hear one of the world's great orchestras.) Still more poignantly, one family, which included six children who called themselves "music lovers," wrote to a representative of the orchestra requesting a photograph of the ensemble "in action." They could not afford tickets to the regular concerts and had no television, but they hoped to place a picture of the group next to the radio during its live broadcasts. "Please forgive us for making this rude request," they wrote, "but we hope that you will fill it for us." The family got their wish. One can only imagine the joy this large, music-loving family experienced upon receiving the photograph, and the feelings it would have engendered toward the American musicians and perhaps even toward the United States itself.²⁴

With the tour at an end, conductors Hendl and Johnson sat down and reflected upon the experience, their words suggesting the blend of musical idealism and national self-interest that characterized the orchestral journeys in those years. One is also struck by the unsavory Western-centric chauvinism that crept into the maestros' observations. Thor Johnson spoke of the way the "untutored natives took to" Western classical music, noting that it was in many cases their first exposure to the form. For his part, Walter Hendl was disdainful of "the Orient's music," claiming it had "little therapeutic value for its peoples." But according to Hendl, Western music "meets their mid-century needs better than their own." Wherever the orchestra played in Asia, Hendl noted, the "natives ... responded best to the best music," and he called Beethoven's *Eroica* the "greatest piece" he had conducted on tour. The ecstatic response the orchestra received after playing it led Hendl to deduce that "man's most important messages hit humanity everywhere in the same way."

For Hendl, the universality of music was clear; peoples of disparate cultures responded to music—even unfamiliar music—in largely the same way. In the political realm, Hendl stated that the orchestra's impact was undeniable, a point leading diplomats in the region conveyed repeatedly to him and others on the tour. The orchestra "had accomplished more good in a few weeks than they could in a lifetime," they told him. And the Asian people let the musicians know how important a trip it was, Hendl claimed, a point confirmed in their frequent cry of "take home your armies and send us your symphonies." Sounding a familiar political note, Johnson observed that the tour had weakened the claim that the United States had "no culture of any kind." The symphony's journey had "disarmed the intellectuals," Johnson averred, and proved Americans were not just "money-mad." Hendl, too, spoke of money, though from a different vantage point. Linking high culture to politics, he considered how economical the tour had been in achieving its geopolitical objectives. Perhaps the trip was expensive, he said, but it was "peanuts in terms of what our government usually pays to accomplish much less in the way of East-West solidarity." Hendl spoke, finally, of music's capacity to narrow the gap between peoples, claiming he was struck by the "power of music" to serve as "a bridge without end." The maestro was convinced that the Symphony of the Air had "brought America and the Orient artistically closer than they ha[d] ever been."[25] For those who doubted this assertion, one only had to reflect upon a performance of Beethoven's Fifth Symphony played jointly by the American ensemble and Japan's NHK Symphony. The 180-piece orchestra thrilled the audience, which included the crown prince and twenty thousand others, who seemed to recognize the "symbolism involved in Japanese and American musicians sitting side by side" in the first combined mass concert Japan had ever seen.[26] Clearly, observers and participants believed the tour was enormously successful, a notion embraced by musicians, conductors, critics, political leaders, and thousands of regular people in postwar Asia, many of whom were touched by the music they heard and by the human interactions that were an essential part of the orchestra's visit.

The New York Philharmonic's celebrated trips with Leonard Bernstein on the podium were another example of American diplomatic outreach. In 1958, the orchestra ventured to Latin America on an extended tour that was followed closely by the press in the United States and by local residents, including journalists, music critics, and ordinary people who could not get enough of the American-born maestro and were swept up in the excitement of hearing a world-class ensemble, often for the first time. Given Bernstein's gifts as an artist and cultural communicator, the charismatic conductor inevitably became the focal point of the trip, which seemed to serve America's overseas interests and, according to some, help build bridges between peoples.[27] The tour, which lasted from April to June, saw Bernstein lead the New Yorkers in twelve countries and twenty-one cities over a seven-week period, with the dashing American conducting the majority of the concerts. (The eminent Dimitri Mitropoulos was the orchestra's other principal conductor.)[28]

On the eve of the trip, the Philharmonic was feted by hundreds of well-wishers who gathered to send the orchestra on its way with a lavish New York reception. Leaders in business, the arts, and politics lent enthusiastic support to the Philharmonic's diplomatic mission, the purpose of which was articulated by a US State Department official who called the orchestra a "brilliant manifestation of cultural achievement in the United States." Suggesting that the trip's objectives were varied, the State Department's representative told the assembled group that the Philharmonic would engender appreciation among foreign peoples, provide a "picture of U.S. life" for all to see, and "help further our national Good Neighbor Policy" in the Western Hemisphere.[29]

If this was one way to characterize the diplomatic aims of the trip, a more idealistic understanding of the orchestra's goals was articulated in the *New York Times,* which called the ensemble the "ideal spokesman" to serve as the country's "cultural ambassador." The *Times'* language suggested it was possible to emphasize a more humanistic, inclusive dimension of the foreign journey, which, the paper observed, would enable the musicians to "transcend geography or the tongues of men" by participating in an endeavor that was intrinsically linked to the music they would perform. The "power of Beethoven [and] the devotion of Bach" would be understood in whatever country the orchestra performed, the editors observed. This was so, the article said, because music was an "all-embracing language" capable of bringing "peoples of all kinds into closest spiritual communion."[30] The words of a State Department official and the language of a leading newspaper thus reflected a bifurcated understanding of the motives underlying the Cold War tours of the 1950s, as notions of both national interest and idealism were advanced to explain the objectives of the United States' program of cultural outreach.

Though many Latin Americans already harbored considerable animosity toward the United States in this period, the Philharmonic's trip was highly successful. As we shall see, the hostility aimed at the political leadership of the United States, which exploded on the streets of Lima and Caracas in the spring of 1958, stood in sharp contrast to the overwhelming enthusiasm and affection the Philharmonic encountered in concert halls and stadiums throughout Latin America. Across the region, reaction to the tour was euphoric, as some two hundred thousand people witnessed orchestral performances for the first time or, for the more experienced concertgoer, heard concerts unlike any they had ever known.[31] In city after city, the ovations were nothing short of delirious. In Rio de Janeiro, eighteen thousand people heard the orchestra, many of whom wept as the New Yorkers concluded the concert with the Brazilian national anthem. More than thirty thousand heard an afternoon performance played outdoors in downtown São Paulo, a special event for those who could not squeeze into the concerts in the local theater. According to a local paper, mothers carried their children, the young sat with the old, and "well-dressed aristocrats rubbed elbows with workers." In the hills above Caracas, seven thousand heard Bernstein conduct; fifteen thousand attended a Sunday morning concert in Mexico City; and one million Venezuelans watched on television as the orchestra performed at the university in Caracas. When the New York musicians and their conductors walked the streets of cities across the continent, they heard expressions of appreciation from countless local people, grateful that the orchestra had come to play for them. Many of the performances saw heads of state in attendance, several of whom received Leonard Bernstein during intermission.[32]

Bernstein, Mitropoulos, and the orchestra garnered rave reviews everywhere they played. Lauding Bernstein, one Chilean paper, *El Siglo,* said the conductor knew how to "give to each of the interpretations an exceptional sparkle," while another, *El Mercurio,* spoke of the "rare and precious present" the US State Department had bestowed on Chile.[33] In Lima, Peru, which, as will be discussed, had been the scene of recent anti-American unrest, the editors of *La Prensa* wrote about the importance of the ensemble's visit, claiming it was "indisputable that cultural ambassadors such as the New York Philharmonic are much more effective than words in the task of accomplishing a better understanding between the peoples of the United States and those of Latin America."[34] The *Journal* in Caracas described the Philharmonic's trip as a notable event in the musical history of the country and called the presence of Bernstein and the orchestra a "genuine tonic" that was "bound to be beneficial."[35]

In every city, along with the national anthems of the United States and the host country, the orchestra played at least one piece by an American composer—Samuel Barber, Aaron Copland, George Gershwin, Roy Harris, or William Schuman—as stipulated by the US government. As was the case in this period, the American compositions Bernstein and Mitropoulos selected were vetted by the Music Advisory Panel, a US government–appointed committee charged with evaluating the suitability of the music to be played in Latin Amer-

Figure 5.1. Leonard Bernstein with a group of Peruvian musicians on the 1958 tour to Latin America.
Source: New York Philharmonic Leon Levy Digital Archive.

ica.³⁶ The idea that foreign audiences should hear music written by US composers was consistent with one of the primary objectives of the orchestral tours—and the Eisenhower cultural initiative more generally—namely, that people overseas should be made aware that the United States was not a nation of cultural underachievers. The goal was to show that America valued high culture and that the country had the compositions to prove it. Based on their reactions, audiences apparently enjoyed such pieces, though it is difficult to gauge with much certainty to what extent local concertgoers absorbed the larger musico-ideological message.³⁷

In discussing the New York Philharmonic's Latin American tour, one must consider Leonard Bernstein's impact on the overall success of the venture. The conductor was adored wherever he went, and despite the arduous demands of the journey, he relished the opportunity to showcase the orchestra.³⁸ But Bernstein's talents were not confined to the podium. Throughout the tour, he demonstrated his capabilities outside the concert hall, serving as a cultural ambassador for the United States. The man who had long been a fierce critic of the American government and a target of its investigators represented the United States with devotion and vigor.³⁹ According to the orchestra's president, he "attended press conferences without number, luncheons, dinners, celebrations of local playing and dancing, good, bad, and indifferent," and "charmed the old and fascinated the young." Moreover, Bernstein could communicate in Spanish, an invaluable asset given the orchestra's goals.⁴⁰

While the New York Philharmonic was making history in Latin America, the worlds of music and international politics intersected as Bernstein and Vice President Richard Nixon crossed paths in the region. In the spring of 1958, seeking to shore up relations with US allies to the south, Eisenhower sent Nixon to visit the South American continent. While abroad, the American leader attended the inauguration of the Argentine president and made stops in Uruguay, Peru, and Venezuela, among other places. He encountered an angry reception in several cities, especially Lima and Caracas. In Peru, Nixon and his wife, Pat, were spat on by youthful Latin Americans, and in Caracas, their limousine was stoned by enraged citizens who were no doubt upset that the United States had earlier supported the dictator Marcos Pérez Jiménez, whom the Venezuelans had overthrown a few months before. Nixon's driver managed to escape the melee and the car sped off, but not before its occupants had feared for their lives.⁴¹

Soon after, when Nixon reached Quito, Ecuador, the conductor and the future president had the chance to exchange thoughts on

Figure 5.2. Leonard Bernstein, stopping for a shoe shine, frolics with a group of children in Lima, Peru, on the 1958 Latin American tour.
Source: New York Philharmonic Leon Levy Digital Archive.

politics and music. While Nixon was holding a press conference at the US embassy, Bernstein made his way over. Upon learning that the conductor was there, the vice president offered praise for the musician and spoke fondly about his collection of Bernstein recordings. Never reluctant to engage a crowd, the maestro noted that the two men were on similar missions in Latin America, though he acknowledged Nixon's job was tougher, since the Philharmonic was sharing music while Nixon was discussing tariffs and other less sublime matters. Bernstein praised Nixon for the good job he was doing, and that was that—or so it seemed.[42]

That evening, at a diplomatic dinner, the two wound up next to one another and got to talking about their respective challenges, a conversation Bernstein recalled later with characteristic idealism. "I reported to the Vice President tumultuous receptions; record crowds; cheering, stamping audiences; kisses; roses; embraces; while he reported to me the unpleasant, distasteful incidents" he had endured. Bernstein reflected upon their different experiences. Both were on goodwill missions, after all, and both were "vulnerable to the same demonstrations of anti-Yankee feelings." For Bernstein, the answer was clear. The difference lay "in music: in the exchange of the deepest feelings and revelations of which man is capable—those

Figure 5.3. Leonard Bernstein speaking with Vice President Richard Nixon on the 1958 Latin American tour.
Source: New York Philharmonic Leon Levy Digital Archive.

of art." The conductor invoked the power of music, which he believed could transform the world. "If we are really serious about communicating with one another," he said, serious about "peaceful civilization—then we can never overestimate the good that comes from artistic communication." For Bernstein, the significance of the Philharmonic's global mission was undeniable. "When we touch one another through music," he observed, "we are touching the heart, the mind, and the spirit all at once."[43]

The significance of the orchestra's mission was made clear to the ensemble upon its return from Latin America by the American president and vice president. Writing to the president of the Philharmonic, Dwight Eisenhower emphasized the idealistic component of the trip, praising the orchestra for its "excellent accomplishment" overseas. By sharing its skills with the United States' neighbors to the south, he noted, the country had "drawn closer to the ideal of mutual understanding and friendship which is our goal."[44] More intriguing was the vice president's message, in which Richard Nixon, who had actually become a part of the tour's narrative, spoke not just about his "delight at the success" of the Latin American journey and his wish to see such programs continue. In the days ahead, he said, he hoped America's "friend-making program" would go on, noting that future trips would allow the United States "to reach even deeper into the hearts and minds of our friends around the world."[45] Nixon's choice of words spoke to one of the fundamental aims of the program, which sought to draw the world's peoples, allies in this instance, closer to the United States by using music to appeal to both emotion and reason. In this formulation, the ineffable effect of music could enhance existing relationships between the United States and peoples across the world, who, it was hoped, would link a splendid cultural event to the distinctive attributes of the American political, economic, and social order. Clearly, American policy makers believed that if people perceived an intrinsic connection between art and the American system, this would enhance the country's international position.

With the trip at an end, the artists spoke memorably about its significance. At a welcoming ceremony at New York's City Hall, the Philharmonic's conductors candidly appraised the tour and reflected upon the link between art and politics. Leonard Bernstein contrasted the orchestra's experience with Richard Nixon's, explaining, with a hint of contempt, that his players had come "only to speak music," whereas the "other mission came to present a new policy for the future, and didn't have one." But the Philharmonic had "a mission for all time—Haydn, Gershwin, and so on." Of course, those who clapped for the musicians were "not necessarily" the same people who attacked the vice president, Bernstein said. But the maestro's message was clear: US foreign policy in the region was inadequate, while music had no such limitations. For his part, Dimitri Mitropoulos (a Greek citizen) spoke less critically about the United States, emphasizing, instead, the difference between art and politics. Proclaiming a truism, the distinguished conductor asserted that the "world ha[d] more love for art than for politicians," and concluded with some advice to the diplomats in Washington. Were they clever in seeking to achieve their goals, he said, they would "make more use of the arts."[46]

If the New York Philharmonic's musicians had journeyed to Latin America "only to speak music," as Leonard Bernstein claimed, one wonders what they were trying to say. And in reflecting on that question, one might also ponder matters central to this volume, namely, the extent to which music can illuminate the course of international relations, and, more specifically, whether focusing on music can enrich our understanding of America's concerns during the Cold War. It is clear that US policy makers believed in music's power to influence the contours of world politics, and they were convinced that brilliant performances by distinguished American ensembles could advance the country's diplomatic goals. By sending symphony orchestras to Latin America and Asia, the United States sought to fortify its relations with regions thought vital to American interests in a divided world. It was hoped that the Asian and Latin American journeys would compel friends and allies to realize that liberal capitalism was capable of producing artistic institutions of the highest caliber, which might alter what Dwight Eisenhower had identified as the widespread sense that the United States was better at manufacturing automobiles than "worthwhile cultural works." By playing symphonic music, policy makers believed that Americans could prove they were not simply a "race of materialists" and that that could influence the shape of international politics.

From the perspective of the American musicians who traversed the globe during the Cold War, the evidence suggests something more. While some (or even most) likely supported the United States' diplomatic goals in the East-West struggle, the record points to a different set of motives. In speaking the language of music, as Bernstein put it, American artists hoped to contribute to the creation of a more peaceful international order. Among America's symphonic musicians, many seemed to embrace the notion of the universality of music and believed superb orchestral performances could help transform the character of interstate relations. When the Symphony of the Air played a special outdoor concert in Japan for young people who could not afford tickets to a regular performance, one imagines that altruism, rather than nationalism, inspired them to do so. Indeed, in researching the history of the Cold War symphonic tours, I have been struck by the character of the musician-to-listener encounters that occurred across the world, which evinced the American musicians' sincere belief that their artistic endeavors could help overcome the perils of world politics, their musical labors serving to strengthen the bonds among peoples and nations, whether friend or foe.

As one reflects upon the extent to which music can enrich our understanding of international relations, one must also consider the perspective of those who heard the extraordinary concerts offered by American orchestras. In trying to understand this experience from the listener's vantage point, I would suggest that additional study in local (i.e., overseas) sources is necessary, though it is possible to offer a few observations here. From the material I have examined—overseas and American music reviews, listener comments in the foreign press, and letters sent directly to the ensembles—the response to America's symphonic ambassadors was supremely positive, in both a musical and a humanistic sense. Again and again, listeners, whether professional reviewers or ordinary music lovers, were enthralled upon hearing an American orchestra. Most Latin American or Asian audiences had never encountered performances of such sonic brilliance, instrumental virtuosity, and interpretive depth. While music's emotional power is difficult to measure and its impact hard to quantify, the evidence suggests that the effect on local audiences of attending such concerts was overwhelming.[47]

Finally, one is left to meditate upon the connection between international relations and music. In so doing, I would contend that the history of international relations cannot be disentangled from the subject of human emotions, and I would suggest that the emotions of a people are central to the way nations perceive and, ultimately, interact with one another. The proposition that international relations are intertwined with emotions and perceptions, and that such elusive matters might inform the interactions among states, surely merits further study.[48] What seems clear is that as the US government deployed symphony orchestras around the world to counter the belief that American society was unsophisticated and materialistic, the emotional element inherent in all music resonated in powerful and possibly unfathomable ways with the needs, dreams, and aspirations of listeners across the world. Thousands were awed by what they heard and perhaps inclined to imagine that the American people were not, as many had been told, uncultured barbarians. While such observations are somewhat conjectural, one is on firmer ground in asserting that during a perilous era, the orchestral tours represented a collective cultural enterprise that aimed to utilize music to transform interstate relations and reconfigure the dynamics of world politics. Whether one considers US policy makers, American performers, or listeners in Asia and Latin America, it seems clear that each group, in its own way, believed in music's power to accomplish exactly that.

Notes

1. US Congress, House, Subcommittee on the Committee on Appropriations, *The Supplemental Appropriations Bill, 1956,* 84th Cong., 1st sess., 13, 14, 20 June 1955, p. 388.
2. "Text of Speech by Eisenhower Outlining Proposals for Peace in the World," *New York Times,* 17 April 1953. On the speech, see also James Reston, "Eisenhower Said to Force Hand of Kremlin on Peace," *New York Times,* 17 April 1953.
3. Kenneth Osgood, *Total Cold War: Eisenhower's Secret Propaganda Battle at Home and Abroad* (Lawrence: University Press of Kansas, 2006), 65.
4. Ibid., 217.
5. Osgood convincingly makes this point in his assessment of US perceptions of Soviet policy (ibid.). For an illustration of government officials expressing concern about Soviet cultural policy and the need for an American response, see US Congress, House, Congressmen Richards (South Carolina), Thompson (New Jersey), Udall (Arizona), Judd (New Jersey) speaking on behalf of S. 3116, 84th Cong., 2nd sess., *Congressional Record* 14100-104 (23 July 1956).

6. Dwight Eisenhower to Edgar N. Eisenhower, 22 November 1955, Ann Whitman File, Eisenhower Diary Series, Box 11, Eisenhower Diary-November 1955, Eisenhower Library, Abilene, Kansas. I encountered this source in Osgood's *Total Cold War* and obtained a copy of the document from the Eisenhower Library.
7. Osgood, *Total Cold War*, 218. According to one report, peoples around the world perceived American culture as barren and saw Americans as a "gadget-loving people produced by an exclusively mechanical, technological and materialist civilization." Quoted in Operations Coordinating Board, "Position Paper, President's Emergency Fund for International Affairs," 4 January 1955, OCB Central Files, Box 14, OCB 007 (File #1), Eisenhower Library, Abilene, Kansas. I encountered this source in Osgood's *Total Cold War* and obtained a copy of the document from the Eisenhower Library. On American cultural diplomacy, see two works by Frank Ninkovich: *The Diplomacy of Ideas: U.S. Foreign Policy and Cultural Relations, 1938–1950* (Cambridge: Cambridge University Press, 1981); *U.S. Information Policy and Cultural Diplomacy* (New York: Foreign Policy Association, 1996).
8. Thomas Bender, *A Nation Among Nations: America's Place in World History* (New York: Hill and Wang, 2006), 6–7. On this approach, some key texts include Thomas Bender, ed., *Rethinking American History in a Global Age* (Berkeley: University of California Press, 2002); Ian Tyrrell, *Transnational Nation: United States History in Global Perspective since 1789* (New York: Palgrave, 2007). For more focused studies, see Daniel T. Rodgers, *Atlantic Crossings: Social Politics in a Progressive Age* (Cambridge, MA: Harvard University Press, 1998); Jonathan Rosenberg, *How Far the Promised Land? World Affairs and the American Civil Rights Movement from the First World War to Vietnam* (Princeton, NJ: Princeton University Press, 2006).
9. Quoted in Naima Prevots, *Dance for Export: Cultural Diplomacy and the Cold War* (Middletown, CT: Wesleyan University Press, 1998), 11.
10. Ibid.
11. Debate and discussion on the merits of this approach continued throughout the mid-1950s in congressional committee chambers and on the floor of the US Congress. I examine this in "Fighting the Cold War with Violins and Trumpets: American Symphony Orchestras Abroad in the 1950s," in *Winter Kept Us Warm: Cold War Interactions Reconsidered*, ed. Sari Autio-Sarasmo and Brendan Humphreys (Helsinki: Aleksanteri Cold War Series, 2010), 23–43. Note that my discussion of American policy during this period in this chapter is based on my more extensive treatment in "Fighting the Cold War with Violins and Trumpets."
12. "International Exchange Program," *ANTA Newsletter*, May 1955, 4. See also "Symphony of the Air to Tour Far East Under International Exchange Program," *New York Times*, 23 February 1955.
13. For a description of ANTA, see US Congress, House, Subcommittee on the Committee on Appropriations, *The Supplemental Appropriations Bill, 1956*, 84th Cong., 1st sess., 13, 14, 20 June 1955, pp. 270–72. The most comprehensive history is Mary Widrig John, "ANTA: The American National Theater and Academy, Its First Quarter Century, 1935–1969" (PhD diss., New York University, 1965), esp. 289–302.
14. Howard Taubman, "Orchestra Tours," *New York Times*, 27 February 1955.
15. "Pacific Ambassadors," *Musical America*, June 1955, 4.
16. "Concerts in Tokyo," *New York Times*, 7 May 1955.
17. "Rhee Joins 13,000 at Concert in Seoul to Hear Symphony of the Air Perform," *New York Times*, 27 May 1955. The orchestra played on a special stage constructed by US Army engineers.

18. "Symphony of Air is Heard in Taipei," *New York Times*, 2 June 1955. In Manila, President Ramon Magsaysay was a special guest and patron at one of the concerts, which was attended by three thousand Filipinos. See "Symphony of Air Enchants Manila," *New York Times*, 7 June 1955.
19. US Congress, House, Subcommittee on the Committee on Appropriations, *The Supplemental Appropriations Bill, 1956*, 84th Cong., 1st sess., 13, 14, 20 June 1955, p. 406.
20. Ibid.
21. Ibid., 387.
22. Ibid., 388.
23. Paul Renzi Jr., "Symphony of the Air: Ambassadors of Good Will," *Musical Courier*, June 1955, 19. Renzi was a member of the orchestra's woodwind section.
24. Howard Taubman, "'No End of Jolly,'" *New York Times*, 29 May 1955.
25. Jay Harrison, "Symphony's Tour Brings East Closer," *New York Herald Tribune*, 28 August 1955.
26. US Congress, House, Subcommittee on the Committee on Appropriations, *The Supplemental Appropriations Bill, 1956*, 84th Cong., 1st sess., 13, 14, 20 June 1955, p. 389.
27. On Leonard Bernstein's career and his influence as a conductor and cultural figure, see Humphrey Burton, *Leonard Bernstein* (New York: Doubleday, 1994); Barry Seldes, *Leonard Bernstein: The Political Life of an American Musician* (Berkeley: University of California Press, 2009). On Bernstein's years at the New York Philharmonic, see Howard Shanet, *Philharmonic: A History of New York's Orchestra* (New York: Doubleday, 1975), 333–66. The trip was sponsored by the President's Special International Program for Cultural Presentations, administered by ANTA. The other celebrated trip undertaken by Bernstein and the New York Philharmonic was the 1959 journey to Europe and the Soviet Union. For an examination of that tour, see Rosenberg, "Fighting the Cold War with Violins and Trumpets."
28. See "Philharmonic's Forthcoming Tour of Latin America," 20 February 1958, Box 022-03, Folder 6, New York Philharmonic Archives, Lincoln Center, New York City (hereafter NYPA). See also the agreement (dated 18 April 1958) between the International Cultural Exchange Service of ANTA and the New York Philharmonic, signed by Robert C. Schnitzer (ANTA) and George Judd of the Philharmonic, Box 022-03, Folder 14, NYPA. On the sources of the relatively small amount of corporate funding for the trip, see "Two Corporations Aid Orchestra Tour," *New York Times*, 23 April 1958. The itinerary and programs for each stop on the 1958 tour can be found in Box 022-03, Folder 2, NYPA. My discussion of the Latin American tour in this chapter draws on the following: Jonathan Rosenberg, "An Idealist Abroad," in *Leonard Bernstein, American Original: How a Modern Renaissance Man Transformed Music and the World During His New York Philharmonic Years, 1943–1976*, ed. Burton Bernstein and Barbara B. Haws (New York: Harper Collins, 2008), 117–33.
29. "Celebration in Honor of Forthcoming Latin American Tour Given Bernstein, Mitropoulos and Members of New York Philharmonic," 26 April 1958, Box 022-03, Folder 45, NYPA. The State Department official was James Magdanz, chief of the Cultural Presentations Program staff.
30. "The Philharmonic on Tour," *New York Times*, 30 April 1958.
31. See Carlos Moseley, "The Philharmonic Hath Charms," *New York Times*, 25 May 1958.
32. "New York Philharmonic Tour of Latin America," Box 022003, Folder 18, NYPA. The description of the São Paulo concert is from *Diario de Sao Paulo*, 18 June

1958, which was found in Box 022-03, Folder 13, NYPA. See also "New York Philharmonic Triumphs in South America," *Musical America,* July 1958, 16.
33. "Foreign Service Despatch" from the US embassy in Santiago, Chile, 12 June 1958, Box 022-03, Folder 36, NYPA.
34. "New York Philharmonic Latin American Tour: Excerpts from Press Comments," Lima, Peru, Box 022-03, Folder 18, NYPA. The *La Prensa* editorial was dated 14 May 1958.
35. "Adios Philharmonic! Come Again!" *Caracas Journal,* 4 May 1958. In Quito, Ecuador, a leading paper called the appearance of Bernstein and the orchestra "the most brilliant artistic triumph" the city had ever seen. See "The New York Philharmonic Orchestra: Outstanding Artistic Triumph," *El Comercio* (Quito), 12 May 1958. Both pieces are from "New York Philharmonic Tour: Excerpts from Press Comments," Box 022-03, Folder 6, NYPA.
36. In the manuscript I am preparing, I examine in detail the workings of the Music Advisory Panel. Comprised of scholars, composers, and music critics, the panel wielded considerable power in selecting who would perform (ensembles, soloists, and even conductors) and what would be played. Concerning the orchestral tours, some relevant documents, all of which are held at the Bureau of Educational and Cultural Affairs Historical Collection, J. William Fulbright Papers, University of Arkansas, Fayetteville, include the following: Memorandum to the Music Advisory Panel (hereafter MAP), 10 August 1955, Box 100, folder 1; International Exchange Program, undated (probably 1955), Box 100, folder 1; MAP meeting, 16 October 1957, Box 100, folder 3; MAP, 18 December 1957, Box 100, folder 3; MAP, 15 January 1958, Box 100, folder 2; MAP, 19 February 1958, Box 100, folder 2.
37. See "U.S. Music to be Heard," *New York Philharmonic,* 15 April 1958. Relevant correspondence on this subject includes the following: Robert Schnitzer (ANTA general manager) to Bruno Zirato (managing director of the New York Philharmonic), 26 June 1957, Box 022-03, Folder 22, NYPA; Zirato to Schnitzer, 1 July 1957, Box 022-03, Folder 22, NYPA; Schnitzer to Zirato, 14 November 1957, Box 022-03, Folder 22, NYPA; Schnitzer to Leonard Bernstein, 26 December 1957, Box 022-03, Folder 22, NYPA. In addition, the Music Advisory Panel hoped the orchestra would perform music by Latin American composers while on tour, although a government official assured a New York Philharmonic administrator that playing such music "is only a suggestion, not a requirement." As it happened, the orchestra complied with this request only occasionally. See Schnitzer to Zirato, 26 July 1957, Box 022-03, Folder 22, NYPA.
38. The New York Philharmonic's president, David Keiser, wrote about Bernstein's boundless energy and irrepressible spirit. See Keiser to Bruno Zirato, 30 May 1958, Box 022-03, Folder 3, NYPA. See also Carlo Moseley to Jack (unknown last name), 22 May 1958, Box 022-03, Folder 3, NYPA.
39. On Bernstein's political views, see Seldes, *Leonard Bernstein,* esp. chaps. 2–4.
40. David Keiser to Bruno Zirato, 30 May 1958, Box 022-03, Folder 3, NYPA.
41. On Nixon's trip to Latin America, see Walter LaFeber, *America, Russia, and the Cold War, 1945–2006,* 10th ed. (New York: McGraw Hill, 2008), 214–16; Mark T. Gilderhus, *The Second Century: U.S.-Latin American Relations Since 1889* (Wilmington, DE: Scholarly Resources, 2000), 155–57. See also the following contemporary accounts and perspectives on the Nixon trip: "The Peruvian Incident," *New York Times,* 10 May 1958; "Anti-Nixon Drive Found Concerted," *New York Times,* 10 May 1958; "Eisenhower Hails Nixon's Courage in Peru," *New York Times,* 10 May 1958; "Anti-Nixon Riots Stir U.S. Reviews of Ties to Latins," *New York Times,*

11 May 1958; "Bogota Hails Nixon," *New York Times*, 12 May 1958; "Statements by Eisenhower and Nixon," *New York Times*, 16 May 1958; "Mounting U.S. Troubles: Why and What to Do," *New York Times*, 18 May 1958; "Venezuela: Anti-U.S. Case History," *New York Times*, 18 May 1958; "Beneath the Boiling-Up in South America," *New York Times*, 25 May 1958.

42. The description of the encounter is in a packet of letters from Carlos Moseley to Jack (unknown last name). See the 20 May letter in Box 022-03, Folder 3, NYPA.
43. Quoted in Leonard Bernstein, *Findings* (New York: Simon and Schuster, 1982), 220–21. The *Wall Street Journal* spoke of the contrast between Nixon's experience and that of the New York Philharmonic. See "Music Hath Charms to Please Volatile Latins," *Wall Street Journal*, 15 May 1958. See also "Counterpoint to Caracas," *New York World-Telegram*, 19 May 1958.
44. Dwight Eisenhower to David Keiser, 8 July 1958, Box 022-03, Folder 24, NYPA.
45. Richard Nixon to David Keiser, 8 July 1958, Box 022-03, Folder 23, NYPA.
46. "Musical Diplomacy Called Successful," *New York Times*, 18 June 1958. See also "Orchestra's Tour Ends at City Hall," *New York Times*, 17 June 1958; "City to Welcome Home New York Philharmonic," 13 June 1958, Department of Commerce and Public Events, City of New York, Box 022-03, Folder 45, NYPA; "New York Philharmonic-Symphony Orchestra Welcome Home Ceremony," 16 June 1958, Box 022-03, Folder 18, NYPA.
47. On music and emotion, see Philip Ball, *The Music Instinct: How Music Works and Why We Can't Do Without It* (New York: Oxford University Press, 2010), 254–321; Charles Rosen, *Music and Sentiment* (New Haven, CT: Yale University Press, 2010); Christopher Small, *Musicking: The Meanings of Performing and Listening* (Middletown, CT: Wesleyan University Press, 1998), 130–43; Derek Matravers, "Expression in Music," in *Philosophers on Music: Experience, Meaning, and Work*, ed. Kathleen Stock (New York: Oxford University Press, 2007), 95–116; Paul Boghossian, "Explaining Musical Experience," in Stock, *Philosophers on Music*, 117–29.
48. For a pathbreaking study of music, emotions, and interstate relations, which offers a genuinely novel way of understanding German-American relations, see Jessica C.E. Gienow-Hecht, *Sound Diplomacy: Music and Emotions in Transatlantic Relations, 1850-1920* (Chicago: University of Chicago Press, 2009). See also Jessica C.E. Gienow-Hecht, "Trumpeting Down the Walls of Jericho: The Politics of Art, Music, and Emotion in German-American Relations, 1870-1920," *Journal of Social History* (Spring 2003): 585–613. For a work that illuminates the entanglement of perception, emotion, and interstate behavior during World War II, see John Dower, *War Without Mercy: Race and Power in the Pacific War* (New York: Pantheon, 1986). On the origins of the Cold War, see Frank Costigliola, "'Unceasing Pressure for Penetration': Gender, Pathology, and Emotion in George Kennan's Formation of the Cold War," *Journal of American History* (March 1997): 1309–39. For the work of two political scientists who examine the link between emotion and international politics, see Neta Crawford, "The Passion of World Politics: Propositions on Emotion and Emotional Relationships," *International Security* (Spring 2000): 116-56; Jonathan Mercer, "Human Nature and the First Image: Emotion in International Politics," *Journal of International Relations and Development*, 2006, 9 (288–303). A forum in *Diplomatic History* on music and international affairs is suggestive for its wide-ranging examination of the connections between western classical music and international affairs. See "Special Forum: Musical Diplomacy: Strategies, Agendas, Relationships," *Diplomatic History* 36 (January 2012): 17–75.

Bibliography

Archives

Bureau of Educational and Cultural Affairs Historical Collection, J. William Fulbright Papers, University of Arkansas, Fayetteville

New York Philharmonic Archives, Lincoln Center, New York City

Printed Sources

Ball, Philip. *The Music Instinct: How Music Works and Why We Can't Do Without It.* New York: Oxford University Press, 2010.

Bender, Thomas. *A Nation Among Nations: America's Place in World History.* New York: Hill and Wang, 2006.

———, ed. *Rethinking American History in a Global Age.* Berkeley: University of California Press, 2002.

Bernstein, Leonard. *Findings.* New York: Simon and Schuster, 1982.

Boghossian, Paul. "Explaining Musical Experience." In *Philosophers on Music: Experience, Meaning, and Work,* ed. Kathleen Stock, 117–29. New York: Oxford University Press, 2007.

Burton, Humphrey. *Leonard Bernstein.* New York: Doubleday, 1994.

Dower, John. *War Without Mercy: Race and Power in the Pacific War.* New York: Pantheon, 1986.

Gilderhus, Mark T. *The Second Century: U.S.-Latin American Relations Since 1889.* Wilmington, DE: Scholarly Resources, 2000.

Gienow-Hecht, Jessica C.E. "Trumpeting Down the Walls of Jericho: The Politics of Art, Music, and Emotion in German-American Relations, 1870-1920," *Journal of Social History* (Spring 2003): 585–613.

LaFeber, Walter. *America, Russia, and the Cold War, 1945–2006.* 10th ed. New York: McGraw Hill, 2008.

Matravers, Derek. "Expression in Music." In *Philosophers on Music: Experience, Meaning, and Work,* ed. Kathleen Stock, 95–116. New York: Oxford University Press, 2007.

Ninkovich, Frank. *The Diplomacy of Ideas: U.S. Foreign Policy and Cultural Relations, 1938–1950.* Cambridge: Cambridge University Press, 1981.

———. *U.S. Information Policy and Cultural Diplomacy.* New York: Foreign Policy Association, 1996.

Osgood, Kenneth. *Total Cold War: Eisenhower's Secret Propaganda Battle at Home and Abroad.* Lawrence: University Press of Kansas. 2006.

Prevots, Naima. *Dance for Export: Cultural Diplomacy and the Cold War.* Middletown, CT: Wesleyan University Press, 1998.

Renzi, Paul, Jr. "Symphony of the Air: Ambassadors of Good Will." *Musical Courier* (June 1955): 19.

Rodgers, Daniel T. *Atlantic Crossings: Social Politics in a Progressive Age.* Cambridge, MA: Harvard University Press, 1998.

Rosen, Charles. *Music and Sentiment.* New Haven, CT: Yale University Press, 2010.

Rosenberg, Jonathan. "Fighting the Cold War with Violins and Trumpets: American Symphony Orchestras Abroad in the 1950s." In *Winter Kept Us Warm: Cold War Interactions Reconsidered,* ed. Sari Autio-Sarasmo and Brendan Humphreys, 23–43. Helsinki: Kikimora Publications, 2010.

———. *How Far the Promised Land? World Affairs and the American Civil Rights Movement from the First World War to Vietnam.* Princeton, NJ: Princeton University Press, 2006.

———. "An Idealist Abroad." In *Leonard Bernstein, American Original: How a Modern Renaissance Man Transformed Music and the World During His New York Philharmonic Years, 1943–1976,* ed. Burton Bernstein and Barbara B. Haws, 117–33. New York: Harper Collins, 2008.

Seldes, Barry. *Leonard Bernstein: The Political Life of an American Musician.* Berkeley: University of California Press, 2009.

Shanet, Howard. *Philharmonic: A History of New York's Orchestra.* New York: Doubleday, 1975.

Small, Christopher. *Musicking: The Meanings of Performing and Listening.* Middletown, CT: Wesleyan University Press, 1998.

Tyrrell, Ian. *Transnational Nation: United States History in Global Perspective since 1789.* New York: Palgrave, 2007.

US Congress, House. Congressmen Richards (South Carolina), Thompson (New Jersey), Udall (Arizona), Judd (New Jersey) speaking on behalf of S. 3116, 84th Cong., 2nd sess. *Congressional Record* 14100-104 (23 July 1956).

US Congress, House, Subcommittee on the Committee on Appropriations. *The Supplemental Appropriations Bill, 1956.* 84th Cong., 1st sess., 13, 14, 20 June 1955.

Widrig John, Mary. "ANTA: The American National Theater and Academy, Its First Quarter Century, 1935–1969." PhD diss., New York University, 1965.

Chapter Six

MUSIC DIPLOMACY IN AN EMERGENCY
Eisenhower's "Secret Weapon," Iceland, 1954–59

Emily Abrams Ansari

Under President Eisenhower, the United States government orchestrated the best-funded and most far-reaching program of music diplomacy in its history. Through the State Department's Cultural Presentations Program, American orchestras, choirs, soloists, jazz bands, and folk groups were heard in concert halls across the globe. For many in Washington DC, the program's aims were long term—building friendship and nurturing respect for the United States to build Cold War alliances—a feature that differentiated it from the more short-term, strategically motivated information programs.[1] In 1954, such attitudes led Eisenhower to grant responsibility for short-term psychological warfare to a newly created organization, the United States Information Agency, while the State Department retained control over cultural and educational exchanges, including those involving the arts.

Most of the existing studies of Eisenhower's Cold War music diplomacy focus on these friendship-building State Department tours, employing archival materials housed at the University of Arkansas at Fayetteville to assess music's role in the cultural Cold War.[2] While the State Department was certainly the most important facilitator of US music diplomacy, the almost exclusive focus on its programs has led scholars to overlook musical deployments intended to address urgent foreign relations crises, which essentially bypassed State De-

---

Notes for this section begin on page 183.

partment procedures. These unusual tours were controlled directly by the Operations Coordinating Board (OCB), an executive committee that reported to the National Security Council (NSC). Documentation of the OCB's activities in the realm of music diplomacy can be found in the Eisenhower Presidential Library. This collection has been little utilized in the study of Cold War music diplomacy, although it offers revealing insights into one US president's awareness of music's ability to shape international relations. Meanwhile, the emergency tours documented in the collection show that Eisenhower and his staff thought of music as something capable of achieving very immediate and significant psychological results, in addition to more incremental changes in attitude.

When Eisenhower spoke in public about music diplomacy, he tended to emphasize the affective impact of the art form. Music, as he understood it, had social power, which meant that musicians had "a very special responsibility."

> They express America's concepts of beauty, decency, and morality. ... Theirs is a vital responsibility because it affects the morale of our country, indeed, it affects our soul. Artists fully aware of and dedicated to their responsibility strengthen our national spirit. Artists cognizant of their opportunity and willing to seize it contribute to our national aspirations.[3]

In his speeches as president, Eisenhower used similarly evocative language to describe the effect of tours by musicians and other cultural leaders, which, he said, were poised to "contribute to the better understanding of the peoples of the world that must be the foundation of peace."[4]

While Eisenhower clearly believed that music could help make the world a better place, his correspondence with Washington insiders and other confidantes speaks much more overtly of its potential uses for addressing the United States' current international challenges. Music, he argued, could be used to the nation's advantage overseas because it possessed the ability to change attitudes. To Vice President Richard Nixon, Eisenhower wrote that arts diplomacy could demonstrate "the superiority of the products and cultural values of our system of free enterprise."[5] Similarly, he encouraged Secretary of State John Foster Dulles to broaden his conception of psychological warfare to include "the singing of a beautiful hymn."[6] A 1955 letter to his brother Edgar provides a particularly far-reaching description of the political benefits of "using musicians in our propaganda work abroad":

> It is possible that you do not understand how ignorant most of the world is about America and how important it is to us that some of the misunderstanding be corrected. One of them involves our cultural standards and our artistic tastes. Europeans have been taught that we are a race of materialists.... Our successes are described in terms of automobiles and not in terms of worthwhile cultural works of any kind. Spiritual and intellectual values are deemed to be almost non-existent in our country.
>
> This picture of their misunderstanding is not overdrawn—in fact, in some areas we are believed to be bombastic, jingoistic, and totally devoted to the theories of force and power as the only worthwhile elements in the world....
>
> One of the ways to help is to send abroad some of our better productions in the fields of dramatics, music, painting and the like.[7]

Thus, for Eisenhower, the most significant purpose of musical propaganda in an era of ideological competition was to communicate an image of the United States that could effect international political change.

Leading figures close to Eisenhower made similarly bold assertions about music's capabilities as a tool of psychological warfare. Senior White House staff member Elmer Staats, for example, described it as "a secret weapon" in the Cold War context, capable of attracting foreigners to the United States.[8] For Staats, music had benefits that written propaganda did not because it is "direct and speaks for itself."[9] Other White House documents argued that music was able to depict key characteristics of the United States to foreigners, including: "basic American spiritual values and motivations";[10] "our democratic values in education, our freedom in creative expression, American opportunities for self-development without regard to social, racial or religious origin";[11] and the United States' commitment to international "cultural cooperation."[12] Music could also help shatter stereotypes of Americans as "preeminently a gadget-loving people."[13] According to one White House memo, such negative preconceptions about American ability, creativity, and opportunity had unfortunately brought about "a distrust of American preparedness for world leadership."[14] The best way to reduce this distrust, according to another report, was to initiate programs that would help build "respect and prestige" for the United States abroad.[15]

Ultimately, of course, we can gain the greatest insights into the Eisenhower administration's political perspective on music by examining its use in specific international situations, especially those that were controlled by top officials. While the State Department tours allowed for somewhat limited OCB involvement, since they were arranged through the American National Theatre and Academy (ANTA) and its panels of private citizen experts, emergency situations would sometimes lead the OCB to coordinate their own tours directly.[16] Shawn Parry-Giles sees the OCB as the controlling force in an unusually "militarized" structure for propagandistic activities under Eisenhower. This structure "virtually eliminated congressional oversight, allowing Eisenhower and his closest advisers to oversee and coordinate his international message through the various government bodies responsible for propagating it."[17] In this context, OCB-organized tours can reveal much about attitudes to music among officials at the very top of the Eisenhower administration.

This chapter examines one such emergency deployment of music by Eisenhower's OCB, extending our understanding of Eisenhower's belief in music's powers as a tool of persuasion. The crisis in relations between the United States and Iceland in the mid-1950s demonstrates that Eisenhower and his staff not only thought of this art form as a long-term friendship builder, but also as a device that could be used in short-term crisis management. In midcentury Iceland, music not only helped in the hasty reorientation of an international relation. It also contributed to both the articulation of Cold War power and resistance to it.

Music Diplomacy and the Iceland Crisis

Throughout the Cold War, US foreign relations experts devoted large amounts of their time to neutral or communist-leaning countries because these were the places where the global reach of the Kremlin might most easily be expanded.[18] Iceland was one such country. Despite its small population, an alliance with Iceland was highly desirable to both superpowers because of its location. As an unnamed military strategist explained to the *Washington Post* in 1956:

> Stand in the middle of Iceland and look toward Moscow.... You're just about halfway between New York and Moscow. Take a right face, and there's Britain less than 1000 miles away; another right face and there's New York, 2400 miles; another, and there's Greenland, with other important bases, less than three hours' flying time away. Iceland is a vital link in our NATO defense base chain.[19]

The United States had a history of close relations with Iceland, but also a history of Icelandic opposition to the presence they wished to secure there. During World War II, the United States had taken responsibility for Iceland's defense, but nationalist and neutralist sentiments grew with the country's independence from Denmark in 1944 and the end of the hostilities on the Continent. This led many Icelanders to demand that the American forces stationed on the island be sent home. Meanwhile, as the Cold War began, the Soviets worked hard to bolster growing support for communism in Iceland by purchasing massive stocks of fish—the country's principal export. American journalists were fearful about where such assistance might lead, speculating that if the USSR gained a strong footing in Iceland, "submarines and aircraft could turn the North Atlantic into a Soviet lake."[20] In 1951 the North Atlantic Treaty Organization (NATO) finally persuaded the Icelandic parliament to sign a treaty that gave the United States responsibility for Iceland's defense as representatives of NATO. Almost immediately, several thousand US personnel arrived to establish an Air Force base in the southwestern coastal town of Keflavík.[21]

The growing Keflavík base quickly became controversial among Icelanders concerned about the Americanization of their country. Nationalists, communists, and, increasingly, the more centrist Progressive Party and Social Democratic Party all argued that the base brought unwanted foreign control and influence: the communist People's Alliance Party, for example, spoke regularly of the need to "rid Iceland of its colonial fetters."[22] Such expressions of nationalism, which White House staff construed as "fanatic," were not only the result of the country's recent independence.[23] They also rested on a long history of pride in its Viking roots, its language, and its traditions.[24] Particularly troubling to many was the interaction of American soldiers with Icelandic women in Keflavík. The resulting relationships sometimes led to marriage and thereafter the departure of young Icelandic brides for the United States, including one winner of the Miss Iceland competition (see figure 6.1).[25] Icelanders were deeply troubled by any emigration from Iceland because of the small size of their population (around 160,000). Their opposition to such marriages was also a consequence of a strong patriarchal tradition, which revered women and prioritized their protection.[26] In a study of postwar Germany, Petra Goedde has argued that American soldiers "feminized" that defeated nation by defying bans on fraternizing with local women and assuming the role of protectors in the absence of the millions of young German men lost in the war.[27] Icelandic nationalists recognized a similarly "masculine," protectionist stance among American servicemen in their country, an attitude that injured their national pride.

Alongside these sociological effects, the base also brought undesired cultural influences. Like many other Europeans, Icelanders

Figure 6.1. Sergeant Haddix and Miss Iceland.
Source: Demaree Bess, "Uncle Sam's Reluctant Ally," *Saturday Evening Post,* 29 December 1956.

were profoundly troubled by the steady influx of American media and popular music into their country, a flow only hastened by the military presence.[28] American television became available in Iceland in 1955, when the US Department of Defense began transmitting programming for the entertainment of the troops through channels that were also accessible to local people. Since no Icelandic channels yet existed, American shows defined many Icelanders' first interactions with the new medium, much to the horror of nationalists.[29] Another ongoing problem was the broadcasts of bebop from the base's radio station, which again was intended for the troops but receivable on local radios.[30] For a proportion of Icelanders, these American popular culture products represented a threat to their way of life. As a 1951 editorial in the Icelandic newspaper *Tíminn* argued, "[I]t is a fact that Iceland's culture is not so strong that it can resist all foreign influence represented by the troops."[31] NSC staff correctly recognized that these objections posed a threat to the American presence in Iceland, as this 1954 memo enclosure demonstrates: "There is a real fear among older Icelanders that their one thousand-year-old language and culture will be corrupted by the impact of the Americans on their population of less than 160,000. They are exceedingly sensitive about anything that happens at the Keflavík base that might change the island's life."[32]

The growing backlash against a perceived American sociocultural invasion meant that by the mid-1950s the presence of the base, as one White House document stated, was "by far the most important foreign policy issue in Iceland and usually also the most prominent domestic issue."[33] While Iceland's politicians debated the appropriate course of action, its people built a fence around the base and introduced a pass system (see figure 6.2). This fence, as one NSC document recorded, was "not intended to keep intruders out, but rather to keep the G.I.'s in—to 'protect' Icelanders from too much contact with Americans."[34] These restrictions were more severe than at any other US base in Europe, making Keflavík one of the least popular places to be posted.[35]

The OCB decided to respond to these concerns about American cultural imperialism in Iceland with a heavy dose of cultural diplomacy. In July 1954, a White House National Security Council State-

Figure 6.2. The fence at Keflavík.
Source: Demaree Bess, "Uncle Sam's Reluctant Ally," *Saturday Evening Post,* 29 December 1956.

ment of Policy on Iceland (NSC 5426) laid out a series of strategies for reducing Icelandic anti-Americanism, which included the use of touring musicians. The ultimate goal, according to the document, was to maintain Iceland "as an independent and economically viable nation with a stable government friendly to the United States and actively cooperating in NATO defense efforts." Thirteen courses of action were proposed, listed in abbreviated form in table 6.1. Projects pertaining to culture were numbers five and six on the list, where "stop-over visits by U.S. concert artists and leaders" were specifically suggested.

With the OCB retaining control over the actual projects resulting from this list, the State Department and its advisers were left out of the loop, despite the heavy emphasis on music.[36] Indeed, one-third of the projects proposed on an early list of possible actions were music-related.[37] OCB strategic documents called for "concerts in Iceland by at least four prominent artists per year and an equal number of promising young artists." "To the extent possible," this same report urged, "encourage these artists to give concerts in outlying communities as well as in Reykjavík."[38]

The OCB's decision to emphasize music resulted in a massive influx of American musicians—notably only classical musicians—into this small island nation in the mid- to late 1950s. Visiting ensembles

Table 6.1. NSC 5426, Statement of Policy on Iceland: Courses of action (abbreviated from original)

1. Adhere to Defense Agreement of 1951, taking into account Iceland's special circumstances
2. Promote harmonious relations in carrying out military activities
3. Encourage Icelandic participation in NATO
4. Continue US technical assistance, especially regarding labor relations
5. Maintain intensified USIA program
6. Strengthen US-Icelandic cultural relations
7. Increase trade
8. Increase fish markets
9. Economic assistance
10. Assist Iceland in obtaining US credit
11. Prepare to assist in case of war
12. Avoid appearing to lead an attack at the United Nations on Iceland's position on territorial waters
13. [Redacted]
Source: Draft Statement of Policy proposed by the National Security Council on Iceland, NSC 5426, 12 July 1954, White House Office, NSC Staff, Papers, 1948–61, Disaster Series, Box 49, Iceland (1), EPL.

included the Air Force Symphony, the Robert Shaw Chorale, and various chamber groups drawn from the Boston Symphony Orchestra. Because flights to Iceland were only possible by military plane and were thus expensive, solo recitals were particularly frequent, performed by musicians such as James Wolfe and Ervin Laszlo (both pianists); Betty Allen, Robert McFerrin, and Blanche Thebom (opera singers); and Jeanne Mitchell, Roman Totenberg, and Isaac Stern (violinists). These musicians played well-known European classical repertoire and also fulfilled a mandate of the State Department's Cultural Presentations Program, which required an American work at every concert.

The photograph reproduced as figure 6.3, which shows three brass players from the Boston Symphony Orchestra being transported to Iceland in a military aircraft, evokes the mind-set underlying Eisenhower's deployment of musicians. Each musician practices his instrument amid the military paraphernalia of a US Air Force plane, powerfully demonstrating music's co-optation as a weapon of

Figure 6.3. Boston Symphony Orchestra musicians en route to Iceland, 1956. Roger Voisin (trumpet), Ralph Pottle (horn), and Arthur Kerr (trombone). Photographer unknown.
Source: Boston Symphony Orchestra Archives.

war during the 1950s and the militarization, as Parry-Giles describes it, of US propaganda under Eisenhower's watch.[39] In this image, musicians and their instruments occupy a space normally reserved for servicemen and their weapons. These performers are part of Eisenhower's Cold War army of private citizens—cultural diplomats employed to safeguard the future of a military alliance essential to US and NATO security.

The wording of NSC flight requests provides more concrete evidence that Eisenhower's security officials saw the music program in Iceland as an American defense tool. After violinist Isaac Stern toured Iceland in January 1955, he decided to donate a set of high-fidelity record playing equipment to the University of Iceland. The OCB asked the Military Air Transport Service to transport both the machinery and a technician to install it, justifying the cost by claiming that the donation was "considered of importance in our effort to win over Icelandic university students, among whom anti-defense propaganda has made considerable headway."[40] In this case, granting young people access to recorded sound is construed as a military opportunity. The writer of this document also used militaristic language to justify the use of similar transportation for touring musicians: these men and women were needed in Iceland in order to "counter" the Soviet Union's "cultural offensive."[41]

The Icelandic tours made by various groups formed from within the Boston Symphony Orchestra (BSO) serve as particularly illuminating case studies for exploring OCB goals in Iceland. The State Department was forced to rule out an extension to Iceland of the BSO's 1956 tour of Europe due to the very high cost of transportation.[42] Nevertheless, BSO musicians performed frequently in Iceland between 1954 and 1958. First, the orchestra's organist, E. Power Biggs, toured Iceland as a soloist in 1954.[43] A year later, he returned to the island with seven first-chair BSO instrumentalists.[44] In 1956, several of these musicians returned once again, bringing along additional BSO colleagues. Rather remarkably, inclement weather at the end of this tour resulted in the creation of an entirely new ensemble. Stuck in Reykjavík for three days, George Humphrey (viola) and Carl Zeise (cello) found themselves playing string quartets with Björn Ólafsson and Jón Sen, concertmaster and assistant concertmaster of the Iceland Symphony Orchestra. The foursome enjoyed the experience immensely and pondered opportunities to repeat it. On his return to the United States, Humphrey traveled to Washington, where he pitched to officials a tour of Iceland by an "American-Icelandic String Quartet"—a concept he likely knew would be recognized as a potent political vehicle. He was right, and the foursome received money from the US taxpayer to tour first Iceland in 1958 and then a host of Icelandic immigrant towns in the United States in 1959.⁴⁵

These various BSO-connected ensembles visited an extensive network of cities, towns, and villages in Iceland, helping to demonstrate American cultural achievements to a wide array of Icelandic voters. During the 1955 tour, the musicians took part in solo concerto performances with the national orchestra in Reykjavík and undertook chamber ensemble tours of outlying communities.⁴⁶ The larger group that came the following year performed concerts in the capital and then split into two groups, with six musicians touring the east of Iceland and five the west.⁴⁷ The Icelandic-American String Quartet similarly aimed for a wide geographic reach, playing fifteen concerts in eighteen days in small towns across Iceland. "Unbelievably," George Humphrey writes in his autobiography, "each concert was attended by a good 90 percent of the towns' populations."⁴⁸ These itineraries demonstrate that White House and State Department officials were not only interested in wooing political and cultural leaders in Iceland's major cities, as they were in some other countries, but instead sought a nationwide attitude change among the voting public through an art form that most Icelanders already appreciated.

The US embassy in Reykjavík worked hard to ensure an organizational structure for these concerts that demonstrated respect for Icelandic attitudes and sensibilities, presumably in the hope of counterbalancing the perceived bad behavior of US servicemen. The US ambassador John Muccio had noticed that the "independent" Icelanders felt uncomfortable with the Soviets' free concerts. He therefore suggested that the first BSO touring group charge a small sum for tickets—high enough to avoid denting Icelandic pride but low enough to be affordable to most. The result, Humphrey writes, was that they "were besieged to the point where each of [the] concerts was sold out, a very different result from the Russian giveaway of their attractions."⁴⁹

Of all the groups that toured, the Icelandic-American String Quartet sheds the most light on US policy toward Iceland because it owed its very existence to the United States' cultural diplomatic strategy. A crucial source in this narrative is a letter from cellist Humphrey to C. D. Jackson, who was both a BSO trustee and one of Eisenhower's most trusted propaganda advisers. Humphrey explained to Jackson that the State Department had funded only the Icelandic members of the quartet, and not the Americans, for their US tour in 1959. This is not surprising, because the Smith-Mundt Act of 1948 had prohibited government departments from directing any American Cold War propaganda toward the American people. The Icelanders, by contrast, could be justified as exchange participants. Indeed, the State Department very much wanted the US tour to go ahead. According to Humphrey's letter, the American members' travel costs were therefore covered by the Farfield Foundation—an organization that, it later transpired, was a dummy foundation funneling Central Intelligence Agency (CIA) money.[50] In his autobiography, however, Humphrey complicated this account, claiming that "a gentleman" named James Lombard was the principal financial contributor to their tour.[51] He added that State Department staff had told the group that they would cover their travel expenses, but that the rules changed during their tour, leaving them out of pocket.[52] Despite this confusing picture, it is quite possible that all of these individuals and organizations played a role in funding the quartet's US tour. Cultural diplomatic staff across Washington frequently turned to covert funding and private donors when overt funding was illegal or otherwise politically problematic.[53]

Because of the quartet's success in the United States and Iceland and its members' awareness of their political usefulness, Humphrey decided that the quartet's next destination should be the Soviet Union. In the spirit of the group, they hoped to find a Russian pianist who might join them on the tour: the work Humphrey had in mind for performance was the Shostakovich Piano Quintet.[54] Initially, according to Humphrey, enthusiasm for the tour within the State Department was "instantaneous."[55] Soon, however, the director of the State Department's Cultural Presentations Program, James Magdanz, told Humphrey that the tour would not, in fact, be possible. According to Humphrey, Magdanz said that because the USSR placed such strict limits on artistic exchange between the two countries, the State Department must restrict their presentations to those that represented a "purely American achievement." Magdanz wrote that he did not believe the quartet could "reasonably qualify" for State Department sponsorship to visit any country other than Iceland because only half of the group was American. Indeed, Humphrey continues, Magdanz "did not suggest that there was anything admirable to the plan" for a Soviet tour: clearly he was only interested in utilizing the quartet's ability to demonstrate Icelandic-American friendship to Icelanders.[56]

Nevertheless, the organization charged by the State Department with arranging the tours and organizing the advisory panels that approved them, ANTA, apparently felt differently about the quartet's potential as a diplomatic tool. ANTA's general manager, Robert Schnitzer, told Humphrey that he would put him in touch with "foundations which might see the project through."[57] Yet ultimately Humphrey's efforts to obtain assistance, including his letter to Jackson, were all in vain: US diplomatic relations with the USSR changed dramatically on 1 May 1960, when an American U-2 plane was brought down over Russia, bringing a swift end to discussions about the tour.[58]

The Icelandic-American String Quartet's successful and unsuccessful tour bids demonstrate the limited political circumstances in which foreign relations experts considered music propaganda to be useful and/or fundable through overt government channels. The State Department, White House, and CIA supported the quartet's visits to Iceland and to Icelandic immigrant strongholds in the United States, believing the group could transmit Eisenhower's urgently needed message of respect and friendship to Icelandic citizens and their international relatives while showing that the United States shared their commitment to high art. Yet this message was only deemed politically beneficial to the United States when shared with Icelanders and the Icelandic diaspora. Washington had no interest in bringing the quartet's powerful symbolic depiction of Icelandic-American friendship to a broad cross section of Americans or, indeed, to European or Soviet audiences.

Music's Message

So what was classical music's message to Iceland and why was the art form so frequently utilized by Eisenhower's OCB? One significant reason for the classical emphasis was the success of recent musical missions to Iceland initiated by the Soviet Union and other communist nations; indeed, most US cultural diplomacy was reactive rather than proactive. By 1956, the volume of attractions sent from communist countries to Iceland was strikingly high. The NSC was particularly concerned about the vast arts program run by the Soviet-Icelandic Cultural Society, which "provide[s] ample cover for domestic and Soviet agents to make contact in the country."[59] Another White House report from 1956 noted that the People's Republic of China had recently sent the Peking Opera Company to Reykjavík, while Poland would shortly send four of its own musicians.[60] By responding in kind to communist attractions, the Americans showed the Icelanders that a democratic, capitalist society like the United States could produce great works of art as well as the popular culture that some despised.

The OCB strategy was also an attempt to demonstrate shared cultural values, because the Icelanders were known to hold classical music in high esteem. A 1955 article entitled "Music vs. Guns" by US Congressman Carroll D. Kearns (R-PA) demonstrates that officials in Washington were well aware that political opportunities to better relations with Iceland could be created if the United States emphasized its commitment to European traditions of high art. Having recently returned from a trip to Iceland with the US Air Force, Kearns argued that American classical music could help the United States regain the Icelanders' respect. The Icelanders, he wrote, were "a highly cultured people" with "the oldest Parliament in the world"; they were "real lovers of music," with "critics ... as astute and discriminating as any ... in New York."[61] Kearns's article is rooted in the long-standing European attitude that "highly cultured," "discriminating" people are inevitably lovers of Western classical music. If the United States could demonstrate that it also valued high culture, the theory went, Icelanders were more likely to feel a connection to it. Receiving this message through high-quality classical music performances across their country, Icelanders would simultaneously be shown the great cultural benefits they might enjoy through a continued alliance with the United States.

Third, in deploying only classical stars, White House staff attempted to prove that the United States had absolutely no intention of dominating Iceland culturally through the Air Force base. White House security documents make plain that this was a major strategic priority, describing the urgent need to "demonstrate the non-imperialistic nature of U.S. political actions and the friendship and sympathy of the people of the U.S. towards Iceland."[62] By offsetting the presence of bebop on the local radio station with concerts of classical music, it was hoped that cultural traditionalists might be appeased. This group represented the greatest threat to the American military presence, hence the decision to prioritize their tastes over those of younger audiences who enjoyed American popular music.

Local objections to bebop in particular may well have been influenced by Icelandic racism, given bebop's roots in African American musical traditions. Racism was at the root of much Icelandic nationalist sentiment, fueled by a desire to keep Norse bloodlines and traditions untarnished. US officials had historically proven themselves more than willing to accommodate such attitudes. From World War II through the 1970s, the government of Iceland refused to permit African American soldiers to be posted to the US base in Keflavík: Valur Ingimundarson has argued that "the presence of blacks was seen as posing a direct threat to Icelandic women and, by extension, to the Icelandic nation."⁶³ Very unusually and very quietly, the United States agreed to this stipulation because of Iceland's strategic importance, despite refusing similar requests from other countries after 1950.⁶⁴

In this context, it seems rather unsurprising that the US government favored classical music over jazz for Iceland, even as black jazz musicians were sent to a host of other countries from 1956 onward.⁶⁵ In sending only classical music and not jazz, it initially appears that Eisenhower was further emphasizing the message implied by his deferment to Iceland's policy on black soldiers: that he was willing to respect Iceland's cultural and racial biases, however offensive Americans might find them, in exchange for their allegiance. The story is not quite this straightforward, however, because the State Department did in fact send several black opera singers to the island. An Iceland tour was planned for Marian Anderson in 1954, but this was called off because of her debut at the Metropolitan Opera.⁶⁶ Over subsequent years, the African American baritone Robert McFerrin (1958) and mezzo-soprano Betty Allen (1960) performed in highly acclaimed tours.⁶⁷ No government documents explain why these African American stars were chosen for tours while popular jazz musicians were not sent, but a number of possible reasons suggest themselves. Officials in Washington may have hoped that the sight of black musicians performing in a widely respected style might gently encourage Iceland to reconsider its policy on black soldiers, which they knew would cause a storm of controversy if the American public learned of it.⁶⁸ At the same time, black classical musicians, like their colleagues in jazz, served to counterbalance global media reports of American racial inequality, which had significantly undermined efforts to build international respect for the United States.⁶⁹

As Richard Nelson and Foad Izadi have put it, American public diplomacy has been consistently characterized by "image building rather than ... genuine dialogue and symmetrical relationships."⁷⁰ In funding a one-way deployment of American classical musicians, officials in Washington attempted to show the Icelanders that the United States respected their nation's traditions and understood their concerns about cultural infiltration from overseas. As a result, the picture of American culture presented to the Icelanders was left deliberately incomplete in order to accomplish vital political objectives in the fastest time possible.

Ultimately the United States was successful in averting Icelandic efforts to close the Keflavík base. The crisis came to a head with the June 1956 election, when Iceland's three left-wing parties robbed the Conservative Party of its apparent victory by forming a coalition, unified by their commitment to investigating the closure of the base. Two events that occurred shortly thereafter, however, brought a sudden end to the debate. First, the US government agreed to help Iceland out of an impending financial crisis with millions of dollars in grants and loans.[71] Second, in the fall of 1956 the Soviets invaded Budapest to suppress the Hungarian Revolution, a move that significantly reduced Icelandic support for communism.[72] At the same time, the parties now in power had begun to realize that there was more public support for the base, which brought many financial and security benefits, than they had previously thought.[73] Money and international developments thus played the most significant roles in ensuring the survival of the base, not music.

Nevertheless, OCB progress reports made the case that the American cultural program had made the Icelanders feel less ambivalent about their decision to permit a continued American presence in Keflavík.[74] Even as early as the end of 1955, a poll conducted via a third country for the USIA showed that the "prestige" of the United States and its culture was, in the eyes of the Icelanders, "way above Russia," suggesting that the first cultural missions had had the desired effect.[75] Reviews of individual concerts also spoke to the positive reception of American cultural attractions: one audience that heard baritone Robert McFerrin, for example, was reported to have been "enraptured."[76] A growing appreciation for US culture and values thus appeared to the OCB to have sweetened the American bribe. The touring musicians had seemingly been quite successful in transmitting Eisenhower's message that the United States was both culturally sophisticated and respectful of the aesthetic preferences of other nations.

Yet, of course, not all Icelanders were delighted with Eisenhower's cultural campaign. Many on the political left saw straight through Eisenhower's musical messengers, as is demonstrated by this excerpt from a 1954 article in a socialist newspaper:

> The U.S. Air Force Band was not here in the service of noble art. It is made up of men who obey military discipline and they were ordered here only as sly propaganda for the occupation. Their goal was to try to diminish the public opposition to the foreign army, to increase communication between Icelanders and the military forces.... The money raised by these warriors [for Icelandic charities] is stained with the shame and humiliation of the military settlement.[77]

Another journalist for the same paper used biting sarcasm to describe the patronizing and "outrageously simplistic speeches" made by Congressman Kearns during his tour of Iceland in support of the US presence there: "Before the U.S. Air Force orchestra played its concerts in Reykjavík this spring, Icelanders believed that the U.S. was populated with savage barbarians, who excelled in nothing but killing other people. This tidbit on the cultural level of Icelanders is brought to us by the American senator who joined the orchestra here."[78] Although these sources show that many disinclined toward the US occupation mocked the message from Eisenhower communicated through the tours, they also make clear that the message itself was getting through. Whether or not individual Icelanders wanted to hear Eisenhower's desperate plea for friendship and collaboration, by 1956 enough Icelanders were willing to listen to ensure the survival of the base.

If OCB officials sought to demonstrate to the Icelanders that the United States had no "imperialistic" intentions toward their country, we can only assume that these same officials considered classical music, in contrast to the popular songs dispersed via the Air Force base's radio station, to be without "imperialistic" features. If not, they would surely have found a covertly funded vehicle to bring American musicians to the island to avoid exacerbating the situation. Their apparent attitude demonstrates the prevalence of a commonly held view that classical music exists apart from capitalism, which is, of course, the political system that enables cultural imperialism. That is, they understood art and commerce to be entirely distinct entities. Conceptualized in such terms, classical music cannot possibly serve an imperialistic purpose, making it appear a particularly attractive, and thus effective, mechanism for persuasion. American insecurities about national contributions to high art may also have been at play, encouraging political leaders to think of American classical music as something that could only ever appear "friendly" and never culturally dominating or manipulative.

This kind of foreign policy strategy would today be called "smart power": "the ability to combine the hard power of coercion or payment with the soft power of attraction into a successful strategy," according to Joseph Nye's recent definition.[79] In seeking this "attraction," officials in Washington employed "nonimperialistic" classical musicians to assuage concern about "imperialistic" bebop and cross-national intermarriage. How ironic, therefore, that what this deployment actually represented was an imperialistic move far more deliberate and calculated than any of the offense-causing bebop records and TV shows that the classical concerts were intended to outweigh. Sent to convince the Icelanders that Americans shared their values and did not seek to dominate them, these musicians were used to ensure continued US control and influence in Iceland. Eisenhower's musical messengers, innocent and charming as they may have appeared to many Icelandic audience members, in fact served as vital mechanisms of coercion. In neutral countries like Iceland, these men and women were as essential as any military tool in Eisenhower's arsenal.

The United States' short-lived musical bombardment of Iceland in the late 1950s shows that artistic, cultural, and political interactions were consistently intertwined in the history of relations between these two countries. Of course, Icelandic-US relations were far from unique in this respect, especially during the Cold War, when international cultural dialogues were never merely a sideline to major policy decisions and actions. Indeed, as the case of Iceland proves, they were sometimes sufficiently significant that they could derail an international relation—or get a relationship back on track.

Notes

1. The nature of this separation is described in detail in Hans N. Tuch, *Communicating with the World: U.S. Public Diplomacy Overseas* (New York: St. Martin's Press, 1990), 18–21; Richard T. Arndt, *The First Resort of Kings: American Cultural Diplomacy in the Twentieth Century* (Washington DC: Potomac Books, 2005), 255–78.
2. For example, see Lisa E. Davenport, *Jazz Diplomacy: Promoting America in the Cold War Era* (Jackson: University Press of Mississippi, 2009); Penny Von Eschen, *Satchmo Blows Up the World: Jazz Ambassadors Play the Cold War* (Cambridge, MA: Harvard University Press, 2004); Danielle Fosler-Lussier, "Cultural Diplomacy as Cultural Globalization: The University of Michigan Jazz Band in Latin America," *Journal of the Society for American Music* 4, no. 1 (February 2010): 59–93; Emily Abrams Ansari, "'Masters of the President's Music': Cold War Composers and the United States Government" (PhD diss., Harvard University, 2010).
3. Dwight D. Eisenhower, "The Creative Purpose," in *Creative America,* by John F. Kennedy et al. (New York: Ridge Press, 1962), 109.
4. Dwight D. Eisenhower, quoted in press release from James C. Hagerty, Press Secretary to the President, 29 June 1956, White House Office, National Security Council (NSC) Staff, Papers, 1948–61, Operations Coordinating Board (OCB) Central File Series, Box 18, OCB 141.31 (5), Dwight D. Eisenhower Presidential Library, Abilene, Kansas (hereafter EPL).
5. Dwight D. Eisenhower to the President of the Senate, 27 July 1954, White House Office, NSC Staff, Papers, 1948–61, OCB Central File Series, Box 14, OCB 007 (File #1) (1)–(8), EPL.
6. Memo from Dwight D. Eisenhower to the Secretary of State, 24 October 1953, C. D. Jackson Papers, 1931–67, Box 50, Eisenhower, Dwight D.—Correspondence, 1953 (1), EPL.

7. Dwight D. Eisenhower to Edgar Eisenhower, 22 November 1955, Eisenhower, Dwight D., Papers as President, 1953–61, DDE Diary Series, Box 11, DDE Diary—November, 1955 (1), EPL.
8. Memo, Elmer B. Staats to Dale O. Smith, Subject: Briefing Notes on Porgy & Bess to Moscow, 19 September 1955, White House Office, NSC Staff, Papers, 1948–61, OCB Central File Series, Box 15, OCB 007 (File #2) (6), EPL.
9. Memorandum for the OCB, Subject: "President's Emergency Fund for International Affairs," 7 January 1955, White House Office, NSC Staff, Papers, 1948–61, OCB Central File Series, Box 14, OCB 007 (File #1) (3), EPL.
10. Ralph E. Becker, "Program for Expansion of United States Exchange in the Field of the Cultural Arts," White House Office, NSC Staff, Papers, 1948–61, OCB Central File Series, Box 16, OCB 007 (File #4) (5), EPL.
11. Memorandum for the OCB, Subject: "President's Emergency Fund for International Affairs," 7 January 1955.
12. [A. R.?] Walmsley to Secretary of State, 21 March 1956, White House Office, NSC Staff, Papers, 1948–61, OCB Central File Series, Box 15, OCB 007 (File #3) (5), EPL.
13. Memorandum for the OCB, Subject: "President's Emergency Fund for International Affairs," 7 January 1955.
14. Ibid.
15. President's Emergency Fund for Participation in International Affairs, Third Quarterly Report, 1 January 1955–31 March 1955, White House Office, NSC Staff, Papers, 1948–61, OCB Central File Series, Box 14, OCB 007 (File #1) (5), EPL.
16. For an assessment of the ANTA Music Advisory Panel's influence on US music diplomacy, see Emily Abrams Ansari, "Shaping the Policies of Cold War Musical Diplomacy: An Epistemic Community of American Composers," *Diplomatic History* 36, no. 1 (January 2012): 41–52.
17. Shawn J. Parry-Giles, *The Rhetorical Presidency, Propaganda, and the Cold War, 1945–1955* (Westport, CT: Praeger, 2002), xxiii.
18. Extract from OCB Minutes, 6 February 1957, White House Office, NSC Staff, Papers, 1948–61, OCB Central File Series, Box 16, OCB 007 (File #4) (6), EPL.
19. James E. Warner, "Iceland is Called 'Vital' to NATO Chain of Bases," *Washington Post and Times Herald*, 20 June 1956, White House Office, NSC Staff, Papers, 1948–61, OCB Central File Series, Box 35, OCB 091 Iceland (File #4) (4), EPL.
20. "Iceland: Where U.S. May Lose a Base," *U.S. News and World Report*, 13 April 1956, 43.
21. This paragraph's historical overview is based upon Þór Whitehead, *The Ally Who Came in From the Cold: A Survey of Icelandic Foreign Policy, 1946–1956* (Reykjavík: University of Iceland Press, 1998); Jussi M. Hanhimäki, *Scandinavia and the United States: An Insecure Friendship* (New York: Twayne, 1997).
22. Quoted in Donald Edwin Nuechterlein, *Iceland, Reluctant Ally* (Ithaca, NY: Cornell University Press, 1961), 121; original source not provided.
23. Draft: Outline Plan of Operations for Iceland, OCB, no date, White House Office, NSC Staff, Papers, 1948–61, OCB Central File Series, Box 35, OCB 091 Iceland (File #2) (2), EPL.
24. Valur Ingimundarson, "Immunizing Against the American Other: Racism, Nationalism, and Gender in U.S.-Icelandic Military Relations During the Cold War," *Journal of Cold War Studies* 6, no. 4 (2004): 65–88.
25. Demaree Bess, "Uncle Sam's Reluctant Ally," *Saturday Evening Post*, 29 December 1956, 21, 56.
26. Ingimundarson, "Immunizing against the American Other," 67.
27. Petra Goedde, "From Villains to Victims: Fraternization and Feminization of Germany, 1945–47," *Diplomatic History* 23, no. 1 (1999): 1–20.

28. For more on the Americanization of Europe, see, for example, Richard Pells, *Not Like Us: How Europeans have Loved, Hated, and Transformed American Culture since World War II* (New York: Basic Books, 1997).
29. Hanhimäki, *Scandinavia and the United States*, 339; Bess, "Uncle Sam's Reluctant Ally," 20–21, 55.
30. G. L. Rockwell, "No Wonder Iceland Hates Us!," *American Mercury* 84 (January 1957): 10.
31. Editorial, *Tíminn*, 1 June 1951, translated and quoted in Nuechterlein, *Iceland, Reluctant Ally*, 109.
32. Enclosure (1) to Op–616 Memo of 17 November 1954, Excerpt from *U.S. News and World Report*, 19 November 1954, White House Office, NSC Staff, Papers, 1948–61, OCB Central File Series, Box 35, OCB 091 Iceland (File #1) (7), EPL.
33. Draft: Outline Plan of Operations for Iceland.
34. Enclosure (1) to Op–616 Memo of 17 November 1954.
35. Memorandum for Mr. James S. Lay Jr., Exec. Secretary, NSC, from Elmer B. Staats, Subject: Progress Report on Iceland (NSC 5426), 27 September 1955, White House Office, NSC Staff, Papers, 1948–61, OCB Central File Series, Box 35, OCB 091 Iceland (File #2) (9), EPL; Ingimundarson, "Immunizing Against the American Other," 66.
36. "The Panel members are reminded that President's Program funds are rarely used for Iceland appearances." Music Advisory Panel Minutes, 18 December 1957, Box 100, Folder 3, Bureau of Educational and Cultural Affairs Collection, MC468, Special Collections, University of Arkansas, Fayetteville (hereafter CU Collection).
37. Agenda: OCB Working Group on Iceland, Meeting 12 May 1955, White House Office, NSC Staff, Papers, 1948–61, OCB Central File Series, Box 35, OCB 091 Iceland (File #1) (11), EPL.
38. Draft: Outline Plan of Operations for Iceland.
39. Parry–Giles, *The Rhetorical Presidency*, xxiii.
40. Request for MATS Transportation in Implementation of NSC 5426 (Iceland), no date, White House Office, NSC Staff, Papers, 1948–61, OCB Central File Series, Box 14, OCB 007. (File #1) (5), EPL.
41. Ibid.
42. Naomi Huber, American Embassy in Iceland, to Thomas Perry, 8 March 1956, MGT 48, Tour and Trip Files 1956–57, Box 5, "Iceland," Boston Symphony Orchestra Archives, Symphony Hall, Boston, MA (hereafter BSO Archives).
43. E. Power Biggs, European tour, April, May, June, 1954 (itinerary), MGT 54X, Managers' Subject Files, 1914–73, Box 1, Biggs, E. Power (organ), 1948–55, BSO Archives.
44. See George Norwood Humphrey, *Becoming a Musician* (Philadelphia: Xlibris, 2007), 116; Mary Stewart French to Thomas Perry, 25 April 1955, MGT 54X, Managers' Subject Files, 1914–73, Box 1, Biggs, E. Power (organ), 1948–55, BSO Archives.
45. See Humphrey, *Becoming a Musician*, 118–19; "String Quartet Born of Storm in Iceland to Play Here June 3," *New York Times*, 21 May 1959, 36.
46. Humphrey, *Becoming a Musician*, 116.
47. Ibid., 117; Eighth Quarterly Report, President's Emergency Fund for Participation in International Affairs, 1 April–30 June 1956, White House Office, NSC Staff, Papers, 1948–61, OCB Central File Series, Box 16, OCB 007 (File #4) (2), 10, EPL.
48. Humphrey, *Becoming a Musician*, 118.
49. Ibid., 117.
50. George Humphrey to C. D. Jackson, 16 March 1959, C. D. Jackson Papers, 1931–67, Box 111, Washburn, Abbott (2), EPL. The magazine *Ramparts* and the *Saturday Evening Post* first revealed the CIA's funding of major anticommunist organiza-

51. Humphrey, *Becoming a Musician*, 118. I have been unable to establish who James Lombard was.
52. Ibid., 119.
53. There is an extensive literature on this topic; the most comprehensive recent examination of the ways in which the US government collaborated with private foundations is Wilford, *The Mighty Wurlitzer*.
54. Humphrey, *Becoming a Musician*, 119.
55. George Humphrey to C. D. Jackson, 16 March 1959.
56. Ibid.
57. Ibid.
58. Humphrey, *Becoming a Musician*, 120.
59. Analysis of Internal Security Situation in Iceland and Recommended Action, Draft, 9 February 1956, White House Office, NSC Staff, Papers, 1948–61, OCB Central File Series, Box 35, OCB 091 Iceland (File #3) (3), EPL.
60. Memo for Mr. Roy M. Melbourne from R. P. Crenshaw, Subject: 6 Months' Schedule for OCB Working Group on Iceland, 3 August 1956, White House Office, NSC Staff, Papers, 1948–61, OCB Central File Series, Box 35, OCB 091 Iceland (File #4) (6), EPL.
61. Carroll D. Kearns, "Music vs. Guns," *Etude* 73 (1955): 14.
62. Analysis of Internal Security Situation in Iceland and Recommended Action, Draft, 9 February 1956.
63. Ingimundarson, "Immunizing against the American Other," 69.
64. By the mid-1950s, Iceland was the only country in the world where the United States still agreed to such a request, although in the years immediately after the war a similar policy had been in place in Canada, Greenland, and various other countries. Whitehead, *The Ally Who Came in From the Cold*, 62.
65. For more on the jazz tours, see Davenport, *Jazz Diplomacy*; Von Eschen, *Satchmo Blows Up the World*.
66. Music Advisory Panel Minutes, 8 November 1954, Box 100, Folder 1, CU Collection.
67. "Foreign Service Despatch," American Embassy Reykjavík, to State Department, 27 March 1958, RG 59, Central Decimal File 1955–59, 032 McFerrin, Robert/3-2758, National Archives and Records Administration II, College Park, Maryland (hereafter NARA II); "Foreign Service Despatch," American Embassy Reykjavík, to State Department, 3 February 1960, RG 59, Central Decimal File 1960–63, 032 Allen, Betty/2-360, NARA II.
68. Ingimundarson details anxieties in Washington DC about the policy and the furor in the United States when the *Amsterdam News* revealed it to the public in 1959. Restrictions were not removed until some time in the 1970s: Ingimundarson has found no evidence to suggest the change was ever publicly acknowledged by the US government. Ingimundarson, "Immunizing against the American Other," 80.
69. Von Eschen, *Satchmo Blows up the World*, 5.
70. Richard Nelson and Foad Izadi, "Ethics and Social Issues in Public Diplomacy," in *Routledge Handbook of Public Diplomacy*, ed. Nancy Snow and Philip M. Taylor (New York: Routledge, 2009), 343.
71. Memorandum for the President from D. A. Fitzgerald, 26 April 1957, White House Office, NSC Staff, Papers, 1948–61, OCB Central File Series, Box 35, OCB 091 Iceland (File #5) (5), EPL.

72. Whitehead, *The Ally Who Came in From the Cold*, 81.
73. Nuechterlein, *Iceland, Reluctant Ally*, 165.
74. OCB: Progress Report on Iceland, 19 September 1956, White House Office, NSC Staff, Papers, 1948–61, OCB Central File Series, Box 35, OCB 091 Iceland (File #4) (6), EPL.
75. Memorandum of Meeting: OCB Working Group on NSC 5426 (Iceland), 26 October 1955, White House Office, NSC Staff, Papers, 1948–61, OCB Central File Series, Box 35, OCB 091 Iceland (File #2) (10), EPL.
76. Excerpt from *Visir*, 3 March 1958, in "Foreign Service Despatch," American Embassy Reykjavík (Iceland), to State Department, 27 March 1958, regarding performances by Robert McFerrin, RG 59, Central Decimal File 1955–59, 032 McFerrin, Robert/3-2758, NARA II.
77. "Kr. 40.840,00," *Þjóðviljinn*, 26 March 1954, 6. Translated for the author by Árni Heimir Ingólfsson.
78. "Hljómsveit flughersins kom Íslendingum af þeirri skoðun að villimenn byggi Bandaríkin," *Þjóðviljinn*, 17 July 1954, 5. Translated for the author by Árni Heimir Ingólfsson.
79. Joseph S. Nye Jr., "The Future of Soft Power in U.S. Foreign Policy," in *Soft Power and U.S. Foreign Policy: Theoretical, Historical and Contemporary Perspectives*, ed. Inderjeet Parmar and Michael Cox (London and New York: Routledge, 2010), 9.

Bibliography

Archives

Boston Symphony Orchestra Archives, Symphony Hall, Boston
Bureau for Educational and Cultural Affairs Historical Collection, MC468, Special Collections, University of Arkansas, Fayetteville
National Archives and Records Administration, College Park, Maryland
Dwight D. Eisenhower Presidential Library, Abilene, Kansas

Printed Sources

Ansari, Emily Abrams. "'Masters of the President's Music': Cold War Composers and the United States Government." PhD diss., Harvard University, 2010.

———. "Shaping the Policies of Cold War Musical Diplomacy: An Epistemic Community of American Composers." *Diplomatic History* 36, no. 1 (January 2012): 41–52.

Arndt, Richard T. *The First Resort of Kings: American Cultural Diplomacy in the Twentieth Century.* Washington DC: Potomac Books, 2005.

Davenport, Lisa E. *Jazz Diplomacy: Promoting America in the Cold War Era.* Jackson: University Press of Mississippi, 2009.

Eisenhower, Dwight D. "The Creative Purpose." In *Creative America*, by John F. Kennedy, James Baldwin, Louis Kronenberger, John Ciardi, Robert Frost, Mark van Doren, Dwight D. Eisenhower, Harry S. Truman, and Joseph Wood Krutch, 108–9. New York: Ridge Press, 1962.

Fosler-Lussier, Danielle. "Cultural Diplomacy as Cultural Globalization: The University of Michigan Jazz Band in Latin America." *Journal of the Society for American Music* 4, no. 1 (February 2010): 59–93.

Goedde, Petra. "From Villains to Victims: Fraternization and Feminization of Germany, 1945–47." *Diplomatic History* 23, no. 1 (1999): 1–20.

Hanhimäki, Jussi M. *Scandinavia and the United States: An Insecure Friendship.* New York: Twayne, 1997.

Humphrey, George Norwood. *Becoming a Musician.* Philadelphia: Xlibris, 2007.

Ingimundarson, Valur. "Immunizing Against the American Other: Racism, Nationalism, and Gender in U.S.-Icelandic Military Relations During the Cold War." *Journal of Cold War Studies* 6, no. 4 (2004): 65–88.

Kearns, Carroll D. "Music vs. Guns." *Etude* 73 (1955): 13–14, 64.

Nelson, Richard, and Foad Izadi. "Ethics and Social Issues in Public Diplomacy." In *Routledge Handbook of Public Diplomacy,* ed. Nancy Snow and Philip M. Taylor, 334–351. New York: Routledge, 2009.

Nuechterlein, Donald Edwin. *Iceland, Reluctant Ally.* Ithaca, NY: Cornell University Press, 1961.

Nye, Joseph S., Jr. "The Future of Soft Power in U.S. Foreign Policy." In *Soft Power and U.S. Foreign Policy: Theoretical, Historical and Contemporary Perspectives,* ed. Inderjeet Parmar and Michael Cox, 4–11. London and New York: Routledge, 2010.

Parry-Giles, Shawn. *The Rhetorical Presidency, Propaganda, and the Cold War, 1945–1955.* Westport, CT: Praeger, 2002.

Rockwell, G. L. "No Wonder Iceland Hates Us!," *American Mercury* 84 (January 1957): 7–13.

Pells, Richard. *Not Like Us: How Europeans have Loved, Hated, and Transformed American Culture since World War II.* New York: Basic Books, 1997.

Saunders, Frances Stonor. *Who Paid the Piper? The CIA and the Cultural Cold War.* London: Granta Books, 1999.

Tuch, Hans N. *Communicating with the World: U.S. Public Diplomacy Overseas.* New York: St. Martin's Press, 1990.

Von Eschen, Penny. *Satchmo Blows Up the World: Jazz Ambassadors Play the Cold War.* Cambridge, MA: Harvard University Press, 2004.

Whitehead, Þór. *The Ally Who Came in From the Cold: A Survey of Icelandic Foreign Policy, 1946–1956.* Reykjavík: University of Iceland Press, 1998.

Wilford, Hugh. *The Mighty Wurlitzer: How the CIA Played America.* Cambridge, MA: Harvard University Press, 2008.

Chapter Seven

INTIMATE HISTORIES OF THE MUSICAL COLD WAR
Fred Prieberg and Igor Blazhkov's Unofficial Diplomacy

Peter J. Schmelz

> "One thing about music: it doesn't like borders."
> —William Christie in Joshua Jampol, *Living Opera*

In February 1959, nearing the end of an eventful survey of the Pacific Ocean as part of the International Geophysical Year (1957–58), the Russian oceanographic vessel *Vitiaz* ("warrior" or "hero" in old folk poetry) docked in Honolulu's harbor.[1] Cliff Coleman, a Honolulu businessman, World War II veteran, newspaper record reviewer, radio disc jockey, and classical music fan, encountered little resistance as he impulsively walked up the gangplank and asked to meet the crew. After several attempts, a female crew member (A. Pavlova—not to be confused with the famous ballerina) was found who could speak with him. Coleman immediately offered to show the scientists the local sights. Over fifty years later, he recalled the encounter with enthusiasm. Coleman drove three or four of the Russians around Honolulu in his car before taking them home for dinner and an LP listening session. One of the recordings he played was Shostakovich's Symphony no. 5.

The response from his audience was immediate and emphatic. Pavlova suddenly sat up and declared, "We heard you on the radio!" While en route to Hawaii, the scientists had tuned into American radio broadcasts and had stumbled upon Coleman's radio program.

Notes for this section begin on page 216.

"We were so happy and surprised that they were playing Shostakovich on the radio," Pavlova continued. "When I mentioned I was on the radio," Coleman recalled, "that changed the whole situation. The next day the woman and three different scientists (she spoke the best English) went on a tour. Then two others the next day." When the *Vitiaz* left, Coleman "put together a batch of LPs and sent them off." Sometime later he received a box of Russian LPs in return. The *Vitiaz* returned to Honolulu after a year or so and Coleman repeated the tours (likely in August and September 1961). He and the scientists periodically exchanged notes and Christmas (or New Year) cards, and when Coleman moved to the United Kingdom later in the decade he spoke with them by phone.[2]

In November 1959, the Soviet general interest music periodical *Muzykal'naia zhizn'* published an account of the visit by Pavlova, titled "On the Hawaiian Islands."[3] She described the warm greeting that had been extended to the Soviet visitors in Honolulu, and the article featured two photographs of crowds, comprising officials and the general public, gathered to greet and gawk at the ship. (It was apparently open to visitors at its ports of call.) Pavlova further detailed her meetings with a variety of Hawaiians, including a visit to the University of Hawaii, where students danced the hula for the Soviet scientists, and her several encounters with John Kelley (1919–2007), surfer, peace activist, and musician.[4] Near the end of the article, Pavlova also mentioned Coleman's radio programs, as well as the visit to his house, where "we listened to the excellent recording of Shostakovich's Fifth Symphony performed by the Philadelphia Orchestra and Rachmaninov's Third Piano Concerto performed by Gilels." Pavlova also marveled at the large number of Russian and Soviet composers in Coleman's extensive record collection.

In Kiev, in the Ukrainian Soviet Socialist Republic, the enterprising young conductor Igor Blazhkov read Pavlova's article, became intrigued by the "astonishing" (his word) Coleman—and by the promise of his abundant record collection—and sent off a letter addressed only to "Cliff Coleman, Honolulu Radio." Coleman miraculously received the letter, and the two became pen pals for "many years," as Blazhkov described. But they became more than pen pals, for Coleman became an important source of recordings for the circle of young Soviet composers actively studying new compositional trends in Kiev at the time. Blazhkov recounted, "I sent him records of Russian music that he was lacking, and he sent me (at my request) recordings (both tapes and records) of works by Stravinsky, Bartók, Hindemith, Honegger, Varèse, Boulez, Stockhausen, and others," among them Schoenberg and Milhaud. These recordings, Blazhkov said, "played a leading role in the study of the classics of modern music by the members of our circle: [Valentin] Silvestrov [b. 1937], [Leonid] Hrabovsky [b. 1935], [Vitaliy] Hodzyatsky [b. 1936], [Galina] Mokreeva [1936–68; Blazhkov's first wife], and others."[5]

The impromptu encounter on the Hawaiian Islands had far-reaching effects on musical life not only in Kiev, but also in Moscow, Leningrad, Tallinn, and Yerevan (among others). The young composers in Kiev had several similar avenues of foreign support, and Blazhkov became an important conduit. The Coleman connection reveals how far afield Blazhkov ventured in search of scores and recordings. Although Blazhkov's role has been acknowledged previously, his story and the tragic story of his wife, the musicologist Galina Mokreeva, deserve to be told more fully.[6] Only recently, thanks to materials from his personal archive and other newly located sources, has the extent of Blazhkov's and Mokreeva's networking and propagandizing on behalf of new music during the 1960s become clearer.[7] Alongside his many other activities, Blazhkov's correspondence with West German music writer Fred K. Prieberg (1928–2010), the focus of the discussion below, helps present a new perspective on music and international relations during the Cold War, and the type of history I think they exemplify: an intimate history.

Intimate History and the Cold War

The *Vitiaz*'s expedition epitomizes the complicated, interconnected layering of Cold War exchanges: the official cooperative, international reason for its travels (the International Geophysical Year); the recriminations surrounding its apparent brush with radioactive fallout from US nuclear weapons testing in the Marshall Islands; the mistrustful accusations of US congressmen about its alleged spying near the US coast and sensitive US missile installations; official visits by the Soviet scientists with local Hawaiian dignitaries; and Coleman's unofficial encounter, leading to unofficial exchanges between Coleman and Blazhkov. The first items in that list—the more public side of Cold War exchanges—have received much recent scrutiny, but the final two—the intimate side—remain understudied. Scholars have addressed Soviet tourism and radio transmission both into and out of the USSR during the Cold War.[8] Nonetheless, unofficial, personal transnational networks between the USSR and the West have received little examination, although they formed a crucial nexus for information exchange, and especially for music, during the Soviet thaw of the 1960s.

By intimate history, I have in mind not only a microhistory, but also a type of history that touches on the hidden corners of Soviet musical life during the thaw and the Cold War, especially the intensely subjective corners that music is especially (and perhaps uniquely) prone to activating.[9] In her recent book *The Inner Life of Empires,* historian Emma Rothschild proposes "new kinds of microhistory" that offer "a new way of thinking about one of the oldest historical inquiries, or the history of the inner life." "This is a history," she continues, "in Adam Smith's description, that recounts the unfolding of public events by leading the reader 'into the sentiments and mind of the actor.'" Although Rothschild calls it "an eighteenth-century sort of history," it also seems appropriate for the Cold War—the most public yet private of modern conflicts.[10]

As in Rothschild's "new type of microhistory," the intimate history presented below reveals close personal connections that reflect larger trends, among them questions of style, globalization, democracy, national identities, and modernism. Intimate history both reframes and refines microhistory, while also sounding in counterpoint to grander public histories. It carries a different emphasis, especially in the Soviet context, with its stark oppositions between public and private, where public surfaces, while illuminating in their own right, often obscured individual lived, felt, and sounded experiences.[11] Intimate history also teases out the subtle ramifications of musical encounters, and especially the connections between "texts" (recordings, scores, live performances, radio broadcasts) and personal responses.

In many respects this approach builds upon Danielle Fosler-Lussier's research on the University of Michigan jazz band tours under the auspices of the US State Department, but it expands to consider actors working outside official channels.[12] Blazhkov and his young Soviet colleagues undeniably benefited from US government cultural propaganda (including scores and recordings), as demonstrated by lexicographer Nicolas Slonimsky's important visit to Kiev in 1962. But Slonimsky and Blazhkov also had an ongoing relationship separate from the US State Department, as did Blazhkov and Prieberg. Their correspondence, independent of any official channels, preserves a snapshot of crucial moments from the 1960s, including the various freezes and thaws of official Soviet artistic policy, the politics of tamizdat, and the role of unofficial spaces (whether imagined or actual) within Soviet musical life.[13]

What do we gain by thinking of Blazhkov's actions as diplomacy, rather than a normal (and necessary) kind of musical entrepreneurship? To be sure, this is diplomacy of a very particular sort: Blazhkov mediated between official Soviet pronouncements and Prieberg's goals—including Prieberg's idealistic interpretations of official Soviet pronouncements—all the while asserting his own (Blazhkov's) desires and aspirations. Blazhkov and Prieberg's interactions are thus akin to "track two" or citizen diplomacy, the "unofficial, non-structured interaction" described by career diplomat Joseph V. Montville that often carried as much, if not more, weight than official actions.[14] Exchanges such as Blazhkov and Prieberg's formed a significant type of international relation, framing each side's opinion of the other on a personal level and producing significant and tangible results alongside more diffuse changes in perspective and behavior. The interactions were ongoing processes, offering a developing feedback loop of creation and reception akin to a network in Bruno Latour's sense.[15]

Rather than addressing only how Russians imported new music from abroad in the 1950s and 1960s, a topic that I have considered in greater detail elsewhere, the discussion below expands to include materials exported and the interconnections between the two (imports and exports).[16] Many of Blazhkov's activities qualify as forms of musical tamizdat, or material disseminated unofficially abroad, the international form of the domestic samizdat. But as they involved music, the problems were different, involving arranging publications as well as performances, with all of the associated logistical hiccups. Scholars have recently begun reevaluating samizdat and its relatives (including tamizdat and magnitizdat, or recordings), yet there have been no studies of musical tamizdat—musical transmission beyond the Soviet Union's borders—and the ongoing reciprocal networks of information exchange that resulted.[17]

As many recent studies of samizdat have highlighted, this behavior was not explicitly dissident.[18] Instead, it was more complicated: Blazhkov carefully avoided politics, demonstrating an interest only in furthering musical knowledge and his friends' musical careers. For his part, as we shall see, the West German Prieberg's agenda remained more political, despite his declaration to Russian pianist Maria Yudina that "it is bad if a musical piece becomes a demonstration for or against something."[19]

Despite their best intentions, the Cold War persistently threatened to engulf Blazhkov and Prieberg. While most of the discussions in Blazhkov's correspondence center on the practicalities of exchanging scores, books, and recordings, they also touch on more overtly political matters—especially the traumatic results of Soviet prohibitions for Blazhkov and his first wife, Galina Mokreeva. The most notable of these prohibitions concerned questions of style—and, by extension, freedom and democracy—which were always implicitly (and often explicitly) linked to the Cold War. Accessible tonal music became associated with Soviet orthodoxy, while difficult atonal compositions became emblematic of Western freedoms.[20] Prieberg's letters demonstrate uncertainty about the flexibility of these official Soviet expectations; the contrast between the two sides generated a push and pull about tonality and accessibility, modernism and novelty. Blazhkov remained in the middle, negotiating among shifting Soviet dictates, his own aesthetic preferences, his colleagues' compositional careers, and his foreign audiences' desires (both perceived and actual).

Given this political and stylistic background, the business discussions that dominate the correspondence take on new implications for our study of both musical production and reception and Cold War transnational exchanges. Prieberg's letters reveal the various assumptions about supply and demand under which Western publishers operated—and the extent to which "avant-garde Soviet music" represented a potentially lucrative brand.[21] Blazhkov's advocacy of new music in the Soviet Union highlights the degree to which composers' reputations are engineered by others: they are beholden to networks of individuals. This was especially the case for Soviet composers writing in a nonsanctioned style who desperately wanted to be heard outside the USSR. Since official Soviet institutions did not support—and often actively suppressed—the music Blazhkov championed, he disseminated it himself, becoming a one-man propaganda bureau. As we shall see, Blazhkov's letters thus prove especially valuable for understanding the early international career of Valentin Silvestrov, a leading composer from his generation.

"I am very interested in new works of your friends, the composers . . ."

Blazhkov was born in 1936 in Kiev, Ukraine. He studied conducting at the Kiev Conservatory under Alexander Klimov, graduating in 1959, and won the Conducting Competition of the Republic of Ukraine the same year. He served as conductor with the State Philharmonic Orchestra of Ukraine from 1958 to 1962 and the next year moved to Leningrad, where from 1963 to 1968 he acted as one of the assistant conductors of the Leningrad Philharmonic under Yevgeny Mravinsky.[22] He cultivated a highly modern repertoire and took a special interest in Stravinsky. Blazhkov even met and assisted the famous émigré during his celebrated 1962 return visit to the USSR.[23] But Blazhkov soon leaned toward more difficult fare, instigating a number of key unofficial music performances of works by Edison Denisov (1929–96) and Alfred Schnittke (1934–98), as well as the premiere of Andrey Volkonsky's important song cycle *Laments of Shchaza* (*Zhaloby Shchazy,* 1962) on 27 and 28 April 1965.[24]

Blazhkov corresponded with a number of noted non-Soviet musicians, among them Stravinsky, Edgard Varèse, Ernst Krenek, and the Russian-American musical polymath Nicolas Slonimsky—in addition to Britten, Hindemith, Barber, Boulez, Hartmann, Henze, Nono, and Dallapiccola.[25] His correspondence with the older composers was more routine: they shared information, scores, and books. But with Prieberg, closer to Blazhkov in age, more than just scores were exchanged: ideas about freedom and control were debated and reputations were cultivated. The two kept the postal system busy, with Blazhkov requesting materials ranging from Telemann and Schütz to Szymanowski, Webern, and Stravinsky.[26] Prieberg, in turn, sought more obscure Soviet fare, as in a letter from early January 1962 in which he requested Georgiy Sviridov's *Pathetic Oratorio* (*Pateticheskaia oratoriia,* text by Mayakovsky, 1959) along with "some interesting political cantata or mass songs."[27] Prieberg (figure 7.1) was also interested in far-flung trivia, including details of a Kiev version of the conductorless Moscow ensemble Persimfans (the Kiev Symphonic Ensemble, which first performed on 27 December 1926).[28] The correspondence lasted from 1961 until the mid-1980s, becoming infrequent after 1970, and consisted of forty-one letters and postcards: eighteen from Prieberg and twenty-three from Blazhkov.

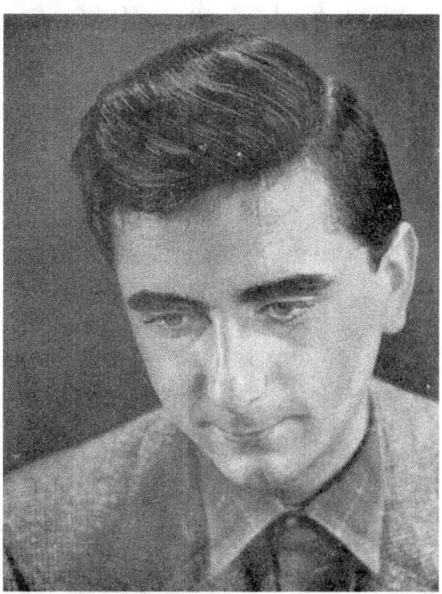

Figure 7.1. Fred Prieberg. Photographer unknown.
Source: public domain.

Prieberg first wrote to Blazhkov on 20 June 1961, obtaining

his address from leading West German modernist composer Karlheinz Stockhausen, with whom Blazhkov and Yudina had already corresponded.[29] Prieberg, based in Baden-Baden, described himself to Blazhkov as a "radio author and writer with a strong interest in modern music," noting in the letter's postscript his *Lexikon der neuen Musik* (Freiburg: K. Alber, 1958) and "a survey of electronic music," *Musica ex machina: Über das Verhältnis von Musik und Technik* (Berlin: Ullstein, 1960).[30] Prieberg had traveled to Moscow and Leningrad with the Radio Hamburg Symphony Orchestra in April 1960 and was writing Blazhkov because he was "very much interested in new works of your friends, the composers ... *muzyka sovremennaia* [modern music] in our sense." Prieberg dangled the possibility of performance as his carrot:

> I am able to have broadcast any partition [score] which you might care to send me.... [T]here is much interest in Russian music of the youngest composers whom ... *spravochnik* [the directory] 'Sovetskie kompozitory' does not yet list—works like the Eleventh [Symphony] of Shostakovich come by themselves, but music of the youngest composers would remain unknown.

As these excerpts suggest, the two corresponded most frequently in (often broken) English, their only common language, although when pressed for time Blazhkov reverted to Russian, which Prieberg was forced to translate with the assistance of friends.[31]

Prieberg was in touch with several other Soviets, among them the musicologists Liudmila Poliakova (1921–94), Yuri Keldysh (1907–95), and Grigoriy Shneerson (1901–82), many of whom Prieberg believed showed more ideological flexibility in their correspondence than in their published work.[32] "Even the discussion by correspondence that I have with Keldysh and Shneerson suggests a revaluation of principles of Formalism and Realism," Prieberg declared in his letter to Blazhkov from 7 January 1962. "A certain schematic ruling seems to be discontinued." "Would not dodecaphonic [i.e., twelve-tone] music be accepted, as soon as large masses of the public ask for it?" he innocently proposed. Blazhkov's response was telling: "Well, I do not think I quite agree with you that the esthetical frame is rapidly changing. And Shneerson is far from being dialectically thinking; writing his 'Vivid and dead music' [i.e., *Muzyka zhivoi i mertvyi (Music Living and Dead)*, first edition, 1960; second edition, 1964] sufficed to be convinced of that."[33] Prieberg had a great deal to learn about sorting official propaganda from the lived reality of the Soviet state, and about sorting public proclamations from intimate confidences.

Soon after hearing from Prieberg for the first time, Blazhkov wrote on 22 July 1961 to the pianist Maria Yudina about him, relaying Prieberg's wish for "dodecaphonic works by our young composers," which he had promised to have performed. Blazhkov excitedly urged Yudina to "get from Volkonsky everything dodecaphonic and from the Estonians too—don't put it off." Blazhkov also expressed his desire for Yudina to help him organize tighter connections between the new music groups in Moscow, Tallinn, and Kiev: "So that we may immediately share all the latest, so that all of the works appearing to composers in our association will be well-known in our circle." Blazhkov was simultaneously building exchange networks within and without the Soviet Union, facilitating the circulation of materials at home and abroad.[34]

Blazhkov's response to Prieberg's first letter, apparently from September 1961, did not survive. Evidently, he sent a list of scores he wished Prieberg to gather. He also sent some piano music by Silvestrov, including the piece that Prieberg refers to in a letter from 2 October 1961 as "snaka" (i.e., "Signs" ["Znaki"] from the 1961 Five Pieces for Piano). Prieberg responded that he was willing to continue programming Silvestrov ("your friend") on concerts and radio programs as long as he "does not object." Any proceeds from the performances would be used to purchase scores for the Ukrainians. Prieberg also promised to send copies of his recent books to Blazhkov, and asked for biographical information about the unofficial composers while begging for "more interesting compositions of your friends, for string trio or quartet, for instance." Prieberg was excited to have contact with Blazhkov because he previously had been limited to the materials sent him by the Soviet Composers Union, which only "present the official view of contemporary music." Prieberg was fascinated by the unofficial side.

Blazhkov's response of 22 October 1961 continued to refer to Silvestrov anonymously as "my friend." Blazhkov concluded by noting that "I hope that I could help you considerably more." But the exchange remained rather lopsided: Prieberg offered more tangibly to Blazhkov, serving to arrange performances and make contacts with the Western European music market for him and his colleagues. By providing information about the young Soviet composers and other unfamiliar Russian and Soviet music, Blazhkov, in turn, helped bolster the authority of Prieberg's books. Prieberg also served Blazhkov as a crucial source for Western scores, as became clear when a frantic Blazhkov wrote Prieberg in early December 1962 asking for the words for Stravinsky's Four Russian Peasant Songs.[35]

Prieberg's letter of 8 November 1961 suggested that he was effective in his advocacy: the first performance of Silvestrov's piano pieces was slated for late November with the Bavarian Radio in Munich, performed by "the famous Baden-Baden pianist Maria Bergmann." Prieberg also indicated his desire to "interest one of the traveling pianists in the piece and even to place it with a publisher here." But the complications, especially financial, of arranging the performance of unofficial Soviet music quickly became apparent, as Prieberg urged "your friend" to provide written authorization for Prieberg to serve as his legal proxy regarding artistic rights. "This is most important as performance fees are to be expected," Prieberg concluded.

As mentioned in the letter of 7 January 1962, Silvestrov's piano pieces were indeed performed on 22 November 1961. What did the radio listeners hear? Prieberg himself described the pointillistic, "twelve-tonish" pieces in an article published in the January 1963 issue of the London journal *Survey*:

> The four "Signs" are idylls of an utterly unromantic kind, brief, pregnant, and pellucid. They possess an aphoristic quality. Each of these short pieces has a compositorial "point," and none has anything in common with Tchaikovsky's broad symphonic sweep or Khachaturian's folkloristic pathos. The five piano pieces—*Preludio, Toccatina, Melodia, Chorale,* and *La Sonatina Sospesa*—form an extremely succinct and tense little suite, composed in the twelve-tone manner and modeled on Schoenberg, it is true, but far from pedantic and imbued with a very personal, almost "Russian" *espressivo*.[36]

The expectations apparent in this review are curious yet suggestive. Why should Silvestrov sound like Tchaikovsky or Khachaturian? Prieberg's otherwise sympathetic conclusions are typical, especially the emphasis on the "Russian" *espressivo*—misguided (or at least more complicated) given Silvestrov's actual nationality. Prieberg was not the only one bowled over by the young Ukrainian's work: "Mr. [Hans Heinz] Stuckenschmidt [1901–88] wrote me [Prieberg]: 'The piano pieces from Kiev did interest me extraordinarily.' He is going to analyze and publicize them."[37]

Although performances of Silvestrov's music had been easy to arrange, publishing them proved more difficult, as Prieberg reported in January 1962: "I have already tried to place it [Silvestrov's piano pieces] with the UE [Universal Edition], but they are reluctant to take it; moreover they did not react on my request to send modern partitions to you, free of charge. Thus they do not deserve publishing the pieces. However I shall contact several other publishers about this."³⁸ But publication was not the only way to build a career. Prieberg and Blazhkov also frequently discussed composing competitions, among them the International Gaudeamus Music Week, to which Prieberg suggested that Silvestrov send his Piano Quintet, even offering to pay the application fee himself.³⁹ Blazhkov also constantly prodded Silvestrov to engage in European musical life (including sending scores directly to Prieberg himself), as his letters from Leningrad to his friend in Kiev attest.⁴⁰

Throughout the early stages of the correspondence, Blazhkov avoided mentioning Silvestrov's name.⁴¹ Prieberg reciprocated, usually referring to Silvestrov as "our friend," as in his letter from 20 February 1962, which also relayed new information on the performance and possible publication of the young composer's music:

> Our friend has a very fascinating face, "unlike what we think is Russian," as my wife observed when I showed her the photograph. I tried to explain to her the difference between Russian and Ukrainian. News of his work were eagerly appreciated here; consequently I have contacted a publisher for the piano pieces. Please let him know this. Tonight I shall copy our radio registration of the pieces and mail it to you. ... I hope he will be satisfied by Mrs. Bergmann's art; she is a specialist for Boulez, Messiaen, Stockhausen etc.

Blazhkov and his circle were more than satisfied with Bergmann's performance. In March 1962 he wrote to Prieberg: "We are charmed with the subtlety of Bergmann's art. Please give her our best wishes."⁴²

"Letter from Kiev" and Its Fallout

The radio broadcasts continued. In Prieberg's letter of 17 May 1962, he details the three performances that Silvestrov's Five Pieces for Piano had received on Radio Munich, Radio Frankfurt, and an unspecified station (likely Baden-Baden), in addition to an upcoming broadcast to take place on Radio Bremen "in combination with a lecture of mine about modern trends in Soviet music."⁴³ Prieberg added, "However I have not yet any account of the performance fees; radio bureaucracy takes a lot of time, you know." He continued, again begging for more scores to perform, while acknowledging the potential political fallout:

> I shall be able to have broadcast or publicly performed any partition of Silvestrov or his friends-in-style; last week I was in Hamburg and Bremen in order to discuss matters with leading persons of the radio.

Moreover I shall see that any "Pasternak effect" in connection with such performances is being avoided—as is the case with the piano pieces. As you see from the program, our friend is in good international company; there is no spoken introduction and no indication as to where he lives. There is a certain possibility of the pieces being printed here by a specialized publisher.

Prieberg followed this with one more plea for scores, "especially with up to 15 musicians." He remained most interested in the renowned yet mysterious Andrey Volkonsky, especially his *Suite of Mirrors* to texts of Federico Garcia Lorca (*Siuita zerkal,* 1960).[44]

By this point, Prieberg was flouting protocol: he named Silvestrov multiple times, not adhering to the convention they had been following of calling him "our friend" or "your friend." Even worse, he closed with a pointed criticism: "I was upset to read the silly accusations in Khrennikov's speech at the composers congress; certainly he does not know how to understand historical events. The renown of Soviet music in the West cannot rest forever on Shostakovich or Khachaturyan."

Blazhkov offered a cryptic yet pointed reply on 26 May 1962: "Thank you very much for your letter of May 17. You have imparted me many gratifying things. Nevertheless your letter sins with considerable mistakes. Please think over your last letter: I hope you will draw a proper conclusion for future." Clearly Prieberg had gone too far by mentioning the "Pasternak effect," tying Silvestrov directly to the foreign performances of his compositions, and criticizing Soviet Composers Union head Tikhon Khrennikov.[45] The rest of Blazhkov's letter was confined to business—reportage and no requests other than a postscript recommending that Prieberg read Blazhkov's wife's recent article in a Polish music journal.

Blazhkov's tense tone stemmed from the effects he and his wife, Galina Mokreeva (figure 7.2), were feeling from her "Letter from Kiev," which had appeared in the Polish journal *Ruch muzyczny* on 1 May 1962. From the outset of the article, the 26-year-old Mokreeva had adopted a combative attitude. Describing an official review (*smotr*) of young Kiev composers that had taken place in December 1961, she noted that "among the mass of epigonous, dead, and helpless compositions, interesting and daring works by the youngest of our musicians (a majority of whom are still conservatory students) unexpectedly shined with marvelous brilliance and displayed a high level of compositional craft."[46] She named the central composers in Blazhkov's circle—Silvestrov, Hrabovsky, Hodzyatsky, Huba, and Vitaly Patsera—but especially singled out Silvestrov's Piano Quintet for its "great stylistic maturity." She called attention to the way he "leaves the bounds of tonality and in places approaches twelve-tone techniques." But this was dangerous, so Mokreeva made sure to caution that despite Silvestrov's apparent emulation of Bartók and Schoenberg, he had come to his style "intuitively." In fact, "Silvestrov is a born dodecaphonist, he employs the system with such freedom.... It is difficult to compare his present style with any of the well-known dodecaphonists." Mokreeva also praised Hrabovsky, and in so doing criticized other Ukrainian composers. "The heavy, foggy,

Figure 7.2. Galina Mokreeva.
Source: Igor Blazhkov; date unknown.

and one-sided style of Glazunov's orchestration is preserved here with surprising stubbornness," she wrote, adding that "many of the works astonished with their technical helplessness, dilettantism, and absence of musical erudition." Mokreeva had thrown down the gauntlet; no wonder her article incited a strong response.

The article caused Blazhkov and Mokreeva considerable grief, as Blazhkov revealed in a letter he wrote to Yudina the very same day that he chastised Prieberg. "Huge trouble befell us," Blazhkov reported, because in the article:

> the successes of our young dodecaphonists were noted as a deeply positive phenomenon. As a result, after perusing that article here, there were endless meetings in the Central Committee, the Ministry of Culture, the Conservatory, and the Composers Union. They ascribed to Galya [Galina Mokreeva] being against the people [*antinarodnyi*], being against socialist realism, rejecting the classics, and propagandizing musical formalism. Insofar as it was declared that "all of that is a result of the influence of I. Blazhkov," the Central Committee took action—and immediately removed Galya and me from our jobs.

Blazhkov ended with two pleas to Yudina: the first to help him find employment in Russia (suggesting that his troubles were local to Kiev and Ukraine), the second to play Silvestrov's piano music—"right now." His conclusion is chilling: "My mood is such right now that I could hang myself."[47]

Prieberg's later letter from August 1962 hints at this trauma. In Prieberg's letter to Blazhkov from 19 June 1962, however, he obviously remained unaware of these events, and of Blazhkov's perilous emotional state. Instead, Prieberg expressed, yet again, his desire to hear any of Volkonsky's works, but especially his setting of Lorca (*Suite of Mirrors*). The letter reveals the complications and contradictions of unofficial musical politics at the time:

> Obviously [Volkonsky] is very reluctant about sending any partition of his abroad, at least this is what Mme. Yudina writes me.[48] I know also that here are certain people who tend to dramatize musical events in the SU [Soviet Union] and think of the young composers as "victims" out of political reasons. However, I have the best connections with Radio Hamburg and Radio Cologne—besides others—and could see too much connotations being avoided with radio performance. At least, both stations are eagerly interested in performing modern Russian music of the more advanced type. The work of [Estonian composer Arvo] Pärt that was played at some Yugoslavian festival has been retransmitted by either of these broadcasting stations—and without any ill side effects.

Just when Blazhkov and his wife were suffering the effects of demonstrating an affinity for a Western style—and had become "victims" for "political reasons"—Prieberg was decrying those who "dramatized" musical events in the USSR. Furthermore, heedless of the now-amplified risks, Prieberg continued to spell out the means for sending scores unofficially abroad: "So, if you know a way of getting new works of Volkonsky, Pärt, Silvestrov or any other promising composer, please let me know. They could be sent to me inofficially, and I would than distribute them to Hamburg and Cologne. Thus the composer's contact with abroad would be kept purely private."[49]

Blazhkov's response is missing, but it obviously related the dire results of Mokreeva's Polish article. Prieberg's reply on 4 August 1962 reveals his dawning awareness of how overly idealistic his views of the situation had been. Because of the unparalleled light it sheds on Prieberg's evolving thinking at this time, it is worth sampling at length:

> I have got and understood all your words. Do I need to tell you how angry and horrified I am? From here the impression arose that after the 20th Congress of the Party there was a new trend towards a more liberal view of artistic events going on; obviously, this was too optimistically reckoned, and a grave error. The situation is really confusing to me. Once a year—or so—some modern West European piece is broadcast by Radio Moscow as recorded by a foreign guest conductor (I remember Frank Martin's partly twelve-tone "Symphonie Concertante" [1946])

... and then this and the sly press campaign against "experimenting." Does the decree mean a separation from your wife? There is a dialectical point in it: She has made known to us an artistic trend in the USSR which could serve to emphasize and heighten the prestige and international standing of the USSR in the eyes of our avantgardists. Up to now these think that the Union may be a realm of bourgeois reactionaries; but the article told them: There are others.... Now it seems that writers of articles underlining the glory and modernity of the State are punished for their good intentions.

Prieberg's confused optimism was symptomatic of many outsiders, who, despite ample precedents, remained unable (or unwilling) to imagine how harsh and fickle the byzantine Soviet bureaucracy could be. It also showed that Prieberg maintained an artificially high opinion of the avant-garde, typical among certain Western Europeans and Americans; Stuckenschmidt, Steinecke, and Nicolas Nabokov also strongly advocated the connection between modernism and freedom. It was left to Blazhkov to attempt to explain from within the fluid, mutable world of Soviet music in the early 1960s. Even as he remained cautiously hopeful about performing new Soviet music, at times the clouds parted and Prieberg appeared to understand: "Sometimes I have the impression they [the young Soviet composers] are very reluctant to part with their works, which would be quite understandable for me."[50]

This 4 August 1962 letter from Prieberg ends with an intriguing statement: "In case, our friend wants to write the article for '... Beiträge' without his name being mentioned, I can relay the manuscript, of course. I am going to find out that idiot who has written him via the Composers Union (as he obviously has, for how would they know else?)." Presumably about Silvestrov, this comment yet again suggests the persistent danger of corresponding with foreigners—the very real possibility of governmental surveillance.

After finally obtaining Mokreeva's article, Prieberg wrote Blazhkov on 25 August 1962 that he found it "very good, well written and necessary; it gives information and the opinion of the writer in modest language and without any polemic intent. Please, relay cordial congratulations to your wife."[51] The message feels particularly ineffectual given what Prieberg knew of Mokreeva's plight at the time and the real dangers posed by foreign contact.

Meanwhile, Prieberg had become so concerned with Blazhkov and Mokreeva's troubles that he wrote to Grigoriy Shneerson, the Soviet journalist best known for his book-length rant against new music, *Music Living and Dead.* Shneerson, in turn, reported to Prieberg that he had called the Kiev Composers Union asking for more details. Shneerson conveyed the official spin: Mokreeva had not been fired and Blazhkov's stint with the State Philharmonic Orchestra of Ukraine had come to its slated conclusion. Indeed, Blazhkov had been promoted: he was to be second conductor of the Donetsk Symphony Orchestra. Rather than promotion, Blazhkov properly viewed this as exile. He wrote to Prieberg on 6 October 1962: "Not long ago I have come from Donetsk (new place of my job) and I irrevocably decided not to leave Kiev." In Shneerson's letter to Prieberg, he further underscored the official line:

> There was no kind of decision made about Mokreeva's article by the Central Committee of the Communist Party of Ukraine. The article by that young, beginning musicologist [*muzykovedka*] ... truly called forth a critical response from the Ukrainian Union of Composers, insofar as she very tendentiously described to Polish readers the creative successes of the young composers of Kiev, playing up those composers who experiment with "series" and disdainfully talking about all the rest, among them the much more talented.

"Therefore," Shneerson continued, "the information that you and your opponents have received about the 'case of Mokreeva and her husband' is largely untrue, or to put it simply, a lie. I do not know the source of that information, but I am convinced that he is unfriendly to the culture of our country."[52] Shneerson even gave Prieberg permission to publish sections of his letter.

After conveying this information, Prieberg felt it necessary to remind Blazhkov that "[w]e have some problems of our own: A few politicians here have taken to clamoring for folklore-based modern music. Even if they do not have any power to enforce this, it is quite a nuisance." Yet the "power to enforce" aesthetic edicts was a critical distinction between East and West. After all, Blazhkov was cowed enough by the reaction to Mokreeva's article that he submitted under a pseudonym—Andrzej Kowalewski—his account of Stravinsky's fall 1962 visit to the USSR, published in January 1963 by the Polish *Ruch muzyczny*.[53]

Mokreeva's travails had not ended. As Blazhkov documented in his letter to Prieberg from 12 February 1963, Mokreeva presented a lecture on 26 December 1962 at the Kiev House of Architects called "Music of the Twentieth Century" that was attended by Silvestrov, Huba, and Hrabovsky. Representatives from the Communist Party organization of the Kiev Conservatory also appeared, caused a disturbance, and reported the misdeeds to the "higher party organizations of Kiev."[54] Blazhkov later recalled that Coleman played a role in the scandal. During her talk Mokreeva played examples from reel-to-reel tapes sent by Coleman on which he announced each selection in English. Some in the audience, hearing English, accused Mokreeva of using excerpts from illegal Voice of America radio broadcasts.[55]

Blazhkov continued his report to Prieberg:

> Again passed endless conferences and meetings, which continue to the present day. They mocked the young composers and my wife as much as possible. The party officials have called for her musicology degree to be taken away, depriving her of any chance to be involved with music. As a result of all of this, my wife has become a nervous wreck.

Blazhkov concluded with a plea: "Dear friend, I urgently ask you to discuss all of this injustice in the press."[56] Prieberg complied, writing at length of Mokreeva's difficulties in the July 1963 issue of *Survey*, borrowing many of the details from Blazhkov's own letters. (Some of Prieberg's sentences are direct paraphrases or translations of Blazhkov's, especially from the 12 February 1963 letter.)[57] In his article, Prieberg concluded: "Now her situation is worse than ever.... [H]er story illustrates the kind of thing that can throw an artist far off his course if he fights against conformism. Nevertheless, there is a full-scale contest going on between the unruly artists and conservative party authorities."[58]

By the time the *Survey* article appeared, Blazhkov had obtained employment with the Leningrad Philharmonic. In his letter from 9 April 1963, Prieberg congratulated him: "This would be the right place for young challenging people like you and your valiant wife." Blazhkov definitively announced the move, and his new address, in his letter of 6 September 1963.

Reprisals I

Despite the difficulties that had forced the young couple's relocation, Prieberg kept pressing to publish unofficial Soviet music. On 11 December 1962, he acknowledged receipt of three more piano pieces, but expressed urgency about acquiring larger compositions, apparently in response to market demands. On 25 January 1963, Prieberg noted that he was still shopping Silvestrov's scores around, but that "Dr. [Hermann] Moeck [b. 1922] seemed to me more interested in orchestral pieces which have a better market here. And there should be more composers, more new names. Please try to find them. I wonder if Pärt, Andrey [Volkonsky] or several others of the avant-garde would be inclined to have a work published here?"

He also inquired after the idiosyncratic Leningrad composer Galina Ustvolskaya (1919–2006).[59] Prieberg provided Blazhkov an update on the publishing situation in his 9 April 1963 letter:

> The publisher ... thinks that some of the partitions are excellent and most could be used if the situation on the market for chamber and piano music would be better. He even gave me a preliminary draft of an agreement with the composer; yet he has no use for the small forms. Any orchestra piece will have his interest, and if it is good it will be published. My next move in behalf of the partitions is with the radio stations; it takes some time however.[60]

Overall, in 1963 Prieberg took on a greater role as a writer about new Soviet music. We have already noted his July 1963 *Survey* article. This article was preceded by one that he announced to Blazhkov in his letter from 5 January 1963, an "extensive study [in *Survey*] about the state of modern music in the USSR, citing names and facts and success of our mutual friends, Valentin [Silvestrov], Andrey [Volkonsky], Arvo [Pärt], etc. Their status in Soviet society is well demonstrated by official criticism poured over works like [Pärt's] 'Nekrolog' [*Obituary*]."[61] Prieberg's letter indicates how badly Soviet criticism backfired by drawing excessive attention to the material it was trying to squelch.

Up to this point, Prieberg had continued to maintain ties, however frustrating, with the Soviet Composers Union in Moscow. He was invited by *Sovetskaya muzyka* to write articles about musical life in West Germany, but they were never published.[62] Prieberg acknowledged that "in exceptional cases the Composers Union is of assistance," but complained that "the Composers Union has not yet sent me a recording of [Pärt's] 'Nekrolog.' Schnittke's oratorio 'Nagasaki' which has reached me after half a year of waiting and begging seems to be the summit of their good will."[63]

Any goodwill between the Soviet Composers Union and Prieberg evaporated entirely in 1963. The immediate catalyst was an article called "The New Music in the Soviet Union" that Prieberg published in *Die Zeit* on 12 April 1963, although his articles in *Survey* from January and July 1963 likely furthered the split. In the April article, Prieberg began by noting the "fierce campaign underway against the young Avantgardists in the USSR"—referring here to the fallout from the infamous Manezh exhibition of late 1962, at which Khrushchev memorably critiqued a display of avant-garde visual art.[64] Volkonsky and other young Soviet composers, notably Pärt, were caught up in the recriminations that followed, as Khrushchev himself inveighed against "dodecaphony" as a type of "cacophony."[65]

Given this backdrop, Mokreeva's talk at the House of Architects on 26 December 1962 was particularly ill timed. It coincided exactly with one of the first official speeches in Moscow by Central Committee ideological watchdog Leonid Ilichev, in which he attacked Volkonsky (among other creative figures). Prieberg's newly pessimistic articles were meant to counteract this "campaign" and to demonstrate that, as he put it in the January *Survey* article, "official speeches and articles paint a far too rosy picture of Soviet Russia as a musical country."[66] For Prieberg, the young composers were signs of life: "Naturally, the salvation of music does not lie in dodecaphony, but Russian twelve-tone music proves that the isolation of creative forces is not a permanency."[67]

In his letter to Blazhkov from 9 April 1963, Prieberg advised Blazhkov that he was going to "mail you another article about new music in the Soviet Union," likely referring to the forthcoming *Die Zeit* article. He also reflects on the recent crackdown, admitting:

> You were right: There is no "new course" in musical policy; I was shocked when reading the speeches of Ilichev and Khrushchev himself. He ought to know that the public explanation of his dislikes in music is identical with a taboo, the extreme counterpart of liberty. Some of my friends do not think it advisable to write of the inside situation; they fear that retaliations could be provoked. On the other hand, it is important to know of everything going on ... and I had the hope that at least dodecaphony would be tolerated in due time!

His friends were right to be apprehensive; Prieberg pressed on regardless. In his *Die Zeit* piece, Prieberg recognized the difficulties in programming the new Soviet music: "The first 'modern'—in our sense—pieces by Soviet composers have arrived in the West and were played here casually. So as to avoid any Pasternak effect, no fuss has been made around them." Prieberg's continued worrying about the "Pasternak effect" reveals the real effect the Soviet clampdown on the author of *Doctor Zhivago* had provoked: it raised rather than diminished interest in Soviet creative figures. Despite his worries, and despite the very real repercussions for Blazhkov and Mokreeva, Prieberg avidly kept programming unofficial Soviet music, convinced of the value of twelve-tone music as both a marker of and a stimulus for "liberty" in the USSR.

In *Die Zeit*, Prieberg further proclaimed the "great talent" in "modern" Soviet works, singling out Silvestrov as the "leader of the Kiev circle of friends."[68] Prieberg heard both the Schoenberg of 1925 and Webern in Silvestrov's music, but claimed that they had been "revived and heightened by him in such a way that one can speak not only of a Russian or Ukrainian twelve-tone style, but also of a pronounced personal style."⁶⁹ He also called attention to Volkonsky and the displaced Romanian Filipp Gershkovich (Herschkowitz) (a former pupil of Berg and Webern), as well as others in Kiev and Tallinn, among them Pärt and his much-discussed but little-heard orchestral *Obituary* (*Nekrolog*).

A string of Soviet denunciations of Prieberg's work quickly followed, initiated by the musicologist Israel Nestyev and joined by Sergey Aksyuk and Khrennikov—excerpts from the latter two were even translated and published in *Die Zeit* in November 1963 along with a response by Prieberg.⁷⁰ In an October 1963 *Sovetskaia muzyka* article tellingly titled "From the Position of the Cold War," Nestyev denounced Prieberg and other Western (and Central European) music critics, among them Stuckenschmidt, Antoine Goléa, André Hodeir, Colin Mason, Boris Schwarz, and Leon Markiewicz.⁷¹ He also took issue with Mokreeva's "Letter from Kiev" and criticized the Polish *Ruch muzyczny*'s "attempts ... to take upon itself the leadership of our musical youth," attempts "which are doomed to complete failure, all the more so since that decadent little group is increasingly meeting sharp criticism in our own country."

Nestyev then turned to Prieberg: "It is well-known that Prieberg, living in Baden-Baden, actively corresponds with several young Soviet musicians and even receives scores of their new compositions from them."⁷² The criticisms are sharp but familiar, the thinly veiled threats really aimed at Nestyev's young Soviet readers: "The young friends of Fred Prieberg, one should think, will soon overcome their 'childhood illnesses' if they are truly talented."⁷³ Nestyev, like many contemporary Soviet critics, adopted a condescendingly paternalistic tone, using his targets' youth as both cudgel and saving grace: this too shall pass, it is only a phase. Yet responses such as Nestyev's suggest Soviet music officials scrambling to deal with unfavorable information unofficially flowing, despite their best efforts, in and out of the country.

Never Pure

In his 17 August 1963 letter to Yudina, Prieberg observed that "gradually here they are beginning to be interested in the music of Valentin [Silvestrov]; it is purely musical interest, I try to impede all the rest."⁷⁴ Yet the interest was never purely musical. As Silvestrov (and the other young Soviets) were heard more widely outside the USSR, they also encountered for the first time criticism from non-Soviet sources, much of it betraying the larger sociopolitical and aesthetic assumptions lurking behind the ostensibly "purely musical interest." More specifically, the new music was consistently heard in relation to the Cold War.

Representative is the 4 September 1964 letter from Prieberg to Blazhkov, which reports on recent and upcoming performances of Silvestrov's music, notably at the Berliner Festwochen, where "no undue publicity is made and for the program book I have written but few sentences in the form of a short biography stating quite optimistically that it is possible to compose like this in the USSR and that 'western influence' means influence from Warsaw and Prague ... (I hope this will be true in the long run)."[75] The bulk of the letter concerned the judgment of noted German philosopher and musical thinker Theodor Adorno regarding Silvestrov's music. Prieberg continues,

> Adorno wrote me about his piano pieces. He thinks that Valentin is extremely gifted, yet he feels that it would be a pity if Valentin would repeat for himself the musical development after Schoenberg. This is exactly what makes me uneasy. He should by no means imitate the idiotic fads of certain of our young composers, e.g., in regard to "aleatoric" techniques. Musical creation has certain limits. To go beyond these is artistically irresponsible and, in his situation, even unwise as it might provoke rage in Mr. Tikhon [i.e., Khrennikov, the head of the Soviet Composers Union].[76]

Following this capsule summary of Adorno's 1955 essay "The Aging of the New Music," Prieberg launched his own evaluation of Soviet musical politics.[77] Here he further reflects his own preconceptions about his role as musical "importer" of advanced Soviet music:

> For the time being [Silvestrov's] pieces and their quality have provided me with the reasonable foundation to tell the public: the USSR has composers who can be superior to ours in the field of contemporary music, and surely this is what Tikhon [Khrennikov] would like to hear. Perhaps this is the way to induce him to grant "export licenses" for partitions. But how weak is my foundation if Valentin goes to the extreme of composing in the short-lived trend of aleatorics that cannot be justified by any critic. I want him to understand me correctly, and this is a cordial and friendly advice due to my experience with our musical scene.[78]

Prieberg then advised Silvestrov (through Blazhkov) to "concentrate on the development and intensification of the style of the trio [Silvestrov's Trio for Flute, Trumpet, and Celesta, 1962], for instance; this seems to be a good point of departure." (Not coincidentally, Silvestrov had dedicated the trio to Prieberg.) Prieberg then warned, "No imitation, please; at his musical standard there are no great models for him to be found here. For Valentin, there is a personal way of development." The letter conveyed Prieberg's assumptions in capsule form: about musical modernism, history, innovation, audience expectations, Cold War cultural competition, and authentic "Russian" or "Ukrainian" music. Blazhkov passed along Prieberg's (and Adorno's) comments to Silvestrov, but it is unclear what either Ukrainian musician made of them.[79]

The responses of Prieberg and Adorno trapped the young Soviet between two competing models of artistic production, West and East. Silvestrov was criticized from all sides. He apparently adopted the attitude recommended by his colleague Edison Denisov, who wrote in a 1965 letter to Blazhkov about the reviews of his (Denisov's) Paris premieres (presumably *Sun of the Incas*): "All of them are of a very low professional standard (although also positive-condescending). Tell Valya [Silvestrov] not to pay them any mind."[80] In early September 1966, Denisov further wrote to Blazhkov, "I don't trust Prieberg very much. He writes about our music in a way that plays right into Khrennikov's hands."[81] Apparently Silvestrov heeded the advice: Silvestrov's compositions from the mid-1960s to the early 1970s made ample use of the "aleatorics" that Prieberg scorned so severely.

In his letter to Blazhkov from 8 January 1965, Prieberg was still seeking a publisher for Silvestrov's music despite his ill-advised recent compositional choices: "As for publishing Valentin's works I am in contact with a publisher; if I could be sure to get more and all of his compositions, I myself would found a publishing agency for young music from USSR ... a nice idea, isn't it? But of course I would have to have also works by the other composers, so that expenses are not higher than the reward." Market forces consistently tempered Prieberg's entrepreneurial ambitions. Prieberg also sent along a tape of the "Bremen performance" of Silvestrov's music (presumably the Five Pieces for Piano).

Blazhkov replied in his letter of 28 February 1965: "We listened [to] the tape with a great joy. And Valentin was glad as a child. It is an enormous stimulus for his creative work." Through Prieberg (and Blazhkov), Silvestrov was able to gain something that he and many other young Soviet composers lobbied for whenever they could in the 1960s: performances.[82] In fact, the "first public performance of Silvestrov's works in the USSR" came only on 8 December 1965, when Blazhkov conducted the premiere of his *Spectrums* (*Spektry*, 1965) for orchestra.[83] The young Soviet composers wanted to hear their music in order to continue developing artistically, but because of their perceived stylistic indiscretions, they had few opportunities. As a result, they stuck to less noticeable forms—for piano or smaller ensembles, precisely those groupings that Prieberg and Western publishers like Moeck found so unmarketable. Perhaps because of the prodding from Prieberg, mediated by Blazhkov, Silvestrov began writing larger compositions in the second half of the 1960s. One of these, his gigantic Symphony no. 3, *Eschatophony,* was awarded a Koussevitzky Prize in 1967 and was performed in Darmstadt the following year; the orchestral *Hymn* (1967) won second prize at the International Gaudeamus Composers' Competition in 1970.[84] It is telling that *Eschatophony* had to wait another eight years for a performance in the Soviet Union (on 2 October 1976 in Kiev).[85]

By mid-1965, Blazhkov had become extremely active in his new post in Leningrad and his correspondence with Prieberg became sporadic. Mokreeva had begun graduate work in music theory at the Leningrad Conservatory, researching a dissertation on Stravinsky.[86] In his lengthy letter of 28 September 1965, Blazhkov updated Prieberg on the creative and personal lives of his *confrères* and urged him to adopt a new project: "It seems to me that you must work at new book on young Soviet composers solely." By the letter of 10 September 1967, Blazhkov apparently had taken on that—hitherto uncompleted—task himself. In his letter from 5 October 1966, Blazhkov reminded Prieberg of his intent to find publishers for the young Soviets: "Could you renew your negotiations with Dr. Hermann Moeck as well as with the UE [Universal Edition]? I think [Silvestrov's] "The Spectrums," [Denisov's] "The Sun of the Incas" [1964], and [Volkonsky's] "The Laments of Shchaza" could adorn their business." Universal Edition published the *Laments of Shchaza* in 1970, and the *Sun of the Incas* in 1971; *Spectrums* was only recently published by Belaieff.

In addition, Silvestrov's *Serenade* from his *Triad* (*Triada*, 1962) appeared in 1968 in the collection *New Soviet Piano Music,* edited by Rudolf Lück and published in Cologne by Gerig.[87] Upon hearing of Prieberg's (limited) involvement with the project, Blazhkov urged him (in vain) to cut the works by Gliére, Kabalevsky, and Sviridov from the collection: "These pieces are very mediocre and in addition they have nothing in common with the title 'New Soviet Piano Music.'" Blazhkov also asked (again in vain) that the other two movements of Silvestrov's *Triad* be included, in addition to Volkonsky's *Musica Stricta* and Zahortsev's *Rhythms.* Prieberg justified the "several really mediocre pieces" that Blazhkov had noted, demonstrating an awareness of the musical market similar to that in his 8 January

1965 letter: the publisher "had some business reasons, one of them being the idea that the Russian State Publisher should be pleased (for some intended cooperation the nature of which I do not know), the other being the expectation that not all of the buyers are friends of avantgardistic styles nor able to play complicated music."[88] For perhaps the first (but not last) time, the young Soviet modernists were stymied by the fickle tastes of the open market. The world was not black and white: what was condemned in the USSR was not necessarily welcomed with open arms in Europe.

Reprisals II: Tragedy

In his letters from 1966 and 1967, Blazhkov remained upbeat. He was brimming with projects, and his composer friends were faring well. Yet the same year the German piano volumes finally appeared, Blazhkov suffered several terrible shocks. In late June 1968, he was removed from his post at the Leningrad Philharmonic because of his advocacy of new music, or, in the sterile language of the official pronouncement, for "insufficiencies in the repertoire of the Leningrad Philharmonic."[89]

By the middle of 1968, Mokreeva and Blazhkov were enduring a painful separation. He was having a spiritual crisis as well: he visited the philosopher Yakov Druskin in late May asking whether he should be baptized.[90] A distraught letter dated 22 July 1968 from Blazhkov to Silvestrov records his distressed state:

> Believe me, I am in a condition that prevents writing to anyone about anything. Beginning from the moment of the preparations for our concert at the end of March to the present day, I find myself without breathing space, in a constant vortex.[91] I have in mind more internal factors than external. For already fate truly decided to set up tests of strength for me in all possible spheres—spiritual, intimate, and others. Therefore, even my expulsion from the [Leningrad] Philharmonic passed by me unnoticed somehow. Most likely I'll have a chance to feel that sometime later.

Blazhkov and Mokreeva's situation only deteriorated. On 2 December 1968, Mokreeva committed suicide.[92] She was thirty-two. Blazhkov's belated announcement to Prieberg was blunt: "As to me, my personal life turned out very unfortunately. In 1963 I was invited to work as a conductor in the Leningrad Philharmonic. I with my wife Galya moved in Leningrad where she teached a musical branches. And on December 1968 she perished. We buried her in Kiev." After this stunning revelation, Blazhkov's matter-of-fact recitation of his new life is particularly poignant: "I came back to Kiev again and now am an artistic leader and conductor of the Kiev Chamber Orchestra. A lot of time passes in concert tours through the country ... I often conduct by the scores which you sent me once and remember you with great warmth." In his postscript he asked for scores by Couperin, Vivaldi, and others.[93]

Prieberg's immediate response, if he responded at all, does not survive. His next letter from 3 August 1973 returned to more mundane matters. An epistolary silence ensues for over a decade. The final letter that survives is from Blazhkov to Prieberg, dated 4 July 1985:

> Yes, my friend, our friendly relations are already lasting 25 years. We are advancing in age. My son Kirill is now 8. He studies piano at a musical

Figure 7.3. Valentin Silvestrov and Igor Blazkhov, 1975.
Source: Larisa Bondarenko.

school. Please Fred write me about your work and your family life.... I should be very grateful if you would get for me D. Scarlatti's Oboe Concerto (score) or Concerto for 2 Violins (score). I sincerely hope you will be able to help me in this matter.

Conclusion

Over the past decade, musicologists have gradually approached a consensus about reception that, in the formulation of diplomatic historian Jessica C. E. Gienow-Hecht, "what matters about music is not only what is played but what people hear and think while giving or attending a performance."[94] And what they hear, think, say, and write before and after a performance. This list should be further expanded, as Christopher Small does, to include performances in a much broader sense, including listening to recordings in the privacy of one's home or other intimate spaces.[95] Furthermore, despite the damage it does to the sanctified image of the canonic masterpiece, it is becoming clear that music's meanings are directly related to how it is bought and sold or otherwise disseminated. With this more holistic, "thicker" conceptualization and contextualization of the musical act, we begin to understand to what degree the history of music's reception is an intimate history, or, more specifically, a very private history with very public ramifications. The same might easily be said of international relations, as suggested, for example, by Costigliola's study of the effects of Kennan's personal, intellectual, and emotional experiences on "his ostensibly realistic prose," especially the well-known long telegram of 1946.[96]

What can Blazhkov's networks of exchange tell us about international relations? A great deal, it turns out. Both sides took their roles very seriously, and both sides often misunderstood each other. Prieberg's idealistic preconceptions about freedom of expression and musical style were counterpoised by Blazhkov's idealistic expectations about foreign publication and performance as well as by naïve official Soviet ideas about acceptable and unacceptable music and the results of criticism, just or not. How else to explain the missteps Soviet officials made with Pärt and Volkonsky? Denunciations that attempted to silence them only drew the eager attention of foreigners. But this was the little-mentioned flip side of the "Pasternak effect" that Prieberg cited so frequently. The Iron Curtain had become rather porous by the 1960s, and information, although intermittent, flowed nonetheless. Competing worldviews collided and fed one another as acceptable ensembles, techniques, and styles were heatedly debated. Yet the Cold War and its rhetoric of freedom suffused everything, rising to the forefront in many of Prieberg's pronouncements, as we have seen.

What can international relations tell us about music? As the intimate history of Blazhkov, Prieberg, Mokreeva (and Silvestrov) indicates, during the Cold War, seemingly apolitical music became politicized to the core, implicated in all sorts of international relations as it was constructed, framed, bought, and sold. Music enjoyed a vibrant social existence that often spilled across national boundaries. Yet, as musicologist Mary Ann Smart cautions,

> [m]usicologists sometimes need to be reminded that "society" is more than simply another word for the people who made and consumed music in a particular place or time. It is also a set of collective practices partially shaped or willed by their participants, its contracts constantly in flux, formed by conversation, exchange of opinion, and print culture.[97]

And, I might add, formed in the twentieth century by new types of aural and material culture: radio, television, telephone, LPs, and tape recordings. Intimate history both comprises and elucidates the kinetic "collective practices" Smart identifies.

Finally, historians and musicologists alike could benefit from the reminder that, to borrow historian Andrew Zimmerman's potent phrase, the "historically miniscule can transform the historically enormous."[98] This is what intimate histories promise: discerning the enormous in the miniature. Intimate histories—such as that informed by Prieberg and Blazhkov's correspondence—offer models for tracing similar dynamic intersections of music and society, both close and vast.

Acknowledgments

I am greatly indebted to Igor Blazhkov for providing me with crucial assistance and materials in the preparation of this chapter, particularly his correspondence with Prieberg, Denisov, and Silvestrov. I dedicate this essay to Igor Blazhkov and to the memory of Galina Mokreeva. I would also like to express thanks to the Washington University in St. Louis interdisciplinary faculty seminar "Intimate Histories of the Cold War and Decolonization," convened by Jean Allman and Andrea Friedman. Our lively discussions helped propel this project forward. They coined the phrase "intimate history." Finally, I am grateful to Danielle Fosler-Lussier and Jessica C. E. Gienow-Hecht for their careful readings of the text. A forthcoming article of mine in the *Journal of Musicological Research* called "'Shostakovich' Fights the Cold

War: Reflections from Great to Small" continues the present discussion of intimate history during the Cold War.

Notes

Dedicated to Igor Blazhkov and in memory of Galina Mokreeva.
1. A picture of the *Vitiaz* along with detailed specifications can be found in N. N. Sysoev, "Ekspeditsionnoe sudno 'Vitiaz,'" *Trydy instituta okeanologii* 16 (1959): 3–23. The ship became part of Soviet and American Cold War tussling when it was forced to return to port in late May 1958 as a result of alleged contamination resulting from US nuclear testing on the Marshall Islands. See V. Petelin, "'Vitiaz' vozvrashchaetsia dosrochno," *Sovremennyi vostok*, no. 10 (1958): 22–24 (esp. the final paragraphs on p. 24); "Russians Say Ship Fled U.S. Fall-Out: Pravda Asserts Atomic Rain Menaced Craft 2,000 Miles From Tests in Pacific," *New York Times*, 7 June 1958, 9; "Soviet I.G.Y. Ship is Home," *New York Times*, 21 June 1958, 5; "Soviet Ship Contaminated," *New York Times*, 8 August 1958, 7.
2. The information in this and the preceding paragraph was drawn largely from my telephone interview with Coleman on 20 October 2010. His memories have been corroborated by correspondence and conversations with Igor Blazhkov and by consulting contemporary publications, including: A. D. Dobrovol'skii, "'Vitiaz' v okeane," *Nauka i zhizn'*, no. 7 (1958): 35–38; Sysoev, "Ekspeditsionnoe sudno 'Vitiaz,'" 3–23; "Soviet Vessel in Pacific," *New York Times*, 2 February 1959, 17; "Space Group Asks About Soviet Ship; House Panel Member Says Science Vessel Lingers at Pacific Missile Area," *New York Times*, 17 February 1959, 4; Walter Sullivan, "Sea Depths Yield Secrets in I.G.Y.," *New York Times*, 5 January 1959, 4; "Scientists Open Pacific Congress; Honolulu Sessions to Study Problems of Area," *New York Times*, 22 August 1961, 17; "Soviet Scientists Invite Foreigners on a Cruise," *New York Times*, 2 September 1961, 37.
3. A. Pavlova, "Na Gavaiskikh ostrovakh," *Muzykal'naia zhizn'*, no. 11 (1959): 16–17. All quotations in this paragraph are from this article.
4. Catherine E. Toth, "1919–2007: Hawaii Surf Activist John Kelly Dies," *Honolulu Advertiser*, 5 October 2007, A1. See also Dzhon Kelli, "Pis'mo iz Gonolulu," *Muzykal'naia zhizn'*, no. 15 (1960): 14.
5. Igor Blazhkov, interview with author, telephone, digital recording, 27 April 2009; emails from 19 July 2011 and 22 October 2010.
6. See Peter J. Schmelz, *Such Freedom, If Only Musical: Unofficial Soviet Music during the Thaw* (New York: Oxford University Press, 2009), 46.
7. An important recent source on Mokreeva is Igor' Blazhkov, ed., *Galina Mokreeva: Stat'i, pis'ma, vospominaniia* (Kiev: Dukh i litera, 2013).
8. See Simo Mikkonen, "Stealing the Monopoly of Knowledge? Soviet Reactions to U.S. Cold War Broadcasting," *Kritika: Explorations in Russian and Eurasian History*, n.s., 11, no. 4 (2010): 771–805; Anne E. Gorsuch and Diane P. Koenker, eds., *Turizm: The Russian and East European Tourist under Capitalism and Socialism* (Ithaca, NY: Cornell University Press, 2006); Anne E. Gorsuch, *All This Is Your World: Soviet Tourism at Home and Abroad after Stalin* (Oxford and New York: Oxford University Press, 2011); Diane P. Koenker, *Club Red: Vacation Travel and the Soviet Dream* (Ithaca, NY: Cornell University Press, 2013); Peter J. Schmelz, "Alfred Schnittke's *Nagasaki*: Soviet Nuclear Culture, Radio Moscow, and the Global Cold War," *Journal of the American Musicological Society* 62 (2009): 413–74.

9. For a cogent introduction to microhistory, see Carlo Ginzburg, "Microhistory: Two or Three Things That I Know about It," in *Threads and Traces: True False Fictive*, trans. Anne C. Tedeschi and John Tedeschi (Berkeley: University of California Press, 2012), 193–214.
10. Emma Rothschild, *The Inner Life of Empires: An Eighteenth-Century History* (Princeton, NJ, and Oxford: Princeton University Press, 2011), 7 (see also p. 6).
11. Thus, to varying degrees the work of Orlando Figes, Irina Paperno, Alexei Yurchak, and Sergei I. Zhuk all might be characterized as intimate histories. See Orlando Figes, *The Whisperers: Private Life in Stalin's Russia* (New York: Metropolitan Books, 2007); Figes, *Just Send Me Word: A True Story of Love and Survival in the Gulag* (New York: Metropolitan Books, 2012); Irina Paperno, *Stories of the Soviet Experience: Memoirs, Diaries, Dreams* (Ithaca, NY, and London: Cornell University Press, 2009), esp. 17–24; Alexei Yurchak, *Everything Was Forever, Until It Was No More: The Last Soviet Generation* (Princeton, NJ: Princeton University Press, 2006); Sergei I. Zhuk, *Rock and Roll in the Rocket City: The West, Identity, and Ideology in Soviet Dniepropetrovsk, 1960–1985* (Baltimore: Johns Hopkins University Press, 2010).
12. Danielle Fosler-Lussier, "Cultural Diplomacy as Cultural Globalization: The University of Michigan Jazz Band in Latin America," *Journal of the Society for American Music* 4, no. 1 (2010): 59–93. See also Danielle Fosler-Lussier, *Music in America's Cold War Diplomacy* (Berkeley: University of California Press, forthcoming 2015). Note that this emphasis on private connections is distinct from W. Scott Lucas's research into state-private networks during the Cold War. See W. Scott Lucas, "Mobilizing Culture: The State-Private Network and the CIA in the Early Cold War," in *War and Cold War in American Foreign Policy, 1942–62*, ed. Dale Carter and Robin Clifton (New York: Palgrave, 2002), 83–107.
13. Blazhkov was not alone: pianist Maria Yudina—herself a major figure worthy of greater attention—carried out a voluminous correspondence with foreign musicians, most of which has now been published. See the citations to this correspondence below (and the bibliography below) for more detailed bibliographic information.
14. See William D. Davidson and Joseph V. Montville, "Foreign Policy According to Freud," *Foreign Policy* 45 (1981–82): 145–57, esp. 155; and Ross Mackenzie, *When Stars and Stripes Met Hammer and Sickle: The Chautauqua Conferences on U.S.-Soviet Relations, 1985–1989* (Columbia: University of South Carolina Press, 2006), 3. Colorful examples of quasi-official (if not unofficial) "non-structured interaction" between American diplomats and Russian diplomats and others (including ballerinas) appear in Frank Costigliola, "'Unceasing Pressure for Penetration': Gender, Pathology, and Emotion in George Kennan's Formation of the Cold War," *Journal of American History* 83, no. 4 (1997): 1309–39, esp. 1314–20.
15. See Benjamin Piekut, *Experimentalism Otherwise: The New York Avant-Garde and Its Limits* (Berkeley and Los Angeles: University of California Press, 2011), esp. 8–9, 15. See also Benjamin Piekut, "Actor-Networks in Music History: Clarifications and Critiques," *Twentieth-Century Music* 11, no. 2 (2014): 191–215.
16. See Schmelz, *Such Freedom, If Only Musical,* chap. 1.
17. See, for example, the two special issues of *Poetics Today,* "Publish and Perish: Samizdat and Underground Cultural Practices in the Soviet Bloc," volume 29, no. 4 (2008) and volume 30, no. 1 (2009), especially Peter Steiner, "Introduction: On Samizdat, Tamizdat, Magnitizdat, and Other Strange Words That Are Difficult to Pronounce," *Poetics Today* 29, no. 4 (2008): 613–28.
18. See, for example, Serguei Oushakine, "The Terrifying Mimicry of Samizdat," *Public Culture* 13, no. 2 (2001): 191–214; see also several articles in the *Poetics Today*

"Publish and Perish" special issues, volume 29, no. 4 (2008) and volume 30, no. 1 (2009).
19. Prieberg to Yudina, 30 May 1962, in Mariia Iudina, *Dukh dyshit, gde khochet: Perepiska 1962–1963 gg.* (Moscow: Rossiiskaia politicheskaia entsiklopediia, 2010), 208.
20. There is by now a sizable bibliography on this topic. See, for example, Danielle Fosler-Lussier, *Music Divided: Bartók's Legacy in Cold War Culture* (Berkeley: University of California Press, 2007), as well as the articles in Peter J. Schmelz and Elizabeth Bergman, eds., "Music in the Cold War," special issues, *Journal of Musicology* 26, nos. 1 and 2 (2009).
21. For more on the branding of the Soviet avant-garde in the late Cold War period, see Peter J. Schmelz, "Selling Schnittke: Late Soviet Censorship and the Cold War Marketplace," in *The Oxford Handbook of Musical Censorship*, ed. Patricia Z. Hall (Oxford: Oxford University Press, forthcoming).
22. In 1965 there were two primary conductors, Mravinsky and Jansons, and three assistants, Blazhkov, Serov, and Alyev. Boris Schwarz, *Music and Musical Life in Soviet Russia, Enlarged Edition, 1917–1981* (Bloomington: Indiana University Press, 1983), 465.
23. Blazhkov's recordings are difficult to obtain. Those on compact disc worth seeking out include: Igor Blazhkov, conductor, Kiev Symphony Orchestra, *Prokofiev-Tchaïkovsky-Kabalevsky*, Analekta Fleur dy Lys CD, FL 2 3036, 1995; Dmitri Shostakovich, *Symphony no. 2 and Symphony no. 10*, with Blazhkov conducting Leningrad Philharmonic Choir and Orchestra in the Symphony no. 2, Russian Disc CD, RD CD 11 195, 1993.
24. I discovered the date for this premiere only after the publication of Schmelz, *Such Freedom, If Only Musical* (see p. 125, note 139). It is taken from the program for the concert that Blazhkov kindly provided me. The first half of the program featured various works by Frescobaldi. The second half consisted of Franco Donatoni's *Doubles* for harpsichord (1961), followed by Volkonsky's new composition.
25. From the unpublished transcript of Blazhkov's January 2008 interview with Tat'iana Frumkis, a condensed version of which (missing this information) appeared as: Tat'iana Frumkis, "'Trudnosti udesiateriali moiu energiiu,'" *Evropa-Ekspress*, no. 7 (11 February 2008), http://www.euxpress.de/archive/artikel_8402.html (inactive link; last accessed 31 July 2013); now available at http://archive.today/Z55S (accessed 9 October 2014). Blazhkov kindly provided me with a copy of the full transcript of the interview.
26. Letters of 22 August 1964, 28 September 1965, 31 March 1963, 6 October 1962, 5 December 1962, and 15 June 1963, among others. Blazhkov graciously provided me copies of both Prieberg's and his letters (which he kept copies of). Blazhkov maintains the originals in his personal archive.
27. Prieberg to Blazhkov, 7 January 1962.
28. Prieberg to Blazhkov, 2 October 1961.
29. Blazhkov interview with Frumkis, January 2008, unpublished transcript. In Blazhkov's letter to Prieberg from 28 January 1962, he requests Prieberg to ask Stockhausen to send him several recordings (*Kontra-Punkte, Klavierstücke I–IV*, and *Klavierstück XI*), plus volumes 1–4 of the English edition of the journal *Die Reihe*. Prieberg sent Stockhausen's *Study* to Blazhkov himself (1 February 1962 letter from Blazhkov to Prieberg). Blazhkov asked again about *Die Reihe* in his 6 September 1963 letter.
30. For more basic facts about Prieberg, including a bibliography of his writings, see Oliver Kopf, "Prieberg, Fred K.," in *Musik in Geschichte und Gegenwart: Personen-*

teil, vol. 13, 2nd, new edition, ed. Ludwig Finscher (Kassel: Bärenreiter, 2005), 931–32.
31. I have preserved most of the syntax and other meaningful idiosyncratic aspects of these exchanges (including the foreign words that appeared in both their prose), but have corrected obvious small errors and misspellings and made proper names uniform. Unless otherwise noted, all translations are mine.
32. See also Prieberg to Yudina, 22 December 1961, in Mariia Iudina, *V iskusstve radostno byt' vmeste: Perepiska 1959–1961 gg.* (Moscow: Rossiiskaia politicheskaia entsiklopediia, 2009), 721.
33. Blazhkov to Prieberg, 1 February 1962.
34. Blazhkov to Yudina, 22 July 1961, in Iudina, *V iskusstve radostno byt' vmeste*, 606–7. A significant detail emerges at the end of the letter to Yudina: Wolfgang Steinecke (1910–61), critic and founder of the Darmstadt new music courses, had recently ("the other day") sent Blazhkov an official invitation for Blazhkov, Silvestrov, and Grabovsky to visit Darmstadt that summer, all expenses covered. The request was predictably denied by the central music officials in Moscow—to whom Steinecke had also apparently sent copies of the invitations through Karen Khachaturyan, whom Steinecke had met at a music festival in Zagreb. The three young Ukrainians never attended the Darmstadt courses, although Silvestrov's Symphony no. 3, *Eschatophony,* was heard there in September 1968.
35. Blazhkov to Prieberg, 5 December 1962.
36. Fred K. Prieberg, "The Sound of New Music," *Survey: A Journal of Soviet and East European Studies,* no. 46 (January 1963): 99.
37. Brief mention is made of "Konstantin" [sic] Silvestrov's *Trio* in H. H. Stuckenschmidt, *Twentieth Century Music,* trans. Richard Deveson (New York and Toronto: McGraw-Hill, 1969), 228.
38. Prieberg to Blazhkov, 7 January 1962.
39. Blazhkov to Prieberg, 26 December 1961; Prieberg to Blazhkov, 7 January 1962.
40. An example is Blazhkov to Silvestrov, 12 September 1966. This correspondence is available in the Sammlung Valentin Silvestrov at the Paul Sacher Stiftung in Basel, Switzerland.
41. See, for example, Blazhkov to Prieberg, 13 February 1962.
42. Blazhkov to Prieberg, 31 March 1962.
43. Compare with Prieberg's 30 May 1962 letter to Yudina, in Iudina, *Dukh dyshit, gde khochet,* 208.
44. See Schmelz, *Such Freedom, If Only Musical,* 98–112.
45. For more on the "Pasternak Effect," see the recent Peter Finn and Petra Couvée, *The Zhivago Affair: The Kremlin, the CIA, and the Battle Over a Forbidden Book* (New York: Pantheon Books, 2014).
46. Halina Mokrejewa [Galina Mokreeva], "List z Kijowa," *Ruch muzyczny,* no. 9 (1 May 1962): 18–19. This is a translation from the Russian version of the text prepared by Blazhkov, which he kindly provided to me. It has subsequently been published in Blazhkov, ed., *Galina Mokreeva,* 253–56.
47. Blazhkov to Yudina, 26 May 1962, in Iudina, *Dukh dyshit, gde khochet,* 219–20, 272–74. For Yudina's response to the Silvestrov request, see her letter to Blazhkov and Mokreeva from 20 July 1962, in Iudina, *Dukh dyshit, gde khochet,* 274. Yudina had initially responded with a troubled, sympathetic telegram on 3 June 1962; subsequent, longer letters followed as she scrambled to help the couple. Blazhkov found temporary work with the second orchestra of the Leningrad Philharmonic during its summer stay in Sochi; he conducted open-air concerts and rehearsed compositions by Stravinsky with the ensemble in preparation for the composer's visit that October. According to a letter from Mokreeva to

Yudina from late 1962, the couple remained in dire financial circumstances. See Blazhkov, ed., *Galina Mokreeva,* 343–50 and 355; Iudina, *Dukh dyshit, gde khochet,* 275–76n6.

48. He likely refers to Yudina's letter from 21 May 1962. Note also Prieberg's response from 30 May 1962. See Iudina, *Dukh dyshit, gde khochet,* 199–207, esp. 201–2, 204–5 (nos. 6 and 9); see also 207–8.
49. Prieberg to Blazhkov, 19 June 1962.
50. All the quotations in this paragraph are from Prieberg to Blazhkov, 4 August 1962.
51. Prieberg to Blazhkov, 25 August 1962 (resent on 18 September 1962).
52. Grigorii Shneerson to Fred Prieberg, undated insertion (original in Russian) to letter of 5 October 1962 from Prieberg to Blazhkov.
53. Andrzej Kowalewski [Igor Blazhkov], "Strawiński w ojczyźnie," *Ruch muzyczny,* no. 1 (1963): 14–16. I am grateful to Igor Blazhkov for providing me with a copy of the Russian version of this article.
54. Blazhkov to Prieberg, 12 February 1963 (original in Russian).
55. Blazhkov, ed., *Galina Mokreeva,* 7.
56. Blazhkov to Prieberg, 12 February 1963 (original in Russian). At this time Mokreeva only possessed an undergraduate degree in musicology from the Kiev Conservatory (and that not without controversy). She subsequently was denied admission into the graduate musicology program at the Kiev Conservatory because of a poor score on the Marxism section of the entrance exam. See Mokreeva's letters to Yudina on 7-8 July 1961 and 8 October 1961 in Blazhkov, ed., *Galina Mokreeva,* 329–30 and 334–35.
57. The *Survey* material on Mokreeva, in turn, appeared in Prieberg's *Musik in der Sowjetunion* (Cologne: Verlag Wissenschaft und Politik, 1965), 343.
58. Fred K. Prieberg, "Music," *Survey: A Journal of Soviet and East European Studies,* no. 48 (July 1963): 31–32.
59. Moeck, the son of Moeck Verlag's founder, was actively recruiting avant-garde Polish music at this time, as Prieberg also reported in this letter.
60. In his previous letter, from 12 February 1963, Blazhkov had sent Silvestrov's *doverennost'* (proxy) to Prieberg, i.e., the document that granted Prieberg authority to collect royalties and conduct other business transactions on his behalf.
61. Prieberg also mentioned that "a second article will appear in the German journal *Osteuropa* soon," but this seems never to have been published; perhaps it went to *Die Zeit* instead.
62. See Prieberg to Yudina, 18 January 1962; Yudina to Prieberg, 21 May 1962; Prieberg to Blazhkov, 19 June 1962. The first two are in Iudina, *Dukh dyshit, gde khochet,* 21–22, 201, 204–5, 206–7n11.
63. Prieberg to Blazhkov, 9 April 1963. In his letters of 6 October 1962 and 30 November 1962, Blazhkov mentioned searching for the Pärt score, but he was complaining a year later that "I have a friendly relations with Andrey and Arvo, but it is a year yet as I am waiting for their promises" (6 September 1963). See also Schmelz, "Alfred Schnittke's *Nagasaki.*"
64. Fred K. Prieberg (misspelled as "Priebeie" in the *Die Zeit* online archive), "Die neue Musik in der Sowjetunion," *Die Zeit,* 12 April 1963.
65. See Schmelz, *Such Freedom, If Only Musical,* 111–12, 5.
66. Prieberg, "The Sound of New Music," 95. Blazhkov acknowledged receiving a copy of this article in his 9 April 1963 letter to Prieberg.
67. Prieberg, "The Sound of New Music," 101.
68. Prieberg [Priebeie], "Die neue Musik in der Sowjetunion."
69. Prieberg [Priebeie], "Die neue Musik in der Sowjetunion."

70. S. Akssjuk [Sergei Aksiuk], "Fred Priebergs Irrtümer," *Die Zeit,* 29 November 1963 (originally in *Sovetskaia kul'tura,* 5 October 1963); Tichon Chrennikov [Tikhon Khrennikov], "Für die Musik der kommunistischen Zukunft," *Die Zeit,* 29 November 1963 (originally in *Sovetskaia kul'tura,* 19 October 1963); and Fred Prieberg, "Fred Priebergs Antwort," *Die Zeit,* 29 November 1963.
71. Blazhkov had warned him of Nestyev's impending article in his letter from 6 September 1963.
72. I. Nest'ev, "S pozitsii 'Kholodnoi voiny,'" *Sovetskaia muzyka* 10 (1963): 125–30 (quotation on p. 129). See also Prieberg [Priebeie], "Die neue Musik in der Sowjetunion." This supports Blazhkov's contention that the KGB carefully monitored all of his foreign correspondence and, as a result, prevented him from obtaining visas to travel abroad. Blazhkov interview with Frumkis, January 2008, unpublished transcript.
73. Note also Yudina's ironic comment to Pierre Suvchinsky about Prieberg's Soviet woes in her letter of 14–15 April 1964. In Mariia Iudina, *Nereal'nost' zla: Perepiska 1964–1966 gg.* (Moscow: Rossiiskaia politicheskaia entsiklopediia, 2010), 72.
74. In Iudina, *Dukh dyshit, gde khochet,* 580.
75. Silvestrov's Trio for Flute, Trumpet, and Celesta (1962) was premiered at the Berliner Festwochen on 24 September 1964, with Aurele Nicolet on flute, Frizz Wesenigk on trumpet, and Rolf Kuhnert on celesta.
76. Adorno's letter from 25 May 1964 to Prieberg is reprinted in Tat'iana Frumkis, "Dukh riskovannoi svobody," in *Symposion [ΣΥΜΠΟΣΙΟΝ]: Vstrechi s Valentinom Sil'vestrovym,* ed. Alla Vaisband and Konstantin Sigov (Kiev: Dukh i litera, 2012), 353–54; an excerpt appears in Tatjana Frumkis, "Vorwort/Preface," in Valentin Silvestrov, *Klavierwerke (Werke von 1961 bis 1979),* vol. 1 (Frankfurt/M.: M. P. Beliaeff, 2006), v.
77. Theodor W. Adorno, "The Aging of the New Music (1955)," in *Essays on Music,* ed. Richard Leppert, trans. Susan H. Gillespie (Berkeley and Los Angeles: University of California Press, 2002), 181–202.
78. Prieberg made similar comments in his 12 February 1964 letter to Yudina. See Iudina, *Nereal'nost' zla,* 28.
79. See also Prieberg, *Musik in der Sowjetunion,* 346.
80. Denisov to Blazhkov, 30 July 1966.
81. Denisov to Blazhkov, 6 September 1966.
82. See, in reference to this, Silvestrov's comments in the section "Slovo molodezhi," *Sovetskaia muzyka,* no. 5 (1968): 22.
83. Blazhkov to Prieberg, 12 September 1966.
84. The prize was 1,000 guilders. See *Gaudeamus Information,* November–December 1970.
85. For more on *Eschatophony,* see Peter J. Schmelz, "Valentin Silvestrov and the Echoes of Music History," *Journal of Musicology* 31, no. 2 (2014): 235–38.
86. Iudina, *Dukh dyshit, gde khochet,* 16n1.
87. Rudolf Lück, ed., *Neue sowjetische Klaviermusik,* 2 vols. (Cologne: Gerig, [1968]), 1:23–26.
88. Prieberg to Blazhkov, 12 December 1967. This restates his market awareness from his 8 January 1965 letter.
89. The decree in question was from the Directorate of Musical Institutions of the Ministry of Culture of the USSR, dated 20 June 1968. Its full title was "O nedostatkakh repertuara Leningradskoi filarmoniia" (On insufficiencies in the repertoire of the Leningrad Philharmonic). See also Schmelz, "Selling Schnittke."
90. See Iakov Druskin, *Pered prinadlezhnostiami chego-libo: Dnevniki 1963–1979* (Saint Petersburg: Akademicheskii proekt, 2001), 385–88.

91. Silvestrov's Symphony no. 2 was premiered in Leningrad on 1 April 1968 with Blazhkov conducting the Leningrad Chamber Orchestra.
92. See Blazhkov, ed., *Galina Mokreeva,* 8; see also Druskin, *Pered prinadlezhnostiami chego-libo,* 435 (see also p. 368 on Mokreeva's baptism).
93. Blazhkov to Prieberg, 27 November 1971.
94. Jessica C. E. Gienow-Hecht, *Sound Diplomacy: Music and Emotions in Transatlantic Relations, 1850–1920* (Chicago: University of Chicago Press, 2009), 223.
95. Christopher Small, *Musicking: The Meanings of Performing and Listening* (Middleton, CT: Wesleyan University Press, 1998).
96. Costigliola, "'Unceasing Pressure for Penetration,'" 1309.
97. Mary Ann Smart, "Commentary: A Stroll in the Piazza and a Night at the Opera," *Journal of Interdisciplinary History* 36, no. 4 (2006): 621.
98. Andrew Zimmerman, *Alabama in Africa: Booker T. Washington, the German Empire, and the Globalization of the New South* (Princeton, NJ, and Oxford: Princeton University Press, 2010), 247–48. For another recent consideration of the points of intersection between history and musicology, see Jane F. Fulcher, "Introduction: Defining the New Cultural History of Music, Its Origins, Methodologies, and Lines of Inquiry," in *The Oxford Handbook of the New Cultural History of Music,* ed. Jane F. Fulcher (Oxford and New York: Oxford University Press, 2011), 3–14.

Bibliography

Adorno, Theodor W. "The Aging of the New Music (1955)." In *Essays on Music,* edited by Richard Leppert, translated by Susan H. Gillespie, 181–202. Berkeley and Los Angeles: University of California Press, 2002.
Akssjuk, S. [Sergei Aksiuk]. "Fred Priebergs Irrtümer." *Die Zeit,* 29 November 1963. Originally in *Sovetskaia kul'tura,* 5 October 1963.
Blazhkov, Igor', ed. *Galina Mokreeva: Stat'i, pis'ma, vospominaniia.* Kiev: Dukh i litera, 2013.
Chrennikov, Tichon [Tikhon Khrennikov]. "Für die Musik der kommunistischen Zukunft." *Die Zeit,* 29 November 1963. Originally in *Sovetskaia kul'tura,* 19 October 1963.
Costigliola, Frank. "'Unceasing Pressure for Penetration': Gender, Pathology, and Emotion in George Kennan's Formation of the Cold War." *Journal of American History* 83, no. 4 (1997): 1309–39.
Davidson, William D., and Joseph V. Montville. "Foreign Policy According to Freud." *Foreign Policy* 45 (1981–82): 145–57.
Dobrovol'skii, A. D. "'Vitiaz' v okeane." *Nauka i zhizn',* no. 7 (1958): 35–38.
Druskin, Iakov. *Pered prinadlezhnostiami chego-libo: Dnevniki 1963–1979.* Saint Petersburg: Akademicheskii proyekt, 2001.
Figes, Orlando. *Just Send Me Word: A True Story of Love and Survival in the Gulag.* New York: Metropolitan Books, 2012.
Figes, Orlando. *The Whisperers: Private Life in Stalin's Russia.* New York: Metropolitan Books, 2007.

Finn, Peter, and Petra Couvée. *The Zhivago Affair: The Kremlin, the CIA, and the Battle Over a Forbidden Book.* New York: Pantheon Books, 2014.
Fosler-Lussier, Danielle. "Cultural Diplomacy as Cultural Globalization: The University of Michigan Jazz Band in Latin America." *Journal of the Society for American Music* 4, no. 1 (2010): 59–93.
Fosler-Lussier, Danielle. *Music Divided: Bartók's Legacy in Cold War Culture.* Berkeley: University of California Press, 2007.
Fosler-Lussier, Danielle. *Music in America's Cold War Diplomacy.* Berkeley: University of California Press, forthcoming 2015.
Frumkis, Tat'iana. "Dukh riskovannoi svobody." In *Symposion [ΣΥΜΠΟΣΙΟΝ]: Vstrechi s Valentinom Sil'vestrovym,* edited by Alla Vaisband and Konstantin Sigov, 338–77. Kiev: Dukh i litera, 2012.
Frumkis, Tat'iana. "'Trudnosti udesiateriali moiu energiiu,'" *Evropa-Ekspress,* no. 7 (11 February 2008).
Frumkis, Tat'iana [Tatjana]. "Vorwort/Preface." In Valentin Silvestrov, *Klavierwerke (Werke von 1961 bis 1979),* vol. 1, iv–v. Frankfurt: M. P. Beliaeff, 2006.
Fulcher, Jane F. "Introduction: Defining the New Cultural History of Music, Its Origins, Methodologies, and Lines of Inquiry." In *The Oxford Handbook of the New Cultural History of Music,* ed. Jane F. Fulcher, 3–14. Oxford and New York: Oxford University Press, 2011.
Gienow-Hecht, Jessica C. E. *Sound Diplomacy: Music and Emotions in Transatlantic Relations, 1850–1920.* Chicago: University of Chicago Press, 2009.
Ginzburg, Carlo. "Microhistory: Two or Three Things That I Know about It." In *Threads and Traces: True False Fictive,* translated by Anne C. Tedeschi and John Tedeschi, 193–214. Berkeley: University of California Press, 2012.
Gorsuch, Anne E. *All This Is Your World: Soviet Tourism at Home and Abroad after Stalin.* Oxford and New York: Oxford University Press, 2011.
Gorsuch, Anne E., and Diane P. Koenker, eds. *Turizm: The Russian and East European Tourist under Capitalism and Socialism.* Ithaca, NY: Cornell University Press, 2006.
Iudina, Mariia. *Dukh dyshit, gde khochet: Perepiska 1962–1963 gg.* Moscow: Rossiiskaia politicheskaia entsiklopediia, 2010.
Iudina, Mariia. *Nereal'nost' zla: Perepiska 1964–1966 gg.* Moscow: Rossiiskaia politicheskaia entsiklopediia, 2010.
Iudina, Mariia. *V iskusstve radostno byt' vmeste: Perepiska 1959–1961 gg.* Moscow: Rossiiskaia politicheskaia entsiklopediia, 2009.
Jampol, Joshua. *Living Opera.* Oxford and New York: Oxford University Press, 2010.
Kelli, Dzhon. "Pis'mo iz Gonolulu." *Muzykal'naia zhizn',* no. 15 (1960): 14.
Koenker, Diane P. *Club Red: Vacation Travel and the Soviet Dream.* Ithaca, NY: Cornell University Press, 2013.
Kopf, Oliver. "Prieberg, Fred K." In *Musik in Geschichte und Gegenwart: Personenteil,* vol. 13, 2nd, new edition, ed. Ludwig Finscher (Kassel: Bärenreiter, 2005), 931–32.

Kowalewski, Andrzej [Igor Blazhkov]. "Strawiński w ojczyźnie." *Ruch muzyczny*, no. 1 (1963): 14–16.

Lucas, W. Scott. "Mobilizing Culture: The State-Private Network and the CIA in the Early Cold War." In *War and Cold War in American Foreign Policy, 1942–62*, edited by Dale Carter and Robin Clifton, 83–107. New York: Palgrave, 2002.

Lück, Rudolf, ed. *Neue sowjetische Klaviermusik*. 2 vols. Cologne: Gerig, [1968].

Mackenzie, Ross. *When Stars and Stripes Met Hammer and Sickle: The Chautauqua Conferences on U.S.-Soviet Relations, 1985–1989*. Columbia: University of South Carolina Press, 2006.

Mikkonen, Simo. "Stealing the Monopoly of Knowledge? Soviet Reactions to U.S. Cold War Broadcasting." *Kritika: Explorations in Russian and Eurasian History*, n.s., 11, no. 4 (2010): 771–805.

Mokrejewa, Halina [Mokreeva, Galina]. "List z Kijowa." *Ruch muzyczny*, no. 9 (1 May 1962): 18–19.

Nest'ev, I. "S pozitsii 'Kholodnoi voiny.'" *Sovetskaia muzyka* 10 (1963): 125–30.

Oushakine, Serguei. "The Terrifying Mimicry of Samizdat." *Public Culture* 13, no. 2 (2001): 191–214.

Paperno, Irina. *Stories of the Soviet Experience: Memoirs, Diaries, Dreams*. Ithaca, NY, and London: Cornell University Press, 2009.

Pavlova, A. "Na Gavaiskikh ostrovakh." *Muzykal'naia zhizn'*, no. 11 (1959): 16–17.

Petelin, V. "'Vitiaz' vozvrashchaetsia dosrochno." *Sovremennyi vostok*, no. 10 (1958): 22–24.

Piekut, Benjamin. "Actor-Networks in Music History: Clarifications and Critiques." *Twentieth-Century Music* 11, no. 2 (2014): 191–215.

Piekut, Benjamin. *Experimentalism Otherwise: The New York Avant-Garde and Its Limits*. Berkeley and Los Angeles: University of California Press, 2011.

Prieberg, Fred K. "Fred Priebergs Antwort." *Die Zeit*, 29 November 1963.

Prieberg, Fred. K. *Lexikon der neuen Musik*. Freiburg: K. Alber, 1958.

Prieberg, Fred K. "Music." *Survey: A Journal of Soviet and East European Studies*, no. 48 (July 1963): 30–35.

Prieberg, Fred K. *Musica ex machina: Über das Verhältnis von Musik und Technik*. Berlin: Ullstein, 1960.

Prieberg, Fred K. *Musik in der Sowjetunion*. Cologne: Verlag Wissenschaft und Politik, 1965.

Prieberg, Fred K. "The Sound of New Music." *Survey: A Journal of Soviet and East European Studies*, no. 46 (January 1963): 94–101.

Rothschild, Emma. *The Inner Life of Empires: An Eighteenth-Century History*. Princeton, NJ, and Oxford: Princeton University Press, 2011.

Schmelz, Peter J. "Alfred Schnittke's *Nagasaki*: Soviet Nuclear Culture, Radio Moscow, and the Global Cold War." *Journal of the American Musicological Society* 62 (2009): 413–74.

Schmelz, Peter J. "Selling Schnittke." In *The Oxford Handbook of Musical Censorship,* ed. Patricia Z. Hall. Oxford: Oxford University Press, forthcoming.

Schmelz, Peter J. "'Shostakovich' Fights the Cold War: Reflections from Great to Small," *Journal of Musicological Research* (forthcoming).

Schmelz, Peter J. *Such Freedom, If Only Musical: Unofficial Soviet Music during the Thaw.* New York: Oxford University Press, 2009.

Schmelz, Peter J. "Valentin Silvestrov and the Echoes of Music History." *Journal of Musicology* 31, no. 2 (2014): 231–71.

Schmelz, Peter J., and Elizabeth Bergman, eds. "Music in the Cold War." Special issues, *Journal of Musicology* 26, nos. 1 and 2 (2009).

Schwarz, Boris. *Music and Musical Life in Soviet Russia, Enlarged Edition, 1917–1981.* Bloomington: Indiana University Press, 1983.

Silvestrov, Valentin. *Klavierwerke (Werke von 1961 bis 1979),* vol. 1. Frankfurt/M.: M. P. Beliaeff, 2006.

Sil'vestrov, Valentin. "Slovo molodezhi." *Sovetskaia muzyka,* no. 5 (1968): 22.

Small, Christopher. *Musicking: The Meanings of Performing and Listening.* Middleton, CT: Wesleyan University Press, 1998.

Smart, Mary Ann. "Commentary: A Stroll in the Piazza and a Night at the Opera." *Journal of Interdisciplinary History* 36, no. 4 (2006): 621.

Steiner, Peter. "Introduction: On Samizdat, Tamizdat, Magnitizdat, and Other Strange Words That Are Difficult to Pronounce." *Poetics Today* 29, no. 4 (2008): 613–28.

Stuckenschmidt, H. H. *Twentieth Century Music.* Translated by Richard Deveson. New York and Toronto: McGraw-Hill, 1969.

Sysoev, N. N. "Ekspeditsionnoe sudno 'Vitiaz.'" *Trudy instituta okeanologii* 16 (1959): 3–23.

Yurchak, Alexei. *Everything Was Forever, Until It Was No More: The Last Soviet Generation.* Princeton, NJ: Princeton University Press, 2006.

Zhuk, Sergei I. *Rock and Roll in the Rocket City: The West, Identity, and Ideology in Soviet Dniepropetrovsk, 1960–1985.* Baltimore: Johns Hopkins University Press, 2010.

Zimmerman, Andrew. *Alabama in Africa: Booker T. Washington, the German Empire, and the Globalization of the New South.* Princeton, NJ, and Oxford: Princeton University Press, 2010.

Chapter Eight

"WHERE I CANNOT ROAM, MY SONG WILL TAKE WING"
Polish Cultural Promotion in Belarus, 1988

Andrea F. Bohlman

Among the passengers on board a charter plane from Warsaw to Vitebsk on 21 July 1988 was Mirosław Hermaszewski, the first Polish citizen to travel into space. The entire Polish delegation, predominantly Communist Party officials and cultural organizers en route to the Belorussian Soviet Socialist Republic (SSR) (now Belarus), were about to attend the final concert of the Festival of Polish Song, planned for the evening of 22 July, the forty-fourth anniversary of the Polish People's Republic. Over the course of the program, two cosmonauts were to be honored: Hermaszewski, whose 1978 mission had been sponsored by the Soviet Union, and Valentina Tereshkova, a Soviet pilot of Belarusian origin and the first woman in space. The two officially recognized "Heroes of the Soviet Union" symbolized the positive contributions of satellite states, in the case of Poland, and SSRs, in the case of Belarus, to Soviet society. At the climactic gala concert of the Festival of Polish Song, Polish cultural promoters hoped to drive home a celebration of cultural vitality—of Soviet culture in Eastern Europe—through musical performance.

"*Pieśń* and *piosenka* are interwoven into every nation's fate," the emcees began their opening address for the festival's final concert. They cited the two Polish words that index the English "song" as they set the tone for the historical survey of Polish popular music that was to come (see appendix 1 for the address's complete text). Endowing both serious and light song—a distinction I discuss below—with

---

Notes for this section begin on page 248.

tremendous personal, cultural, and political weight, the hosts outlined a litany of song's animation of individual humanity, national identity, and international friendship. They proclaimed that from love and camaraderie to loss and conflict, tunes and texts accompany people through history, through their lives. Laden with specific regional and historical references, the text, vetted by the Central Committee of the Polish United Workers' Party (PZPR), was at once diplomatic and emotional in tone.[1] One goal was to underscore the harmony of Polish-Soviet friendship. The event's programming demonstrated the interconnectivity of the two musical cultures, providing evidence of international fraternity. To be sure, the speakers offered up a naïve vision of universality through music, in which song, broadly conceived, was the best cultural ambassador. They continued, "*Pieśń* and *piosenka* exceed the boundaries of nations and the barriers of language, bringing us nearer each other and uniting us through the feeling of community and friendship." This ascription of popular music to a constructive capacity on the part of the communist PZPR is the product of the calculated cultivation of national music culture that could simultaneously represent Polishness while also cementing an affiliation with popular music traditions beyond the eastern border of the Polish People's Republic.[2] Officials looked to the east, in contradistinction to those at the helm of contemporary music institutions, so often lauded for their openness to the Western avant-garde.

The 1988 Festival of Polish Song in Vitebsk—one of the few festivals the PZPR curated beyond Polish borders—presents us with the opportunity to understand more fully the aesthetic value with which songs were endowed and the diplomatic function invested in popular culture, broadly conceived. I suggest that in the festival's particular case, popular music offered the Polish state the opportunity to formulate and celebrate a shared Soviet, and thus socialist-international, music history, strongly nuanced by specific regional contributions. The focused locality of the festival lends particular insight into national and international visions of history at the end of the Cold War, for in their playlist for Vitebsk, Polish delegates projected a sweeping history of "Polish song" that depended on and contributed to the international relations of the region. Two international histories emerged in the pinnacle concert: one orchestrated by the PZPR through soft diplomacy behind the event and another performed by Polish, Russian, and Belarusian artists through song.

Popular music's lyrical intimacy foregrounded the interpersonal, and its generic hybridity revived the vital multinational music history of the region, a potential party organizers appreciated could be used to personalize Polish-Belarusian relations. In other words, music performed an international relation that was understood to be divorced from current state policies. The stage facilitated direct, personal address by cultural dignitaries and beloved singers, all of whom articulated long visions of cherished cultural warmth and familiarity. Parsing the pomp and circumstance of the festival's choreography and rehearing the subtle musical potpourri, I contend that music was more than a symbol of international harmony between two countries. Musical performance reveled in the complex harmony and discord of the cultural histories of the Polish People's Republic, the Belorussian SSR, and the Soviet Union without undermining the united vision of party propaganda. After elaborating on the festival's diplomatic, bureaucratic, and discursive background, I return to the final gala concert, a celebration of "roaming" Polish songs.

The very existence of the Festival of Polish Song in the Belorussian SSR bore witness to a shifting understanding of the westernmost border of the USSR from both sides in the late 1980s. Just over a year before it took place, a declaration in April 1987 between Polish premier Wojciech Jaruzelski and Mikhail Gorbachev after the latter's appointment as Soviet head of state had focused upon reciprocal Polish-Soviet relations that interwove arts and culture.[3] The plan suggested building bridges between cultures through two reciprocal channels: by circulating print materials and by establishing regular exchanges between cities. As part of the 1987 cultural normalization instigated by the PZPR's Central Committee, the Department of Culture first turned specifically to Polish-Belarusian relations and the festival in Vitebsk. This Festival of Polish Song, the first outside of Poland or Moscow, was conceived of as a model for collaboration between socialist countries.[4] Polish ministers hoped it would launch a series of SSR festivals to cultivate close and direct cultural ties with the Ukrainian and Lithuanian SSRs, thereby recognizing distinct local contributions to a shared socialist cultural history. The targeted geographical region was not without historical significance: the lands had been the domain of the Polish-Lithuanian Commonwealth from 1569 to 1795, and the legacy of this shared, multinational history and forced postwar migrations haunted this contested borderland.[5] At the festival, the emcees conjured up the long history of the region when they quoted the nineteenth-century epic poem *Konrad Wallenrod*, by Adam Mickiewicz, in their opening address. They gave voice to the work of a Lithuanian writer born in the western region of what was in 1988 Belarus—whose entire literary output was in Polish—when they recited Mickiewicz's verse: "Where I cannot roam, my song will take wing."[6] Through a writer whom Belarusians, Poles, and even Russians could claim as their own, the emcees portrayed music as transcending both political boundaries as well as the limits of human mortality. Invoking the Polish romantic bard (*wieszcz*), however, did more than ground their optimistic vision of song in literary authority. They urged that song and musical culture could rekindle a closeness among those living across the multinational region regardless of political strife or division. Mickiewicz invests song, written in the future tense, with the potential to negotiate, narrate, and endure multinational histories.

The Party's Musical Stage

How much did the PZPR subsidize and monitor musical culture? A brief exploration of the Central Committee's attitude toward music, and specifically popular music, is necessary before unpacking the organization and programming of the Vitebsk festival. Enduring discussions of music's value and repeated attempts at cultural reform emerge from the Department of Culture's correspondence, plenary meetings, and reports in the 1980s. The Department of Culture was just one of the Central Committee's subdivisions; assigned primary responsibility for music, literature, theater, film, the visual arts, and more, its leaders operated in tandem with other units (see table 8.1).[7] Beneath the Central Committee's Executive Council, the Politburo and administration connected offices and divisions with other governmental organizations, such as the Secret Police. Beneath the central administration, each department focused on a particular sector, theoretically occupying equal standing in the hierarchy, so that communication across the wide range of bureaus was one of the main accomplishments of the bureaucratic—and archival—paper trail.

The rise of the Solidarity Independent Trade Union, culminating in its legalization in 1980, and the subsequent declaration of martial law in 1981 in many ways distinguished the decade's policy making from the previous thirty years of the Polish People's Republic. In particular, two waves of cultural reform, framed as "normalization," in 1984 and 1987 brought increased support of popular culture. At the same time, the exceptional freedom jazz musicians, contemporary composers, and rock bands had experienced in Poland relative to other Warsaw Pact nations continued to play out in the party's attitude toward music, which was generally permissive. Party officials

Table 8.1. The distribution of power in the Central Committee of the PZPR (1981–85).

Central Committee (KC)	
Politburo	
Secretariat	
Office of the Secretariat, KC	Bureau of the Central Party Control Commission (CKKP)
Bureau of Letters and Inspection	Bureau of the Central Auditing Commission (CKR)
General Department	Department for Ideological-Educational Work
Central Archive of the KC	Press, Radio, and Television Department
Bureau of Parliamentary Matters	Department of Learning and Education
Department of Organization	Department of Culture
Personnel Department	Department of Agricultural and Food Economy
Department of Administration	Department of Industry, Construction, and Transport
Socio-Professional Department	Department of Trade and Finance
Department of Public Organization, Sport, and Tourism	Institute for Basic Problems of Marxism-Leninism (became the Academy of Social Sciences, 1984)
Foreign Sector	

imagined that diverse musics successfully represented the socialist society throughout its existence, from the early years of Stalinist socialist realism to the punk rock festivals of the 1980s. Whether in history lessons, films, on avant-garde theatrical stages, or in the policies of the musical organizations supported through party funding—the Polish Composers Union is just one example—music was to be heard more often than it was to be repressed. The Polish musical avant-garde, for example, was nurtured by the state-supported Warsaw Autumn International Festival of Contemporary Music, a Cold War institution widely celebrated for its position at the crossroads between musical modernisms of the East and West.[8]

In the 1980s, music's strength in Polish culture made it a platform for political play: the party took music seriously. The purview of the Department of Culture bespeaks an inclusive approach toward musical styles and subcultures. Directors and secretaries kept tabs on wide-ranging musical domains: hard rock, cabaret, contemporary music, Polish early music, folk music, punk, singer-songwriters, and more. The party's cultural organizers and bureaucrats planned and reviewed specific events. With numerous state-sponsored artists' organizations in consistent competition for financial attention and the privilege of ideological nonintervention, the desk of the Department of Culture was often the last stop a set of regulations made before approval (see table 8.2).[9] Here written and spoken discourse gathered in print, capturing the party's means of engagement with culture.[10] The individual associations in table 2 received funding because they reported to and were observed by the party, often for the primary purpose of monitoring the modest flow of cash.[11] One need only glance through the diverse constituencies represented—luthiers, jazz musicians, Chopin enthusiasts, and more—to understand the confusing aggregate of musical concerns the Department of Culture faced.

The mandate to "normalize" focused on matters at home, but the Department of Culture was more than aware of the international nature of the music scene. Global sounds and stars played multiple roles in Polish popular music, even though the cultural field was nurtured as a Polish product that spoke to Polish audiences. On the one hand, events linked American and Soviet entertainment cultures. For example, with its eye on the prize, a state-sponsored popular music organization planned a concert in Warsaw, "In Defense of Peace," in 1986 to which organizers hoped to invite the "most popular artists in the world, known for their progressive and anti-war activities."[12]

Table 8.2. Musical associations receiving funds from the PZPR in 1983.

Wieniawski Musical Society of Poznań
Polish Jazz Clubs
Polish Association of Contemporary Music
Authors' Guild—Union of Authors and Composers for the Stage
Association of Polish Musician-Artists
Association of Polish Musical Youth
Frederic Chopin Society
Szymanowski Musical Society in Zakopane
Polish Composers Union
Union of Polish Entertainment [*Rozrywka*] Authors and Composers
Union of Polish Luthiers
Polish Branch of the International Society for Music Education
Folk Institute of Music
Polish Union of Choirs and Orchestras

Paul McCartney, Jane Fonda, Bulat Okudzhava, Stevie Wonder, Bob Dylan, Kenny Rodgers, and Dolly Parton were all to appear on stage in the same evening. Though the predicted cost was enormous, the international extravaganza, according to the secretary of the Department of Culture, Adam Kaczmarek, had tremendous potential to aid in confirming Poland's profile as an international example. A huge "political and artistic event" that Kaczmarek explicitly indicated would be "in the spirit of the Helsinki Accords," the concert was designed to participate in global peace promotion. It never came to pass, but the conversations in the mid-1980s set the tone for public concerts devoted to performing international harmony in Poland.

The phase of normalization instigated upon martial law's conclusion was directed specifically at evaluating music in the Polish People's Republic: the Department of Culture established a subdepartment, the Department of Music, in 1984, tasked with this responsibility. Such campaigns of cultural reform took place after public conflicts with society and consisted of efforts to perform a healthy Polish society to the public in the domains of culture and education.[13] Music was an ideal target for building what historian Padraic Kenney has called a "new democratic facade" precisely because the composers and performers of Western art music had achieved such prominence as the internationally recognized "Polish School."[14] The Vitebsk Festival of Polish Song was planned as part of the second wave of normalization, which began in 1987 and continued almost until the convocation of roundtable negotiations in early 1989 brought the PZPR's power to an end. While the new Department of Music targeted music education for reform, the major assessment of Polish musical culture three years later located the area of greatest concern in so-called *rozrywka,* or entertainment.

Rozrywka as Music

Perhaps the most inclusive sphere of the arts within Polish cultural activity and for the republic's Department of Culture was that of *rozrywka.* Translated variously as entertainment, recreation, amusement, pastime, and diversion, the term refers to an expanding group of cultural activities frequently associated with popular culture or the public sphere. A prerequisite reform that the Department of Culture delegated was grasping just what *rozrywka* encompassed: the struggles to define *rozrywka* were at the core of the 1987 shifts in cultural policy.[15] By 1988 the party could still only confirm *roz-*

rywka's widespread presence and lowbrow aura while evading clear definition:

> *Rozrywka* is a broad concept. It includes: stage arts, music, the circus, cabaret, variety shows, amusement parks, and even that so-called 'gastronomic *rozrywka*,' as well as records and video as media for transmission and dissemination.
>
> In such a large field of activity it is unusually important to penetrate the cultural domain, to formulate its political judgments, to delineate its tasks. In particular it is precisely *rozrywka*—mass culture—that has a very large influence on the patterns of life, relaxation, and the preference of particular ideas and values.
>
> In Warsaw, as in the whole country, there has never been a fully developed definition of popular and mass culture. *Rozrywka* was always used for art of a lower quality and treated as thus by both policy makers and art criticism.[16]

The deployment of "mass culture," a critical concept for any Department of Culture under Soviet state socialism, in the 1988 brief suggests why the party maintained a sense of authorial control over *rozrywka*. In its name, the department engineered cultural experiences presumed to be more fleeting and thrilling than lasting and substantial. Correspondingly, *rozrywka* indexes a cultural activity's presumed value and function more than the activity itself; the entertainment's content is fundamentally elusive.

As a cultural sector at the heart of the normalization reforms of 1984 and 1987, *rozrywka* functioned as an umbrella framework in which the "light" arts were discussed and evaluated. The term sparked conversations about mass culture, technology, and artistic success, all in the Marxist sense, within the Department of Culture, which supported a subdepartment devoted to *rozrywka*. It encompassed domains of culture judged to have lesser value, without the intellectual gravitas of "serious music" (*muzyka poważna*) or "beautiful literature" (*literatura piękna*). The activities toward which party officials directed their attention were invested with much of the idealism that foresaw unity across society, profession, age, religious heritage, and ethnicity. Following the aggressive, even "hegemonic," rise of Polish punk rock on the popular music scene in the 1970s and early 1980s, the official reform of *rozrywka* had the potential to reach out to a broader public left wanting entertainment with a less hardened sound.[17]

Rozrywka's wide-ranging and variable presence in Poland primed it for influence.[18] As the party had consistently invested in classical music education and the dissemination of *rozrywka*'s higher-brow brethren during Stalinist socialist realism, cultural organizers now ensured that *rozrywka* was incorporated into music curricula. Better music education would attract large and impressionable audiences and enable the recognition of both the vitality of their socialist state and an event's sheer splendor. Key to understanding the Central Committee's obsession with *rozrywka* is noting party members' frequent acknowledgment that, via the recording industry, American popular music was able to travel more easily than ever.[19] And if Poles were to learn of their own long national history of cabaret, music theater, and popular lyric song—all of which fell under the rubric of *rozrywka*—the party would have to invest significant capital into its promotion.[20]

The debates surrounding the establishment of computer cafés and amusement parks in Warsaw hardly focused upon musical matters, but music was consistently present in a number of state-sponsored *rozrywka* events. During the mid-1980s, music was discussed throughout the Department of Culture, in tandem with the Departments of Music and *Rozrywka*. Composer and cultural organizer Zbigniew Adrjański's report of the extensive list of concerts supported by a Warsaw city governmental organization (the Capital City Bureau of Artistic Events) provides a sense of the "broad" reach of *rozrywka* and the generous conception of musical activity ascribed to this cultural sphere. He took credit for the creative activity of an "artistic or popular artistic" vein, including the formation of experimental avant-garde theater; three cabaret artists' employment; "political and parapolitical" concerts of historical and patriotic popular song; and several weddings, civil funerals, and name day celebrations that involved music. The bureau supported the seasons of two chamber orchestras, a big band orchestra, a ballet ensemble, and two series of light classical music. Numerous rock and punk bands performed under Adrjański's wings, demarcated as young musicians playing for young audiences, and he sponsored the seasons of three Polish bands. A number of other touring heavy metal and punk bands (including Iron Maiden) as well as prominent Polish punk bands (Dezerter, TSA, and Kult) put on notorious concerts in Warsaw.

Though the umbrella term *rozrywka* was specific to the Polish People's Republic, the efforts to reinvigorate, reform, and then normalize the cultural activities associated with it were directed at a sphere of performances in a sector of state-sponsored culture modeled directly on a Soviet model: *estrada,* or the stage. Discourse in numerous Slavic languages in the twentieth century organized popular music into two branches: *narodnaya* and *estradnaya muzyka,* in Russian.[21] In many ways these embodied the nationalist/socialist dichotomy that served as the basis of socialist realism under Stalin. Both genres framed the goals of Soviet culture for international performance. *Narodnaya* referred broadly to "folk," "national," "people's," and "popular" in both its meaning and practical application to the enormous official national folk ensembles that cultivated regional folk song in a pan-Warsaw Pact aesthetic. On the other hand, *estradnaya muzyka,* itself borrowed from Spanish and French, was developed alongside a state-sponsored school of popular musicians that came to be referred to by the same name as the light, cabaret-influenced lyric song genres they performed. In his three-volume history of Soviet popular song, Russian literature scholar David Mac-Fadyen frames the songs of *estradnaya muzyka* as recasting internationalist ideology in intimate and personal lyrics, though he is careful not to suggest that *estrada*'s performers represented the party line. Soviet popular music was well-known and cherished, and "hundreds of millions of lyric songs that took the callous metaphors of Soviet fraternity and reclaimed them on a small, private, and sincere scale were sold in the Soviet Union."[22]

Rozrywka facilitated international exchange at home and abroad. Institutions brought together performers in Poland so that, because of *estrada,* performers from across the Soviet Union, Western Europe, and North America sang out one after the other on stage. Audience members in Poland were certainly familiar with the music of Soviet *estrada* and American rock, but they saw celebrities from East and West perform alongside leading national voices at the International Song Festival at Sopot. At the festival's band shell on the Baltic Sea, Poles cheered for bands and singers from both sides of the Cold War divide every summer. From its inception, the Sopot festival had embraced competition as a means of generating momentum for up-and-coming artists based on its model and rival in Western Europe, the Eurovision Song Contest.[23] From 1961 to the present day, various prizes have been awarded to songs in Polish, to songs by Soviet performers, and to international stars who headlined in Sopot. Money, publicity, and international tours brought megastars such as Alla Pugacheva from Soviet *estrada* and, in 1987, Johnny Cash, a living legend of American country music.

Musical diplomacy—in this case the sponsorship of artists' foreign travel by the state—took on many shapes and forms under the auspices of the Central Committee of the PZPR.[24] In the early 1980s, cabaret singer-songwriters Andrzej Rosiewicz and Jan Pietrzak toured North America and Canada singing almost exclusively at Polish American community centers. In 1987, a delegation of Polish musicians traveled to Moscow on official business, meeting with artists' associations, performing, attending local concerts, and disseminating Polish music history books through schools. After the Solidarity Independent Trade Union's rise and fall, the Polish government set out to improve their relationships with the Soviet Socialist Republics as well as Czechoslovakia; the promotion of SSRs' contemporary music scenes at festivals in Poland was also a part of the normalization process. The Polish Composers Union welcomed Czechoslovak, Bulgarian, Hungarian, and Georgian composers to concert series.[25] Polish composers also furthered their socialist colleagues' music in programming across Poland, occasionally in the name of countering an Austro-German canon, occasionally in the name of socialist brotherhood.[26]

The "Polish song" sent abroad under the umbrella of *rozrywka*, as we shall see, was orchestrated to appeal broadly and address time-honored emotional domains that were not perceived to threaten society. The hits of Mieczysław Fogg, Michał Bajor, Anna German, and Czesław Niemen had none of the rough-edged individualism of Polish punk and hard rock. But the ballads and pop tunes the Department of Culture fueled funds into at Vitebsk challenge narratives of cultural resistance in Polish music history.[27] The energy devoted to *rozrywka* models a vision of Polish music at once national and international through the singers' intimate and sentimental narratives of love and loss.

Toward Polish Song

At the Festival of Polish Song in Vitebsk in 1988, party officials rattled off the powers of song, playing with songs' similarities and differences through their welcoming oration. Diverse genres of song—from popular to revolutionary to children's, and not excluding operatic arias—provide a perspective on Poles' musical agency. *Pieśń* or *piosenka*, the two terms that referenced short musical works sung to instrumental accompaniment, could refer to diverse musics, even music that was relegated to the Department of Culture's Department of *Rozrywka* and excluded from the rubric of the Department of Music. Many genres traded on "song," and thus its traces in committee memos, resolutions, and organizational matters are plentiful. Conceptually, too, song was debated and theorized with reference to concrete examples as a unit of the larger, abstract artistic practice of "music."

It is worth pausing a moment to define "song" rigorously within the Polish context, because a pair of terms refers to what in English is termed a song, in German a *Lied,* in French a *chanson,* and in Russian a *pesnia. Pieśń* and *piosenka* might roughly be translated as "song" and "little song," since they are technically differentiated by the diminutive ending *-ka.* But the primary distinction between the two terms is one of register instead of genre. Both terms cross the divide between classical music and its others in Poland: for example, German *Lieder* and church hymns are both called *pieśni,* a term that emphasizes their status rather than musical sophistication. In Polish discourse there can be folk (*ludowe*) *pieśni,* as in the case of Oskar Kolberg's monumental collection *Pieśni ludu polskiego* (*Songs of the Polish People,* 1842), and *piosenki.* Within a specified genre, *pieśń* and *piosenka* indicate scope and weight. For example, legion songs (*pieśni legionowe*) tell histories of battles and bear the burdens of blood loss in their balladic forms, while the lively refrains of war songs (*piosenki wojenne*) cajole soldiers into militant spirit and charmingly portray them lost in love. Most dictionaries fail to distinguish between the two words even though, as is evident in the Vitebsk invocation's rhetoric, they are not interchangeable. The terms are dependent not only upon the music they describe, but also upon who is using them and why, and so I have chosen to keep the Polish original throughout this chapter.[28]

While the conceptualization of song in the Polish People's Republic emerges as broad—even vague—and generous, songs themselves remained discrete musical units, less intimidating to unpack than music lacking semantics. The compact musical pieces circulated easily on cassette and in print. Lyrics could, of course, be memorized or circulated as broadsides or in songbooks. Both the Department of Culture and the Censorship Bureau processed these reductions of songs to text. The Department of Culture interpreted unsystematically and inconsistently. For example, the fear that American music would infiltrate Poland's airwaves and concert stages manifests itself in concern for positive representations of life in the United States. One official drew attention to the performance of Agnieszka Osiecka's song "Susanna" ("Zuzanna," 1985) by rock balladeer Maryla Rodowicz at the concert in celebration of the fortieth anniversary of Warsaw's liberation, for example.[29] The assemblage of disco, Cadillacs, and African Americans was, for him, a positive sketch of Western commerce. At the same time, Halina Frąckowiak was invited to sing her 1984 hit, "Tin Pan Alley," which likewise follows a young woman chasing her heart, a man, and a car through an American urban space, as an official Polish representative at the Vitebsk Festival of Polish Song.

Here I am in San Francisco,	Siedzę sobie w San Francisco,
Black Bobby, he's my type.	Czarny Bobby to mój typ.
He's already abducted me to the disco,	Już porywa mnie na disco,
Shifting life's gears for me,	Zmienia dla mnie życia tryb,
We're already speeding along in a Cadillac,	Już pędzimy cadillakiem,
We're already entering a sharp bend …	Już wchodzimy ostro w zakręt …

—"Zuzanna," Agnieszka Osiecka

A yellow taxi, just like in China Town,	Taksówka żółta tak jak China Town
We move suppressing the fire in our hearts,	ruszymy tłumiąc pożar serc,
In music that knows no truth nor lies,	w muzykę, która nie zna prawd i kłamstw,
But it is, it always is.	ale jest, ciągle jest.

—"Tin Pan Alley," Halina Frąckowiak

Side-by-side, the songs' lyrics send mixed messages; they reveal a similar sense of enamor with glamor and technology, which, in each song, is supported by a summer beat reminiscent of Duran Duran.

Songs are—and were—much more than their texts. In the Polish People's Republic, they became fundamentally associated with their performers and even certain performances, captured on musical media. Polish radio and television broadcast concerts and variety shows that lined singers (in Polish, literally "songers," or *piosenkarzy*) and their hits up back-to-back-to-back. Cassette tapes and LPs published by state-sponsored record labels promoted Polish artists at home and abroad, whether they sang *Lieder,* metal, poetry, or Bible verses. The music of Polish *rozrywka* contained self-conscious Soviet and American influences. Blues and a bustling rock 'n' roll aesthetic formed the basis of the Polish stars' sound of the 1970s and 1980s as much as did the auteur and lyric textual conventions of Russian popular song. For example, the underlying funk sound accompanying Czesław Niemen's wailing blues attracted attention from Western labels as well as the adoration of the Polish public, while Marek Grechuta's frivolous love songs had their roots in the same Jewish cabarets in Lwów and Saint Petersburg that inspired Nikolai Gnatiuk's nostalgic fox-trots. Musicians and ensembles increasingly conceived of their work in the popular music domain as hybrid, borrowing bass lines, lyrics, song forms, and dance forms from across high and low, serious and light, poetic and entertainment divides.[30]

Programming Polish Music for the International Stage

The "big four" song festivals of the Polish People's Republic—the International Song Festival in Sopot, the National Festival of Polish in Opole, the Soldiers' Song Festival in Kołobrzeg, and the Festival of Soviet Song in Zielona Góra—offered the enthusiastic Polish public variety shows, pageants, gala concerts, and song competitions. On the stages of these events, songs became part of a broader musical context and explicitly choreographed the mission of the Department of Culture. Building upon recent successes touring Moscow, the Department of Culture set out to connect the Polish stage with that of a neighboring Soviet Socialist Republic where the language barrier was minimal: Belarus. The Festival of Polish Song in Vitebsk, held 19–22 July 1988 to coincide with the anniversary of the Polish socialist state's establishment, brings together the twin musical themes of promotion and nation and drives home the point that song offered constructive and creative possibilities for the Department of Culture. In many ways, the event's format mirrored that of the festivals hosted in Poland: a litany of concerts with programs devoted to themes ("Friendship") and genres (rock) were held in the brand-new amphitheater outside of the Belarusian city. Local cultural officials in Vitebsk and the organizers of the Festival of Soviet Song in Zielona Góra shared the stage with artists from the Soviet Union and Poland. A smaller cast of Polish stars traveled as members of the delegation to Belarus than had been originally anticipated, but megastar Maryla Rodowicz, velvet crooner Michał Bajor, and prolific composer Seweryn Krajewski headlined nearly every concert, drawing what were reported to be large crowds.[31]

As self-conscious counterpoints to the celebrations of Soviet culture in Poland, the Festivals of Polish Song held in the Soviet Union were planned with the confidence that they would be well-received: the Polish Ministry of Culture and Arts was even prepared to commit continued financial and organizational support. A Festival of Polish Song in Moscow, the first such extravaganza, in early March 1988 received positive acclaim from its Soviet audiences. On the scene in the Soviet Union, representatives from various professions and social circles—a student, a hairdresser, and a theater director—had described being floored by the level of artistry, according to the official report. The logic was clear: further Festivals of Polish Song would continue to offer proof that the Polish People's Republic fostered cultural success in concert programs that pleased audiences and provided well-crafted songs and interpretations of note.[32] Through their musical offerings, both Festivals of Polish Song, in Moscow and in Vitebsk, articulated what the party imagined as *rozrywka*'s broad relevance, the concrete success of Polish popular music in the twentieth century, and the significance of song for Polish culture.

The Festivals of Polish Song abroad most closely mirrored the Festival of Soviet Song in Zielona Góra, which held its own among the quartet of high-profile song festivals founded in the 1960s. Coordinated by the Polish-Soviet Friendship Society, the festival made exchange possible and promoted Soviet culture. In the mountains of western Silesia, singers from across Warsaw Pact nations competed for the best *estrada* song, singing in multiple languages: Russian, their native language, and, often, Polish. The difficulty of multilingualism drew attention to cultural barriers while confirming an embrace of multinationalism. The Zielona Góra festival did launch the careers of a number of Polish pop stars, among them Michał Bajor, the male vocalist with the highest billing at the final gala concert in Vitebsk.

The concert on the ultimate evening of the Vitebsk Festival of Polish Song celebrated the vital history and present of popular song in Poland while simultaneously reveling in its cosmopolitan flavor over the course of two hours (see appendix 2). The Vitebsk concert's program, a mixture between a retrospective and a survey of up-and-coming talent, was a variety show that attempted a comprehensive tour of Polish song, from the cabaret hits of Mieczysław Fogg to the rock anthems of Maryla Rodowicz to the synthesized Euro-pop of the 1980s—the latter of which represents the final state-subsidized song genre in the Polish People's Republic. The entire event in Vitebsk placed value in song and a world in which *pieśń* and *piosenka* interface. The emcees of the festival declared songs' vitality to an audience of Belarusian and Polish listeners repeatedly through their opening address, to which I have already alluded. Their pronouncements drove home one of the key concepts behind the party's musical reforms in 1983 and 1987: songs can shape as well as narrate a nation's history. Furthermore, they generously opened the category of song over the course of the address, which took the form of a cyclical concatenation of definitions. Songs' power grows out of their plurality of affect and effect: youthful rebellion, national spirit, ironic subversion, and sublime transcendence. References to Gorbachev as a musical inspiration and a friend of Poland in the opening address emphasized that the event was to perform the political ties between the Polish People's Republic and the USSR through culture. Though theirs was an encomium to *Polish* song, what emerged on the musical stage was an interpretation of popular music previously assumed to be anchored as belonging on either side of the eastern Polish border as "taking wing"—to evoke Mickiewicz—among international audiences.

The program of the gala concert, painstakingly assembled by the Department of *Rozrywka* and the Union of *Rozrywka* Authors and Composers, narrates a history of popular song in Poland during the twentieth century that is notable because of the reciprocal influence it implies between Polish and Soviet song. This final evening began with a "potpourri" of songs popular among Polish and Soviet audiences accompanied by a symphonic jazz ensemble that had traveled from Poland. The combination of the tangos and hits of the Warsaw-trained songwriter Jerzy Petersburski, which were already popular on Russian stages in the 1920s, with numbers from the 1934 hit Soviet musical film *Jolly Fellows* (*Vesyolye rebyata*) staged the urban musical life of the interwar period anew. A string of so-called Schlager (*szlagier*) tunes gave hit love songs or socialist-realist tunes that were central to music education across the Eastern Bloc a big band sound. One of the Polish tunes, "Colorful Markets," had been prominent at the scenes of the Solidarity Independent Trade Union's strikes, where it was supplied with new and subversive texts.[33] The organizers confidently sidestepped historical detail when programming soldiers' songs from World War II, selecting only lighter songs that elided the differences between the national legions. The potpourri's hits, designed to elicit audience recognition and delight, concluded with Soviet *estrada* hits in multiple languages.

The evening's spectacle continued by nuancing popular music history of the early Cold War. The careful presentation of the Soviet Union as a land rich in popular song of various registers and regional significances dominated the middle portion of the program. First came the music of the postwar Polish girl group Valentines (Walentynki) intermingled with Soviet tunes that were themselves popular in Poland in the 1960s, such as "Tblisi." The organizers nodded to local Belarusian folklore—a small but significant gesture, as we shall see—when they commissioned a Polish band to cover a folk song. Finally, before the program's climax, Maryla Rodowicz and Michał Bajor transformed the music of the Russian bards from singer-songwriter ballads to rock anthems. They performed the PZPR's embrace of Soviet unofficial music culture, which had so often been under scrutiny in the USSR as well as in translation in Poland.[34]

No doubt one of the greatest celebrities of the Socialist musical stage was Anna German (1936–82), the most internationally renowned *estrada* singer trained in Poland and a figure crucial to understanding the aesthetic ambition of the 1988 Vitebsk festival.[35] Her career was at the heart of the gala program in Vitebsk, precisely because she was exceptionally beloved in the Soviet Union, a fact the emcees foregrounded in their commentary on stage.[36] "Once a Year the Gardens Bloom" ("Odin raz v god sady tsvetut"), sung by the up-and-coming starlet Alicja Majewska, concluded the historical portion of the evening and was preceded by an announcement commending German's tremendous significance. Catapulted to fame through her performance of Katarzyna Gaertner's "Dancing Euridices" ("Tańczające Eurydiki") and victories at the Sopot and Opole festivals in the early 1960s, German recorded albums in Russian and Polish and toured the East and West until her death from cancer in 1982. Though she frequently sang as a kind of musical tourist, adding songs in the local language when appearing abroad, she was anything but a chameleon on the stage.

German's demure performance aesthetic captured the Polish *estrada* ideal: she rarely glanced at television cameras and, in the sighs and fermatas that heighten lyric song's drama, she often restrained her voice in the back of her throat, maintaining intensity through reserve. Polish state *rozrywka* picked up on German's fame from the start. In her, the organizers had found a kind, intelligent, and humble musical representative—a voice speaking as much to the Polish general public as she did to the world. The biography written as a liner note for a compilation album released by the Polish state label depicts her success as accidental and frames the act of singing as one of pleasure: "Anna German is by profession a geologist ... but, to keep herself going, what she enjoys most is singing."[37] The same blurb goes on to balance exceptional musical skill with a down-to-earth, girl-next-door character: "Apart from the unusual quality of her voice, it is obvious that this Slav[ic] looking, tall, and blue-eyed girl is extremely musical." The racial undertones of the text confirm brotherhood with the Soviet Union while valorizing the local vis-à-vis the unspoken: others at home in Poland.

German's understated performance presence narrated the nostalgic melancholy of lyric repertory. It was her own recorded performance of "Odin raz v god sady tsvetut," which ends with a confident embrace of the lonely singularity of spring—"only once,"—that functioned as a means to remember German's connection to Soviet popular culture when audiences replayed it after her death. With a soaring violin counterpoint as her primary partner, German sang, sotto voce, of the recurrent hopes spring brings, its promise inevitably thwarted by loneliness. The tribute to German on the stage at the Vitebsk festival captured the warm sentiment of *estrada* even against the musical growing pains of synthesized keyboards, drums, and brass ever present in orchestrations in the late 1980s. Reviving her song and remembering her voice through musical performance rather than extensive colloquy also implicitly made the case that I have made over the course of this article: songs perform intimate international relations.

Though it was the most prominent, the Polish Festival of Song in Vitebsk was only one of the cultural ventures charged with the task of bringing Poles and Belarusians closer together in 1988. Three additional projects underscored that the two socialist states shared both musical past and present. The party approached expanding their international musical projects with plans to send a diverse set of musical resources across the border: an opera company, music pedagogy books, and the staff of the Polish Artists' Agency.[38] First, the Department of Culture predicted "interesting" fruit would be born from collaboration between two major opera companies: the Wrocław Opera and the National Academic Bolshoi Theatre of Minsk would exchange personnel. Second, the festival in honor of the nineteenth-century opera composer Stanisław Moniuszko, an annual event in Lower Silesia, was responsible for developing educational outreach in their namesake composer's hometown, a district in Minsk. Children who attended schools in the Polish People's Republic and the Belorussian SSR named after the composer would cocurate a room dedicated to the composer near his birthplace, scores of his works would be given to the Belarusian capital's conservatory, and plans were in the works for the performance of one of Moniuszko's operas by a Belarusian company. The third collaboration was almost strictly organizational: the artists' agencies were to target each other's countries reciprocally when arranging travel for their artists.[39]

The strategic nature of the subsequent cultural diplomatic projects the Department of Culture planned provides the Vitebsk Festival of Polish Song a larger context within the Polish government. The diversity of the popular song concerts abroad, however, underscores the diplomatic resonance and nuance musical performance can bring in comparison with the more common practice of the exchange of standing musical ensembles and the import and export of materials. I contend that music's presence on historical international stages—performed—is a crucial source for illuminating international history, in particular as a cultural-political mode of address. Musical analyses and the critical interpretation of performances expand and elaborate scholars' understanding of the nuance governments frequently invest in planning and negotiating international cultural exchanges. Performances provide a stage for *pieśni* and *piosenki* to be heard one after the other, a means to link conflicting and contrasting aspects of the cultural history of Eastern Europe.

The history of Belarus and the history of Poland have been interwoven since the formation of the Polish-Lithuanian Commonwealth in 1569. The scope of the Commonwealth, which included lands that are now Poland, Lithuania, Ukraine, and Belarus, defined the region as multiethnic, multilingual, and—as divergent ideas of the modern nation-state developed—multinational. As historian Timothy Snyder has shown, Poland and Belarus continued to experience a sense of shared cultural history in the twentieth century, even though their national histories diverged drastically. When World War I brought the three-part partition of Poland to an end, the new nation-states grappled to respond to the needs and political organization of the multinational population that lived in the region between Warsaw and Minsk.

The question of Polish-Belarusian relations was thus entwined not only in drawing a border between the Belorussian Soviet Socialist Republic, formed in 1922, and independent interwar Poland, formed in 1918, but in such social aspects as the state support for schools and universities that taught in Belarusian. While aggressive policies in Poland closed all institutions catering to ethnic Belarusians in the 1920s, those in the Belorussian SSR enjoyed backing from Moscow at first.[40] It was only under Stalin in the 1930s that the Belarusian language and its infrastructure came under censure and condemnation. This attitude was not relaxed until Gorbachev came to power, that is, in the very moment when the PZPR was reconsidering its diplomatic approach toward the Belorussian SSR and nurturing its cultural ties. Furthermore, the connections many Belarusian activists in the 1980s had with the formerly Polish lands in the west inspired them to invest activist resources in the Polish context, in solidarity with the opposition movements rooted in nineteenth-century Polish nationalism.[41]

It was precisely this cultural history of the region that came across in the dramaturgy of the gala concert of the Polish Festival of Song, which acknowledged specifically *Belarusian* regional culture—their cosmonaut, their folk tune, and their local rock bands—alongside that of the Soviet empire's center: the Russian Soviet Federative Socialist Republic. Many heard in the Polish-language epic poetry of Vilnius-born Adam Mickiewicz odes to their own people and nation—just one example of the shared legacy of nineteenth-century culture for this region that figured prominently on the stage in Vitebsk.[42] The party's musical orchestrations emphasized the confluence of Poland's music history with that of other Warsaw Pact nations without confirming a centralized vision of the USSR: in speech and song, they acknowledged Gorbachev's politics of decentralization. On the stage in Belarus, performers brought to life a confident vision of a rich program peppered with music from across the Soviet Bloc. The constructive revision of *rozrywka* in Polish music history of the twentieth century matched a forward-looking and multinational understanding of an Eastern Europe rooted in multinational culture.

Appendix 1

Welcoming Address for the Festival of Polish Song

Pieśń and *piosenka* are interwoven into every nation's fate.

Pieśń and *piosenka* are an inherent part of the culture of every nation, part of its many colors. They contain the strength to release the feeling of joy, the capacity to build a sense of community. They are a foundation, a meditation, and a reflection on life.

Pieśń and *piosenka* exceed the boundaries of nations and the barriers of language, approaching and uniting through the feeling of community and friendship.

The *piosenka* is the smile of youth, its manifestation. With a *piosenka* close to your heart and to love, to friendship and to joy.

Pieśń and *piosenka* can serve as a heartfelt connection to other times, a bridge between years gone by and the present.

The *piosenka* is a musical mirror of desires and hopes and—as it happens—the rebellion and anger of the younger generations. It circulates through a variety of human emotions and feelings. It can amuse and touch. Sometimes it is a poetic and musical manifestation of youth. Now the next generation writes and paints its portrait through *pieśń* and *piosenka,* word and music. From the *pieśni* and *piosenki* of every nation one can create a unique spectacle in which history wanders arm in arm with today and the desire of a happy tomorrow.

I wish that for you all, the *piosenki* sung in Vitebsk will prove to be a symbolic, yet another missive of our friendship. That they will wake in you joy and good feelings. That you will listen to Polish *pieśni* and *piosenki* and think about Poland, about close, heartfelt, Polish-Soviet ties of friendship.

In Poland we know Soviet *pieśni* and *piosenki*; both the old, the legionary, and those of today. And there are those among these for which we've already forgotten when they were written, but they function as ours precisely because they speak about our shared desires. Such as the one that made its way through probably all of our Polish homes, schools, and kindergardens: "Let There Always Be Sun."[43]

Survival, joy, and the experiences of generations gain in *piosenki* their universal measure.

As the Polish poet says, we love *pieśni*:

> Because the *pieśń* births and the *pieśń* resurrects
> The *pieśń* gives strength, the *pieśń* saves ...[44]

The *pieśń* of each nation has its own marks, its own contents. After all, it is nourished by the history of that nation, by the fortunes, by its desires, sensations, and feelings. The history of Polish *pieśni* reveals their great spiritual strength and vitality.

Pieśń grows out of history and the history of its comrades.

Pieśń was the spark of insurgent action. It survived historical turbulence, was a support in years of captivity, a challenge to and a summons to during the Nazi years of contempt. Polish and Soviet soldiers, on the shared fronts and paths of the war, sang shared *pieśni* and *piosenki*. Thus the brotherhood of *pieśni* came to be and the weapon of brotherhood was strengthened.

Pieśń and *piosenki* are the foundation of the nation in hard times.

It is in *Konrad Wallenrod*, a poem straight from Lithuanian soil, that Adam Mickiewicz beautifully wrote:

> Heroic paintings will succumb to a flame;
> Sword-wielding looters will rob and prevail,
> But the song remains ...[45]

In the same poem he writes that:

> Where [in the land] I cannot roam, my song will take wing.[46]

A few days ago we experienced a visit by the Soviet leader M. Gorbachev deeply and sincerely in our country. In many cities, during meetings with youths, with people on the street, as expressions of friendship and joy upon meeting with him during his stay: a *pieśń* spontaneously broke out, a *piosenka* appeared. It has become a symbolic sign of this visit, a sign and beautiful link of our Polish-Soviet friendship. May it remain, may it build new bridges of heartfelt, brotherly feelings of mutual friendship and kindness. May it be a shared smile for the young generation, an expression of joy, faith, and hope for a good shared tomorrow. Let it be a message of our shared desire for peace and happiness. And, if it becomes necessary, let it be a shout, a protest, a reproof.

I wish you, dear friends, that in the landscape of our friendly ties, that the Festival of Polish Song in Vitebsk will become a colorful musical connection, as is the Festival of Soviet Song in Zielona Góra.

Appendix 2

Script for the Final Gala Concert, "Stars of the Polish Stage"

- Jazz Orchestra "Alex Band" (conducted by Aleksander Maliszewski): one-minute introduction.
- Zbigniew Wodecki performing "Ta ostatnia niedziela": A cabaret song by Jerzy Petersburski.
- Alex Band presents a selection of popular *pieśni* and *piosenki* from the army (1943–45), performed by Polish and Soviet soldiers, as well as other works immediately popularized upon liberation. These *piosenki* sung in Polish and Russian have become a part the friendship between our nations. Most of them have endured in our tradition to today.
- The potpourri concludes with fragments of the most popular contemporary Polish and Soviet pieces, performed in both of our countries, as well as three contemporary Soviet compositions (from the repertories of [Alla] Pugacheva and [Valerii] Leont'ev). The survey concludes with the piece by Isaac Dunayevsky, "Heart," from the film *Jolly Fellows* (1934).
- Emcees: Welcome. Recognition of the cosmonauts in the audience. Laudatory comments about Polish postwar *rozrywka*. [Polish hits from the 1950s and 1960s]: Ensemble Spektrum covers hits by the Filipinki, Trubadurzy, and Filipinki Garżyna Świtała: "Tblisi" (Georgian song popularized in Poland in the 1960s); "Zwodzony most" (Irena Santor).
- Emcees: Announcement of the special new version of a Belarusian folk song by the band Spectrum.
- Spectrum: Belarusian *piosenka*.
- Emcees: Announcement of two songs of poetic character from the repertories of Vladimir Vysocky and Bulat Okudzhava, performed by Michał Bajor and Maryla Rodowicz.

- Emcees: Some words remembering the singer Anna German, who was unusually popular in the USSR. Announcement of *piosenki* from her repertory, recalled for us by Alicja Majewska.
- Alicja Majewska—"Odin raz": *piosenka* performed in the Russian language.
- Emcees: Announcement of the portion of the concert that presents current hits of the polish *estrada*.
- Alex Band: Selection of contemporary Polish hits.
- Emcees: Presentation of the representatives of the youngest generation of Poles on the stage: Halina, Katarzyna Ulicka, Wojciech Blond, Majka Jeżowska, Papa Dance Band, Maxi Singiel.
- Emcees: Introduction of the next singers, who are known for their appearances in the Soviet Union as stars of the Polish *estrada*: Halina Frąckowiak ("Tin Pan Alley"), Grażyna Świtała, Krystyna Prońko, Zbigniew Wodeck, among others.
- Emcees: Announcement of the guests of the Polish concert: Soviet stars.
- Anna Veski: Recital consisting of three songs.
- Konferansjerzy: Announcement of the next performers, among them Michał Bajor, laureate of the Festival of Soviet Song in Zielona Góra, actor, representative of the literary *piosenka*.
- Michał Bajor
- Alicja Majewska
- Maryla Rodowicz
- Emcees: Announcement of the conclusion.

Note: Both appendices drawn from LVI-1740, WK KC PZPR, AAN and translated by Andrea F. Bohlman.

Acknowledgments

Sincere thanks to Philip V. Bohlman, Louis Epstein, Jessica C. E. Gienow-Hecht, Alexander Rehding, Emily Richmond Pollock, and Anne C. Shreffler for feedback on this article in its various stages.

Notes

1. The edited draft, in Polish, can be found in folder LVI-1740 of the Department of Culture in the Archive of the Central Committee, Polish United Workers' Party, at the Archive of Modern Acts in Warsaw (hereafter WK KC-PZPR, AAN). All translations are my own unless otherwise noted.

2. Such rhetoric was shaped by Stalin's infamous "Friendship of the Peoples" campaign. See Terry Martin, *The Affirmative Action Empire: Nations and Nationalism in the Soviet Union, 1923–1939* (Ithaca, NY: Cornell University Press, 2001), 432–61.
3. "Notatka dot. polsko białoruskiej współpracy kulturalnej" [Note on Polish-Belorussian cultural collaboration], 11 July 1988, LVI-1749, WK KC-PZPR, AAN. The relationship between Jaruzelski and Gorbachev had involved a series of collaborations upon reform; see "Jaruzelski Visits Gorbachev, Reaffirms Support for Soviet Leader's Reforms," *Los Angeles Times*, 22 April 1987. For a fuller and contemporary discussion of the mutual respect between the two leaders, see Charles Gati, "Gorbachev and Eastern Europe," *Foreign Affairs* 65, no. 5 (1987): 958–75.
4. Report on the Moscow Festival of Polish Song by Wacław Janas, 15 March 1988, LVI-1749, WK KC-PZPR, AAN.
5. See Timothy Snyder, *The Reconstruction of Nations: Poland, Ukraine, Lithuania, Belarus, 1569–1999* (New Haven, CT, 2003), 72–89, 154–201.
6. Mickiewicz, Adam, *Konrad Wallenrod and Grażyna*, trans. Irene Suboczewski (Lanham, MD, 1989), part VI, line 233.
7. The precise allotment of tasks shifted subtly after 1970. Departments were divided and recombined, but the basic structure of the Executive Council, followed by the Politburo and then the departments, remained stable. Table 1 is based on Krzysztof Dąbek, *PZPR: retrospektywny portret własny* [PZPR: A retrospective self-portrait] (Warsaw: Wydawnictwo TRIO, 2006), 45. Translations of department names are based, when possible, on Paul G. Lewis, *Political Authority and Party Secretaries in Poland, 1975–1986* (Cambridge: Cambridge University Press, 1989), xviii–xix.
8. Lisa Jakelski explores the careful negotiation of Polish music as "in between" on the aesthetic and political levels in her dissertation, "The Changing Seasons of the Warsaw Autumn: Contemporary Music in Poland, 1960–1990" (PhD diss., University of California at Berkeley, 2009).
9. Culled from the Department of Culture's 1983 report, 536 897l88, WK KC-PZPR, AAN.
10. Studies of earlier Cold War archival trails have been able to make clearer distinctions between communist parties' plans for action, their verbal debates, and the public sphere outcomes. See, for example, Rachel Beckles Willson's attention to adjudication boards at the Hungarian Composers Union: *Ligeti, Kurtág, and Hungarian Music in the Cold War* (Cambridge: Cambridge University Press, 2007), 34–42; see also Joy H. Calico's discussion of the fabrication of censorship in the case of Paul Dessau's *Lukullus*: "The Trial, the Condemnation, the Cover-up: Behind the Scenes of Brecht/Dessau's *Lucullus* Opera(s)," *Cambridge Opera Journal* 14, no. 3 (2002): 313–42. In the context at hand, transcriptions of meeting minutes are few and far between in the PZPR's practice.
11. A summary of jazz's growth in Poland until 1985 details the financial stability of jazz; see, for example, "Stan aktualny i perspektywy rozwoju ruchu jazzowego w Polsce: Wyprowadzenie do dyskusji" [Current state of and perspective on the growth of the jazz movement in Poland: Introduction for debate], 1185 930l9, WK KC-PZPR, AAN.
12. "Notatka w sprawie organizacji międzynarodowego koncertu estradowego 'W obrowie pokoju'" [Note on the matter of organizing an international concert on stage, "In Defense of Peace"], LVI-1745, WK KC-PZPR, AAN.
13. Padraic Kenney, *A Carnival of Revolution: Central Europe 1989* (Princeton, NJ: Princeton University Press, 2003), 26. See also Lewis, *Political Authority and Party Secretaries in Poland*, 218–52, for reforms within the party.

14. Speaking to the Department of Culture, luthier Włodzimierz Kamiński deployed Polish music's strength of identity as a bait and switch in a speech addressing the status quo. "Poland's musical society is too strong to allow a general collapse of musical arts," he claimed; LVI-210, WK KC-PZPR, AAN. For a discussion of contemporary music's "Polishness," see Ruth Seehaber, *Die "polnische Schule" in der neuen Musik: Befragung eines musikhistorischen Topos* (Cologne: Böhlau, 2009).
15. Having undertaken fieldwork in the culture houses (*domy kultury*) of Poland, Hungary, and the USSR, Anne White observed a similar need to refashion the hardened division between art and entertainment in the events hosted in these countries' cities: *De-Stalinization and the House of Culture* (London and New York: Routledge, 1990), 69–78.
16. "Rozrywka to pojęcie szerokie. Obejmuje ona: sztukę estradową, muzykę, cyrk, kabaret, variete, widowiska, lunaparki, a także tzw. 'rozrywkę gastronomiczną' oraz fonografię i video jako formę przekazu i upowszechniania. Przy tak dużym zakresie działania niezwykle ważne jest penetrowanie tego obszaru kulturowego, wyrażanie politycznych ocen i wyznaczanie zadań. Zwłaszcza, że właśnie rozrywka, kultura masowa wywiera bardzo duży wpływ na wzorce życia, wypoczynku, preferowanie określonych idei i wartości. W Warszawie podobnie jak i w całym kraju nigdy nie opracowano całościowej koncepcji kultury popularnej i masowej. Rozrywka zawsze była uważana za sztukę gorszego gatunku a co za tym idzie lekceważąco traktowana zarówno przez decydentów jak i część krytyki artystycznej." In "Ocena stanu rozrywki w Warszawie" [Appraisal of the state of *rozrywka* in Warsaw], 1988, LVI-1750, WK KC-PZPR, AAN.
17. "Program SBIA na lata 1986/89 /skrót—też programowych/" [Program of the Capital Bureau of Artistic Events for the years 1986–89 (abbreviated—also programming)], LVI-1748, WK KC-PZPR, AAN: "Emphasis on events not only for youth, but also for the middle as well as older generations. Rehabilitation of sensational *rozrywka* (melodic *piosenki*, literary cabaret, musical spectacle!). Of *rozrywka* of social value and engagement." (Nacisk na imprezy nie tylko dla młodzieży, lecz i dla średniego oraz starzego pokolenia. Rehabilitacja rozrywki senseownej /Melodyjnej piosenki, kabaretu literackiego, widowiska muzycznego!/. Rozrywki społecznie wartościowej i zaangażowej.)
18. Cezar M. Ornatowski comes to similar conclusions with respect to the fate of rhetoric's pedagogy: "Reform often compensated for the failings of other projects through the [Polish People's Republic], but in the 1980s one observed the a general dulling of the party's hardest socialist agendas, the economic and political collapse ... demonstrated, among other things, the failure of the education project." In "Writing, from Stalinism to Democracy: Literacy Education and Politics in Poland, 1945–1999," in *Traditions of Writing Research*, ed. Charles Bazerman et al. (London, 2010), 91.
19. "An audience of youths, in its great size, decidedly prefers *rozrywka* addressed to them and understandable only to them, putting signs and symbols of their own subculture to use, of primitive or apparent non-conformism or demonstrative ambivalence toward everything. [It prefers] *rozrywka* with cosmopolitan features, but near to the anglosaxon style of rock." (Młodzieżowa widownia w swojej masie zdecydowanie preferuje rozrywkę adresowaną i zrozumiałą tylko dla niej, posługującą się znakami i symbolami swoistej subkultury, prymitywnego często pozornego nonkormformizmu lub demonstrowanej obojętności na wszystko, rozrywkę, o cechach kosmopolitycznych, ale bliższych anglosaskiemu stylowi rozrywki.) "Czym jest SBiA na dziś?" [What is SBiA today?], LVI-1748, WK KC-PZPR, AAN.

20. When Johnny Cash performed at the Sopot festival in 1988, the government prepared to balance this American with a significant battalion of Polish stars (LVI-1750, WK KC-PZPR, AAN), noting that his music was a "matter of personal taste" (letter from Mirosław Słowiński to A. Wasilewski, 16 February 1988, LVI-1749, WK KC-PZPR, AAN). In organizing the "Country Picnic" portion of the festival, the Department of Culture also insisted that singers' language be Polish and country of origin be Poland, even if this was not true for the songs they covered (LVI-1738, WK KC-PZPR, AAN).
21. Donna A. Buchanan, "Review of Sabrina P. Ramet, ed., *Rocking the State: Rock Music and Politics in Eastern Europe and Russia*," Notes 51, no. 4 (1995): 1284.
22. David MacFadyen, *Estrada?! Grand Narratives and the Philosophy of the Russian Popular Song since Perestroika* (Montreal: McGill-Queen's University Press, 2005), 175. See also MacFadyen, *Songs for Fat People: Affect, Emotion, and Celebrity in the Russian Popular Song, 1900–1955* (Montreal: McGill-Queen's University Press, 2003); MacFadyen, *Red Stars: Personality and the Soviet Popular Song, 1955–1991* (Montreal: McGill-Queen's University Press, 2001).
23. Mieczysław Pawłów gives a register of the stars from Western Europe and the Soviet Union who appeared at the festival in *Sopockie Międzynarodowe Festivale Piosenki* [Sopot's International Festivals of Song] (Legnica: Biblioteka Publiczna, 2007).
24. As one mode of cultural politics, cultural diplomacy is, of course, contextually specific and not always limited to the activities of the state. Though one could also focus on top-down policies, Annika Frieberg makes an argument for understanding cultural diplomacy in Poland during the Cold War as a series of interpersonal networks rather than as a single program with a unified vision in her study of the West German–Polish relations in the year of the Polish millennium: "Catholics in Ostpolitik? Networking and Nonstate Diplomacy in the Bensberger Memorandum, 1966–1970," in *Searching for a Cultural Diplomacy*, ed. Jessica C. E. Gienow-Hecht and Mark C. Donfried (Oxford: Berghahn Books, 2010), 109–34. Danielle Fosler-Lussier likewise emphasizes the role of the individual by drawing attention to the dialogic exchange that American musicians experienced abroad: "Cultural Diplomacy as Cultural Globalization: The University of Michigan Jazz Band in Latin America," *Journal of the Society for American Music* 4, no. 1 (2010): 73.
25. Izabela Zymer, *50 lat Związek Kompozytorów Polskich* [50 years of the Polish Composers Union] (Warsaw: Polish Composers Union, 2005), 181. Programs for the Bulgarian (19 December 1983, 19 December 1988), Czechoslovak (3 December 1984, 14 June 1985), Hungarian (9 March 1985), East German (19 January 1987), and Georgian (17 November 1988) events are held in the concert archives of the Composers Union Archives (Zarząd Główny Archives: Koncerty).
26. "Kommentarz do materiałów informacyjno oceniających działalności instytucji artystycznych /w okresie 1980–85/" [Commentary on materials evaluating the activities of artistic institutions (in the period 1980–85)], February 1986, LVI-210, WK KC-PZPR, AAN.
27. For one explanation of the allure of rock as a weapon of change in Poland, see Jolanta Pekacz, "Did Rock Smash the Wall? The Role of Rock in Political Transition," *Popular Music* 13, no. 1 (1994): 41–49. Daphne Carr writes with skepticism toward exceptional dissidence in East-Central European culture, noting that a focus on "rock around the bloc" has left much popular music out of Eastern European history: "Perhaps that is because [punk and rock] movements fueled the romantic ideology of rock as power for the powerless, an obvious mapping of how pop can serve as cultural resistance. Western scholars and historians of

Slavic popular music during communism have relatively ignored musical genres that did not correspond to this ideology." Daphne Carr, "Dancing, Democracy, and Kitsch: Poland's Disco Polo," in *Listen Again: A Momentary History of Pop Music*, ed. Eric Weisbard (Durham, NC: Duke University Press, 2007), 274.

28. The more analogous comparison with German, thus, is the distinction between *Lied* and *Gesang*. The latter includes information about social and cultural context.
29. "Notatka informacyjna nt. koncertu z okazji 40-lecia wyzwolenia Warszawy" [Informational note on the topic of the concert on the occasion of the 40th anniversary of Warsaw's liberation], 1185 930 | 9, WK KC-PZPR, AAN.
30. The practices I observe in the networks of the musical community in Poland in the 1980s mirror what Robert Walser has claimed as the domain of popular music: "Nowhere are genre boundaries more fluid than in popular music.... Musicians are ceaselessly creating new fusions and extensions of popular genres." Robert Walser, *Running with the Devil: Power, Gender, and Madness in Heavy Metal Music* (Middletown, CT: Wesleyan University Press, 1993), 27. David MacFadyen spins Walser's claim more empirically, and with reference to a popular scene geographically more proximal to Poland: "Soviet performers mixed these songs [romances, waltzes, fox-trots, tangos, and folk numbers—postrevolution songs] with theatre, while composers used wit and whimsy in popular melanges of vocal music, comedy, and poetry. This tradition, born before the Revolution, had outlasted all forms of international butchery. It still rolls on today with relative ease, surviving even the demise of socialism." MacFadyen, *Red Stars*, 4. See Fabian Holt, *Genre in Popular Music* (Chicago: University of Chicago Press, 2007), for a rigorous study of the stakes of contesting genre in popular music.
31. The festival's organizational record and final programming is filed in three folders at the Archive of Modern Acts: LVI-1740, 1749, and 1750, WK KC-PZPR, AAN.
32. "Notatka informacyjna. Dotyczy: działań przygotowawczych zmierzających do realizacji Festiwalu Piosenki Polskiej w Witebsku" [Informational note on the matter of the preparations for the Festival of Polish Song in Vitebsk], LVI-1750, WK KC-PZPR, AAN.
33. *Grudzień—Sierpień: Piosenki i wiersze wybrzeża* [December—August: Songs and poems of the coast] (Warsaw: Zespół BL i H, 1980).
34. J. Martin Daughtry has written that the Russian poetic-musical practice, *avtorskaia pesnia*, attracted listeners with diverse political allegiances: "'Sonic Samizdat': Situating Unofficial Recording in the Post-Stalinist Soviet Union," *Poetics Today* 30, no. 1 (2009): 46.
35. As her surname suggests, German was not of Polish heritage, though her father was of German descent and born in Łódź. Born in what is contemporary Uzbekistan, German and her mother moved to Wrocław with her Polish stepfather after World War II. Whether or not she had Jewish heritage was not public during her life and has only recently become a topic of speculation among right-wing contingents in Poland.
36. It is no coincidence that the first biography of German was published in the Soviet Union: Aleksandr Zhigarev, *Anna German* (Moscow, 1988).
37. J. Ch., *Anna German: Tanczące Euridiki* (Polskie Nagranie, XL 0284).
38. "Notatka dot. polsko białoruskiej współpracy kulturalnej" [Note on Polish-Belorussian cultural collaboration], 11 July 1988, LVI-1749, WK KC-PZPR, AAN.
39. The substantial difficulty Belarusian artists would have traveling to Poland was conceived of as a problem, but not necessarily a hindrance, when setting this agenda point.
40. Snyder, *The Reconstruction of Nations*, 65.

41. Ibid., 284.
42. Ibid., 91.
43. The Soviet children's song "Pust' vsegda budet solntse" was well-known for its bright outlook on the future. Ronald Reagan quoted a few lines in his New Year's Day address in 1986, found at http://www.reagan.utexas.edu/archives/speeches/1986/10186a.htm (accessed 14 January 2012).
44. From Jerzy Żuławski's "Riposte," in *Poezje*, vol. 2 (Warsaw and Lwów, 1903), 51.
45. Mickiewicz, *Konrad Wallenrod and Grażyna*, part IV, lines 187–89. The Frederic Chopin monument in Łazienki Park in Warsaw has borne the same quote since its restoration after World War II.
46. Ibid., part VI, line 233.

Bibliography

Archives

Department of Culture in the Archive of the Central Committee, Polish United Workers' Party, at the Archive of Modern Acts, Warsaw
Polish Composers Union, Polish Music Information Center, Warsaw

Printed Sources

Beckles Willson, Rachel. *Ligeti, Kurtág, and Hungarian Music in the Cold War*. Cambridge: Cambridge University Press, 2007.
Buchanan, Donna A. "Review of Sabrina P. Ramet, ed. Rocking the State: Rock Music and Politics in Eastern Europe and Russia." Notes 51, no. 4 (1995): 1283–286.
Calico, Joy H. "The Trial, the Condemnation, the Cover-up: Behind the Scenes of Brecht/Dessau's *Lucullus* Opera(s)." *Cambridge Opera Journal* 14, no. 3 (2002): 313–42.
Carr, Daphne. "Dancing, Democracy, and Kitsch: Poland's Disco Polo." In *Listen Again: A Momentary History of Pop Music*, ed. Eric Weisbard, 272–85. Durham, NC: Duke University Press, 2007.
Dąbek, Krzysztof. *PZPR: Retrospektywny portret własny* [PZPR: A retrospective self-portrait]. Warsaw: Wydawnictwo TRIO, 2006.
Daughtry, J. Martin. "'Sonic Samizdat': Situating Unofficial Recording in the Post-Stalinist Soviet Union." *Poetics Today* 30, no. 1 (2009): 27–65.
Fosler-Lussier, Danielle. "Cultural Diplomacy as Cultural Globalization: The University of Michigan Jazz Band in Latin America." *Journal of the Society for American Music* 4, no. 1 (2010): 59–93.
Frieberg, Annika. "Catholics in Ostpolitik? Networking and Nonstate Diplomacy in the Bensberger Memorandum, 1966–1970." In *Searching for a Cultural Diplomacy*, ed. Jessica C. E. Gienow-Hecht and Mark C. Don, 109–34. Oxford: Berghahn Books, 2010.
Gati, Charles. "Gorbachev and Eastern Europe." *Foreign Affairs* 65, no. 5 (1987): 958–75.

Grudzień—Sierpień: Piosenki i wiersze wybrzeża [December—August: Songs and poems of the coast]. Warsaw: Zespół BL i H, 1980.
Holt, Fabian. *Genre in Popular Music.* Chicago: University of Chicago Press, 2007.
Jakelski, Lisa. "The Changing Seasons of the Warsaw Autumn: Contemporary Music in Poland, 1960–1990." PhD diss., University of California at Berkeley, 2009.
Kan, Alex, and Nick Hayes. "Big Beat in Poland." In *Rocking the State: Rock Music and Politics in Eastern Europe and Russia,* ed. Sabrina P. Ramet, 41–53. Boulder, CO: Westview Press, 1994.
Kenney, Padraic. *A Carnival of Revolution: Central Europe 1989.* Princeton, NJ: Princeton University Press, 2003.
Lewis, Paul G. *Political Authority and Party Secretaries in Poland, 1975–1986.* Cambridge, 1989.
MacFadyen, David. *Estrada?! Grand Narratives and the Philosophy of the Russian Popular Song since Perestroika.* Montreal: McGill-Queen's University Press, 2005.
———. *Red Stars: Personality and the Soviet Popular Song, 1955–1991.* Montreal: McGill-Queen's University Press, 2001.
———. *Songs for Fat People: Affect, Emotion, and Celebrity in the Russian Popular Song, 1900–1955.* Montreal: McGill-Queen's University Press, 2002.
Martin, Terry. *The Affirmative Action Empire: Nations and Nationalism in the Soviet Union, 1923–1939.* Ithaca, NY: Cornell University Press, 2001.
Mickiewicz, Adam. *Konrad Wallenrod and Grażyna.* Translated by Irene Suboczewski. Lanham, MD, 1989.
Ornatowski, Cezar M. "Writing, from Stalinism to Democracy: Literacy Education and Politics in Poland, 1945–1999." In *Traditions of Writing Research,* ed. Charles Bazerman, Robert Krut, Karen Lunsford, Susan McLeod, Suzie Null, Paul Rogers, and Amanda Stansell, 85–96. London, 2010.
Pawłów, Mieczysław. *Sopockie Międzynarodowe Festivale Piosenki* [The Sopot International Festivals of Song]. Legnica: Biblioteka Publiczna, 2007.
Pekacz, Jolanta. "Did Rock Smash the Wall? The Role of Rock in Political Transition." *Popular Music* 13, no. 1 (1994): 41–49.
Ryback, Timothy W. *Rock Around the Bloc: A History of Rock Music in Eastern Europe and the Soviet Union.* London and New York: Oxford University Press, 1990.
Seehaber, Ruth. *Die "polnische Schule" in der neuen Musik: Befragung eines musikhistorischen Topos.* Cologne: Böhlau, 2009.
Snyder, Timothy. *The Reconstruction of Nations: Poland, Ukraine, Lithuania, Belarus, 1569–1999.* New Haven, CT: Yale University Press, 2003.
Walser, Robert. *Running with the Devil: Power, Gender, and Madness in Heavy Metal Music.* Middletown, CT: Wesleyan University Press, 1993.

White, Anne. *De-Stalinization and the House of Culture.* London and New York: Routledge, 1990.
Zhigarev, Aleksandr. *Anna German.* Moscow: Iskusstvo, 1988.
Żuławski, Jerzy. *Poezje.* Vol. 2. Warsaw and Lwów, 1903.
Zymer, Izabela, ed. *50 lat Związek Kompozytorów Polskich* [50 years of the Polish Composers Union]. Warsaw: Polish Composers Union, 2005.

INDEX

Adorno, Theodore, 209–10
Adrjanski, Zbigniew, 234
African Americans, 179–80
"Aging of the New Music" (Adorno), 209
Air Force Symphony, 174
Akademie der Künste, 74–75
Aksyuk, Sergey, 208
Alfred of Saxe-Coburg and Gotha, 46
Allen, Betty, 174, 180
American Forces Network, 108
American-Icelandic String Quartet, 175–78
American Music Control office, 105–6
American National Theater and Academy, 147, 168, 177–78
Anderson, Marian, 180
anti-war activists, 231–32
Armstrong, Louis, 6
Arnaud, Jean, 101–2
Ars Viva, 76–78, 82
Asia, 7, 146–51
Atlanta Constitution, 34, 51, 54
avant-garde music, 203

Bach, Johan Sebastian, 98, 101
Bajor, Michal, 236, 239–41, 247–248
Barber, Samuel, 100, 153, 195
Barcelona, as location for ISCM festival, 71–72
Barrison, Abelone, 39, 42–43, 49–50
Barrison, Ethel, 44–45
Barrison, Gertrude, 38, 43
Barrison, Lyseus, 37
Barrison, Mabel, 44
Barrison, Sanders, 37

Barrison, Sophie, 38, 43
Barski, Sergei, 105–6
Bartók, Bela, 190, 201
Bax, Arnold, 70
BBC German Service, 107, 110
bebop, 179–80, 182
Beethoven, Ludwig von, 3, 98, 101, 103, 150
Belorussian Soviet Socialist Republic, 226, 244–45
Berendt, Joachim-Ernst, 107–8
Berg, Alban, 62, 65, 77
Bergmann, Maria, 192, 199
Berliner Festwochen, 209
Berlin Philharmonic, 98, 103
Bernstein, Leonard, 10, 15, 142, 151–58
Bernstorff, Albrecht Graf von, 43
Bernstorff, Wilhelm von, 43–44
Biggs, E. Power, 175
Binet, Jean, 70
Blazhkov, Igor, 16, 191–92, 194–99, 205, 209–15
Blomay, André de, 81
Blond, Wojiech, 248
Blüthner, Hans, 108
Bornoff, Jack, 105–6
Boston Symphony Orchestra, in Iceland, 174–77
Boulez, Pierre, 190, 195
Brezhnev, Leonid, 144
British Force Broadcasting Service, 108
Britten, Benjamin, 195
Brubeck, Dave, 6
Bulcher, Harry, 94–95
Bulten, Benjamin, 100
Bush, Alan, 61–62, 64, 78

Capital City Bureau of Artistic Events, Warsaw, 234
Carlyle, Thomas, 52
Casella, Alberto, 70
Cash, Johnny, 235
Casino Roof Garden, New York, 49
Castelnuovo-Tedesco, Mario, 70
Censorship Bureau, Poland, 237
Central Committee of the Communist Party, 75
Central Intelligence Agency, 82, 177
"Chance for Peace" speech by Eisenhower, 141–42
Chiang Kai-shek, 148
Chinese Women's Anti-Aggression League, 148
Christie, William, 189
Clara Morris touring company, 37
classical music, 17
    culture of, in United States, 143–44
    initiatives in Eisenhower years, 141, 145–59
    meaning of culture of, 142–43
    message to Iceland in 1950s, 178–83
    orchestral tours to Iceland, 172–77
    tool of U.S. diplomacy, 142
    tours to Iceland, 173–78
Claxton, Kate, 38
Cliburn, Van, 10
Cohen, Alfred J., 34
Cold War
    classical music initiatives, 141, 145–59
    Iceland crisis and music diplomacy, 169–83
    impact on composition and performance, 9–11
    and intimate history, 191–94
    jazz in context of, 5–6, 109–10
    layering of Soviet-U.S. exchanges, 191–92
    music diplomacy in Eisenhower years, 166–83
    Soviet peace initiative, 141–42
    symphony tours, 14–15
    and U.S. policymakers, 145
Coleman, Cliff, 189–91, 204–5, 207
"Colorful Markets," 241
communication, music as mode of, 11, 18–19

communism, composers under, 18
Concert for Nine Instruments (Webern), 62, 65–67, 81–82
Congress for Cultural Freedom, 82
Contemporary Music Festival, Stuttgart in 1947, 108
Copland, Aaron, 153
Costigliola, Frank, 214
Couperin family of musicians, 215
cultural diplomacy
    to counteract negative perceptions of the United States, 142
    effort by Polish Department of Culture, 243–44
    Eisenhower's request for funds for, 145–46
    for Iceland in 1950s, 172–77
    music in postwar Germany, 98–111
    as smart power, 14, 18, 182–83
    of Soviet Union in 1950s, 141–42
    See also music diplomacy
cultural festival of Konstanz, 1946, 100
cultural history of Poland-Belarus era, 244–45
Cultural League for the Renewal of Germany, 100
Czech Philharmonic, 64–65

Dahlhaus, Carl, 3
Dale, Alan, 34, 49, 53–54
    critique of Barrison Sisters, 51
Dallapiccola, Luigi, 78, 195
"Dancing Euridice," 242
Darmstädter Ferienkürse für Neue Musik, 82, 106
Das Echo, 68
Debussy, Claude, 9, 60
democracy, U.S. defense of, 144
denazification, 96s, 103–4
Denisov, Edison, 195, 210
DeNora, Tia, 3
Dent, Edward J., 64–65, 70–71, 73–74, 76–78, 82
Department of Commerce (U.S.), 146
Department of Culture, Poland, 16, 237
    big four song festivals, 239
    cultural diplomacy effort, 243–44
    and Department of Music, 231–32
    inclusive approach to music, 230–32

normalization goal, 231–32
rozrywka as music, 232–36
Department of Defense (U.S.), 171
Department of Music, Poland, 232, 234
diplomacy, total, 19. *See also* cultural diplomacy; music diplomacy
Doctor Zhivago (Pasternak), 297
Donetsk Symphony Orchestra, 204
Druskin, Yakov, 212
Dulles, John Foster, 167
Dumas, Alexandre, 39
Dunayevsky, Isaac, 247
Durrani, Osman, 7
Dvorak, Antonin, 9
Dylan, Bob, 232

East Germany, impact of jazz and rock in, 6
Eden Musee, 39
Eimat, Hans, 106
Ein deutsches Requiem (Brahms), 3
Eisenhower, Dwight D., 11, 93–94, 111, 140–42, 145–46, 157, 178
   on music diplomacy, 167–68
Eisler, Hanns, 13, 64, 70–74, 75–76, 81
Ellington, Duke, 6
Elysium, 39
Ensemble Spectrum, 247
entarte Musik, 66
ernste Musik, 17
Eroica (Beethoven), 150
estradnaya muzyka, 234–35
ethnomusicology, 2–4
Europe
   cultural upheaval of 1890s, 46–47
   music and politics in 1930s, 59
   negative perceptions of the United States in, 142
European art music, 105–6
Eurovision Song Contest, 235
Eytinge, Pearl, 37–39

Festival of Polish Song, in Soviet Union, 239–40
Festival of Polish Song, Vitebsk, 16, 226–29, 232, 236, 239–41, 244–47
Festival of Soviet Song, Zielona Góra, 16, 239–40, 247
Fifth Symphony (Beethoven), 150–51
Five Pieces for Piano (Silvestrov), 199
Fleron, William, 39–41, 44–45, 48, 50
Fogg, Mieczyslaw, 236, 240

Folies Bergère, 35, 40–41, 50
Fonda, Jane, 232
foreign policy, in post-Stalin era, 141–42
Fourth Symphony (Tchaikovsky), 98
Frackowiak, Halina, 237–38, 248
Free German Youth, 109
French commemorative festival of 1947, Berlin, 95, 100
Fuller, Loïe, 41, 42
Furtwängler, Wilhelm, 104

Garcia Lorca, Federico, 200, 202
Gerigk, Herbert, 66, 67, 69
German, Anna, 16–17, 236, 241–42, 248
German *Lied*, 237
Germany
   Allied debate on treatment of, 93–95
   denazification of musicians, 103–4
   hip hop, 7, 8
   jazz in postwar years, 106–10
   music and Allied occupation, 95–96, 101
   popular music, 109
   postwar music restoration, 98–111
   short-term objectives of occupiers, 96
   views on reeducation, 93, 97–98
   violence and looting by occupiers, 97
   See also Nazi government
Gerry Society, 37
Gershkovich, Filipp, 208
Gershwin, George, 153
Gilels, Emil, 190
Gillespie, Dizzy, 6
Gnatiuk, Nikolai, 238
Goebbels, Joseph, 104
Goléa, Antoine, 208
Goodman, Benny, 6
Gorbachev, Mikhail, 228, 240, 244–46
Gruenberg, Louis, 78, 82
Grundlingh, Albert, 7

Hába, Alois, 62, 64, 65
Harris, Roy, 100, 153
Hawaii, visit of Soviet ship in 1959, 189–91
Hegel, G. F. W., 52
Hendl, Walter, 146, 148–51

Henze, Hans Werner, 195
Hermaszewski, Miroslaw, 226
Hindemith, Paul, 104, 190, 195
hip hop, 7–8
Histoire croisée (Schmidt-Rost), 5–6
Hitler, Adolf, 3, 144
Hodeir, André, 208
Hodzyatsky, Vitaliy, 191
Hoffmannsthal, Hugo von, 46–47
Honegger, Arthur, 190
Hong Kong, Symphony of the Air tour to, 146–51
Hrabovsky, Leonid, 191, 201
Humphrey, George, 175, 176–77, 178
Hungarian Revolution of 1956, 181

Iceland, 15, 169–83
IG Farben, 93
Ilichev, Leonid, 297
"In Defense of Peace" concert, Warsaw, 231–32
Ingmundarson, Valur, 179–80
Inner Life of Empires (Rothschild), 192
Inter-Allied Music Lending Library, Berlin, 101
International Exchange Program (U.S.), 146
International Gaudemus Composers' Competition, 211
International Gaudemus Music Week, 199
International Geophysical Year, 189
International Music Office, Moscow, 64
international relations
 and Blahzkov's correspondence, 214–15
 and jazz in postwar Germany, 109–10
 and music, 142–45, 159, 215
 music competition in postwar Germany, 102–4
 See also diplomacy; foreign policy
International Society for Contemporary Music, 13, 58–80
International Society for New Music, 75
International Song Festival, Sopot, 235, 239
International Tchaikovsky Piano Competition of 1958, 10
intimate history and Cold War, 191–94

Jackson, C. D., 176, 178
Jalowetz, Heinrich, 65
Jarnack, Philipp, 70
Jaruzelski, Wojieck, 228
jazz
 in context of international relations, 5–6
 in early Cold War years, 109–10
 in French-occupied Germany, 107–8
 in postwar Germany, 95, 106–10
 Soviet opposition to, 107
 University of Michigan band tours, 192
jazz musicians, German, 108–9
Jazz Orchestra Alex Band, 247
Jezowska, Majka, 248
Jirattikorn, Amporn, 7
Jochum, Eugen, 98
Johnson, Thor, 146, 149–50
Jolly Fellows (film), 241, 247

Kabasta, Oswald, 98
Kaczmarek, Adam, 232
Karlsbad, and Prague festival of 1935, 62–64
Käs. Rudolf, 108
Kearns, Carroll D., 179, 182
Keflavik air force base, Iceland, 170
Khrennikov, Tikhon, 200, 208
Khrushchev, Nikita, 10, 144
 denunciation of avant-garde, 206
Kiev Chamber Orchestra, 213
Kiev Composers Union, 203–4
Kiev Symphonic Ensemble, 195
Knappertsbuch, Hans, 98
Kolberg, Oskar, 237
Kolisch, Rudolf, 65
Konrad Wallenrod (Mickiewicz), 228–29, 246
Korngold, Erich Wolfgang, 77
Koster and Bial's music hall, New York, 33, 35–36, 48–50, 54
Kovalewski, Andrezj, 204
Krajewski, Seweryn, 239
Krenek, Ernst, 68–70, 77, 195
Kulturbund zur demokratischen Erneuerung Deutschlands, 100–101, 103, 107

Labroca, Mario, 70
L'Affaire Clemenceau (Dumas), 39

260　　　　　　　　　　　　　　　Index

La forza del destino (Verdi), 69
Laments of Shchaza (Volkonsky), 195
Lampol, Joshua, 189
Laszlo, Ervin, 174
Latin American tour by New York Philharmonic, 151–58
Laux, Karl, 106
Leningrad Philharmonic, 195, 205
Leont'ev, Valerii, 247
Les Songes (Milhaud), 70
Levy, Beth, 4
Lindner, Anton, 47–48
Lombard, James, 177
Lualdi, Adriano, 69
Lück, Rudolf, 211

MacFadyen, David, 235
Magdanz, James, 177
Mahler, Gustav, 60, 99, 101
Majewska, Alicja, 242, 248
Maliszewski, Aleksander, 247
Markiewicz, Leon, 208
Mason, Colin, 208
mass culture, 233
McCartney, Paul, 232
McFerrin, Robert, 174, 180, 181
Mendelssohn, Felix, 98, 99, 101
Menuhin, Yehudi, 104
MHK Symphony, Japan, 150–51
Mickiewicz, Adam, 228–29, 241, 244, 246
Midnight Bell, 38
Milhaud, Darius, 68–70, 191
Military Air Transport Service, 175
Mitchell, Jeanne, 174
Mitchell, Tony, 8
Mitropoulos, Dimitri, 151–53, 157
Moeck, Hermann, 205, 210–11
Mokreeva, Galina, 191, 194, 200–205, 207, 211, 212–13
Moniuszko, Stanislaw, 243
Montgomery, Bernard L., 93–94, 111
Montville, Joseph V., 193
Morris, Clara, 37
Moscow, as location for ISCM festival, 71–72
Mozart, Wolfgang Amadeus, 98, 101
Mravinsky, Yevgeny, 195
Mr. Cupid, 39
Muccio, John, 176
Mucha, Alphonse, 42
music
　　and Allied occupation, 95–96

Blazhkov's role in Cold War, 191–215
borderless nature of, 143
competition in international relations, 102–4
in context of international history, 5–8
in context of modernity, 3
as cultural force, 106–10
cultural historians on, 4–8
effect of *Vitiaz* visit on Soviet Union, 191
as form of communication, 12
genres, 17
impact on international relations, 18
independence from politics, 80–81
as instrument of diplomacy, 14
and international history, 59
and international relations, 142–45, 159, 215
meaning in dissemination of, 214
mode of communication, 18–19
modernist and avant-garde in Germany, 100
Nazi policy, 68–69
new recent music and politicians, 59–60
policy differences among occupiers, 105–6
Polish, for international stage, 239–45
Polish School, 232
and political history, 1–2
in reeducation program, 102
relationship to state, 58–59
restoration in postwar Germany, 98–111
role of state, 19–20
rozrywka as, 232–36
socialist realism in, 81
and Soviet Union, 59
strength of, in Polish culture, 230–31
subsidized and monitored by Party, 229–36
tool in psychological warfare, 167–68
understanding international relations and, 11–12
in Vichy France, 4
See also classical music; popular music

Music Advisory Panel (U.S.), 153
Musica ex machina, 196
musical associations, Poland, 231
musical tamizdat, 193
Musica Viva, 78–79
music diplomacy
    assessment of U.S. success in 1950s, 158
    Eisenhower era, 145–49, 166–83
    in Iceland in Cold War, 169–83
    negative views in Iceland, 181–82
    New York Philharmonic tour, 151–58
    under Polish United Workers' Party, 235–36
    by Soviets in Poland, 226–29
    Symphony of the Air tour, 146–51
    by United States in international situations, 168–69
"Music Festivals and Music Every Day," 78
Music Living and Dead (Shneerson), 203
"Music of the Twentieth Century" speech (Mokreeva), 204–5, 207
"Music vs. Guns" (Kearns), 179
Mussolini, Benito, 69, 144

Nabokov, Nicola, 203
Nagasaki (Schnittke), 206
Nagoya Ahubu Nippon, 148
narodnaya, 234–35
National Academic Theater of Minsk, 243
National Festival of Polish Song, Opole, 239
nationalism, 3, 7, 59, 70–71
National Security Council (U.S.), 11, 68, 167, 172–73, 178
Nazi government, 13, 58–59, 76, 78, 82, 97, 104
NBC Symphony Orchestra, 146
Nelson, Richard, 180
Nestyev, Israel, 208
"New Music in the Soviet Union" (Prieberg), 206
new Soviet music, 194, 205–8
New Soviet Piano Music (ed., Lück), 211
New York Philharmonic, 10, 15, 142, 144, 151–58
New York Society for the Prevention of Cruelty to Children, 37

Nieman, Czeslaw, 236, 238
Ninth Symphony (Beethoven), international significance of, 3
Nixon, Richard M., 154–57, 167
Nono, Luigi, 195
normalization, in Poland, 231–32
Northwest German Radio, Cologne, 100
Northwest German Radio, Hamburg, 105–6
NWDR Symphony Orchestra, 106

"Ode to Joy," 3
Official Journal of the National Socialist Cultural Community, 68
Okudzhava, Bulat, 232, 247
Olafson, Björn, 175
Operations Coordinating Board (U.S.) 167–69, 172–75, 178–83
Osiecka, Agmieszka, 237
Overture to a Midsummer Night's Dream (Mendelssohn), 98

Pallavicini, Arthur, 44–46
Papa Dance Band, 248
Parry-Giles, Shawn, 169, 175
Pärt, Arvo, 205–6, 208, 214
Parton, Dolly, 232
Pasternak effect, 207, 214
Pathetic Oratorio (Sovretsov), 195
Pavlova, A., 189–90
Peabody, Francis, 45
Peking Opera Company, 178
People's Alliance Party, Iceland, 170
People's Republic of China, 178
Peresvetov, Ivan, 106
Permanent Council for the International Cooperation of Composers, 59, 66–71, 80
Petersburski, Jerzy, 241
Pfitzner, Hans, 1
Philadelphia Orchestra, 190
Philippines, Symphony of the Air tour in, 146–51
Pietrzak, Jan, 235
Piston, Walter, 100
Poiger, Uta, 6–7, 110
Poland
    and Belorussian history, 244
    cultural reform, 229
    definition of song, 237
    Department of Culture, 16
    emergence of Solidarity, 229
    end of partition, 244

freedom for contemporary music, 229–30
"In Defense of Peace" concert, 231–32
martial law in 1981, 229
rozrywka as music, 232–36
strength of music in culture of, 230–31
Poliakova, Liudmilla, 196
Polish Artists' Agency, 243
Polish Composers Union, 230, 236
Polish-Lithuanian Commonwealth (1569–1795), 228, 244
Polish Ministry of Culture and Arts, 239
Polish music, programmed for international stage, 239–45
Polish punk bands, 234
Polish School of Music, 232
Polish-Soviet Friendship Society, 240
Polish United Workers' Party, 227–34
politics, independence of music from, 80–82
Popular Front, 13, 59, 72, 74–76, 78
popular music
　in Asia, 7
　bebop, 179–80, 182
　blues, 238
　branches of, in Soviet Union, 234–35
　German passion for, 109
　hip hop, 6–7
　jazz, 5–6
　and Poland-Belarus international harmony, 227–28
　rock, 6, 238
Pottle, Ralph, 174
Prague festival of 1935, 62–63, 64–65, 78–80
President's Emergency Fund for International Affairs, 146
Presley, Elvis, 6
Prieberg, Fred K., 16, 191–93, 195–99, 200, 203, 205–11, 213–14
Progressive Party, Iceland, 170
Pronko, Krystyna, 248
Proust, Marcel, 52
psychological warfare, music as tool in, 167–68
Public Law 63 (U.S.), 146
Puccini, Giacomo, 60
Pugacheva, Alla, 235, 247

Rachmaninov, Sergei, 190
Radio Hamburg Symphony Orchestra, 196
rap music, 6–7
Reichenbach, Hermann, 73–74, 75–76
Reichsmusikkammer, 69
"Report on the Negotiations of the International Revolutionary Theater Association," 73
Rhee, Syngman, 147–48
Robert Shaw Chorale, 174
rock music, 6, 238
Rodgers, Kenny, 232
Rodowicz, Maryla, 237, 239–41, 247–48
Rosiewicz, Andrzej, 235
Rothschild, Emma, 192
Roussel, Albert, 70
Rozrywka, 232–36, 245
Russian Soviet Federative Socialist Republic, 244

Sacher, Paul, 71, 78
Saint-Saëns, Camille, 69
Salomé (Strauss), 69
samizdat, 193
Samson et Dalila (Saint-Saëns), 69
Santor, Irena, 247
Scherchen, Hermann, 62, 65, 68–70, 78, 81
Schlager tunes, 241
Schnitzer, Robert C., 146, 177–78
Schoenberg, Arnold, 62, 65, 77, 191, 201
Schopenhauer, Arthur, 1
Schubert, Franz, 103
Schuman, William, 100, 153
Schütz, Heinrich, 195
Schwarz, Boris, 208
Second Vienna School, 62, 77
Sen, Jón, 75
Seventh Congress of the Comintern, 72
Shneerson, Gregoriy, 196, 203–4
Shostakovich, Dimintri, 101
Shostakovich Piano Quartet, 177
Silvestrov, Valentin, 191, 198–201, 205–11
Simmons, Christina, 34
Slonimsky, Nicolas, 195
Small, Christopher, 214
Smart, Mary Ann, 215
Smith-Mundt Act, 176–77
Social Democratic Party, Iceland, 170

socialist realism, 81, 235
Socialist Unity Party, East Germany, 109
Soldiers' Song Festival, Kolobrzeg, 239
Solidarity Independent Trade Union, 229, 236, 241
song festivals of Poland, 239
South America, Nixon's visit to, 154–57
South Korea, 7, 146–51
Soviet Composers Union, 73, 76, 206
Soviet-Icelandic Cultural Society, 178
Soviet Union
    branches of popular music, 234–35
    Central Committee of the Communist Party, 75
    cultural diplomacy in 1950s, 141–42
    debate on treatment of Germany, 93–95
    Festival of Polish Song, 239–40
    interest in Iceland, 179
    limits on artistic exchange, 177
    and location for ISCM festival, 71–72
    music diplomacy in Poland, 226–29
    openness to modernist music, 59
    opposition to jazz, 107
    and Popular Front, 78
    prohibitions on Blazhkov, 194
    U-2 spy plane incident, 178
    views on German reeducation, 97–98
    visit of *Vitiaz* to Hawaii 1959, 189–91
    worldwide peace initiative, 141–42
Sovretsov, Antonin, 195
Spectrum (Silvestrov), 210–11
Staatsoper ceremony of 1947, 94–95
Stalin, Josef, 5, 141, 144, 235
State control of culture, 19–20
relationship to music, 58–59
State Philharmonic Orchestra, Ukraine, 195
Stefan, Paul, 71
Steinecke, Wolfgang, 106
Steinhard, Erich, 64, 82
Stern, Isaac, 174–75
Steuermann, Edward, 65
Stockhausen, Karlheinz, 190, 196

Strauss, Richard, 68–69, 98
Stravinsky, Igor, 70, 190, 195, 197, 204
Stuckenschmidt, Hans-Heinz, 106, 198, 208
Sudeten German composers, 62
Suite of Mirrors (Volkonsky), 202
Survey, 205, 206
Switala, Garzyna, 248
Symphonic Pieces from *Lulu* (Berg), 62
Symphony No. 3, *Eschatophony* (Silvestrov), 210–11
Symphony No. 5 (Shostakovich), 189–90
Symphony of the Air, 15, 140, 142, 144, 146–51
Syzmanowski, Karol, 195

Taiwan, Symphony of the Air tour in, 146–51
Tamada, Kosaku, 140, 149
Tchaikovsky, Piotr, 98, 103
Telemann, Georg P., 195
Tereshkova, Valentina, 226
Thibom, Blanche, 174
Thimonnier, René, 101, 105
Third International Music Festival, Venice 1934, 68
Third Piano Concerto (Rachmaninov), 190
Thomanerchor, Leipzig, 103
Thompson, Virgil, 102
"Tin Pan Alley," 237–38
Tippett, Michael, 100
Toscanini, Arturo, 146
total diplomacy, 19
totalitarianism, and music wars, 18
Toulouse-Lautrec, Henri de, 42, 50
Treaty of Versailles, failure of, 93
Triad (Silvestrov), 211
Trio for Flute, Trumpet, and Celesta (Silvestrov), 209–10
Trocadero, Chicago, 40–41
Trout Quintet (Schubert), 103
23 (Viennese journal), 68–69

United States
    culture of classical music, 143–44
    debate on treatment of Germany, 93–95
    defense of Iceland, 169–70
    foreign policy in post-Stalin era, 141–42

Latin American hostility to, 157
layering of Cold War exchanges, 191–92
music for psychological warfare, 167–68
negative perceptions of, 142
perception of foreign threats, 145
policymakers and cold War, 145
views on German reeducation, 97–98
University of Michigan jazz band tours, 192
Urbizagastequi, Ruben, 8
U.S. Air Force base in Iceland, 170
U.S. Information Agency, 9
U.S. Special Services, 111
U.S. State Department Cultural Relations Program, 166, 174
Ustvolskaya, Galina, 206
U-2 spy plane incident, 178

Valentines, 241
Varèse, Edgard, 190, 195
Variations for Orchestra (Schoenberg), 62
Verdi, Giuseppe, 69
Veski, Anna, 248
Vichy France, 4
Violin Concerto (Beethoven), 104
Vitiaz oceanographic ship, in Hawaii, 189–91
Vivaldi, Antonio, 215
Voëlvry music, 7
Vogel, Wladimir, 65, 68–69
Volkonsky, Andrey, 195, 197, 200, 202, 205–6, 208, 211, 214
Vysocky, Vladimir, 247

Wang (opera), 38
Warsaw Autumn International Festival of Contemporary Music, 230
Webern, Anton, 62, 65–66, 77, 81–82, 195
Weiner, Clarence, 50
Wicked Barrisons reputation, 33
Wilhelm II, Kaiser, 144
Wilson, Woodrow, 145
Wodecki, Zbigniew, 247–48
Wonder, Stevie, 232
World War I, 145
end of Poland's partition, 244–45
Wroclaw Opera, 243

Yudina, Maria, 193, 196–97, 201, 208

Zhadanov doctrine, 81
Zhukov, Georgi K., 92–94
Ziegfeld, Florenz, 40

www.ingramcontent.com/pod-product-compliance
Lightning Source LLC
Chambersburg PA
CBHW072147100526
44589CB00015B/2130